DOMINICAN SAINTS

Rosary Group

DOMINICAN SAINTS

BY

THE NOVICES

OF THE

DOMINICAN HOUSE OF STUDIES
WASHINGTON, D. C.

✠

WITH AN

INTRODUCTION

BY THE

RT. REV. THOMAS J. SHAHAN, D. D.
RECTOR OF THE CATHOLIC UNIVERSITY OF AMERICA

✠

ST. AIDAN PRESS, LLC
Morning View, Kentucky

Dominican Saints.

First published in 1921 by Dominicana, Washington D.C.

Cover image is *The Genealogical Tree of the Dominicans*, from the Netherlands, c. 1480–1490. Courtesy of the National Gallery of Art, Washington, D.C. Number 1964.8.11 in the National Gallery catalog.

ISBN-13: 978-1-962503-03-7
ISBN-10: 1-962503-03-8

For more information, contact:

www.staidanpress.com
staidanpress@gmail.com

We have made no intentional change from the original text except to correct mistakes in spelling and punctuation.

TO OUR *Holy Father, Saint Dominic, on the occasion of the Seventh Centenary of his birth in the "Celestial Hierarchy," these pages are affectionately dedicated by the*

NOVICES.

Nihil Obstat

Fr. V. F. O'Daniel, O. P., S. T. M.
Fr. M. A. Waldron, O. P., S. T. M.

Imprimatur

Fr. Raymundus Meagher, O. P., S. T. L.
Prior Provincialis.

Neo—Eboraci, die 4ª Aug., 1921.

Imprimatur

✠ Jacobus Hartley,
Episcopus Columbensis.

CONTENTS

Introduction

EVEN HUNDRED years have run on since the great Dominic de Guzman walked this earth, shedding about him the luster of his sanctity and his wisdom. And today many thousands of his spiritual children, the world over, rise up to call him blessed, while hundreds of thousands of ardent admirers pay homage to his Order, which has battled so long and so well for the glory of God and the exaltation of His Holy Name.

Among the many exponents of the ideals of the Order of Saint Dominic, the fourteen canonized saints stand out pre-eminently. It is the purpose of this book to outline briefly the lives of these fourteen saints, and to indicate where further information regarding them may be obtained. The writers have drawn their material from scattered but authentic sources in the hope of showing how the spirit of Saint Dominic was, humanly speaking, the mainspring of the activities of these exponents, the guiding principle in the development of their characters, and the lodestar of their lives.

A cursory glance over the lives of Dominican saints would give the impression that they had no common bond, other than that of charity proper to all Christians, so varied are their methods of advancing toward perfection. Each one stands alone, letting his life flow forth in a reckless torrent, and is apparently controlled only by the passion of love for God and love for neighbor. There is a daring, a freedom, an intensity of life, that is amazing. Each utilizes with a master hand the instruments which time and circumstances have given him, for the promotion of the glory of God and the good of humanity. The casual observer is surprised to find such marked variety and individualism in so many saints of the same Order; but deeper investigation reveals the fact that, notwithstanding all this freedom and individualism, the lives of these saints did not develop haphazardly. They were not merely the result of individual souls trying, each in its own original way, to draw near to God. On the contrary, they had a common, fixed rule of life which bound them together, and upon which their various religious characters were based, developed, and brought to perfection. For this great boon they were all indebted to Saint Dominic, who by the force of his genius had wrought out a system whereby, under God, they were enabled to transcend to such lofty heights. It would be difficult to overestimate the value of this rule of life. It is a model of organization that during seven hundred years has called for but little in the way of reform. It may be said still to represent the rude and vigorous municipal freedom of that age in which it arose and took on the shape in which it has come down to us, a monument of efficiency and fairness in the difficult art of directing men along the higher lines of the spiritual life.

Through a merciful dispensation of the Almighty, there has been vouchsafed to man the supreme gift of Revelation, in the light of and by the aid of which alone is he able to solve the mystery of life. Indeed, how precious little has man by unaided reason been able to understand concerning the purpose of his existence, his destiny, his relation toward his fellow-man and toward his Creator; and when neglecting the aid, or spurning the light of Revelation, how sadly deficient he has been in applying the remedies to the social evils which have vexed the human race down through the ages. By means of Revelation, however, he is able to see and to understand his proper place in the divine plan of creation. Through it he is given a clearer idea of God and His sublime perfections; he is made to appreciate the greatness and high spiritual dignity of his nature, the supernatural end to which he is ordained, and to understand clearly his relations toward his God and his fellow-man. This Revelation throws light upon the questions which reason sees only dimly and in shadow, and admits him into secrets which are far beyond the capacity of his unassisted human intellect. In the transmission of this great inheritance from generation to generation for the past seven centuries, the children of Saint Dominic have held a commanding place; for it has been the special mission of the Dominican Order, since its very inception, to labor for the preservation, in all its purity, of the "Deposit of Faith," and to teach and preach its revealed truths to succeeding generations. As to what great things they have accomplished in this regard, history bears witness.

Who can calculate how much the modern world owes to Saint Pius V, whose courageous resistance to the poisonous falsehoods of heresy, and whose valiant defense of European civilization against Turkish invasion and fanaticism has earned for him the title of "Father of Nations"; or to a Saint Thomas Aquinas, the Angel of the Schools, whose synthesis of the dogmas of revealed truth has been the wonder of all succeeding ages; to a Saint Vincent Ferrer, that undaunted preacher of the Divine Word, and perhaps the greatest thaumaturgus since the days of the Apostles; to a Saint Catherine of Siena, whose incomparable correspondence with Popes, Kings, and republics is at once the pride of Italian letters, the honor of the Papacy, the crown of social endeavor amid hopeless confusion, and is treasured among the purest intellectual glories of her sex; or here, at home, to a Saint Rose of Lima, our New World's first flower of sanctity and mightiest exemplar and guide in the stern but lovely life of the Christian spirit.

To the Dominican Order, ecclesiastical studies and liturgy, as well as the social sciences and the fine arts, are very deeply indebted; for it has been an efficient instrument in garnering the wisdom of the ages and bringing it to the defense of truth; in organizing philosophy and rendering it subservient to theology, thus making the knowledge of Revelation queen of the sciences; in elevating the fine arts and putting them into the service of Christ; in a word, by its preaching and teaching it has exercised upon the earth a civilizing and spiritualizing influence, for which the world will ever be its debtor.

For the devout reader of these short lives there is much in store that is delightful as well as profitable. Perhaps there is no human influence that gives so great a stimulus toward the better things of life than do the saints of God. And here it may truly be said that we have no better example than Saint Dominic. By his peculiar sanctity and by his courage to dare and to do, he has been the inspiration, not only of these eminent canonized saints, but also of a host of martyrs, confessors, virgins, and holy men and women distinguished for learning and for sanctity in almost every branch of human activity—from the lowest and humblest state of domestic servitude to the highest position possible to man, that of Vicar of Christ on earth.

These lives are necessarily short, since all have to be compressed within the compass of a single octavo volume. Their very brevity, however, may add to their charm and induce many to read them; and, having read them, be led to read other and more exhaustive biographies of the same saints. In this way they will experience the rare pleasure of coming into contact with the indescribable charm of these great men and women, and through the irresistible eloquence of their example be moved to a greater appreciation of the good things which God reserves to those who love and serve Him faithfully.

✠ Thomas J. Shahan.

Catholic University of America,
Washington, D. C.

Feast of Saint Hyacinth, 1921.

DOMINICAN SAINTS

Saint Dominic

SEVEN CENTURIES ago battlemented parapets raised their bold turrets around the town of Calaruèga, standing by the Roman road some thirty miles northward from Osma, the episcopal see of Old Castile. These medieval walls guarded the castle of the Guzmans, a family of Visigothic knights whose chivalry was famously jealous of its Christian faith as well as of its family honor.

Within this ancient town and of this blue-blooded Guzman stock Saint Dominic was born, about 1170. His father, Felix, seems to have been happily blessed with the qualities of Chaucer's "perfect, gentle knight," although we know but little more about him. His mother, Joanna d'Aza, had strains of Europe's noblest blood, and so renowned was her sanctity that she was beatified by Pope Leo XII. Besides Dominic, two other children of this union lived saintly lives, one, Mannes, having also been beatified.

Marvels accompanied Dominic's birth. Before her delivery, his mother "imagined," says Jordan of Saxony, the Saint's first biographer, "that she bore in her womb a dog, and that it escaped from her, holding in its mouth a burning torch, with which it set fire to the world." "On the day of his baptism the godmother of the Saint had a vision," relates Thierry of Apoldia, "in which the blessed child appeared to her marked on the forehead with a radiant star, the splendor of which illuminated the entire earth." Were not these fitting auguries of the infant's life-work? Christian art has deemed them such, for they are always associated with Saint Dominic's statues and pictures. The font used on the occasion of Dominic's baptism, it is not without interest to note, was later taken to Madrid, and even now the royal children of Spain are christened in it.

Dominic's infancy was passed amid ordinary circumstances. At the age of seven his parents placed him under the tutelage of his maternal uncle, a parish priest at the collegiate church of Gumiel d'Izan, not far distant from Calaruèga. Here the young lad received his primary instructions, which, according to the medieval custom, consisted mainly in reading from the Latin Fathers. His biographers hint that even now his piety was intense. He would wander into the church to listen to the choral chant; or, when his mood so disposed, he would sit a long while gazing at the paintings in the church, which made their appeal to his religious instincts.

When fourteen, Dominic left his uncle's care and entered the schools of Palencia, then the best in Spain. Even at this youthful age he probably had a canon's title, as Guiraud suggests, which defrayed the expenses of his long education. His course at Palencia lasted about ten years. The first five or six were given to the medieval arts course, including logic; the rest of his time was devoted to the study of theology. A serious student, Dominic is said to have shown rather the mature gravity of an old man than the boisterous vivacity of a university student. Always he blended his studies with pious devotions. His charity was revealed at this period, during one of those terrible plagues which were the frequent scourge of medieval towns. In order to relieve the distress and misery of the poor of Palencia, he sold his books. Those were precious possessions before the invention of printing and were "annotated by his own hand," as Brother Stephen reported at his canonization process.

The date of Dominic's ordination is not certain, but was probably 1194. Soon after this event he undertook his duties as canon at

Saint Dominic
Statue at Dominican House of Studies, Washington

the Osma Cathedral. The canons of this church were living a regular life under the rule of Saint Augustine, with Didacus d'Azevedo as prior. The new priest's reputation for holiness and prudence must have preceded him, for the regular life of these canons was a reform measure, and Dominic was made sub-prior immediately. Two years later, when d'Azevedo became bishop of Osma, he appointed Dominic prior of the canons. The nine years of hidden life at the cathedral were given up to the holy practices of conventual life.

"At once," says Jordan of Saxony, "he began to appear among his brother canons as a burning torch, the first in sanctity, the lowest of all in humility, shedding around him an odor of quickening life, a perfume like incense on a summer's day. Like an olive tree which throws out its branches, like a growing cypress, he grew in holiness. He remained day and night in the church. One special demand he constantly addressed to God, that there might be bestowed on him a true charity, a love which should count nothing too dear for the salvation of men. He was accustomed to read the Gospel of Saint Matthew, the Epistles of Saint Paul, and *The Conferences of the Fathers*, by Cassian. These books, assisted by divine grace, raised him to a purity of conscience, to abundant illumination in contemplation, and to an eminent degree of perfection."

At length this quiet, contemplative life was intruded upon. In 1203 Dominic's bishop, Didacus d'Azevedo, took him on a diplomatic journey to Denmark, there to arrange a marriage for the son of Alfonso IX of Castile. This journey brought them through southern France, and thus occasioned the directive inspiration of Dominic's life. It appears that one night, while lodging in an inn at Toulouse, Dominic discovered his host was an Albigensian, an adherent of the pernicious heresy then demoralizing Languedoc. With a newborn apostolic fervor he ingeniously threw himself, heart and mind, into the work of rooting out his host's errors and of implanting again the true faith in the misguided soul. He argued all night, we are told, with a sweet and kindly charity, and won his host over to the truth of the Catholic faith. "From that time," Bernard Guidonis observes, "he cherished in his heart the project of spending himself for the salvation of misbelievers, and of instituting to that end a preaching Order, to be devoted to the evangelization of the nations."

With this fresh inspiration hot in his heart, Dominic's interest in his bishop's mission must have flagged. Nevertheless, he journeyed to Denmark, made the necessary negotiations, then returned to Spain and with a large retinue began the second trip to the north to fetch the young betrothed. When they reached Denmark the second time he and his bishop attended the obsequies of the fair lady for whom they had come. Then the retinue was dispatched to Spain with the sad news. But Dominic and his bishop went to Rome, presumably because of a mutual desire for missionary work among the heathen Cumans who inhabited the steppes of Russia. For this pious project they sought the papal sanction. Innocent III heard the apostolic desires of the two holy men, but saw a greater need for their preaching among the Albigensian heretics. He instructed d'Azevedo to retain his bishopric and to preach in southern France before returning to Spain. Dominic, likewise, was to preach with his bishop. Leaving Rome with the Pope's blessing, the commissioned preachers went to Languedoc.

Early in 1205, Didacus and Dominic arrived at Montpellier, just as the Cistercian missionaries were holding a conference to discuss whether or not they should discontinue their preaching on account of their meager success.

On becoming aware of the presence in the town of the Bishop of Osma and his companion, the Cistercians asked their counsel on the gloomy outlook of the mission. The Bishop perceived that the rich equipages of the missionaries, while befitting their dignity as papal legates, were a source of scandal and were quite in contrast with the show of poverty practiced by the Albigensian itinerant preachers. With keen insight into the situation, Didacus and Dominic reminded the Cistercians of the importance of example in affecting the simple Midi folk. By pretentious holiness and by evangelical poverty, the heretics predisposed the people for the acceptance of their false teachings. Then Bishop d'Azevedo, speaking also for Dominic, said: "The missionaries of Christ must drive out one nail by another; must put to flight the show of holiness by the practices of sincere religion." He made it clear that the success of their preaching would be proportionate to the intensity with which they imitated the primitive apostolic spirit. This apostolic spirit could be had only by extreme sacrifices. This, in substance, was the Bishop's counsel. Hard indeed it was, but it was received in the spirit in which it was offered. By his encouragement and inspiration, Didacus created a new zeal in the preachers. After the conference was finished the Cistercians sent away their magnificent retinues and, following the example of Didacus and Dominic, went about on foot to preach in any place they could win a hearing.

Besides the feature of evangelical poverty, a systematic method of conducting the instruction of the heretics was now adopted. A series of public debates was arranged, in which the Catholic missionaries matched their arguments with those of the most skilful heretics. This mode of missionary activity, more modern than medieval, seems remarkable. Another striking practice is even more interesting. This was the practice of balloting at the end of each discussion, by which the auditors signified which side they thought victorious. One of the liveliest of these religious debates was held at the town of Servian, in which Saint Dominic had a notable victory. The discussion lasted seven days. Each day the most acute and adroit of the Albigensian teachers hurled at him their most terrific blows. But after the week's debate there was a popular acclamation of Dominic's victory. So pleased were the people that they followed him and his companions for three miles out of the town.

Such success as attended the preaching at Servian was not always achieved. For instance, at Verfeil, Dominic became angry over the obstinacy of its inhabitants and launched his anathema upon them: "Cursed be ye, unmannerly heretics; I should have credited you with better sense!"

Dominic's earnest efforts for the dissemination of Catholic truth continued with varying success—now more, now less. He visited every town and village in the Midi, instructing where and how he could—sometimes on the public square, sometimes in the most spacious room of a castle, sometimes in a church. His headquarters were at Fanjeaux, where the Bishop of Toulouse granted him a chaplaincy. He had six companions. They were all priests, mature scholars and generally well equipped to render the greatest assistance to him in his preaching, which at this time was still under the direction and authority of the Bishop of Osma.

Probably the most consoling incident during this period was the conversion in 1206 of nine female heretics. They came to Dominic, confessing that their hearts had been drawn to him by the beauty of the doctrine he expounded in a recent open-air sermon. They declared that heretofore their minds had been deceived by the heretic leaders, for they truly thought these false teachers were good men. Dominic graciously received these nine women back to the faith, but was not content with this. He threw about them the protection of the cloister. They became the first community of Our Lady of Prouille, the mother house of all Dominican sisters. In this work he was aided by Bishop Foulques of Toulouse, who granted to the community the revenue of the Church of Our Lady. This prelate also donated a neighboring house, in which the little community lived and grew in fervor under the saintly founder's spiritual guidance.

Dominic's joy over this first foundation was counteracted in 1206 by the sorrow of the departure of the Bishop of Osma, who, in accordance with the Pope's orders, returned to Spain.

Shortly after the nuns were established at Saint Mary's, Prouille, a neighboring house was opened for the associates of Dominic.

Besides the preachers, he had a couple of helpers, who later on became lay-brothers. These lay helpers attended to all the business concerns of the nuns. Not until 1215 did the Preachers receive definite organization. This was by the recognition of Bishop Foulques, who approved them as a diocesan congregation.

But this local character was not in keeping with the universal apostolate of which Dominic dreamed. Consequently, when he went to Rome in 1215, as consultor to Bishop Foulques, at the Fourth Lateran Council, he requested Pope Innocent III to give papal sanction to his Preaching Order. Grave difficulties were in the way of such a confirmation, because the council, then in session, expressly laid down restrictions against the multiplication of religious orders, with provision that all future communities must adopt one of the existing rules.

Dauntless characters like Saint Dominic are not distressed by difficulties such as this. He saw a way to the execution of his project and without hesitation followed it. With an eager heart he walked again across Europe, back to Toulouse, and, much to his joy, he found his community increased from six to sixteen members. His first concern was to put the matter of a suitable rule before his religious family. A solemn discussion followed, with the result that the Rule of Saint Augustine was adopted, probably for two reasons: First, it embodied the fundamental features of the new order in its general, broad and free insistence on the essential virtues of the religious life, and, secondly, it was flexible enough to be adapted to the varying conditions incident to a world-wide order, which even then these sixteen preachers must have had a dim consciousness of providing for. Then, too, it was the rule Dominic had lived under at Osma for nine years and he could vouch for its admirable fitness to the needs of his institute.

The noble deference of Dominic toward the wishes of his community on this occasion indicates the singular beauty of his character. Here also is displayed in a most exceptional degree the practical political wisdom which Cardinal Newman called Saint Dominic's "imperial genius for government." In a letter written about this time, Pope Innocent III gave the name to Dominic's Order which later became its official title. He bade his secretary address the letter "To Master Dominic and the Brothers Preachers."

After the decision about the rule and before setting out for the third time to Rome, Master Dominic was given the Church of Saint Romain at Toulouse, and for the time being his community used this as headquarters. He left Toulouse in August, 1216, and could not have gone far before he got the news of Pope Innocent's death, in July, 1216. This news must have been especially distressing.

Innocent III was his friend and he sympathized with his ideas. What might he expect from a stranger? Sustained by a supernatural courage, he proceeded to Rome, arriving there in October, 1216. The new Pope, Honorius III, received him kindly and promised to carry out the policy of his predecessor. Two months elapsed, however, before the formal approval of the Order of Preachers was given. And some one has made the ingenious hypothesis that this delay was due to the embarrassment of the papal chancery officials, who could find in previous approvals no technical forms adequate to cover the privileges of Master Dominic's institute. Heretofore only single foundations or federations of existing monasteries were approved, but now it was a question of bestowing on a central power faculties for universal expansion.

The Bull of approval was signed on December 22, 1216. It read as follows:

> "Honorius, Bishop, Servant of the servants of God, to our dear Son, Dominic, prior of Saint Romain of Toulouse, and to your brethren who have made or will make profession of regular life, health, and Apostolic benediction.
>
> "We, considering that the brethren of your Order will be the champions of the faith and true light of the world, do confirm the Order in all its lands and possessions, present and to come, and

we take the Order itself, with all its goods and rights, under our protection and government.

"Given at Santa Sabina at Rome, on the 11th of the kalends of January, this first year of our Pontificate.

"HONORIUS."

On that memorable day of December, 1216, Dominic's heart must have been by far the most joyous in Christendom, as he stood amidst the cypress trees on the Aventine, in the shadow of the Papal Palace of Santa Sabina, and dreamed of the possibilities for good to the Church which were enshrined in the single parchment page of that Pontifical Bull. How his eyes must have glistened as he fingered the precious "Bill of Rights," and how his buoyant, delicately strung soul must have harmonized the sentiments of the *Te Deum* and the *Magnificat,* as it lifted its prayer and was transfigured beyond human proportions in the presence of God! And we can hardly help dwelling for a moment on his outer appearance, since it was the shrine and expression of the inner soul.

In the words of Father McNabb, O. P.: "Everything about Saint Dominic betokened the finest fabric of a human existence; the figure more than medium; the long, gracefully molded fingers; the shoulders slightly bent, as if in hourly deference to all; the noble head nobly crowned with a corona of auburn, flashing golden in the sun; the sweet smile, so homely on his cheeks; the tender, resolute, pathetic, sympathetic eye—a very lamp of light set in a brow of amber ivory; and then that mystic nebula (frequently alluded to by Sister Cecelia and Blessed Jordan) that glowed from his forehead, filling the dark souls of the despairing with peace and bringing thoughts of God and of the angel-trod cloisters of the Great City nearer to the hearts of men."

After receiving the Bull of Approval, Dominic spent all that winter in Rome. During this sojourn he preached incessantly. His lectures on the Epistles of Saint Paul to the servants, whom he saw idling their time in the corridors of the Papal Palace, gained for him a great reputation, which occasioned his being named "Master of the Sacred Palace." Later on, this title was given to the official known as the "Pope's Theologian," and in memory of Saint Dominic a Dominican always holds this position.

Cardinal Ugolino, who became Gregory IX, befriended Saint Dominic during this winter at Rome. Frequently the Saint discussed with him his ideas for the preaching of the faith, and there is no doubt that the encouragement and counsel of this Prince of the Church were of the greatest importance in shaping the destinies of the Order of Preachers.

At the cardinal's house Dominic met Francis of Assisi; this was the second meeting of the Saints, for they met before, on an earlier visit of Dominic in Rome. The two Saints became the warmest friends. Both had similar aims; both were burning with divine charity for the salvation of souls and, although by diverse means and with distinct spirits and geniuses, both worked harmoniously together. Perhaps no sainted friendship has received such a happy perpetuation. For the last seven hundred years the respective orders which claim these Saints as their fathers and founders have given tokens of a mutual esteem, especially by the beautiful tradition kept up on the feasts of these medieval patriarchs. On the feast of Saint Francis Dominicans celebrate the Mass and are honored guests at the Franciscan friaries, and on the feast of Saint Dominic the compliment is returned by the Franciscans.

After preaching the Lent of 1217 at Rome, Dominic went back again to Languedoc. He spent the summer at Prouille. In the modest convent adjoining the monastery of the nuns he frequently gathered together his sixteen brethren to instruct them in his spirit, and we may reasonably suppose that free discussions were had about the future of the Order.

On August 15 Dominic received the profession of his first sixteen friars. Then he made known to them his intention of dispersing them throughout Europe. It was a bold decision, and nobody but himself, apparently, saw any wisdom in the idea. Saint Dominic acted with the prudence which is of the Holy Ghost. At the time a resumption of crusading hostilities threatened the country about Toulouse. As this not only would have prevented any further development there for some time, but also might have meant destruction, Saint Dominic saw that it was expedient, under the circumstances, to scatter his men, like seeds among the fertile fields, at the centers of civilization.

It is interesting to note the already cosmopolitan character of the first sixteen Preaching Friars. Among them were Castilians, Navarese, Normans, French, Languedocians, and even English and Germans. They were distributed in this way: Four went to Spain; seven went to Paris; two remained at Toulouse; two kept the direction of the sisters at Prouille; lastly, Dominic and Stephen of Metz were to go to Rome.

No incident in Saint Dominic's life represents the great-hearted zeal of his soul quite as strikingly as does this dispersion of the Brethren. He clearly grasped the situation, perfectly gauged his opportunities, and confidently judged the successes ahead. The results afterward proved the remarkableness of his courageous broad-mindedness. By a single stroke of genius, Dominic transformed his diocesan preaching band into a universal order.

In connection with the dispersion of the Brethren an interesting bit of history has come down to us:

> "It is recorded that when the Brethren quitted Prouille to spread all over the world, the Saint bade them set out without money or resources of any kind. One of their number complained of this privation; in vain did Saint Dominic implore him to take his courage in his hands; in vain did he assure him that he should want nothing. John of Navarre refused to give in. Compassionating his weakness, Dominic gave him twelve small coins, and so allowed him to set out. At a later period John of Navarre, reflecting

on a kindness and condescension which had perhaps saved him from throwing up all in a fit of discouragement, was humble enough to tell the story of his own weakness" (Quetif—Échard, Scriptores Ord. Præd., Vol. I, p. 50).

Tradition assigns to this period of Saint Dominic's career the institution of the Holy Rosary of Our Blessed Mother, as a combination of vocal and mental prayers grouped about the fifteen mysteries of Catholic faith. In the Catholic mind, Saint Dominic's name is inseparably associated with the Rosary and many Popes have eulogized the piety of the Saint which left such a devotional treasure to the Church. Certainly no other form of prayer is so clearly stamped with Saint Dominic's spirit. His unique blending of contemplation and action is the essential character of the Rosary. It is pre-eminently a simple spiritual exercise in meditation accompanied by the vocal recitation of the sublimest prayers of Catholic piety.

Shortly after sending forth the Brethren, Dominic received four novices at Prouille, and to train them through his own personal influence he deferred his departure. Some business about revenues had to be settled with his devoted friend, Simon de Montfort, and with Bishop Foulques. When all this was attended to, he was free to set out for the fourth time to Rome.

He and Brother Stephen made the trip in the fall of 1217. Many legends tell us of numerous convents founded on this journey, but the best sources report nothing marvelous. He stopped with the Canons Regular of San Nazzario at Milan; thence he journeyed to Bologna, and at the end of January, 1218, he reached Rome with four new recruits, Brothers Otho, Henry, Albert, and Gregory.

Although Pope Honorius was extremely prodigal of spiritual privileges and temporal protection to Saint Dominic for his Friar Preachers, it is a very significant fact that the primitive foundations were characterized by a charming simplicity and a rigorous poverty. The beginnings of the Order in Rome were unpretentious. The friars had only a tentative abode at San Sisto, which had been deeded to the Gilbertines of England. Preaching and charitable works consumed their energies. The day was given to the ministry of the Word, the night to spiritual refreshment in vigils and penances; and in all this Saint Dominic was, of course, the dominant inspiration. "He exercised with fervor, devotion, and humility the office for which he had been chosen by God and to which the Holy See had appointed him, and this upon the chief theater of apostolic authority. Divine grace was on his lips, and by his mouth the Lord spoke. People were eager to hear him." Thierry of Apoldia makes mention of the sermons given by him. He also went about consoling and directing the numerous recluses who immured themselves in cells adjoining the churches, thus to have opportunity for continual prayer and mortification.

The magnificent successes of the first year's labors at Rome must have increased the confidence of the Pope in the worth of the new Order; for in 1218 he entrusted to Saint Dominic a task requiring great prudence and tact. This was the reform of the convents of women in Rome. Innocent III had made plans for this work by assigning to the Gilbertines of England the Church and Convent of San Sisto for one of their double monasteries, composed of separate communities of priests and nuns. Six years after San Sisto had been granted to the Gilbertines and they had failed to take up their work, Honorius revoked the deed of his predecessor and signed over the church and convent to Saint Dominic and his associates. The Friar Preachers took formal possession of this ancient church on December 3, 1218.

The following incident gives us an insight into the poverty of this first community at San Sisto:

> "When the Brethren were at San Sisto [relates Constantine of Orvieto], the Order being still unknown in the town, they often

had to suffer from hunger. On a certain day it even chanced that the procurator, Giacomo del Mielo, had no bread wherewith to serve the community. In the morning several friars had been sent out to beg, but having given to some poor persons, who appealed to them, the few loaves they received, they had returned to the convent empty-handed. The hour for the meal approaching, the procurator presented himself to the servant of God and unfolded to him the case. Dominic, trembling with joy, blessed the Lord with transport, and, as if penetrated by a confidence which came from on high, commanded that the usual signal for the meal should be sounded. Now there were in the convent about forty persons. The signal being given, the friars came to the refectory and in joyous accents recited the prayers of the grace. Whilst each one, seated in order, awaited the meal, two young men of comely aspect entered the refectory with white cloths hung from their necks, in which they carried bread sent by the Celestial Breadmaker. In silence the two messengers placed loaves first at the lowest table, and so on up to the place occupied by the Blessed Dominic, and then they disappeared without any one having attained to the knowledge of whence they came and whither they were gone."

In commemoration of this miracle, it is customary in Dominican convents to begin serving the meal to the lay-brothers, and so on from the youngest up to the prior.

When the regular observance was well established at San Sisto, Saint Dominic turned his attention to the work of restoring the contemplative spirit among the nuns of the city. He secured an apostolic commission and addressed himself to several communities, but without result. Their indifference could not be overcome, so he patiently waited for their hearts to be changed by divine grace. Not until some sixteen months later did the sisters give heed to his exhortations. Meanwhile important events occurred, which brought him into a broader field of activity.

Saint Dominic's heart was in the universities. No fact verifies this better than his sending three friars to Bologna in 1218, hardly after settling himself at Rome. He seems to have had a clear idea of the ripeness of the harvest at this intellectual center, and could not, therefore, desist from sending his laborers into the fields to gather in the golden grain, that was soon to give the Bread of the Incarnate Word, the Staff of Eternal Life, to all Europe. "That year," says a Bolognese chronicler, "three friars of the Order of Friar Preachers came to Bologna for the first time, saying they had been sent by a certain Master Dominic, a Spaniard. As they seemed to be holy men, the church of Santa Maria della Mascarella was given them." Poverty marked the beginnings at Bologna, as it had at Rome. "The friars," says Jordan of Saxony, "suffered all the misery of extreme poverty."

A most providential acquisition to the Order occurred early in 1218, in the person of Reginald of Orleans, a Doctor of Laws, who had taught with great brilliance at Paris. His reception into the Friar Preachers happened in this way: While stopping at Rome, on his way to the Holy Land, he revealed to a cardinal friend his ardent desire to associate preaching with his life as a canon of Orleans. The cardinal then told him of the great work of Dominic de Guzman, a canon of Osma, who was then in Rome.

Reginald was captivated by Dominic's ideals, and shortly afterward met him to arrange about joining his Order. Before he could receive the habit, however, Reginald fell seriously ill with a high fever. During this illness the Blessed Virgin appeared to him, and with her own hands gave him Extreme Unction, after which she gave him a white scapular with the admonition, "Receive the habit of thy Order." Then the Blessed Mother disappeared, and Reginald felt himself completely cured. The following day he received the habit with the Blessed Virgin's white scapular from the hands of Saint Dominic at San Sisto. From that date this white scapular became the essential part of the habit of the Dominicans, which up to this event had consisted of a linen rochet worn over a white tunic.

Saint Dominic permitted Reginald to visit Palestine, but gave him instructions to assume the priorship at Bologna after his return, which appointment indicates the Saint's shrewd prudence, for no place could have given a better theater for Reginald's genius. His brilliant career as a canonist at Paris would immediately give him and the Friar Preachers prestige at the pre-eminent university of law.

On Pentecost, 1218, Saint Dominic, with several of his disciples, attended the General Chapter of the Franciscans at Portiuncula. These annual gatherings were most impressive scenes. The sons of Saint Francis came in thousands and encamped on the fields under brushwood tents, like the Jews of old at the Feast of Tabernacles. Like the flowerings of the primitive Christian spirit, their simple charity, apostolic poverty, and ardent devotion burst forth on this verdant Umbrian plain bordering Mount Subasio. They gathered in the open air for an essentially religious purpose: to gain in mutual communion new strength from the joys, the example, and the sufferings of the other brethren. At the Chapter Saint Dominic and his friars could not but have been inspired by the religious enthusiasm and generosity displayed on all sides. The incident must have given the Friar Preachers new hopes, new visions of the future.

In the fall of that year, 1218, probably about the middle of October, Saint Dominic set out with his namesake, Brother Dominic of Segovia, to foster with his own presence the Order of Preachers in Spain. The Segovian friar had gone to Spain at the time of the dispersion from Prouille, but becoming discouraged he gave up his work and returned to Rome. To recommence this abandoned apostolate, the Saint decided on accompanying the Segovian to his beloved native land.

The two travelers arrived at Bologna for the Feast of All Saints, 1218. Here the three pioneer friars were zealously struggling against many hardships. Saint Dominic cheered them with the news of Reginald's entrance into the Order, and reassured them that all would be well when Reginald should come to direct the destinies of their foundation. After celebrating the feast with them, he and Brother Dominic set out on the well-known road to Milan, and thence to France.

These journeys of Saint Dominic did not distract his mind from contemplation. His cloister was the world; for he had, as Saint Catherine of Siena afterwards said of herself, "a cell" in his heart. His biographers narrate his speaking continually of God to his companion. His face beamed with a bright radiance. When the road was especially rough or when rain fell, he would begin to sing in a loud voice the *Veni Creator* or the *Ave Maris Stella*. At other times he would instruct his companion, or he might say, "Go on before, and let us each think a little of our Divine Lord," which would be a sign for meditation.

When Saint Dominic and his companion arrived at Toulouse they found the community flourishing. They visited the sisters at Prouille, who were refreshed by Saint Dominic's instructions, encouragement, and consolation.

But he did not delay long in Languedoc, for we find him at Segovia, in Spain, before Christmas. This city was not far from Osma. The revisiting of the familiar scenes of his early life must have been a delight to the Saint, after an absence of nearly fifteen years. For about a month he preached incessantly in the environs of Segovia, and soon attracted a number of vocations, which enabled him in February, 1219, to lay the foundations for the first Spanish convent, with Friar Corbolan as prior. Tradition says that he founded a convent of nuns at Osma, but this is not certain.

Probably in the same month that saw the Order's establishment at Segovia, Dominic journeyed to Madrid. The Order was already flourishing here, and this was a great consolation for him. Friar Peter of Medina had gathered a number of vocations and had founded a convent for nuns, after the model of Our Lady of Prouille.

One of the Saint's letters to these nuns has come down to us. In it was laid down the rule of the sisters, which prescribed a strict contemplative life. The letter has been preserved by the Cardinal of Aragon and it is now in the Archives of the Dominican Order at Rome.

At Palencia, his alma mater, Saint Dominic made plans for a convent, which was realized shortly after his departure from Spain. Late in March, 1219, he crossed the Pyrenees and arrived at Toulouse for Easter Sunday. Some business transactions, a few sermons, a few conferences to his "Elder Daughters" of Prouille, made up his program in Languedoc. From Languedoc he set out for Paris, taking with him Friar Bertrand.

Pious incidents have been recorded of this journey. At the shrine of Our Lady of Rocamadour the friars spent a whole night in prayer. Shortly after daybreak on the morrow, when the cool, bracing air invited a resumption of their journey, they started out northward. As noon drew near they fell in with some German pilgrims, who generously shared with them their provisions that noon and for four following days. Because he could not repay by spiritual food the material benefits offered by these pilgrims, Saint Dominic was grieved. Accordingly he suggested to Bertrand that they both pray for the gift of tongues, so as to be able to speak German to their friends. The prayer was answered, and we read that Saint Dominic and Bertrand instructed these pilgrims in good German for four days. At Orleans the party broke up, the Germans taking the road toward Chartres and the friars the one to Paris. Then Saint Dominic bade Bertrand not to mention the miracle until after his death.

From Orleans the journey was short to Paris. Saint Dominic and Brother Bertrand quickened their pace as the great city loomed up in the distance. It was now the beginning of June. The beautiful country scenes along the road found a perfect response in the bright spirits of the traveling friars. Soon they were at the Convent of Saint James, where, much to the Saint's joy, he found a community of thirty exemplary friars. The new recruits were mostly young students, attracted by the fervor and simplicity of the founders of the convent. After he had taken a little rest, Saint Dominic began a series of conferences. At these not only the community, but many of the students of the university, were present. During one of these talks he described the conversion of Reginald of Orleans. Jordan of Saxony was inspired by the story to imitate Reginald's example. He received the habit the next Lent.

By Saint Dominic's order the friars of Saint James' convent were dispersed and convents were founded by them at Limoges, Rheims, Metz, Poitiers, and Orleans. Several weeks were spent by Saint Dominic at Paris, and then he started out for Rome in July, 1219.

Meanwhile great results had been accomplished at Bologna. Reginald had arrived at the university, after his pilgrimage to Palestine, on December 22, 1218. He began at once to preach. "His words burn," wrote Jordan of Saxony; "his eloquence, like a flaming torch, sets the hearts of his hearers on fire. Bologna is in flames. It is as though a second Elias had arisen." And this very enthusiastic praise seems to have been fully justified by the facts, for Reginald drew into the Order of Preachers the best of the professorial staff of the university. So phenomenal was the increase in the community that early in 1219 the first convent was altogether too crowded and a new house was obtained in a providential way. It happened that at this time Reginald gave the Preachers' habit to the rector of the Church of San Nicola, a learned man and a doctor of laws, who requested his bishop to give the church of which he had been rector to the Dominicans. The bishop granted the request; and, by another generous gift of lands adjoining the church, Reginald was able to begin the foundations of the present convent, which houses the precious tomb of Saint Dominic.

Toward the end of July Reginald and his community at Bologna welcomed Saint Dominic, who remained with them for four months—that is, until the latter part of November. The Saint must have beguiled many an hour with tales of his journey and of the wonderful work accomplished at Paris. But, although he was pleased to entertain his brethren, Saint Dominic's primary purpose in staying so long at Bologna was to train the novices in his spirit.

In the Acts of Bologna we read: "If in the refectory [which he regularly attended] the friars had two dishes on their table, he ate but one, and though exhausted by severe vigils he took little food or drink. He was assiduous at choir office and was at times so plunged in his devotions that no sound could distract him from them." Having trained his disciples after the manner of his example, he sent them forth in every direction.

Christmas, 1219, Saint Dominic celebrated at Rome. After the festivities were over, two matters called for his immediate attention: the transfer of his brethren to new quarters and the establishment of the nuns at the San Sisto Convent. Toward the end of January the friars, numbering about a hundred, moved to Santa Sabina. This convent became the Roman novitiate and was the headquarters of the Masters General up to 1273.

The second task, that of uniting the nuns of the city at San Sisto, was a difficult one. Saint Dominic presented himself before several communities and expressed to them the earnest desire of the Pope that they should be united, under his direction, at San Sisto. Finally, at the Convent of Santa Maria del Trastevere, he obtained a sympathetic response. All the sisters of this community except one promised to go to San Sisto. When the news of the co-operation of this community with Saint Dominic became known to the other sisters, interest in the project spread. The members of the Convent of Santa Bibiana also yielded. Accordingly, on Ash Wednesday, 1220, Saint Dominic, in the presence of Cardinals Ugolino, Orsini, and the Cardinal Bishop of Tusculum, received the professions of the sisters in the chapel at San Sisto. Then, on the first Sunday of Lent, at night, the sisters carried in procession the picture of the Blessed Virgin by Saint Luke from Santa Maria Trastevere to San Sisto, unnoticed by the people, who would have protested against its removal during the day.

The community of San Sisto observed the strictest cloister. Its spiritual direction was given by Saint Dominic and his brethren, while lay-brothers attended to the material provisions. Toward the end of February Mother Blanche of Prouille, with seven companions, arrived at San Sisto. She became prioress, and under her tactful guidance the community grew in contemplative spirit. Early documents tell of Saint Dominic's solicitude for his daughters; how he would give them a conference every night he was in Rome; how he would frequently cheer them by his anecdotes and pleasantries; how after one of his absences from Rome he brought back to each nun a pewter spoon as a token of remembrance.

During the installation of the sisters at San Sisto a great miracle was performed by Saint Dominic. Cardinal Orsini's nephew, named Napoleone, was killed by falling from his horse, on the morning the sisters made their obedience to the Saint in the presence of the three cardinals above mentioned. The messengers broke into the chapel and informed the cardinal-uncle of the youth's misfortune. In extreme grief Orsini whispered the news to Saint Dominic, who with characteristic charity gave orders to have the corpse brought to the convent. The body, having been brought in, was laid on the chapel floor. Before it Saint Dominic said Mass for the youth. Then, standing by the mangled body, he cried in a loud voice, "Young man, Napoleone, I say to thee, in the name of Our Lord Jesus Christ, arise." In the sight of the cardinals, nuns, and friars, the young man arose alive and without a sign of the least injury. Thus the most distinguished witnesses attested to the greatest of Saint Dominic's miracles.

The next event of importance in the Saint's life was the General Chapter of the Friar Preachers, which assembled at Bologna (1220) on Pentecost. Delegates came from all the convents of the order. "Hardly had the first meeting convened, when Saint Dominic said to them: 'I am an unworthy and useless friar. I deserve to be deposed.' But the brethren, touched beyond description by the humility of their father, would not hear of his resignation." When Saint Dominic insisted, they granted him the concession of laying down the burden of the Master Generalship during the sessions of the chapter, when definitors were to rule the Order. When the definitors were chosen, "as long as the meeting lasted he was merely one of the friars. If he took the first place, it was only in abstinence, vigils, fasting, and maceration, setting himself above none, except in holiness and humility."

Bernard Guidonis informs us it was during this first chapter that most of the rules of the Dominican constitutions were decided upon. Humbert of the Romans relates the following incident of the meeting: "The Blessed Saint Dominic, in the chapter-house of Bologna, declared for the comfort of the weaker brethren, that even the rules do not bind under pain of sin, and that if he could think otherwise he would hack every cloister to pieces with his knife." At this first chapter, too, the Order of Preachers formally adopted poverty as a means to personal sanctification. Up to this time this had not been definitely laid down.

After the friars were dispersed again, Saint Dominic went to Lombardy, where the heretics were especially hostile to the Catholic faith. His preaching was most effective, and in order that its fruits might be more enduring he founded the "Militia of Jesus Christ," which at a later date became known as the "Order of Penance of Saint Dominic," and finally the Third Order of Saint Dominic. In this order were enrolled lay men and women. The men pledged themselves to defend the faith, even with arms, while the women were to foster it especially by prayer. From June until December the Saint with his friars worked vigorously for the conversion of the misguided heretics in Lombardy. Blessed Raymond of Capua wrote in the fourteenth century that during this particular mission of Saint Dominic a hundred thousand heretics were converted.

In December, 1220, Saint Dominic was in Rome. At this time he met Bishop Foulques of Toulouse, whose patronage had meant so much for the founding of the Order of Preachers. "How delightful must have been the communion of these two men," says

Lacordaire. "They had seen the office of preacher exalted in the Church by an Order of religious dispersed from one end of Europe to another, they who had so often talked of the necessity for re-establishing the apostolate."

Gerard de Frachet has left us an interesting account of the appearance of Saint Dominic: "Everything about him breathed of poverty—his habit, shoes, girdle, knife, books, and all like things. You might see him with his scapular ever so short, yet he did not care to cover it with his mantle, even when in the presence of great persons. He wore the same tunic summer and winter, and it was very old and patched; and his mantle was of the worst."

On May 30, 1221, Saint Dominic presided over the Second General Chapter of his Order at Bologna. His strongest plea on this occasion was for fidelity to study and especially to the study of Sacred Scriptures, the God-given storehouse of preaching material. At this chapter the Order was divided into eight provinces, determined mainly by national distinctions. Two of these were as yet only planned, those of Hungary and England, but friars were assigned to undertake the establishment of the Order in these two countries. The provinces already established were those of Spain, Provence, France, Lombardy, Rome, and Germany.

Some time in June, after the chapter was over, Saint Dominic journeyed to Venice to see his old friend, Cardinal Ugolino. Along the way he preached. And it was on his return journey that he was taken sick with a high fever, just outside Bologna. He made his way to the convent there, and in spite of his illness prayed in the church until midnight, and then assisted at the choral recitation of Matins. No longer, however, could he rally his energies; so after Matins he went to bed and never arose again. For three weeks the fever consumed his energies, and on August 6, 1221, he died, surrounded by his brethren, whom he consoled by the promise that he would be more powerful to help them in heaven than he had been on earth.

Bernard Guidonis observes: "He died in Brother Moneta's bed, because he had none of his own; and he died in Brother Moneta's tunic, because he had not another with which to replace the one he had long been wearing."

Thirteen years after his death Saint Dominic was canonized by his friend, Cardinal Ugolino, who had become Pope Gregory IX. The ceremonies were held on July 13, 1234.

In the Bull of Canonization Pope Gregory said: "Bound to us by ties of close friendship when we were in a humbler state, he gave us by the testimony of his life certain proofs of holiness, afterwards confirmed by the truth of his miracles, reported to us by faithful witnesses."

Saint Dominic's chief glory among men lies in the broad and free spirit bequeathed to the threefold religious family of friars, nuns and tertiaries which perpetuates in our own times the apostolate of Truth inaugurated by him in the thirteenth century. What, then, was this spirit which he gave to his followers and which is the special mark of his genius? Briefly, we may say the essence of this spirit is embodied in his intellectual ideal, which distinguished Saint Dominic among the great leaders who, by several fashions of religious life, have founded in the Church institutes to lead souls Godward.

By no mere accident the motto of his religious family is "Truth," for this word touches the magic appeal of Saint Dominic's heart. Were we to choose a text to express the peculiar mold of his genius, we could find none better than the Saviour's words: "The truth shall make you free" (John viii: 32). He aimed at truth and attained freedom of soul. His long student life at Palencia, his years of contemplation at Osma, his apostolic preaching in Languedoc, his dispersion of the brethren to the university centers scarcely a decade of years after his Order was founded, and, finally, the astounding influence which his friars straightway exercised at these power-houses of learning—all these facts bring out strikingly clear the intellectual mission of Saint Dominic. And, moreover, was it not this mark of his genius that, in the thirteenth century, charmed the most virile intellect of Europe, Saint Thomas Aquinas, and, in the nineteenth century, attracted to the Order of Preachers our great modern champion of intellectual freedom, Père Lacordaire?

The secret of Saint Dominic's holiness, then, was his fast-knit friendship with Christ, who is the Truth, the model of perfect freedom, the only source of life's full happiness.

BIBLIOGRAPHY

English Works:

JEAN GUIRAUD: Saint Dominic. Benziger Bros., New York, 1901.

MOTHER DRANE: History of St. Dominic. Burns, Oates & Washbourne, London.

REV. J. B. O'CONNOR, O. P.: Saint Dominic and the Order of Preachers. Rosary Magazine, New York, 1917.

C. M. ANTONY: In Saint Dominic's Country. Longmans, Green & Co., London, 1912.

FATHER LESCHER, O. P.: Saint Dominic. Catholic Truth Society, London.

FR. BEDE JARRET, O. P.: The Dominican Order. Catholic Truth Society, London.

French Works:

PP. BALME ET LELAIDIER: Histoire Diplomatique de Saint Dominique. Paris, L'Année Dominicaine.

LACORDAIRE: Vie de S. Dominique. J. de Gigord, Ed. Paris, 1912.

CONSTANTINE D'ORVIETO: Vie de S. Dominique. Edited by Échard, Scriptores Ordinis Præd. Paris, 1719.

Latin:

JORDANUS DE SAXONIA: De Origine Ordinis Fratrum Præd. Ed. Fr. Berthier, O. P. Fribourg.

Acta Sanctorum. Aug. 4. S. Dominici.

Saint Peter Martyr

URING THE FIRST PART of the thirteenth century the Church was confronted by a very formidable enemy. This was a sect of heretics called Cathari, which was in reality nothing other than a revival of the old Manichean heresy, against which Saint Augustine had labored and written. Upper Italy was especially infected with this pestilential heresy, and as its advocates were unusually active in this section, the simple inhabitants were doubly exposed to its poisoning influences. The Church, ever solicitous for the welfare of her children, was energetic in combating the evils of this heresy; but for a time it appeared as though the evil might triumph in spite of the vigilance and activity of the ecclesiastical authorities; for when quelled in one district it would immediately spring up with renewed vigor in another, and thus daily many of the faithful were falling victims to the tricks and seductions of the wily sectaries. God, however, was watching over His Church, and sent to her aid in this time of distress His valiant warrior and champion of Truth, Saint Peter the Martyr.

Peter was born in the year 1205, in Verona, a town of the Province of Lombardy. His parents, according to Augustine Valere, bishop of Verona, belonged to the nobility and had long been infected with heresy, to which they obstinately adhered. The boy Peter, however, was saved by divine grace from all contamination, for his parents, under the directing hand of God, never spoke to him of their religion nor forced him into the society of the heretics who frequented their home.

Saint Peter, Martyr

When Peter was seven years of age he was sent to one of the Christian schools of Verona to learn the rudiments of grammar. The master of this school happened to be a learned and devout Catholic, but this circumstance did not hinder the boy's father from sending him thither, for he thought he could easily destroy by subsequent instruction of his own any Christian ideas the child might acquire. At this school Peter made rapid progress in his studies, and, as might easily be expected from a boy of ardent temperament when surrounded by the best of Catholic influences, he acquired an energetic love for goodness and truth. One day, returning home from school, the boy was stopped in the street by his uncle, a stubborn heretic, who asked him what he was learning from his Christian master. In reply the boy began reciting in a devout manner the "Apostles' Creed." After the words "Creator of heaven and earth," the heretic stopped him, explaining that it was by no means God Who created the earth, but the principle of evil, as has always been the teaching of the Manicheans. Peter could not be prevailed upon to admit this, and ended the discussion by the assertion that none who so believed could hope for salvation. In a frenzy the man hastened to the boy's father, insisting that he be punished and removed from the dangerous surroundings of the Christian school, his argument being that if the child were allowed to continue under his present master he would surely join the ranks of the Catholic Church and later prove dangerous to their religion. We shall see how exactly this prophecy was later fulfilled. Peter's father, however, unconsciously acting under the hand of God, refused to listen to his brother's counsel and the boy was neither punished nor withdrawn from the school. Thus his life began with a "Credo" and ended, as we shall see, with the same word written in his own blood.

At the age of fifteen Peter was sent to Bologna to continue his education. The great university there attracted the youth of all countries, but unfortunately vice was rampant among its students. Fearing contamination, Peter prayed much, kept in retirement, fled occasions of sin, practiced self-contempt, and assiduously applied himself to study. Hence he again merited the watchful help of Providence, which had already preserved him from heresy, and, though surrounded on all sides by temptation, his life became more angelic than human.

In 1221 Saint Dominic, the arch-enemy of heretics, came to Bologna to attend a Chapter General of the Order of Preachers, lately founded by him. During his stay there he often preached in the public places of the city, as was the custom in those days. Peter, having heard the man of God, was immediately attracted by that voice which had labored so hard to destroy heresy and sow the seeds of divine love in the hearts of men. He longed to become one of the Saint's spiritual children, and finally, encouraged by the example of some of his companions and masters, offered himself to Dominic. Although the lad was but sixteen years of age, the holy Patriarch, filled with the assurance that God had sent him a treasure, clothed him with the habit of his Order and sent him to prepare for the priesthood. So he, who was the son of an obstinate heretic according to the flesh, now became the spiritual son of the conqueror of heretics.

Brother Peter quickly acquired the spirit of the Order to which he had given himself, and earnestly endeavored to follow the example of its holy founder. Saint Dominic, however, was not left to him long for emulation; for, worn out from a life of almost continual labor and mortification, he lived but a few months after Peter's reception into the Order. The loss of so inspiring a father was truly a severe blow to Dominic's children, and none felt it more keenly than the young novice, Brother Peter. Nevertheless, one consolation was accorded him, namely, that he was present at the deathbed of the holy patriarch and received his last paternal blessing.

The novitiate days of our Saint were marked by a great love for the observances of the institute which he had embraced. The severe fasts and vigils, disciplines, solitude, and other mortifications enjoined by the rule were in his eyes stepping-stones to heaven. As a novice he made but one mistake. His love of mortification carried him to excess, and he added, without the consent of his confessor, many private penances to those prescribed. As a consequence his health began to fail, and it was only then that he realized his mistake. He understood that the devil inspired these self-imposed mortifications, and ever after was content to observe only those permitted by the rule and his confessors. His exact obedience to his superiors in even the slightest things was a source of edification to all the brethren, while his charity toward all was the wonder of the entire community. Later, when he acted as guest-master, this virtue shone out in the holy friar with increased brilliance, and often he sacrificed himself to an heroic degree for the comfort of those he served.

All through Brother Peter's life his purity was angelic, and from constant vigilance in this regard he preserved unblemished his baptismal innocence. This fact was made known by his directors after his death. While in the novitiate he developed a marvelous and untiring application to study, especially to the study of the Sacred Scriptures. Like his father, Saint Dominic, he was never without a copy of the inspired writings, and thus he prepared himself to fight heresy with the armor of Divine Truth. An interesting fact recorded by his biographers is that God endowed him with a gift of memory so remarkable that he never forgot anything which he had once read.

Shortly after his ordination to the holy priesthood the superiors of the Order commanded Peter to prepare for the ministry of preaching. So the holy friar retired to a quiet convent, where he studied assiduously the fallacies of the heretics, in order to know just where and how to attack their false arguments. When he began to preach the faithful were filled with joy, for they recognized in him a powerful defender of the cause of Catholic truth. The heretics, on the other hand, grew uneasy. They feared that by his ability and indomitable zeal he would quickly bring about their ruin.

We are told by early biographers of the Saint that he was tall and majestic in appearance; that his every fiber breathed forth energy and power. His eyes flashed out the intense ardor of his soul, while his voice, perfectly modulated and controlled, never failed to move and convince his hearers. All these qualities of the Saint, so necessary in an orator, were crowned by a wonderful sanctity of life, and this without doubt served, more than anything else, as the magnet which drew the people in multitudes to his feet.

Our Saint had not been preaching long when God sent him a trial which proved very bitter to him, but at the same time greatly advanced him in the way of perfection. It was always the custom of the holy man to repair to his cell when his duties were completed, and there in solitude pour forth his soul to God in prayer. Celestial visions were often granted to him.

On one occasion he had prayed far into the night and angelic visitors had conversed with him. Some of the brethren, passing his cell, were horrified to see a light streaming from a chink in the door and at hearing what they judged to be the voices of women. Scandalized and furious at the thought of their cloister being broken, they solemnly proclaimed Peter at the conventual chapter the next morning. When questioned by his superior, the holy man meekly replied, "He who can declare himself innocent of all fault has no need of defense." His modesty was such as to forbid an open confession of what had really taken place in his cell. The meaning of the reply he had given his prior was, of course, misunderstood, and as a penance he was banished in disgrace to an obscure convent in Ancona.

Crushed by this unmerited dishonor, he took refuge in the solitude of his cell and there, weeping before his crucifix, asked the Saviour how He could permit one who was innocent to be so severely punished. A voice from the crucifix answered, "And what have I done to be abused and tormented like this? Learn from Me to bear wrongs with patience." These words greatly consoled the friar and he never again murmured against the trials he had to suffer. In due time his superiors, supernaturally enlightened concerning the grave injustice that had been done to the humble and saintly religious, exonerated him from the disgraceful charge. They recalled him from his exile, established him in his former place of honor and reverence among his brethren, and commissioned him to resume the office of preaching.

The eloquence of this servant of God filled the entire provinces of Lombardy and Tuscany, and wherever he went there remained after him the sweet odor of his sanctity. So efficacious were his sermons that often one alone was sufficient to effect the conversion of whole cities. God granted him the gift of miracles, and frequently he proved the truth of some point of doctrine by curing the sick, restoring sight to the blind, speech to the dumb, and the like.

Thomas de Lentino, one of the first to write his life, says that the preaching of Brother Peter fell upon the souls of the people like "spring rains, accompanied by the lightning of his miracles." He would march into the midst of heretical communities boldly bearing aloft the standard of our redemption, and with full confidence in the help of God would denounce their errors, at the same time warning them of the divine wrath. The results of his preaching upon both faithful and heretics were such as to merit for him comparison with the Apostles themselves.

Naturally the preacher's renown was soon established and everywhere he was met by thousands, so that frequently he had to speak in the public squares and from the porches of public buildings. His contemporary biographers tell us that when he was approaching the gates of cities all the inhabitants, headed by their bishop and clergy, went forth to receive him with banners and music and carried him into the public places upon a litter, whence he would bless the sick and afflicted who lined the streets.

One place which enjoyed the privilege of our Saint's preaching on many occasions was the town of Cesena, in the Romagna.

It was here that many of his miracles took place. Once while he was walking through the market-place a young nobleman named John di Biaggio, who had long suffered from a diseased hand, approaching, begged him to cure his ailment. The Saint humbly acknowledged his own inability and would have passed on, but the pleading face and words of the young man touched his heart; so, after having fervently prayed, he made the sign of the Cross over the afflicted member and immediately all traces of the disease disappeared.

On another occasion, when the oil of his host had failed, Peter, wishing to relieve him in his embarrassment, sent a servant to one of his friends, a man named Bonaccorsi, for the necessary quantity. The man went to the vessel in which it was kept, but to his dismay found it quite empty, and, fearing lest the servant might think this untrue, called him to see for himself; but, wonderful to relate, when the cover was again lifted the vessel was discovered filled to the brim. Bonaccorsi was greatly astonished at seeing this miracle, which he attributed to the prayers of the saintly friar, and hastened to call in his neighbors that they, too, might witness it.

Another miracle is said to have happened here and was witnessed by a large crowd of people. The friar was preaching one day in the public market-place before the usual throngs, when suddenly a shower of stones was hurled at him from a neighboring roof. Looking up, he beheld a number of boys, prepared to annoy him during the rest of his sermon, no doubt at the bidding of their heretical parents. Gentle reproof had no effect on them, and even when he commanded that they stop, the stones continued to fall, endangering those listening to the discourse. After suffering for a time in silence, Brother Peter suddenly turned from his audience and, bowing his head in prayer, implored Almighty God to manifest His protection. Immediately the roof and walls of the building fell in, crushing all its wicked inhabitants. There is a tradition that for many years afterward the house could not be rebuilt.

The holy preacher's companion in Cesena was a friar named Brother William Cavozzani. One day he presented himself in great anguish before the Saint, as one of his hands had been bitten by a scorpion and the deadly poison was fast rising in his arm. Unable to stand the agony longer and fearing for his life, the afflicted man implored Peter for some remedy. The latter simply blessed the wound with the sign of the Cross, when suddenly the pain ceased and even the swelling disappeared.

From Cesena our Saint went to Ravenna, and as the Dominicans had no convent there, he received hospitality at the presbytery of Saint John the Baptist. As evening approached, the friar bade the sacristan ring the bells of the church to announce a sermon for the following morning; but the man refused, urging that it would be useless, since the cold was so bitter and the blizzard so severe that no one would come. The Saint, however, protested to him that a great congregation would assemble despite the inclement weather.

About midnight the sacristan was awakened by loud knockings on the door of his room, and upon opening was surprised to find a number of the parishioners, who anxiously inquired the reason for a great light which was burning in the tower of the church. The man, as astonished as they, made known to them his ignorance of why it had been placed there. He then announced to the people that a holy Dominican friar had come to preach the next day, adding his reason for not having rung the bells as ordinarily, and that the light was undoubtedly a miracle intended to supply their place. The people, filled with wonder at the sight of the great torch, burning in the midst of the falling snow and shedding such brilliance around it, hastened to spread the news through the town. When Peter ascended the pulpit next morning he saw his prophecy fulfilled, for in spite of the snow and cold the church was crowded to its very doors. After having heard the sermon, the people saw the significance of the brilliant light which announced to them the presence of so holy and enlightened a preacher.

Let us now follow the Saint to Venice. Here, as everywhere else, his stay was marked by many wonders, the most striking of these being the cure of a little boy who had been dumb from his birth. One day, while hearing the confession of a noble woman in the church of Saint Martin, he noticed a boy wandering about near the confessional. Upon questioning the woman concerning the child, she answered that it was her son and that he had never spoken. Full of pity, Peter called the lad to him, bidding him open his mouth. The child obeyed, and the Saint blessed his tongue, saying, "In the name of the Father, and of the Son and of the Holy Ghost." Marvelous to relate, the boy immediately answered, "Amen," and for the rest of his life had perfect use of his speech.

These are but a few of the miracles of Saint Peter as recorded by his earliest biographers. Like wonders occurred wherever he preached, serving to excite the confidence of the faithful and aiding in the conversion of many heretics to the truth. But, not content with winning souls to salvation by words alone, we are told that he was always a martyr in desire, and daily, while offering to heaven the precious blood of Christ, he would pledge simultaneously the blood of his own heart for the sacred cause of the Christian religion.

It is plainly evident that the advent of this champion of the faith was most timely for the welfare of souls, as the Manichean heresy was fast overrunning Italy. It was spreading everywhere the deadly poison of its doctrines and in many instances whole cities were sadly infected. The Church, alarmed at the spread of this heresy, had instituted the Roman Inquisition. The purpose of this institution was to counteract the harm which was being done, by enlightening the ignorant and by publicly refuting the errors of learned heretics. As a means to this end, the Church utilized the services of her most saintly and learned preachers. The reigning pontiff, Gregory IX, knowing well the powers of Brother Peter of Verona, conferred on him the office of Inquisitor General in 1232.

From this time on the life of Saint Peter was one continuous battle. He bent all his efforts to the extermination of heresy, day after day preaching against its insidious errors, disputing with its proud and insolent advocates, and praying God for light and strength. His wonderful memory and knowledge of the sacred sciences, especially that of Scripture, were a valuable asset to him now, for his office demanded that he be prepared at all times to defend the faith in public disputations. This was no easy matter, because in most instances his adversaries were adepts in argumentation, and a keen and penetrating mind was required to detect their fallacies, cloaked, as they always were, in the guise of seeming truth.

Peter's preaching continued to be accompanied by miracles, and often heretics would be led to abjure their error by the witnessing of some wonder. The most extraordinary of these happened one day at Milan, during a disputation with a Manichean bishop. Hundreds of both faithful and heretics were present, and had been patiently standing for hours under the hot sun listening to the two opponents. The bishop, fearing the outcome of the discussion, suddenly changed his method of procedure, and assailed the Saint from a different angle. "Friar Peter," he cried sarcastically, "if you are a saint, as your people believe, why do you permit that they suffer the terrible heat of the sun? Why do you not roll a cloud over their heads?" Peter calmly made answer that God would do so in an instant, if he and his heretical followers would renounce their errors for the truth. The bishop promised, and accordingly the holy man prayed thus: "Almighty God, for the purpose of establishing Thy honor as Creator of all things, and for the conversion of these heretics, I beseech Thee to send a protecting cloud." He made the sign of the Cross in the air, and a thick cloud suddenly appeared, rolling itself out over the heads of the astonished people.

In 1244, Pope Innocent IV ordered our Saint to Florence, where heresy was rampant. The Dominican Inquisitor for that district, Brother Ruggiero Calcagni, was unable to cope with the situation alone, so Peter hastened to his assistance and began preaching in the plaza of the cathedral and in that of Santa Maria Novella. The same wonderful success attended his efforts here as everywhere else. On two occasions it is said that the devil appeared in the shape of a huge black horse plunging wildly into the crowds of listeners. But both times the demon disappeared, as our saintly religious raised his hand in benediction.

It was during his stay in Florence that the saintly preacher became acquainted with the first members of the Servite Order. They were at that time a band of pious men living in community on Mount Senario, and because of our Saint's great renown for sanctity had chosen him as their spiritual director. Upon visiting these religious in their monastery, Brother Peter was overjoyed at the holiness and regularity of their lives, recognizing in them the subjects of a vision previously vouchsafed him. This had been an apparition of the Blessed Mother of God, during which she opened her mantle before the friar, and there appeared beneath its folds a number of religious clothed in black habits. "See these my children," said the Holy Virgin, "whom I have chosen as my own servants. Their duties are to honor my name, and my habit which they wear, and they must also observe the holy Rule of Saint Augustine." Wherever he went, Brother Peter praised highly the new Religious, recommending them to the charity of the faithful, and it was through his efforts that they were approved first by the Bishop of Florence and later on, under the name of "Servants of Mary," by Pope Innocent IV.

Seeing Peter's wonderful success in Florence, his companion, Brother Ruggiero, was greatly encouraged, and now fearlessly attacked the foes of Christianity. The boldness of the two inquisitors naturally enraged the heretics, so they had recourse to the German Emperor, Frederick II, for means to wage war against the Catholics. This man was a very formidable enemy of the Church. He encouraged heresy everywhere and had actually led armed attacks against the faithful. Innocent IV, who had excommunicated him, wrote to Peter after the Emperor's death, in 1250, that at last he could hope for the extermination of heresy.

Our Saint, conscious of the designs of the sectaries and the impending danger to the faithful, formed immediately a military company, composed mainly of Catholic nobles, which he called the "Society of the Captains of Saint Mary." Their uniform was white, with a large red cross on breast and shield, their purpose being the defense of the faith by arms against the assaults of the heretics. Full approbation was given them by Pope Innocent IV.

These precautions were taken none too soon, for on the feast of Saint Bartholomew, August 24th, a band of heretics, headed by a few civil magistrates and Florentine noblemen, made a most cruel attack upon the Catholics. These latter were present in great numbers in the churches of Santa Reparata and Santa Maria Novella, attending the ceremonies in honor of the Apostle; so the attack was directed upon these two places. Many were killed within the edifices, while others were massacred in the cemetery of Santa Reparata, whither they had fled. In the afternoon of the same day the bishop, together with Peter and the other inquisitor, held council with the citizens, and in the hope of averting further bloodshed promised mercy to all who would come before nightfall seeking pardon and reconciliation with the Church. But, alas! this example of good returned for evil had no effect on the obstinate heretics, and abuses only increased.

Unable to bear longer the insults heaped upon the faithful by the cruel heretics, Peter, after having conferred with Rome, raised his white standard and led a crusade against the Manicheans. The presence of the intrepid friar inspired the soldiers with a wonderful confidence and enthusiasm, and with him as their chief they boldly met the enemy in a street near Santa Maria Novella. Quickly repelled, the sectaries retreated to the castle of the Rossi. Peter, however, fired with determination, urged on his knights, who boldly attacked the castle and in a fierce combat completely defeated the heretics. The victory filled the Florentine Catholics with great joy, as they considered it the downfall of heresy in their community, many monuments to commemorate the event being raised on the scene where the contest took place.

Innocent IV, well pleased with the achievements of the friars at Florence, conferred the episcopate upon Brother Ruggiero, while he commissioned Peter to continue preaching all through northern Italy. Heresy was still very strong in many places, especially in and around Milan, as here it was fostered by the influential Royal party.

The holy man's preaching was, indeed, not in vain, for soon many unbelievers presented themselves to him for reconciliation. Among these the majority were women; and, in order that the fruits of his labors might be permanent, our Saint, in imitation of his Holy Father, Saint Dominic, erected a monastery for them, which he dedicated to Saint Mary, Queen of Virgins. He clothed the new religious in the white habit of Saint Dominic, and under his own prudent direction these saintly nuns became a source of edification to all the faithful. Postulants came in such large numbers that in a remarkably short time he was obliged to erect nine of these monasteries to house them.

In Milan the servant of truth naturally followed the same plan for combating heresy as that which he had employed in Florence—that is, he established a society of armed nobles, whom he called "Crusaders." After the Saint's death, Blessed Humbert de Romains, the Master General, affiliated these "Crusaders" with the Dominican Order, thus forming the "Society of Saint Peter Martyr."

While Peter remained in Milan he often received the hospitality of a certain devout nobleman, whom the heretics, due to his position, were most anxious to win over to their sect. The means used in accomplishing this purpose were extraordinary. It happened that one among them was very proficient in the "black art" and in frequent communication with the devil, who often performed the most astounding feats at his instigation. Persuading the Catholic one day to enter the temple of the sect, the magician announced that a miracle would be performed to show the utter falsity of the Christian religion and of Brother Peter's preaching. Hardly had he ceased speaking when there was a flash of light; the devil appeared as a woman carrying a child, and in a tone most severe declared to the astonished nobleman that it was the Mother of God herself who stood before him. The apparition further commanded him to join the ranks of the "faithful" then and there or suffer the worst torments. Greatly frightened, the man hastened to obey, and returned to his home an ardent heretic.

Peter, returning to Milan from one of his missionary journeys, went, as was his custom, to the home of this man, and immediately noticed a great change in his bearing toward him. When he asked the reason for this the nobleman informed him of all that had taken place, and even invited him to the temple that he might see for himself. The friar readily consented to go the next day; but, fearing some sort of an ordeal, spent the entire night in fervent prayer and mortification. Early the next morning he hastened to the nearest church to say his Mass, during which he consecrated an extra Host and, placing it in a ciborium, hid it under his scapular.

At the appointed time, Peter accompanied his friend to the temple, and there the magician once more summoned the apparition. Immediately the light was seen to flash, and in another instant there stood before them the supposed Virgin and Child.

"Brother Peter of Verona," the demon cried, "you are an enemy to me and to my son. Repent and join my faithful who are here present."

At this Peter held aloft the consecrated Host, crying with a loud voice, "If you are truly the Mother of God, adore your Divine Son, Who is here."

After these words had been uttered, there followed a crash, the apparition disappeared, and the wall of the building was split from top to bottom. The nobleman, falling upon his knees, once more confessed his faith in the religion of Christ, and with him all the heretics who had witnessed this miracle.

In 1250 Peter was elected prior of the Convent of Piacenza. Realizing how hated he was by his enemies and knowing full well of his approaching martyrdom, he began to prepare for it by every manner of mortification. We are told that the friars who lived under his authority feared he would die unless he relaxed the severity of his penances. About this time the holy prior also made many prophecies which were to be fulfilled, as he said, after his death. One of these was the fall, before the Christian arms, of the Castle of Gathi, an heretical stronghold, and the burning of the corpses of two heretical bishops buried there. This actually came to pass, as shortly after the Saint's martyrdom the Inquisition ordered the destruction of the castle and the burning of the same bodies of which he had spoken. Upon revisiting the city of Cesena, favored so often by his eloquence, he informed the inhabitants of his approaching martyrdom. "My children," he said, "this time I leave you never to return; for, though the Romagna be now at peace, soon disturbances will arise, and the heretics will slay me shortly after the next Easter feast." While our Saint was preaching at Milan, a woman named Geralda begged him to dispossess her of a demon which had troubled her for many years. Peter told her that he could do nothing then, but bade her have patience, for she would be liberated before long, at his tomb. This prophecy was likewise fulfilled, for after the death of the saint, the woman, having approached his sepulcher and prayed for a time beside his sacred remains, was delivered entirely from the power of the tormenting demon.

The activities of the fearless Dominican against heresy won loud praise from all the faithful. Pope Innocent IV went in person to Milan to thank him for his untiring efforts, and thus encouraged him to even greater zeal. On the other hand the heretics, both frightened and angered at the success of the Inquisition, determined to assassinate several leading inquisitors. Those bearing authority in Milan, Como, Bergamo, Lodi, and Pavia banded together and placed a price on the head of Brother Rainiero Sacconi, formerly of their following, and also on that of the intrepid Peter of Verona. Brother Rainiero would have been murdered at Pavia had not the plot been discovered and foiled. Hence greater precautions were taken and more complete preparations made to assure the death of Brother Peter, for they were fully determined to destroy him, their chief enemy. This fact, however, was well known to the servant of God, for he spoke frequently to the friars concerning his martyrdom, even naming the place where he would be buried. In a sermon to the Milanese on Palm Sunday, he announced his coming sufferings and death, but added solemnly that after quitting this mortal life he would gain greater power against the heretics.

The first steps toward the consummation of the martyrdom of our Saint were taken on Easter Monday, in the year 1252. Stephen Gonfalonieri, the originator of the plot, had summoned together in Milan three other heretics equally thirsting for the blood of the hated Friar Preacher. They were Manfred d'Olirone, Giudotto Sachela, and Jacobo della Chiusa, and together they had gathered a sum of money sufficient to hire a murderer. The money obtained, Stephen and Manfred searched through the neighboring districts for a man willing to commit the actual murder, and they found him in the person of one Carino, a vicious character, known and feared by all as a man of blood. The wretch promised to perform the deed, insisting, however, that they allow him a companion, Albertino Porro of Lenta, likewise a notorious criminal. His employers willingly agreed, and so this part of the plot was completed.

Our Saint was now prior of the convent in Como and had returned to his community for the paschal festivities. That he well knew of the plotting against his life was evident from the way in which he forewarned his religious. He made known to them the very day of his death, the exact spot where he was to be slain, and even named the sum which had been paid to the murderer. The brethren, who, of course, admired the Saint as a fearless warrior of Christ and loved him dearly as their own spiritual father, beseeched Almighty God in unceasing prayers to protect His servant from harm. The holy prior, though, far from being alarmed, was actually impatient to die for the faith so dearly loved, and thus to become a martyr of Christ.

On Tuesday of Easter week, Stephen, Manfred, and Carino took lodgings in Como, as near as possible to the Dominican convent, where they could watch with ease the comings and goings of the doomed friar. Carino attended all the Masses in the conventual church, and under this disguise of piety was enabled to converse with the Brother Porter. From him the villain learned to his great satisfaction that the prior would depart for Milan on the following Saturday; so, hastening to his companions, Carino informed them of the good news. Final preparations for the success of the deed were quickly made, Albertino summoned, and after his arrival nothing more was necessary save to lie in wait for the victim.

The fatal day finally arrived, and the Saint began it with a fervent confession, after which he sang the solemn conventual Mass. Then followed the Chapter of Faults for the community, during which the holy prior gave what he knew to be his last exhortation to his brethren. Throwing his whole soul into his words, he bade them ever to advance in the love of God and the virtues of holy religion; to be prepared and willing at all times to suffer for the faith, and with a most earnest appeal for their prayers, ended his discourse.

Breakfast over, Peter took his leave for Milan, appointing as his companions three of the friars, among whom one, the lay-brother Dominic, was likewise to fall before the assassin's sword. As the little party passed through the gates of the convent the entire community was there to bid the saint farewell. Fearing for his welfare, the brethren tried every means to induce his putting off the journey, but in vain. Since he had but recently recovered from a fever and was still in a very weak condition, the Father Infirmarian warned that he could never reach Milan that day; but to this the holy friar replied, "If such be the case, we will spend the night at the Abbey of Saint Simplician." These, his last words to the brethren, contained a prediction which we will soon see fulfilled.

Meanwhile Carino and his companion, Albertino, had betaken themselves to a deserted spot along the road to Milan, and concealed themselves in a clump of bushes to await the victim.

On account of their prior's weakness, the friars made their way very slowly. Part of the time they prayed or conversed on holy subjects, while the remainder was spent in singing, as was customary with religious when traveling in those days. It was a significant fact that Brother Peter and Brother Dominic, so soon to be the innocent victims of bloodthirsty heretics, sang together the beautiful Easter sequence, "Victimae Paschalis." As noon approached, Peter sent the other two friars to a farmhouse for their dinner, while he and Dominic sought hospitality from the religious of a near-by convent.

Rested and refreshed, the Saint and his companion, instead of waiting, started on again slowly, expecting that the others would soon be with them. It really seemed as though Peter were impatient for death and could wait no longer for the martyr's palm. As the two religious gradually approached the place where Carino and Albertino were in hiding, the latter, suddenly filled with horror at thought of the deed to be committed, threw down his weapon and fled through the fields to the road. Coming upon the two other companions of our Saint, he notified them of the deed about to be perpetrated, urging them to hasten if they wished to save the man of God. The friars, in great alarm, made all possible speed to aid their beloved superior, but arrived too late, for Peter was already dying, while Brother Dominic lay mortally wounded and Carino struggling in the arms of a farmer, who from his field had witnessed the bloody scene.

The early biographers of the Saint have given us in detail the horrible picture of his cruel martyrdom. Carino, filled with rage at the desertion of his companion, determined to accomplish the deed at all cost; so, when the two religious were passing the clump which concealed him, he suddenly sprang upon Peter, striking his head a terrible blow with a pruning-knife. The martyr, in great agony, sank to the earth, while angels, we may be sure, hovered near, waiting to receive his noble soul.

The assassin then turned to the terror-stricken Brother Dominic, and in his fury struck him several times with the weapon. As the villain turned to make his escape, he beheld Peter writing on the ground the words "Credo in unum Deum" by dipping his fingers into his own blood, and in a frenzy of rage drove his weapon through the breast of the dying martyr.

Thus died the first martyr saint of the Dominican Order, one of Christ's most valiant soldiers, whose life from beginning to end was one long warfare for the defense of that doctrine, "Credo in unum Deum." At the time of his death, which occurred on April 6, 1252, our Saint was forty-seven years of age and had worn the habit of a Friar Preacher for thirty-one years.

In great sorrow the two friars and a few peasants who had arrived on the scene made litters of branches, one for the body of the martyr, the other for the wounded Brother Dominic, who lived six days in great agony. Lifting their precious burdens, they tried to reach the next village, but night overtook them and they were forced to remain at the Abbey of Saint Simplician, thus fulfilling Peter's last words to his brethren in Como. During the night the holy remains reposed in the sanctuary of the abbey church, while the monks kept silent vigil.

The news of the martyrdom spread rapidly, and in the early hours of the morning the Archbishop of Milan, with the clergy and civil authorities, followed by an immense multitude of the citizens, came in procession to escort the body of the Saint to the Dominican church of Saint Eustorgius.

Carino was placed in the city prison to await trial, but soon made his escape and fled to a place called Forli. There, crushed by the horror of his crime, the unfortunate man fell sick and was carried to a hospital close to the Dominican convent. Believing himself near death, Carino begged to see a friar to whom he might confess his sins, and, strange to relate, after having made his peace with God almost instantly recovered. When permitted to leave the hospital, the former murderer, earnestly desiring to make atonement, sought admission into the Dominican Order as a lay-brother. He was received with great kindness into the community, and the remainder of his life was marked by such holiness that Brother Carino came to be known popularly as "Il Beato," "The Blessed." Such was the revenge of the holy martyr upon his assassin.

It was on the last day of the August following the martyrdom that Pope Innocent IV inaugurated the work preparatory to the holy Dominican's canonization by commanding Leon de Perego, Archbishop of Milan, and the bishop of Lodi to gather all the material regarding his life, death, and miracles. The result of these proceedings was the solemn canonization of the martyr on March 25, 1253, less than a year after his death. Pope Innocent IV performed the ceremony in the plaza of the Dominican church at Perugia, surrounded with great pomp and in the presence of a multitude of the faithful. Though the date of the martyrdom was April 6th, the feast day was placed on the 29th, as the former date falls so frequently in Holy Week or within the octave of Easter.

Naturally great devotion to Saint Peter Martyr arose in the Dominican and Servite Orders, while his cult spread rapidly throughout Italy and thence through all Europe. Great churches and shrines were soon erected in his honor, and of these probably the most noted was that which arose over the place of his death. We are told by historians that Saint Charles Borromeo, out of respect for this great sanctuary, never entered within its walls without first having removed his shoes. In a short time societies and confraternities in many lands had chosen the martyr as their patron, as did also many cities and towns of Europe.

The relics of Saint Peter of Verona have become widely distributed in the course of time. The head, however, has been preserved in a magnificent shrine, which to this day occupies a chapel in the church of Saint Eustorgius, in Milan. Numerous miracles have taken place at this tomb, and through these great numbers of heretics have been converted to the true faith. All who had taken any part in the plot against his life were, it is said, soon fervent Catholics, through the martyr's intercession, while a few even became members of religious orders and died in the odor of sanctity. Here we see his prophecy to the Milanese fulfilled. We recall that while preaching to them the Saint had declared, "I shall have far greater power over heretics after death than ever was granted me during life."

When we pray for the conversion of unbelievers, let us remember the great power of Saint Peter the Martyr and beg his intercession. May God infuse a similar zeal for Truth and the same ardent desire for souls in the hearts of those who are continuing at the present time the work of this great Dominican.

BIBLIOGRAPHY

Touron, O. P.: Vie de S. Dominique.

Année Dominicaine, IV, 773.

Martyrdom of Saint Peter of Verona. Rosary Magazine, April, 1897.

Butler: Lives of Saints.

Mortier: Histoire des Maîtres Généraux.

Saint Peter of Verona. Catholic Encyclopedia.

Bullarium Ordinis Prædicatorum, VIII, 759.

Acta Sanctorum. April 29.

Taurisano, O. P.: Catalogus Hagiographicus Ordinis Prædicatorum.

Saint Hyacinth

"The Apostle of the North"[1]

AS WE WRITE, the eyes of all christendom are once more turned in pity toward strickened Poland, even as they were long years before the World War. For almost two centuries the world witnessed the dismemberment of a proud nation by three neighboring powers—Russia, Germany, and Austria. Man has pitied Poland from the day of her defeat, when "Liberty shrieked, as Kosciusko fell," till her struggle today. Hers has been an heritage of persecution, famine, and now grim war. But there are in life things more to be feared than war, famine, or persecution, which afflict the soul and body but for a time. Though she yielded her kingdom, Poland has not bartered her most precious inheritance, the Catholic faith, which was preached by her apostolic sons, chief among whom was the subject of this sketch, Saint Hyacinth, the "Apostle of the North."

Like so many other Saints and Blesseds of the Order he was destined to join, our Saint was of noble lineage. Historians and writers are at variance as to the precise date of his birth, but all agree that he was born at the Castle of Lanka, near Breslau, Silesia, between the years 1183 and 1185. A direct descendant of the ancient house of Odrowatz, one of the most illustrious of Silesia, he numbered among his ancestors some of the most distinguished leaders in Church and State. The paternal grandfather of our Saint

[1] Bull of Canonization; Touron; Stanislaus et Séverin de Cracovie, Acta Sanctorum, etc.

Saint Hyacinth

had achieved renown as a general in the fierce struggle with the Tartars—that mighty horde of haters of the Cross who at the time threatened to overrun Europe. The General's two sons inherited their father's chivalry. The younger, Ivo, entered the rank and file of the Lord's army, where he was afterward promoted to a captaincy, being consecrated Bishop of Cracow, Poland, in 1208. The other son, Eustochius, the fruit of whose virtuous marriage was Hyacinth and Ceslaus, was Count of Konski.

Little Hyacinth's childhood days were uneventful, according to a worldly criterion; but, viewed spiritually and in the light of subsequent history, his training during these tender years was of vital consequence. Almost from infancy he gave promise of more than ordinary sanctity and evinced a remarkable aptitude for virtue. What must have been his devoted mother's holy admiration when, as a child, he asked, "Mother, who is God?" The long picture galleries of the castle were one of his favorite haunts. He never tired of hearing the history of his ancestors' exploits, the portraits of whom adorned the walls. Often while so engaged he was heard to repeat: "Now, if my ancestors have acquired so great renown, I must never disgrace my lineage by any crime or venal act. Their glory was their love of justice, their uprightness and magnanimity. I must never lose sight of their standard of virtue, but strive with all my strength to live up to it; so that, following their example here on earth, I may share their eternal reward." To these gifts in the order of grace, all his biographers add his great personal charms. His comely countenance bespoke an uncommon mind and a will that was strong and energetic. He seemed matured beyond his years, early putting away the things of a child and never so happy as when at his mother's side listening to the lessons of piety she strove to inculcate into his young heart. From his "thrice happy mother" he imbibed a tender love and confidence in his Lord and the Blessed Virgin, under whose special protection he placed the purity of his soul and body. It was to this end, too, that he secretly practiced many penances and mortifications, never seeking his own comfort, often prostrate in prayerful supplication for grace to keep this heavenly virtue unsullied and intact.

Another salient trait in his beautiful character was his love of the poor. This he inherited, for his father was called "the father of the poor." When little more than a child, he used to expend in alms all the money that was given him for his own use. When it was exhausted he would go confidently to his parents for a new supply and then joyfully distribute it. Often he would steal away unobserved to visit his protégés in their humble homes. After hearing their tales of woe he would cheer the dejected and console the suffering, always directing their thoughts and hopes to God and heaven. One day, after making his rounds, he was so moved by all that he had seen and heard that his heart overflowed with burning words. His uncle Ivo, overhearing the child's impassioned outbursts of love and compassion, exclaimed with enthusiasm: "My child, I believe by the grace of God you will one day be a great bishop, or a celebrated preacher, or a saint greater than any that has thus far shed luster on Poland." Not a little of Hyacinth's later success was due to the example and guidance of this holy man.

It was to Ivo Odrowatz, then Canon of Cracow, that the preliminary education of Hyacinth and his brother Ceslaus was entrusted. He was especially interested, and justly so, in little Hyacinth. "Mindful the while," continue the biographers, "that God had confided to him the work of molding and developing a beautiful soul, he watched over Hyacinth as over the apple of his eye, loving him as his own son." Nor would he suffer his little charge to be out of his sight. Here he gradually initiated the youth into such functions of the ministry as were compatible with his age, at the same time instilling into his heart that generosity and zeal in the service of God and that thirst for souls that permeated his whole life. The worthy priest was soon called upon to make a momentous decision. Realizing that his multifarious duties as canon and chancellor left him too little time to educate Hyacinth as he wished, he decided to place him under the best masters of the day, who were then at the celebrated University of Prague.

After completing his classical education at Prague, Hyacinth passed to Bologna. We need scarcely add that his parents or uncle had no misgivings that he would drink in the pleasure-loving atmosphere or be infected by the notorious laxity of morals then prevalent at Bologna. There were no attractions for the future saint in the town's gay haunts of dissipation. He passed unscathed through all the dangers then concomitant with the gaining of a university education. Here his lovable disposition and marked deference made him at once a favorite with students and professors. On holidays he divided his time between his studies, to which he applied himself diligently, and work among God's poor. Sundays and holy days were given over exclusively to prayer and recollection.

Hyacinth's student days at Bologna were drawing to a close when his uncle told him that he showed unmistakable signs of a priestly vocation. Hyacinth received this judgment with joy and immediately commenced his preparations for Holy Orders. After this cherished ambition had been realized, he received a prebend in the Cathedral at Cracow and shortly afterward was elected member of the Episcopal Council. Here he distinguished himself by his prudence, learning, and thoroughness and soon exerted a singular influence over all his associates.

Owing chiefly to the frequent barbarian incursions and continual warfare to which the country was subjected, a spirit of laxity, carelessness, and insubordination had crept in among the secular clergy. Hyacinth studied the alarming situation and threw himself energetically into the work of reform. He soon enlisted a clerical following, his noble birth and talents, but above all the example of his spotless life, playing their part in the great work. He encouraged the good and helped his weaker brothers, securing pardon and reinstatement for all who evinced signs of amendment. On the other hand, he arraigned the obstinate before the Episcopal Tribunal and saw that they were properly punished. Thus a danger that boded ill for the diocese of Cracow was averted and gradually disappeared.

Though now entrusted with the administration of the affairs of a greater part of the diocese, Hyacinth in nowise neglected the work of his personal sanctification. His associates marveled at his capacity for work, but never, withal, did he fail to assist at the community exercises of the canonry, the chanting of the divine office, and meditation. He still continued his frequent colloquies with Our Lord and His Blessed Mother, the secret of his spirit of recollection, which he could not forego. And yet there was time for attending the sick at the several hospitals, and time for regular visits to the poor, on whom he spent his entire income. He had long since been persuaded that his money, as well as that of the Church, could not be used more profitably than in alms for the poor. This continued to be the order of his daily work until his uncle Ivo was elected successor of the aged Vincent, Bishop of Cracow.

The year 1219 was to mark a turning point in our Saint's career. Vincent Kadlubkon, the venerable Bishop of Cracow, after resigning the episcopal dignity, retired to the solitude of retreat to await the call to eternal life. Ivo Odrowatz was elected to succeed him, and lost no time setting out for Rome to receive the confirmation of the Holy See. His retinue included his two nephews, Hyacinth and Ceslaus (who since his ordination held the positions of provost and treasurer of Saint Mary's Church at Sandomir) and two young clerics, known to us by the names of Herman the Teuton and Henry of Moravia.

We next hear of the little group of pilgrims as guests at a monastery near the Via Appia, in Rome, to which it would seem they were providentially directed; for within a few days not only were they to hear and meet the blessed Dominic, but were to be witnesses of the holy patriarch's third, and probably greatest, miracle.

Shortly before his death, Pope Innocent III had tried but failed to gather into one community the various relaxed convents of women in Rome. Honorius, his successor, no less ardently desired the reform of the nuns and their enclosure in some community. He entrusted the work to the saintly Dominic, at the same time promising him as his coadjutors Cardinals Ugolino of Ostia, Stephen of Fossa Nuova, and Nicholas, Bishop of Tusculum. After many delays, disappointments, and difficulties, Dominic had all in readiness for the installation of the nuns in his own convent, which adjoined the basilica of Saint Sixtus, in return for which he later received that of Santa Sabina, on the Aventine. The solemn occasion brought together many celebrities, including the above-named cardinals and a number of bishops, among whom Ivo Odrowatz and his companions took their place.

Scarcely had the ceremonies begun when a messenger rushed in, tearing at his hair and uttering loud cries for help. "Napoleon, the nephew of my lord Stephen," he cried, "has just fallen from his horse . . . he is dead." After viewing the body, Dominic had it removed to a room near by and then began to celebrate the holy sacrifice of the Mass. The Mass over, he now arranged the dead youth's broken limbs and thrice prostrated himself on the ground, weeping and praying the while. Then, standing, he made the sign of the cross over the dead form and with hands extended toward heaven, his own body now lifted above the ground, he cried out in a loud voice, "O young man, Napoleon, in the name of our Lord Jesus Christ, I say to thee, arise." And immediately the young man arose, joyful and unhurt.

None of the witnesses of this miracle were more deeply touched than Ivo Odrowatz and his companions. This admiration soon gave place to love, when on further acquaintance they found that Dominic himself was a prodigy of sanctity. So charmed was Ivo with this man of God, with his consuming zeal and the unction of his conversation, that he begged him to send some of his brethren to labor in the northern countries. Dominic replied, with a note of sadness in his voice, that it was his fervent wish to have done so long ago, and that it were impossible, at least for the present, owing to the lack of disciples. As if at God's suggestion, Dominic then proposed that some of Ivo's attendants receive the habit of his order. "I will return them to you Apostles," said he, "and it is, moreover, the best way to carry out your wishes."

A few days later found Hyacinth, Ceslaus, Henry, and Herman at Santa Sabina. Prostrating themselves before the Saint, they begged admission to his Order. They were joyfully received and forthwith began their novitiate. The event was afterward recorded in an inscription over the entrance of the Chapter Room. And Père Lacordaire writes that "among the several frescos which have been preserved to us in a side chapel at Santa Sabina, there are two which represent and commemorate the reception of Hyacinth and his brother Ceslaus into the Dominican Order. Saint Dominic is represented giving the habit to Hyacinth, who seems to have arisen promptly from the customary prostration and is the first to come forward, while Ceslaus is seen still prostrated before the Saint." The early historians of the Order tell us that Dominic himself was their novice-master.

Hyacinth and his companions spent less than a year in this atmosphere of sanctity, where their progress was as rapid as it was extraordinary. Hyacinth outstripped the others in emulation of their ideal and prototype, Saint Dominic. "Soon," says a biographer, "his religious fervor and austerity of life, zeal for God's glory, and for the salvation of souls was comparable only to that of Saint Dominic." When we read that within six months Dominic considered all sufficiently trained, equipped, and ready to pronounce their vows and to return to their native land, we are constrained to exclaim indeed, "There were giants in those days."

Bishop Ivo had looked forward eagerly to the day when he would return with the four religious to his diocese in Poland; so it must have been a distinct disappointment to the estimable man to learn now that he would have to sacrifice the company of the religious and return home before them. Hyacinth and the others, in conformity with the rule of their Order, could not travel well mounted, but on foot, "with neither purse nor script." It is certain, however, that Ivo had at least the pleasure of their company when they left the Eternal City, after which he proceeded directly to Poland.

While traveling through Lombardy and the Venetian territory, they preached as often as they could, until they reached Freisach, in Upper Corinthia, where the Archbishop of Saltzburg and a large number of the faithful received and welcomed them. The Archbishop told them how he had met the holy Patriarch, Saint Dominic, in Rome at the Lateran Council and had asked him for some of his disciples to labor in his diocese.

Hyacinth and his companions forthwith began preaching. The churches were soon too small to contain the crowds that thronged to hear "the new Apostles" preach. One historian writes that Hyacinth and his brothers seemed to have been accorded a share in the Pentecostal gift of tongues, for their preaching was understood by all the peoples that heard them. The enthusiasm of the entire city was indescribable; Freisach had taken on a new life. Scarcely six months elapsed when priests, clerics, and a number of laymen begged to be clothed in the habit of the Order of Preachers. The Archbishop indorsed the plan, and placed a large monastery at the disposal of the Preachers, in which to house the postulants.

Herman the Teuton, a man of rare virtue, was elected first prior. An interesting anecdote is told of him at this period of his life. Herman was far from being a learned man. His ignorance in certain matters was a source of much concern as well as embarrassment to him. "If I am to fulfill my vocation," he often repeated to himself, "I must also preach and teach what I have contemplated." One day, as he knelt in prayer, he besought the Blessed Virgin, to whom he had a special devotion, to help him. "Mother of the Word and Divine Wisdom," he cried, "obtain for me the gift of speech." His prayer was indeed answered, for he was able thereafter to preach in German, Latin, and several other languages with extraordinary eloquence and success.

With staff in hand, Hyacinth, Ceslaus, and Henry now set out for Poland. They purposely elected to travel through the more populous parts of Styria, Austria, Moravia, and Silesia, in order to reach more people. History is silent as to whether or not their reputation for sanctity and preaching had preceded them into these parts, but it tells us that they accomplished great things during their brief stay. Superstitious practices were checked and many conversions were made.

Never before had Cracow witnessed such a demonstration of joy and enthusiasm as was accorded Hyacinth and his companions on their arrival within the city limits. Bishop Ivo and the entire population had turned out to welcome them and conduct them to the house which the bishop had prepared for them. They were not to remain here long, because the large number of postulants that sought admission to the new Order compelled Hyacinth, for he was the superior, to seek larger quarters. The bishop and his chapter and the city magistrates bestowed on the new Order the convent adjoining the Church of the Holy Trinity. On the feast of the Assumption, in the year 1222, Hyacinth and his community took possession of what may be considered the first Dominican foundation in Poland.

Faithful to the Dominican law of dispersion, we find Hyacinth sending Ceslaus and Henry to labor in Bohemia. He then began his memorable mission in Cracow and its environs. A mission indeed; it was a crusade. Giving full play to his zeal, he inveighed against the evils of the day, attacking and uprooting the public vices that reigned unchecked in the capital city. Superstition, immorality, luxury, and debauchery, once exposed by the Saint, were outlawed and gradually disappeared, being supplanted by a spirit of prayer and penance and a holy and frequent use of the sacraments that recalled the primitive ages of the faith. Vindictive enemies were reconciled; restitution for long-standing injustices was effected; public sinners were converted, and many persons led to embrace the religious state. Among these latter were his mother, now a widow, and his grandmother, whom Hyacinth had the happiness of receiving into the Third Order of Saint Dominic. "Cracow," says an early biographer, "taking on this new life, was quite a different place."

The same biographer tells us in a few words the reason for such unexampled fruitfulness in his ministry. In his native city, Hyacinth found a lamentable state of things. There were crying abuses among the secular clergy, whose lives were far from edifying. There were indeed holy monks, but these were enclosed within their convent walls and held no intercourse with the outside world. Hence, the sight of a "religious" preaching and evangelizing at once captivated the people; and, moreover, this preacher was of noble birth and a fellow-countryman. Hence the crowds he attracted to his sermons. His eloquence, it is true, was unsurpassed, but the great source of the Saint's power is to be found in the example of his sanctity and spotless life, in his incessant prayer, and in the miracles with which God was pleased to bless and confirm his work.

We read that Hyacinth continued faithful to the maxims and example of his father, Dominic. Like Dominic, after studying for several hours, he labored the rest of the day, and at night spent long hours before the Blessed Sacrament. He scourged himself thrice unto blood, and when sleep at length claimed him, he would lean against an altar or prostrate himself on the bare floor. His fasts were almost continual. On all Fridays and vigils of greater feasts he took only bread and water. Neither hunger, thirst, nor weariness, storm nor danger, could in the least abate his ardor to gain a soul for Christ. Such was Dominic, and so too, was Hyacinth.

With Saint Paul, he could indeed say, "It is Christ that liveth in me." When he spoke, it was Christ that spoke; when he blest, it was Christ that blest.

Hyacinth soon began to extend his apostolate to near-by provinces. The same success attended his preaching, and he was able to found more convents of his Order, in which numerous souls consecrated themselves to the work of the apostolate. After founding a convent at Sandomir, Hyacinth started out for Plocko, a town on the far bank of the Vistula, in Moravia. "To reach Wisgrade, he and his companions were obliged to cross the Vistula, which at the time had overflowed its banks. There was neither boat nor boatman to convey them across. No one dared brave the turbulent flood. Placing his trust in God, he addressed his companions, Godinus, Florian, and Benedict: "Beloved brothers, let us ask the God whom the heavens and earth and sea obey, to help us across this perilous river." All knelt in prayer. Hyacinth soon rose and, after making the sign of the cross over the waves, began to walk upon the waters, which grew firm under his feet. Seeing his companions motionless on the shore, he cried to them, "In the name of Christ, follow me; trust in the power of the Most High." They seemed stupefied at the prodigy and dared not advance. Then Hyacinth returned to them and spread his cloak on the waters. "Why, my sons," he said, "do you hesitate?" Again making the saving sign over the troubled waters, he added, "This cloak shall be to us as a bridge given by Christ to pass this swollen river." All then stepped upon the cloak and crossed safely to the other side, where they were received by an immense crowd of wondering spectators. This miracle is mentioned by all the Saint's biographers[2] and is cited in the Bull of Canonization (April 17, 1594).

The River Vistula was the scene of another miracle that was witnessed by a number of the clergy and nobles and hundreds of townspeople. While on his way to celebrate the translation of the relics of Saint Stanislaus, patron of Poland, Hyacinth and his party

[2] L'Année Dominicaine; Touron, etc.

were about to cross the Vistula when a woman showed him a lifeless body. "I am a widow," she said, "and this is the body of Peter, my only son. He was drowned last evening, but the body has just been recovered. I am now alone in the world. I beseech you, venerable father, to have mercy on me and help me." Hyacinth was deeply moved and tears filled his eyes as he approached the lifeless form. Taking the youth's hand, he said, "Peter, may our Lord Jesus Christ, whose glory I preach, restore you to life through the intercession of the Blessed Virgin." Instantly Peter arose and gave thanks to God and to His servant, Hyacinth. Soon after his return to the convent in Cracow the "Thaumaturgus of Holy Trinity," as he was called, worked two more miracles. The touch of his hand cured a paralytic, and on another occasion instantly restored a dying woman to perfect health.

After Hyacinth had preached and renewed the spirit of piety in all the cities and provinces of Poland, his zeal for souls turned his thoughts toward the northern kingdoms, where he knew countless souls were perishing through idolatry. Feeling that he could not delay any longer, he instructed the fervent community at Holy Trinity to continue the work begun in Cracow and neighboring cities.

The feast of the Assumption was at hand and all was in readiness for the departure to the North. Hyacinth knelt at the altar wrapt in contemplation of the mystery of the feast. His heart was full of joy at the thought of his Order being the only one vowing obedience to the Mother of God; and that it had received from her its distinctive habit and so many proofs of her affection. Suddenly a dazzling light filled the sanctuary and the Queen of Heaven, standing before the tabernacle, thus addressed him: "Rejoice, Hyacinth my son, for thy prayers are pleasing to my Son, the Saviour of mankind. All that thou askest of Him in my name will be granted thee." Then, promising to continue protectress of the whole Order, she disappeared, while celestial harmony and a perfume of indescribable fragrance filled the sanctuary. This, thought Hyacinth, is a sign of approval. He confided this vision to Godinus and Florian as they left for the Polish frontiers, to begin the wonderful apostolate, of which we can give but the barest outline in these pages.

Hyacinth and his three companions found Pomerania and Prussia torn by schism and heresy and steeped in idolatry. The snows and floods, impenetrable forests, and the wild beasts that lurked therein, or the still fiercer natives, held no fears and proved no obstacle for these men of God. Not the least among the miracles which he continued to work was his gift of tongues, which enabled him to preach to all these half-civilized peoples in their different languages.

To complete and perpetuate his work, he founded convents at Kulm, Camina, near the Oder; at Presmil and Elbinge, in Prussia. When Hyacinth asked the Duke of Pomerania for Gedan, a little islet in the Baltic, as the site for a convent and church, the Duke laughed at the idea, saying that the place was a wilderness and too isolated to be suitable for the purpose. Finally, he yielded to Hyacinth, who foretold that the site would one day be a magnificent city and port. The prophecy proved literally true within a century, in the great city of Danzig. Danzig became such a Catholic stronghold that the Lutheran heresy, which destroyed or profaned all the other churches in the sixteenth century, did not in the least affect it.

Hyacinth now left Prussia and Pomerania to preach in Denmark, Norway, Sweden, and Scotland. The remarkable success with which he labored is commended in a brief by Pope Gregory IX, dated 1231, which he addressed to "All the princes and peoples of the North." In it he urges them "to follow the instructions of the Friar Preachers, those saintly Apostles who have drawn you from the darkness of error into the path of truth and justice."

Red Russia was the next theater of his activities. Prince Daniel and numbers of his subjects were converted to the true faith and abjured the Greek schism. "When most of the people," continues the historian, "were won over to the cause of Christ, Hyacinth founded convents, lest the devil should destroy the fruits of his labors. These communities of Lemburg and Halitz produced the first bishops of the country, as well as many eminent preachers and holy martyrs."

After a short but fruitful stay near the Black Sea and the islands of the Archipelago, Hyacinth turned northward and entered the great Dukedom of Moscovy, then known as Great or Black Russia. We may make bold to say that he was entering upon the greatest and most difficult period of his apostolate, which extended over five years. Idolatry, schism, heresy, and flagrant abuses met him at every turn.

The Christians who were able to live here were not permitted a church in which to assemble or worship. The Grand Duke Vladimir not only turned a deaf ear to Hyacinth's repeated requests for permission to preach to the Catholics, but strove in every way to discourage the Saint and to thwart his efforts. Again and again Hyacinth's importunities met with flat refusal; but, like Saint Peter, he "must obey God rather than man." The Saint, moreover, would not think of "shaking the dust off his feet" on such a harvest, but increased his prayers, fasts, and austerities and pleaded his cause so eloquently, as the Duke said, that he was constrained to yield to the "brilliant man." And no sooner had he commenced to preach and confirm his mission with miracles than crowds of Mohammedans and schismatics flocked to hear him. Hundreds sought baptism and still more were reunited to the Holy See.

One day he happened upon an assembly of idolaters who were kneeling before a great oak on an island in the Dnieper. In the absence of a boat to convey him across, the Saint walked dry-shod over the rapid current. Arriving on the scene, he struck the oak under which the awestruck idolaters worshiped and it crumbled to dust. At this a demon appeared in human form and challenged Hyacinth. A struggle ensued, in which he drew the demon to the river. The waters sustained the man of God, while they swallowed up the human form the evil one had assumed. Many conversions followed on this event.

The jealous Duke, whose bad faith and insincerity caused Hyacinth no little sorrow, seeing many of his court and numbers of the Greek priests following the Saint, began to fear that his absolute authority was waning. He forthwith gave orders that all preaching was to cease and that Hyacinth was to be expelled from the country. Overt persecution commenced, first against the religious and then against all Catholics. But God's work was not to come to naught.

Historians tell us that the Tartar invasion now visited on Kiev was Heaven's punishment for the obstinacy and impiety of the schismatics and the unmerited persecution of the Christians. The Tartars advanced, burning cities, laying waste to towns with fire and sword, until they reached the capitol. After a long and bloody siege, the city was taken, pillaged, and finally reduced to ashes. From their monastery the friars could hear the din of battle across the river. Religious life continued until one morning, when the door of the convent was suddenly broken in. The novices rushed into the adjoining church, where our Saint had just finished celebrating Mass. "We are lost," they cried; "the Tartars are at the doors. Save us, blessed Father."

A violent struggle arose in Hyacinth's breast, for in his veins flowed the blood of a warrior race. As for himself, he would meet death with joyous fortitude. But he must be quick to decide. Grace triumphed over nature and his duty was made manifest. Taking the Blessed Sacrament in the monstrance, he ordered the community to follow him. What passed within him at that moment? He appeared to hesitate, when a sweet voice called to him, "Hyacinth, my son, to whom art thou leaving me? Wilt thou abandon me to the Tartars and to destruction? Take me with thee."

"O glorious Lady," replied the Saint, as he looked at the immense alabaster statue, "how can I carry such a weight?"

"My Son will make it light for thee," answered the voice.

Approaching the pedestal, he lifted the statue, now no heavier than a straw, and passed through the doorway into the midst of a band of Tartars, who fell back as if paralyzed at the sight of the Saint. When the friars reached the Dnieper they found it impossible to cross, for the foe held the opposite bank. The Saint now bade his companions to imitate him in spreading their cloaks upon the water. In this way they floated down the stream until safely beyond reach of the Tartar hordes. They then landed and repaired to the convent at Halitz. The statue became the object of public veneration, which continued at Lemburg, whither the statue was removed some years afterward. The above miracle, attested by over four hundred witnesses, is cited by all the Saint's biographers. During the process of canonization the footprints which tradition said Hyacinth made in the Dnieper—whence the name, "the way of Saint Hyacinth"—were proven to be authentic by the commission in charge.

Leaving the younger religious at Halitz, our Saint, accompanied by Florian, journeyed on to Danzig. Here he found his fondest hopes realized in Benedict, one of his first disciples, who had surrounded himself with a large and zealous community, that had already evangelized all the neighboring tribes. It was on this journey that Hyacinth founded convents in Bulgaria and Moldavia. Regardless of danger, he went among the heretics of Galicia and Poldovia, preached the Catholic faith, confounded the schismatics, and succeeded in removing the darkness of infidelity and in winning over thousands to Christ. He built churches in each of these places, and then started for Lithuania, where he labored with incredible success. In the year 1241, the fifty-sixth of his life, he re-entered Cracow.

During the following two years, which were spent for the most part at the convent of Holy Trinity, Hyacinth edified all by his regular observance, his spirit of prayer and contemplation. His spiritual conferences to his confrères at Holy Trinity stirred both old and young, while the same crowds, and greater than those that hung on his words years before, flocked to hear the "Wonder

Worker" wherever he preached. It was during this period of his ministry that the following miracles took place.

A noble lady, whose home was in one of the outlying districts, invited Hyacinth to preach there on the Feast of Saint Margaret. Upon his arrival in the town, on the eve of the feast, a terrific hailstorm arose, which completely destroyed the rich harvest of grain and corn. The inhabitants, who were peasants, were fairly overwhelmed with grief. Famine stared them in the face, when they besought Hyacinth to relieve their distress. The Saint's heart was touched at the sight of the desolation and the helpless condition of the inhabitants. His eyes were filled with tears, as he addressed them: "My beloved children, God is the Father of mercies. He will pardon and console after chastising you. . . . Take courage and pray." He watched with them in prayer that lasted throughout the night. What a miracle met their eyes next morning, as the sun rose on the country. The harvest was restored as it was before the storm.

Some days later the following took place: Felicie Grusznow, a pious matron of Cracow, presented herself at the convent of Holy Trinity and told the Saint of her husband's cruel treatment and reproaches because God had not blessed their married life with children. She had borne this cross for nearly twenty years, but now felt her fortitude giving way. She refused to leave the convent until the Saint had promised that God would grant her children. After consoling the distracted woman, Hyacinth foretold that a son would be born to her, and that from her lineage would spring a number of illustrious bishops and nobles. The prophecy, historians assure us, was literally fulfilled.

The next miracle recorded is of a different nature, though not the only one of its kind worked by the Saint. As he was entering the Cathedral of Cracow to preach on the feast of the martyr, Saint Stanislaus, a woman approached him, saying: "Servant of God, behold my twin sons; not only are they blind, but were born without the organs of sight. They have never seen their mother's face. Do help me." The Saint then made the sign of the cross over the children, saying at the same time, "May Jesus, the Son of Mary, Who gave sight to the man born blind, give you your sight." Immediately the children saw. He preached daily in the city and neighboring towns. Crowds followed him wherever he preached.

Like Saint Paul, Hyacinth wished to revisit those countries in which he had planted the faith, and then, if possible, to realize the holy Patriarch Dominic's desire of evangelizing the Tartars. With this twofold object in mind, he set out on what may be called his last great mission. After a stay of a few months among the Prussians and Muscovites, Danes, and Swedes, during which he confirmed the Christians in the faith and incited the several convents of religious to renewed fervor and activity and a more regular observance, he proceeded to the country of the barbarous Cumans. What holy joy must have filled his soul when, just across the Cuman frontier, he discovered traces of surviving Dominican missionaries whom Jordan of Saxony, Dominic's successor, had sent there early in 1228. He was witness to the difficulties surmounted by the sweat and often by the blood of these apostolic men in this long unfruitful corner of the Lord's vineyard, as well as to the blessings the Master had showered on their labors.

The meeting of the brethren, which took place shortly afterward, may be more easily imagined than described. Hyacinth set to work immediately with the others and brought about numerous conversions by his gift of tongues.

Now it will be remembered that the Tartars had forced him to abandon Kiev and also to leave part of his community at Halitz. This, however, did not deter him from entering their country. The man of God well knew that "if God be for us who is against us." Once among the barbarians, he set to work fearlessly and soon had a following. Among his first converts were many of those who had witnessed his miracles at Kiev. Others were inspired to embrace Christianity by the joyful manner in which the Christians at Kiev had met death. Ancient chroniclers tell us that thousands were baptized, and among them a prince of Tartary, who afterwards went, with several lords of his nation, to the first Council of Lyons, in 1245.

We read in the life of Saint Lewis that when he landed on the island of Cyprus, in 1248, he was met by an embassy sent from a powerful Christian prince of the Tartars. After relating the circumstances of their conversion by our Saint, they offered to co-operate with the King and promised him protection and aid in the crusade against the Saracens, the hereditary enemy of the Christians and Tartars. Incredible though it seem, Hyacinth now traversed the vast region of Tartary, preached the Gospel in Tibet, near the East Indies, and penetrated into Cathay, the northernmost part of China. Missionaries who in later times visited these places found emblems and traces of the Catholic faith planted there by our Saint.

The next scene of his apostolic labors is Russia, which he now entered for the third time. Here he preached with great success to all classes. His zeal and prayers won over Prince Coloman and his young wife, Salome, both of whom consecrated the remainder of their lives to religious perfection. After a brief visit to the great convent which he had founded at Vilna, the capital of Lithuania, which became the center of one of the most flourishing provinces the Order has ever known, he entered Cracow.

Though Hyacinth was now in the seventy-second year of his life and the fortieth of his apostolate, it never entered into his mind to retire or to spend his remaining days in the quiet of his convent. Hence we find him preaching daily, visiting the sick, and consoling the afflicted. "In a word," says an early biographer, "Hyacinth was to be seen wherever there was good to be accomplished or a soul to save." It was about this time that his last miracle took place.

Primislava, a noble lady, had sent her only son, Wislaus, to invite the Saint to preach to her vassals on the approaching Feast of Saint James. Wislaus was on his way home when he was drowned in the river Raba. Word was sent to his mother, and she arrived at the river bank as Hyacinth and a companion came on the scene. "O Father," she cried, as she threw herself at the Saint's feet, "what have I done to deserve this? My son, whom I sent to invite you, is drowned. Thou canst help me if you wilt." Hyacinth was moved by her sterling faith and sad bereavement. He consoled the good woman, saying: "Be of good heart; you shall see the glory of God." And with that "faith that worketh by charity," he sent up a fervent prayer and lo! the corpse appeared before the awe-stricken mourners. "Blessed Hyacinth," cried Primislava, "your prayers have recovered his body; they can restore his life." Hyacinth then advanced and touched the lifeless body and said: "Wislaus, my son, may our Lord Jesus Christ, Who giveth life to all things, resuscitate thee." The youth arose full of life, while the multitude gave thanks to God.

The reader will recall that in the vision accorded to Hyacinth at the beginning of his apostolate Mary promised to obtain for him all that he should ask through her intercession. Often, in the course of his long and laborious ministry, did our Saint invoke that aid and never in vain. His thoughts and affections were all for her. Her matchless virtues and prerogatives and her power were the subject of his meditations and the theme of his greatest sermons. All his success in combating error he attributed to her, "who alone has overcome all heresies throughout the world." His filial love and virginal purity must have endeared him to the Immaculate Queen, for it is related that "she often appeared to him, and that he seemed to receive his wonderful powers as well as his inspiration from Mary." "But a greater favor still," says a modern biographer, "was likewise her gift, and this was his profound humility." Hyacinth repeatedly refused the episcopal dignity and, except when constrained by obedience, would accept no superiority in the Order. The last grace this loving client received through Mary's hands was a "death precious in the sight of God," the approach of which she foretold to him.

On the feast of Saint Dominic, 1257, our Saint fell ill with a fever which was to carry him to his grave. From this time the brethren who attended him noticed an unearthly glow on his wan face, and when they heard him repeat, "I desire to be dissolved and to be with Christ," they were convinced that he was on the threshold of eternity. Nor was the final summons long delayed. A few days later, as he stood at the altar, he beheld a brilliant light descend from heaven. In its path filed a long procession of angels, who formed, as it were, an escort for the August Queen of Heaven. They prostrated themselves reverently around the altar until Hyacinth finished the Holy Sacrifice. Then the Blessed Virgin motioned to him saying, "Behold," at which instant the heavens opened. He saw Mary advance majestically to the throne of the Most High, after which there followed one of those silences of which the Apocalypse speaks, while the Eternal Father placed upon her head a crown of flowers and stars. "Behold, Hyacinth," said Our Blessed Lady, as she turned to him, "this crown is for thee." The vision vanished, but the Saint continued kneeling, wrapt in ecstasy. With outstretched arms and heaving breast he gazed longingly toward heaven. He assisted at the first vespers of the Feast of the Assumption, after which he asked the prior to assemble the community. "Brothers and dearly beloved children," he said, with a countenance all radiant with joy, "the time has come when I must leave you. Tomorrow God will call me to Himself. Be not afflicted at this separation, for Jesus Christ is our life and hope and you shall find me in Him. As I have loved you on earth so also will I love you in heaven. And now I leave you all that our Holy Father Dominic bequeathed to me—Guard humility, live in mutual charity, preserve voluntary poverty, love Mary." Although exceedingly weak, he insisted on attending the midnight office, and after this he devotedly assisted at Mass, which he could no longer celebrate. Then, kneeling at the altar, supported by his weeping brethren, he received the Holy Viaticum and Extreme Unction. They carried him to his cell, where he calmly awaited the supreme moment of his release. When he felt the end drawing near, he intoned the 30th Psalm, "In Thee, O Lord, have I hoped," and expired at the words, "Into Thy hands I commend my spirit."

Upon hearing of Hyacinth's death, John Prandotta, the beloved Bishop of Cracow, betook himself to the church of the Friar Preachers to venerate the holy remains and to preside at the funeral. Returning later to his cathedral, he knelt in prayer before the altar of the Blessed Virgin and was wrapt in ecstasy, during which he beheld a double file of young men pass before him, clad in white and bearing lighted candles. Then came two venerable men, one wearing episcopal robes, the other the habit of the Friar Preachers. The latter's scapular was of dazzling whiteness and his brow was encircled with a double diadem of sparkling gems. The former then, turning to Prandotta, said: "I am Stanislaus, thy predecessor in the See of Cracow, and this Friar whom you see is Brother Hyacinth, of the Order of Preachers, who wears the double crown of Doctor and Virgin. I and this train of heavenly spirits are conducting him to the realms of eternal bliss." With this, the martyr bishop intoned the antiphon, "Perpetual light shall shine upon Thy saints, O Lord," and vanished into the abyss of celestial light.

When Prandotta came to himself, he said to his attendants: "Let us return to the Friars and relate to them the marvels which it has pleased God to reveal to His most unworthy servant." Arriving at the convent, he called the prior and the brethren, and then, in the presence of the canons, clerics, and laymen who made up his suite, he related to them all that God had manifested to him regarding the glory of His servant Hyacinth.

The same day a holy religious named Brunislawa, of the near-by Order of Premonstratensians, while meditating on the mystery of the Assumption, beheld in vision a heavenly light envelop the church of the Friars. Countless angels sang in harmonious concert, while the Queen of Heaven, arrayed in vesture of sparkling stones, led a friar whose countenance was radiant and whose garments were lily white. Brunislawa ventured to ask the meaning of what she had witnessed, and the Virgin Queen answered: "This is Brother Hyacinth, and I, the Mother of Mercy, am conducting him to my Son." Then the Glorious Queen intoned the words, "I will go to the mountain of myrrh, and to the hill of frankincense," which were taken up by Hyacinth and the angelic choir as they disappeared into the heavens.

Immediately after the obsequies miracles began to be worked at the Saint's tomb. The day after the funeral a young man who had just met death through an accident was restored to life when his mangled body had touched the Saint's coffin. The mere touching of his tomb healed and cured many who were sick or crippled, in many cases immediately.

The Saint's glory was attested by many prodigies, of which the limitations of this sketch permit us to recount but one. This occurred as a holy hermit, who had foretold Hyacinth's death, was praying at the Saint's tomb. Three brilliant lights descended from heaven and surrounded the Saint's relics. The same prodigy was repeated and was attested by numerous witnesses when the tomb was opened for the first time. When the three lights disappeared, heavenly perfume filled the church.

It has often been said of Saint Hyacinth that he received Saint Dominic's spirit with his habit. He has been called Saint Dominic's greatest son, and not undeservedly. We have but to consider his extensive journeys and the number of nations he evangelized or brought back to the faith and unity; the extraordinary hardships he underwent; the perils he so undauntedly braved, and often single-handed—not to mention his continual fasts and innumerable miracles—to see that the title is not unfittingly bestowed. How well do those words of Holy Writ describe him: "In his life he did great wonders and in death he wrought miracles. He was directed by God unto the repentance of the nation and he took away the abominations of the wicked. He directed his heart toward the Lord, and in the days of sinners he strengthened godliness." No other saint, we make bold to say, with the exception of Saint Vincent Ferrer, ever surpassed him in the number and character of miracles wrought. The mere enumeration of Hyacinth's miracles fills thirty-five pages of the Acta Sanctorum. The bull of his canonization, issued on April 17, 1594, declared his miracles to be "almost countless." After the commission in charge had scrutinized his life and works with that judicial exactitude which is characteristic of the Church in so important a matter, it was shown that in Cracow alone fifty dead persons had been raised to life and seventy-two dying persons restored to perfect health.

Pilgrims came from far and near to pray at the Saint's tomb. Miracles multiplied. Devotion to the Saint spread throughout Poland, France, Italy, Spain, Hungary, and even to Western and Eastern India. Pressing appeals were made to Rome by the Kings and hierarchy of Poland, as well as by the Order, to take up the cause of canonization, but owing either to the wickedness of the times or the sudden deaths of several Sovereign Pontiffs this process was delayed.

In the sixteenth century, when the Lutheran heresy raged with satanic violence against the veneration and invocation of the saints, our Saint's holy relics were hidden to escape profanation. Later on, when the danger had passed, they were uncovered and placed in the sacristy, where they reposed until the chapel destined to receive them was completed. Two bulls were issued, in 1527 and 1530, permitting the Friar Preachers and the Church of Poland to celebrate the feast of their beloved protector and apostle. It was reserved to Clement VIII, 1594, to inscribe the name of Hyacinth on the catalogue of saints, and to Urban VIII to extend his feast, August 16, to the universal church.

"Lux Poloniæ—Flos pulcherrime—Ora pro nobis."

BIBLIOGRAPHY

Acta Sanctorum. Bollandists. August 16.

Bullarium Ordinis Prædicatorum.

MORTIER, O. P.: Histoire des Maîtres Généraux des Frères Prêcheurs.

L'Année Dominicaine. August 16.

TOURON, O. P.: L'Histoire Abrégée des Premiers Disciples de Saint Dominique.

GERARD DE FRACHET: Vitæ Fratrum.

Breviarium Romanum.

DRANE: Lives of Dominican Saints and Blesseds.

Catholic Truth Society, London, 1900. Saints of the Rosary.

REILLY, O. P., T. à K.: Saints and Saintly Dominicans.

Saint Thomas of Aquin

(1225–1274)

IN STUDYING Thomas of Aquin, peerless as a genius and wonderful as a saint, so admirable and at the same time so lovable, whose life-history is so vitally interesting and so rich with inspiration, it is absolutely necessary at the very outset to get a broad, clear, and unobstructed view of the background and setting amid which he lived his great life and performed his grand deeds. Saint Thomas lived during the most glorious period of the thirteenth, the greatest of all the centuries. His age was that of Innocent III, Saint Louis of France, Albert the Great, Roger Bacon, Giotto, and Dante. It saw the birth of the magnificent cathedrals of Cologne and of Amiens, the Divina Commedia, and the Summa Theologica. It saw the signing of the Great Charter, the foundation of the universities of Oxford and Paris and of the Orders of Saint Francis and Saint Dominic. It was a century of great faith, grand ideas, generous impulses, rapid and thorough progress in art and science, which for all ages will stand as lofty monuments of its brilliance.

The noble family of the Counts of Aquino was descended from the Princes of Lombardy and was closely connected with the royal houses of thirteenth century Europe. Count Landulf, our Saint's father, was a nephew of the Emperor Frederick I and Lord of Aquino, Loreto, Acerra, and Belcastro. Countess Theodora, his mother, was of royal blood, being descended from the Norman kings of Naples and Sicily. Thomas, their third son, was cousin to the Emperors

Saint Thomas of Aquin

Henry VI and Frederick II, closely allied to the Kings of Castile, Aragon, and France, and closely related to Saint Louis. On his grandmother's side he could trace descent from the Saxon Kings of England. His godfather was Pope Honorius III, who confirmed the Order of Friars Preachers. His grandfather, Count Thomas, had been Captain-General of the Imperial forces. Landulf, in honor of his own father, gave to his third son this famous name, but little dreamed that the child would make it glorious.

There are several striking incidents recorded in connection with the birth and infancy of this wonderful child. One day a holy hermit, who lived among the mountains near the Castle of Rocca Secca, came to Theodora and predicted that the child she would bear would become great, and that his equal in sanctity and learning would not be found in the whole world. The Countess was a pious woman and rejoiced to hear the prophecy, but considered herself all unworthy to be the mother of so great a child.

In the early days of the year 1225 Thomas was born in the Castle of Rocca Secca, which stood high in the mountains, about seven miles from the little town of Aquino. From his earliest years Thomas was marked by the special providence of God. One night, when he was about three years old, lightning struck the tower in which he slept, but spared him, while it killed his little sister and the horses in the stable below. A halo of light was often seen to encircle his head. He was a gentle child, with deep, bright eyes and a placid and thoughtful expression of countenance, and he showed early signs of an admirable disposition. He was free from the wonted faults of childhood, and if, perchance, he cried, the sight of a book would always quiet him. He would gaze in wide-eyed wonder at the illuminated pages of scripts and turn the leaves with wonderful care, though he was yet too young to read. The first turnings of his mind and heart were to God, and the stillness of the chapel, with its tiny red light, threw a spell of fascination over his tender mind.

In the autumn of 1231, when he was six years old, Thomas was placed in the school for noble youths in the great Benedictine Abbey of Monte Cassino. This famous monastery had been founded in the sixth century by the great Saint Benedict, and in the thirteenth century was at the height of its power and glory. It stood on the summit of a mountain, some six miles from the Castle of Rocca Secca. The Counts of Aquino had always been its protectors, and when Thomas went there, his uncle Landulf Sennebald ruled as Abbot. Under the watchful eyes of this prelate and his learned monks the little Thomas made rapid progress in piety and learning. The good monks, who well understood "the reverence which is due to children," were quick to see the remarkable character of the little scholar who had been given into their charge, and accordingly gave him special care. They taught him to speak and write his mother tongue and gave him the rudiments of Latin and French. He made marvelous progress and was looked upon as the school's model by the masters as well as the pupils. It often happened that he was discovered advising his schoolmates to observe the rules of the college. But modesty often crimsoned his innocent brow and stopped the flow of his earnest words when he detected among his young audience the venerable white head of a monk who had in his wise humility stolen up to listen to him. The memory of his stay in the mighty abbey was treasured up and often rehearsed by those wonderful monks, who loved to remember the refining influence which the little scholar had spread about him as sweetly and as unconsciously as a violet hidden in the tall grass. Especially did they wonder at that precocious, tender mind which used to put such questions as these: "What is God? How can we know Him? What is truth?" Aye, there we have it—Truth, the keynote of his life and labors. Those precious years in the silent cloister worked wonders in the heart and mind of the thinker and the Saint.

In the fifth year of his stay at Monte Cassino, when Thomas was eleven years of age, the Abbot advised the Count to send his son to the University of Naples. Accordingly, Thomas went home for a well-deserved holiday. Here he showed the same tender heart which always marked him. His love for the poor, who often came to beg at the castle gates, was most extraordinary. His great desire to help them forced him to beg far more from his parents than they usually gave, though they always had been generous. He even went into the larders and seized whatever he could lay hands on. The steward, discovering this, reported it to the Count, who began to watch his son. One day as the boy was going out on his mission of mercy, with a huge loaf of bread under his mantle, Landulf met him and asked what he carried. Thomas blushed and was about to explain, when his father plucked the cloak away. But, to the astonishment of both, a shower of fragrant roses fell at their feet. Landulf saw the hand of God in the incident, warmly embraced his little son, and strode away to hide his tears, pondering over what he had often heard of the light seen at times about the strange child's brow.

In the autumn of 1236 Thomas and his tutor set out for Naples. That city was in those days described as "a very paradise of God, but inhabited by demons." The wonderful beauty of the city and surrounding country no doubt made a profound impression upon the saintly boy. Nature charmed him and told him of her God. But Naples was also the capital of the realm, a large, gay, frivolous, and wicked city. His pious tutor, however, and the grace of God preserved young Thomas from all danger. He fled the gaiety and idle pleasures of his fellow-students and devoted himself to prayer and study, as had been his wont at Monte Cassino.

It was not at all surprising, then, that the young scholar should make extraordinary progress in his studies. He stayed at the university for seven years. During his first four years he passed through the trivium, which comprised grammar, logic, and rhetoric. In this course he had for his professor the distinguished Pietro Martini. The quadrivium, a three years' course, consisted of music, mathematics, geometry, and astronomy. These studies he pursued under the celebrated Peter of Ireland. Thomas graduated with honors in both courses. His masters esteemed him highly and spoke of him as a model of diligence. Withal he was very modest and hid his talents from his fellows; nevertheless he early acquired a brilliant reputation both for learning and piety, and even at this time it was said of him that he could repeat the lectures he had heard more clearly and deeply than the learned professors had delivered them. His leisure time he spent to good account among the classics, and his pocket money he devoted to the poor, and while his fellow-students were about their noisy amusements he stole off to the church to pray.

The young student's vocation to the religious state and the priesthood had already shown itself long before he went to study at the University of Naples. When but ten years old he saw at the Abbey of Monte Cassino the solemn canonization Mass of Saint Dominic in the year 1234. The story of the great Preacher's wonderful life was fresh upon every one's lips, and this solemnity made a profound impression upon the tender soul of Thomas. He heard and felt the call of God, and from that time on treasured up his high hopes with joy and quiet anticipation. The Dominicans at Naples often saw him absorbed in prayer in their church. When he was about fifteen years old, he went to the Prior of San Domenico and begged admission to the Order. The prior was a prudent man and advised the boy to foster his vocation, and told him he had better wait until he had reached his eighteenth year. The docile child readily obeyed. Accordingly, in August, 1243, Thomas of Aquin laid aside his worldly rank and hopes, and was clothed in the white and black habit of the Order of Friars Preachers. The ceremony took place before a distinguished assembly. Not a word, however, had been said to his parents about his intentions. Thomas knew that "it is a good thing to hide the King's secret," and answered God's call without show or display.

As soon as the news reached the Castle of Rocca Secca a storm of indignation broke. His mother, pious and reasonable in all else, flew into a passion at the thought that the heir of a princely house should so far have forgotten his dignity and the honor of the family as to put on a friar's habit. She sent her complaints to the Pope and the Archbishop of Naples and threatened the Master-General of the Dominicans and the Prior of Naples. Not content with this, she set out for Naples. But as soon as Thomas heard of this he went by a by-road to the Convent of Santa Sabina, in Rome. Theodora followed him thither, but her son refused to see her, even though he longed to spare her tears and to bring her to understand that he wished to be left to follow his choice in peace. But the Countess was a resolute woman; she had other plans for her son. While Rome rang with the vehemence of her lamentations Thomas hurried to the north toward Paris. Theodora dispatched a mounted courier to her elder sons, Landulf and Raynald, who were then in Tuscany, and had them seize the fugitive. Thomas was captured in the town of Acquapendente. His brothers, rough and ready youths, reviled him cruelly and tried to tear his habit from his back, but were unsuccessful. So they dragged him off to Rocca Secca. His father, finding him resolute, shut him up in the tower of the Castle of Monte San Giovanni. Landulf, too, had great hopes for his boy: Thomas should become either a courtier or Abbot of Monte Cassino, but a friar—never! The Count brought his son a suit of fine apparel and a Benedictine habit, saying that he would be content if Thomas chose either the one or the other.

Thomas still remaining firm in his resolve to consecrate his life to Christ, his mother often sent his two sisters, Marietta and Theodora, to visit him. She hoped that their coaxings and caresses might succeed where her tears and entreaties had failed. But the outcome was far otherwise than she had anticipated; for by his earnest words Thomas completely defeated his sisters and finished the good work by winning them over to God. Marietta later entered religion and died as Abbess of her convent in Capua. Theodora, who later became Countess of Morisco, began a life of great sanctity.

But a sterner battle and a more brilliant victory was yet in store for the young novice. His two brothers were bent upon forcing him to give up his religious vocation and shrank from no means, fair or foul. They stripped him of his habit and forced him to put on secular attire, but one of the friars from Naples succeeded in supplying him with another habit, together with some books of philosophy, the Sacred Scriptures and the Book of Sentences of Peter Lombard. The perfidious brothers now tried another move, as cruel as it was base. They secured a beautiful girl, who had thrown away womanhood's most precious jewel, and shut her up alone with their innocent young brother. The conflict was short, but brilliant as the sweep of an archangel's sword. Thomas saw the poor creature, guessed her errand, seized a burning brand from the fireplace, and in a flash drove her out of the room. Then, tracing the sign of the Cross upon the wall with his flaming weapon, he knelt before it whilst he poured out his heart in thanks to God for the victory.

While he prayed thus an ecstatic sleep stole upon him. Two angels stood beside him, saying: "We come to thee from God to bestow upon thee the grace of perpetual virginity." Then they girded this young knight with a white cord, in token of his bravery in the lists of carnal temptation. They girt him so tightly that he awoke with a cry of pain. The girdle is preserved even to this day in the Dominican monastery of Chieri, in Italy, and the beautiful confraternity, called "The Angelic Warfare," to which it gave rise, is known to all the world.

After Thomas had endured his close imprisonment for about eighteen months, his religious brethren complained to Pope Innocent IV and the Emperor Frederick against such scandalous injustice. The Pontiff was much moved when he heard of the cruelty to which Thomas had been subjected, and sent strict orders for his immediate release. The Emperor did likewise. The ruffians, Landulf and Raynald, could do nothing but obey these commands, but to save their faces they connived at their brother's escape. They told their sisters to inform the Dominicans that it would be possible for Thomas to escape; and on the night arranged, Marietta and Theodora having lowered him from a window in a basket into the arms of his happy brethren, he was soon on his way to Naples. Shortly after regaining his freedom he was admitted to solemn profession. This took place in January, 1245.

But his trials were not over. The Countess, his mother, made one more effort to take him away from his vocation. She went to the Pope and asked him to annul her son's vows. Thomas, in answer to the Pontiff's summons, went to Rome. Theodora and those who sided with her alleged many reasons why the young man's profession should be set aside. But Pope Innocent, having examined Thomas very carefully and listened to the story of his vocation, ratified all he had done. Yet, to please the young friar's family, the Pope offered to make him Abbot of Monte Cassino and still allow him to remain a Dominican. How his mother must have caught at the tempting offer and hoped that he would accept. But Thomas declined; he deemed himself all unworthy of such an honor, and knew how incompatible it would be with the habit he wore and loved so tenderly. The Pope then blessed and dismissed him in peace, at the same time forbidding any further attempts upon the youth's liberty.

John of Wildeshausen, Master-General of the Order, knew well the worth and ability of the young friar, and resolved to send him to study in Cologne under Albertus Magnus, whose fame as a teacher had already spread all over Europe. In October, 1245, the General and the novice set out from Rome toward Paris, where the former had some business to transact. After a short stay they proceeded to Cologne, arriving there in January, 1246, after a journey of over 1,500 miles, which, according to the medieval custom, they had made entirely on foot.

When Thomas entered the schools presided over by Albert, they were in a flourishing condition. The students, among whom

Thomas took up his residence, had heard of his reputation and were impressed by his reserved and studious habits. But Thomas, as was his wont, sought to hide his talents. That he succeeded in doing so for a time is proved by the nickname which his fellow-students soon found for him. His modest manner, his docility and aversion for display were looked upon as signs of stupidity; and so they called him "the dumb Sicilian ox." Even Albert is said to have thought him dull.

The master, however, soon discovered that Thomas was hiding his genius. It happened thus: Thomas had written out his solution of an obscure passage from the "Book of the Divine Names." The paper fell into Albert's hands, who immediately recognized it as the work of a master, and bade him prepare himself to defend in solemn disputation certain thorny questions. Thomas did as he was told. The day for the debate arrived, the faculty and students assembled, and Thomas took his place on the rostrum, full of hope and modest courage. He expounded the questions with such marvelous skill and clearness that the hearers were dumbfounded. The objectors rose again and again to attack his theses, but he met all his challengers with courtesy and dexterity. One of his opponents, losing his patience, said: "You seem to forget that you are not a master, to decide, but a disciple to learn how to answer arguments raised." Brave and chivalrous as any knight, Thomas answered simply: "I do not see any other way of answering the difficulty." Then Albert hurled more difficulties at him. But Thomas never wavered. With distinctions and subdistinctions and retorted arguments he cut and thrust and parried his way to victory. Albert knew he had found a man after his own heart, and could restrain his joy no longer. He turned to the auditory and cried: "You call him a 'dumb ox,' but I declare before you that he will yet bellow so loud in doctrine that his voice will resound through the whole world." From this time on he took special interest in Thomas, procured him a cell next to his own, and made him the friend and companion of his studies and walks.

Thomas had been but six months in Cologne when the General Chapter decided to send Albert and Thomas to Paris; the master to take the Doctor's degree and to fill one of the chairs in the university, the pupil to continue his studies under Albert and profit by all the advantages of the great university. In Paris, Thomas continued the good work which he had begun so well at Cologne. He studied Aristotle, Sacred Scripture, and the Fathers of the Church, especially Saint Augustine. His giant strides in learning were equaled by his progress in holiness, and he was the acknowledged model of the community. But withal he remained most affable and lovable. And it is this singular sweetness of disposition that remained his characteristic all through life.

It was during these years in Paris that Thomas met Friar Bonaventure of the Friars Minor. Their acquaintance grew into an intimacy which lasted till death, and which in its ideal beauty and holiness reflected the friendship that united Jonathan and David, and the love that bound together Saint Francis and Saint Dominic. One day Thomas went to visit Bonaventure, whom he found writing the life of the Seraphic Saint Francis. Not wishing to take his friend away from his holy work, Thomas quickly retired unseen with his companion, saying: "Let us leave a saint to write the life of a saint." Upon another occasion Bonaventure went to Thomas, and in the simplicity of his heart said to him: "From what book do you draw all those wonderful ideas which astonish the world so mightily?" Thomas took Bonaventure by the hand, led him to a large crucifix which hung upon the wall of his cell, and said: "There is my only book."

After two years in Paris, Thomas was raised to the subdiaconate, and about this time his younger brother, Rayner, entered the Order in Naples. During this same year, 1248, the General Chapter met in Paris, and, having erected four new formal colleges for higher studies in the other four principal university centers, Bologna, Cologne, Montpellier, and Oxford, designated Master Albert as Regent in

Cologne, with Thomas as Master of Students. So once more the great master and his favorite disciple journeyed together on foot.

In the capacity of Master of Students, Thomas had all the students under his charge; he superintended their courses, read their dissertations, and directed their disputations. Under the guidance of Albert, he now began to lecture in philosophy and Sacred Scripture. His lectures were attended by great crowds of eager students and his fame spread rapidly. He was also preparing himself for the priesthood, and we can imagine how fervently a man of his saintly character must have prayed and worked to fit himself for the exalted office which he filled so well later on. In 1250 he was ordained priest by Conrad of Hochstaden, the princely Archbishop of Cologne. Little is known about this great event in the Saint's life. But William de Tocco, his pupil and first biographer, has left us a sentence full of meaning: "When he consecrated in Mass, he was seized with such intensity of devotion as to be dissolved in tears, utterly absorbed in its mysteries, and nourished with its fruits."

During the year in which Thomas was ordained a great calamity came upon his family. Because of the Emperor Frederick's growing animosity toward the Holy See, Landulf and Raynald of Aquino left the imperial service and entered that of the Pope. Thereupon the Emperor besieged the castle of Rocca Secca, and, after having beaten down the stout resistance of its defenders, put Raynald to death. Landulf died while bravely fighting in the cause of the Church. The aged Countess Theodora went into exile, where shortly after she died a holy death. Thomas heard all this sad news with sorrow, but he knew how to bow before the will of Providence.

It was during these years in Cologne that Thomas began his writings. The treatises "On Being and Essence" and "The Principles of Nature" were the first products of his pen. Then came a "Commentary on the Book of Sentences" and a treatise "On the Government of the Jews." The latter was composed for Adelaide Duchess of Brabant.

But Thomas was not merely a schoolman, an impractical theorist with his head among the clouds. Besides being a wonderful professor of theology, he was also an ardent and eloquent preacher. Hundreds of students flocked to his lectures, but he was not satisfied to reach only the educated. He wished to teach the truth in the pulpit as well as in the master's chair. Wherever he went he never lost an opportunity of preaching to the people, who always listened spell-bound. And well they might, for who was better prepared for the apostolic work than he who was both saint and scholar?

The students of the University of Paris and his own religious brethren were greatly rejoiced when, in the year 1252, Thomas was recalled thither. Here he again met his dear friend Bonaventure, whom he made the companion of his studies and with whom he shared his thoughts and ideals. They were kindred spirits in everything, living a peaceful life of prayer, study, and teaching, while the noise and bustle of university life surged and eddied around them.

The city and the university were at odds. During a night brawl four students were attacked by the city watchmen. After a short resistance one of the lads was killed and the other three wounded and dragged off to prison. The municipal authorities failed to make satisfaction; the doctors suspended their lectures and closed the schools. The Franciscan and Dominican professors, however, having no interest in the quarrel, continued their lectures as usual. The university authorities were highly incensed at this and passed a new statute, that henceforth no one should be admitted to the Doctorate in Theology unless he swore to observe all the university laws, especially the one newly made, that in case of conflict between the university and the city all public lectures must be suspended until the affair was settled. But the Mendicant Orders held their ground and refused to submit to such a law. The struggle between them and the university lasted about three years. When Thomas was presented to take his degree, it was summarily refused him. Pope Alexander IV ordered the university to confer the doctorate upon Thomas, but even the papal mandate was ignored. Things went from bad to worse, and large numbers of students left Paris and went to Oxford.

William of Saint Amour, a noted professor of the university, wrote a book against the friars, entitled "The Perils of the Last Times." He accused them of teaching false doctrine, of being the cause of all the evils and calamities of the times, and the precursors of Antichrist. The vile book was condemned by the Bishops of France, but many people read and believed every word of it. King Louis IX brought the matter before the Pope, who summoned both parties to Rome. The gauntlet so boldly thrown down by William of Saint Amour, in behalf of the university, was calmly taken up by Thomas and Bonaventure, and a commission of doctors represented the university. This latter body also intended to defend another scandalous work, "The Eternal Gospel," in order to obtain the condemnation of the Mendicants.

Thomas, John of Parma, and Albert were sent to defend the Mendicant orders. William's book was put into the hands of two commissions, one consisting of four cardinals, the other of theologians. Among the latter were the three famous friars. Each gave his opinion in writing, but the hopes of all rested principally upon Thomas. When all was ready, the Pope set a day to hear the defense of the Mendicants. The champions appeared before him in the Cathedral of Anagni and read their confutations. The defense was brilliant and the victory complete. William's book was solemnly condemned on October 5, 1256. All this had taken place before the arrival of the deputation from the University of Paris. When they appeared they protested against the verdict, but afterwards all gave in, except William of Saint Amour, who remained obdurate. Thomas of Aquin's defense, entitled "An Apology for the Religious Orders," not only defeated William and the university, but remains for all times the classic defense of the religious life.

The cause being now finished, Thomas went back to Paris, where his superiors wished him to stand for his degree without more delay. But the university again offered violent opposition, and did not submit until the Pope had sent as many as eleven Bulls in favor of Thomas. He, however, became afraid, thinking himself utterly unworthy of the honor, and it was only under obedience that he at last submitted.

During the night before the ceremony Thomas was praying in his cell, when Saint Dominic appeared to him, encouraged him to take the degree, and gave him a text upon which to base his doctoral discourse. Thomas and Bonaventure were to graduate together, but neither wished to precede the other. Their friends, however, soon settled this courteous rivalry by arranging that Bonaventure, as being older than Thomas, should first receive the doctor's cap and ring. This ceremony took place on October 23, 1257.

The time from his reception of the Doctorate in Theology until his death was the brightest and most fruitful period of his whole life. Raymond of Pennafort was now in Spain, laboring heroically for the conversion of the Jews and Moors. He wrote to ask Thomas to aid him by composing a philosophical exposition of Christian belief. The saintly Doctor answered by writing his first monumental work, "The Sum of the Truth of Catholic Faith against the Gentiles." It met with wonderful success and was soon translated into Greek, Hebrew, and Syriac. From the year 1261 it became the standard text-book in the philosophy of religion.

About this time Thomas also wrote a little work upon "Truth," another on the Epistles of Saint Paul, and a commentary on the Book of Job. In those days the doctors of Paris were much engaged in discussing the manner of Christ's presence in the Eucharist. They referred the matter to Thomas, knowing well that he could give a satisfactory explanation. He took the opinions of all the doctors in writing and retired to study and pray. When he had written, he took his manuscript to the church, laid it on the altar, and prayed. Our Blessed Lord appeared and approved of his writing, telling him that he had solved the difficulty as well as was possible by mere human wisdom. Reginald of Piperno, who had followed his friend Thomas into the church, then saw the holy man lifted from the ground while he prayed.

The reputation for sanctity and learning which Thomas had acquired rapidly spread beyond academic circles. King Louis IX esteemed him highly and made him Privy Councillor. In this connection writers call our attention to the fact that during the years in which Thomas sat at the royal council board King Louis achieved his greatest glory. Students who are familiar with the works of the Angelic Doctor know how eminently he was fitted to advise the saintly King in matters temporal as well as spiritual. One evening, while he was dining with the King, Queen, and a few guests, he became lost in thought. All of a sudden he violently struck the table and cried: "The argument is clinched against the Manicheans!" But when he saw what he had done he humbly begged pardon of King Louis, who smiled and called one of his secretaries to take down the argument, lest it lose some of its force and clarity. About this time the King engaged the holy Doctor and the celebrated Vincent de Beauvais to put the royal library in order.

The year 1260 worked a sudden change in the Saint's life. Pope Urban IV, who had succeeded Alexander IV, was very anxious to heal the schism between the Latin and the Greek Church, and, in order to use the great ability of the now widely celebrated Doctor, called him from Paris to Rome. The university was very unwilling to lose him, but the Sovereign Pontiff's orders had to be obeyed. In the Eternal City, Thomas was set over the school of select scholars which resided in the Lateran Palace. Urban IV was a great patron of learning, and wherever he went he took his school with him, and thus for five years the Saint taught in Rome, Viterbo, Fondi, Orvieto, Anagni, Perugia, and Bologna, as the case might be. Along with the holy Doctor's scholastic work always went his zeal in preaching the Word of God. One day, after one of his sermons, a woman, who was suffering from an issue of blood, came up behind the Saint and with great confidence touched the hem of his mantle, and was cured. About this same time he converted two learned Jewish rabbis, not so much by the force and brilliance of his arguments as by the fervor of his prayers.

The reunion of the Eastern and Western Churches was an undertaking very dear to the heart of the zealous Pope, Urban IV. He imparted to the Angelic Doctor his hopes and plans, and told him to write a treatise against the Greeks. This work, "Against the Errors of the Greeks," the Pope sent to the Emperor of Constantinople. The book became popular and was soon translated into Greek. Thomas then followed it up with another, "Against the Errors of the Greeks, Armenians, and Saracens." He himself never lived to see the Council of Florence at which a portion of the Eastern Church came back to the Chair of Peter, but he had done his part in the great work, and had done it extremely well.

The Fortieth General Chapter of the Order met in London in the year 1263. Three hundred friars took part in it. King Henry III extended to the brethren a truly royal welcome, personally assisted at the opening ceremony, and presented each friar with a new habit. Humbert de Romanis, fifth Master-General, presided over the Chapter. He had borne the heavy burden of government for nine years, and now, because of his infirmities, resigned his office. His wishes were obeyed with regret, but since this Chapter had no power to elect his successor it elected Master Albertus Magnus as Vicar-General for one year. The Chapter was attended by many men of eminence. Saint Thomas was there as Definitor for the Roman Province. Besides him there were present Albertus Magnus, Peter de Tarentaise, now known as Blessed Innocent V; Peter de Luca, David de Ayr, the Masters from Oxford and Paris, the Provincials, Vicars, and Definitors from all the Provinces. The Angelic Doctor exercised a profound influence upon the Capitular Fathers in animating them to a great love for sanctity and learning.

Called to Orvieto by Pope Urban, Thomas proposed to him a special feast in honor of the Blessed Sacrament. Some years previously, Julienne, Prioress of Mont Cornillon; Eve, a recluse of Liege, and Isabel of Huy had seen a vision of the saints petitioning our Lord to establish the feast. They took counsel on the matter with Jean de Laussanne, a very pious and learned Canon of Liege. This holy priest gladly approved of their design and composed an office of the Blessed Sacrament, which was adopted by the Church of Saint Martin in Liege. Jean then took the matter to Urban, who was then Archdeacon of Saint Lambert, in Liege. Furthermore, he consulted the Dominican Provincial, Hugh de Saint Cher; Guy de Laon, Bishop of Cambrai, and the Dominican theologians. All these men thought highly of the plan, and the one-time Archdeacon of Saint Lambert's was not long in the Chair of Peter when he thought of instituting the feast of Corpus Christi. Accordingly, he commissioned the Angelic Doctor to compose a new office for the great festival.

Tradition has it that Pope Urban commanded Saint Thomas and Saint Bonaventure to compose separately an office for the feast. While they were working at their task Saint Bonaventure called upon the Angelical, and in the course of the conversation took up and read the Magnificat antiphon, "O Sacrum Convivium!" He was moved to the depths of his seraphic soul by the beauty and heavenly sweetness of the thought and language. When he reached home he went straight to his cell and cast his own manuscript into the fire. If this tradition is authentic—and there is no serious reason for doubting it—we are forced to regret the great loss to Eucharistic literature caused by this grand act of humility. Who will take it upon himself to say what a wonderful office of Corpus Christi might not have been expected from the graceful pen and burning heart of the Seraphic Doctor?

We are so used to thinking of Saint Thomas as the supreme theologian, the prince of schoolmen, the consummate dialectician, that we are in danger of losing sight of his poetic genius. That this was very great is amply proven by the sublime excellence of the office of Corpus Christi, which ranks among the most beautiful offices in the Breviary. Of the hymns for Vespers and Matins, Archbishop Vaughan writes: "The 'Pange Lingua' and 'Sacris Solemniis,' so exquisitely theological, so tenderly effective, so reverently adoring, so expressive of every want and aspiration of the human heart—where are two hymns so touching, so poetical, so angelical as they are?" Christ's sublime love for us, as shown at the Last Supper, is a theme most dear to the glowing heart of the holy Doctor, and in these hymns he sings of it with the eloquence, sweetness, and fervor of an ecstatic Seraph. No higher tribute could be paid to Saint Thomas than that which the Church gave when she adopted the last two verses of his hymns for Vespers and Lauds and enjoined that they be sung at Benediction. For six hundred years the sweet strains of "O Salutaris Hostia" and "Tantum Ergo Sacramentum" have gone up with the incense to the Blessed Sacrament in the cathedrals and village chapels of the world; and their echo will not die until the end of time. In every line of this magnificent office there breathes the same pure thought and feeling so characteristic of the Angelical. The "Lauda Sion Salvatorem," that glorious hymn of praise, never fails to arouse in the devout heart the noblest aspirations and the purest sentiments, and in grandeur yields only to the "Te Deum." And what shall we say of the "Adoro Te"? Its lyrical beauty is nothing if not exquisite. It comes straight from the heart, grows more poignant and tender with every verse, and ends with such a pitiful, aching cry of longing that not only sums up and expresses all our best aspirations, but leaves us mute in wonderment at the intensity of the Saint's love for Christ. Still we feel that it must have been greater than even he could express.

Poets sing because their hearts are full, and in proportion to the grandeur of their thought and the intensity of their emotion will be greatness and spontaneity of their song. In this respect, as well as in the power of accurately putting thought and feeling into language, the Angelic Doctor stands among the sweetest singers of all times. With his grand intellect ablaze with the vision of the Eucharistic mystery and his tender heart burning with love and devotion for the hidden God, he sang as it was given to none before nor after him to sing. In him the theologian saw, the Saint felt, and the poet sang; and the result is more than a poet's rhapsody—it is an angel's song.

After having finished the office of Corpus Christi the holy Doctor undertook another work at the command of the Pope. This was a commentary on the Four Gospels compiled from the Fathers of the Church, and was entitled "Catena Aurea" or "Golden Chain." This is the fullest commentary ever drawn from Patristic sources, and is a very important work. In 1264, shortly after the completion of the first part, the commentary on Saint Matthew, Pope Urban IV died. In February, 1265, the newly-elected Pontiff, Clement IV, called Thomas to Rome. Here the Saint finished his famous treatise, "On the Unity of the Intellect, against the Averroists." The Order had now been deprived of his services for some years. Accordingly, John de Vercelli, the Master-General, came to an agreement with the Pope, and in 1265 the Chapter of Montpellier assigned Thomas to Santa Sabina in Rome, and put into his hands the direction of studies.

The Angelic Doctor now drew the ground-plan for his greatest work, the immortal "Summa Theologica." The words "Sum of Theology" are few, but they mean much, nothing less than a complete synthesis of the whole body of Catholic doctrine, dogmatic and moral. The very daring of such a gigantic undertaking is nothing short of staggering. For nine years the Angel of the Schools labored incessantly and untiringly at this huge structure, and even then was unable to finish it completely.

A very brief outline of this work will not be out of place here, since it will convey at least a faint idea of the grandeur of the

Angelic Doctor's masterpiece. Under three great headings it comprises all theology: God in Himself and as He is the Creator; God as the end of all things, especially of man; God as the Redeemer. The first part is made up of treatises on God, His existence, nature, and attributes. Then comes the creation of the universe, the angels, and man. The first part is divided into 119 questions, subdivided into 584 articles, and fills a huge folio volume. The second part is divided into two divisions, called the first of the second and the second of the second. The first treats of the end of man, morality, passions, sin, theological and moral virtues, law, and grace. It is made up of 114 questions, subdivided into 619 articles. The second of the second treats in copious detail of the same matter that is covered in the first of the second. This takes up 189 questions in 916 articles. The whole second part fills two folios. The third part treats of the Incarnation, the sacraments in general, and in particular, the Resurrection, and the last things. Saint Thomas ceased writing in the middle of the tract on Penance. The rest is all his, but was embodied in the Summa by some one else and is taken from his Commentary on the Fourth Book of the Sentences of Peter Lombard. The whole part comprises 189 questions, with 981 articles. The whole Summa Theologica contains 497 questions, subdivided into 2,481 articles. Saint Thomas wrote the first part at Rome in two years; the second part took five years, and was written in Bologna and Paris; the third part was written in Naples.

After ten years of retirement William de Saint Amour again appeared on the scene with a book against the Mendicant Orders. The Pope entrusted its examination and refutation to the Angelic Doctor, who composed two treatises: one, an apology for the religious orders, entitled, "Against those who would withdraw others from entering the Religious State," and the other, "On the perfection of the Spiritual Life."

During the Lent of 1267 the Saint preached with great eloquence and success in the Old Basilica of Saint Peter. He was held in the greatest esteem. Churches and halls where he preached and taught were crowded, priests, professors, Bishops, and Cardinals being among the audience. In 1267 he assisted at the General Chapter of Bologna, which, by request of the university, assigned him to that city, where he began again to teach publicly in the schools. He was very happy to live at the tomb of Saint Dominic, whose memory he cherished with filial tenderness, and whose grand ideal he ever strove to realize in his own life and work.

The House of Aquino was in 1268 reinstated in its former position and estates. The holy man received the good news with the same equanimity and submission to the Divine Will which had marked him when years before he had heard of its calamitous downfall. He was called to attend the General Chapter of Paris in 1269, which assigned him to that city as Regent of Studies. At this time he was engaged in writing the second part of the Summa, and several of his minor works. In 1270 he bade farewell to his royal friend, Saint Louis IX, who sailed away to the Crusade in Palestine.

During his stay in Paris he went with the novices one day to visit the Abbey Church of Saint Denis. As the little band sat down to rest on a hill overlooking the great city, one of the young men turned to the holy Doctor, and, with a touch of national pride, said to him: "See Master, how beautiful is the city of Paris. Would you not like to be the lord of this city?" "No," replied Thomas, "I would much rather have Saint John Chrysostom's Homilies on the Gospel of Saint Matthew. What could I possibly do with such a city?" "Well, Father," answered the student, "you might sell it to the King, and build many convents for the Order." "Still," said the Saint, "I should prefer to have the Homilies. If I had the government of this city, it would bring me many cares, hinder me from contemplating the divine mysteries, and deprive me of all consolation. Experience shows that the more a man abandons himself to the care and love of temporal things, the more he exposes himself to the danger of losing Heaven."

In the year 1270 Thomas finished his Commentary on the Epistles of Saint Paul. While writing this the Apostle appeared to him and helped him in explaining the difficult passages. In the following year he was called back to Rome, where he completed the second part of the Summa, and began the third part. Besides this he taught regularly in the schools, and wrote his Commentary on Boetius.

Saint Thomas was a man of strikingly noble appearance. He was tall, heavily built, but well proportioned. His features were regular, his head large and beautifully shaped, his forehead high, and he was slightly bald. If we judge by a portrait said to be authentic, his appearance was noble, engaging, but above all, calm, dignified, and unruffled. His large and clear eyes speak of deep meditation, and his firm mouth betrays great strength of character.

The virtue of humility was at the bottom of his whole life and work. He often said: "Love of God leads to self-contempt, whereas self-love leads to contempt of God. If you would raise on high the edifice of holiness, take humility for your foundation." To his friend Reginald he once said: "Thanks be to God, my knowledge, my doctor's degree, my work, have never been able to take humility from my heart." He could never be prevailed upon to accept dignities. The only office he ever held in his Order was the Regency of Studies, which is neither a mere dignity nor a sinecure. When Pope Innocent IV offered him the Abbacy of Monte Cassino together with the privilege of remaining a Dominican, he resolutely declined, even though he knew that his acceptance would have more than satisfied his mother. Clement IV tried to make him a Cardinal, offered him the Abbey of Saint Peter ad Aram, in Rome, and in spite of his refusal issued a Bull, creating him Archbishop of Naples, but all to no purpose. Thomas refused absolutely to give up his humble position, and when he heard of the Bull he went to Pope Clement and begged so earnestly to be freed from the mitre that the Pontiff at last annulled the document.

To the holy vows to which he had bound himself in youth he remained ever true. He was a model in every respect. Poverty, that sacred heritage which Saint Dominic left to his children, the Holy Doctor cherished most ardently. His habit was always poor and simple.

Friar Nicholas de Marsiliaco, one of his fellow-religious, testified: "I was in Paris with Friar Thomas, and I declare before God that never have I seen in any man such degree of innocence, such love of poverty. In writing his 'Sum against the Gentiles' he had not sufficient copy-books, so he wrote it on scraps of paper, although he might have had books in abundance, had he been so minded, but he had no concern for temporal affairs."

His practice of obedience was marvelous. He often said that an obedient man is the same as a saint. When he was in Bologna, a lay-brother, who was about to go shopping in the city, had leave to ask the first friar he met to accompany him, as the Rule of Saint Augustine prescribes. In the cloister he met a priest whom he did not know. He accosted him and said: "Good Father, the Prior wishes you to go with me into the city." The stranger bent his head in assent, and followed him. As they were walking through the busy thoroughfares, the lay-brother often scolded his companion for not keeping up with him. The stranger was lame, but did not offer this as an excuse. He bore the rebuke patiently and each time humbly begged pardon for his fault. Finally, some of the townspeople recognized the great Doctor and hotly told the brother who his companion was. The poor lay-brother fell on his knees to ask forgiveness, but Thomas answered: "Obedience is the perfection of religious life: thereby a man submits himself to his fellow-man for the love of God, just as God became obedient to men for their salvation."

With regard to holy chastity he was an angel in the flesh. Although in his youth angels had assured him that he would remain pure and innocent all his life, he always prayed and watched against the danger of losing this precious jewel. His friend Reginald testified that the Angelical ever remained as innocent as a child. This virtue espoused him to Christ, gave him his miraculously clear intellectual vision here below, and now that he is in heaven it is his imperishable crown forever.

His great charity was only the outcome of his intense, all-absorbing love for God. He never spoke a harsh or unkind word to any one. He had a mortal hatred for sin and error; but at the same time he was always kind and gentle toward sinners, and while crushing an argument he was invariably considerate for his opponent. He was conspicuous for his refined manners, and happily united the grace and courtesy of a nobleman to the dignity and reserve of a cloistered priest. In spite of the many things that claimed his attention he always found time to tend to the wants of others. He was always accessible. High and low, rich and poor, came to him for advice and help which he always gave kindly and generously. Like the Apostle he was all things to all men that he might save all. There were three things that he loved especially: The Church, whose cause he always championed; his Order, from which he dreaded to be separated by ecclesiastical promotion, and God's poor, to whom he even gave the habit from his back, when he could not otherwise help them.

Prayer was for him a prime necessity. He would often say that a religious who does not pray much and fervently is like a soldier trying to fight without weapons. He distrusted his great natural gifts and had recourse to prayer in order to obtain light in his work. Saint Vincent Ferrer and Saint Antoninus affirm that in his difficulties he would go to the Blessed Virgin as a child runs to its mother. Reginald of Piperno, who knew him so intimately, testifies that the Angelic Doctor used prayer as a preparation for everything, and that he owed his marvelous learning less to the power of genius than to the efficacy of prayer.

One of his most remarkable characteristics was his power of concentration and his perfect command over his senses. He was naturally sensitive and delicate, but by sheer force of intellect he gained such a command over himself that he underwent several surgical operations without even feeling the pain. Once when he was dictating to a copyist, he held the candle in his hand in order to assist the scribe. He became so lost in thought that he let the candle burn out in his hand, without giving any sign of feeling the least pain. Over his mental faculties he even had greater control than over his bodily senses. He could dictate to four secretaries, on widely different subjects, at the same time, without in the least losing the thread of his reasoning.

The General Chapter of 1272 met in Florence. It was besieged by petitions from the Universities of Paris, Bologna, and Naples, asking to have again the benefit of the Angelic Doctor's teaching. But Charles I of Anjou, King of Sicily, and brother of Saint Louis, prevailed. Late in August Thomas left Rome in the company of Reginald of Piperno and Bartholomew of Lucca. At Cardinal d'Annibaldi's residence in the Campagna all three of the friars fell sick of malaria. The holy Doctor recovered first, but his two companions lay in great danger. Taking from his bosom a relic of Saint Agnes, he touched them with it, whereupon they were immediately restored to perfect health.

His entry into Naples was like the coming of a great prince. He was met by a great concourse of people who, with shouts of joy, accompanied him to the Convent of Saint Dominic, where nearly thirty years before he had taken the habit. Very shortly after his arrival an incident took place which shows how perfect was his concentration and how habitual his recollection. The Cardinal Legate and the Archbishop of Capua, a former disciple, went to consult him on some theological questions. Hearing of their arrival, Thomas hastened down into the cloister, but was so intent upon his own thoughts that he passed the illustrious visitors without noticing them at all. Presently they heard him exclaim, "I have found the solution!" The Archbishop plucked him by the sleeve, and, on coming to himself, the holy Doctor so humbly begged pardon of the prelates that both were highly edified.

During this same year, his deceased sister, Marietta, Abbess of Capua, appeared to him and told him that she was in heaven. He inquired of her about Raynald and Landulf. She told him that the former was in heaven, but that the latter was yet in purgatory. Moreover, she assured him that he would die soon, and that he would attain very great glory. Shortly after this Raynald appeared bearing the palm of martyrdom and said: "You are in good state, my brother. Hold fast what you have, and finish your course as you began. Know also for certain, that none of your Order, or very few, will ever be lost."

These revelations were very consoling to him. He went about his work as usual, writing, praying, and teaching as was his wont, but with a certain wistfulness; he was homesick for heaven. Every morning he said Mass at an early hour in the chapel of Saint Nicholas, after which he served the Mass of his friend Reginald. While writing his Commentary on Isaiah, the Apostles, Saints Peter and Paul, appeared and brought him great light and assistance in understanding the great prophet. When this work was finished he wrote an exposition of the first fifty-one Psalms. During the year 1273 the frequency of his raptures and visions increased. He seldom left the convent, except to preach or to deliver his daily lecture in the university. During the Lent of 1273 he preached every day in the Cathedral upon the words, "Hail, full of grace, the Lord is with thee."

On the 6th of December, the Feast of Saint Nicholas, 1273, in that Saint's chapel, the Angelic Doctor fell into a long ecstasy during Mass. He never told any one what he had seen, but from that day on his pen lay idle and he wrote no more. He was often seen raised in the air while engaged in prayer. One day several of the friars saw him thus uplifted before the crucifix in Saint Nicholas chapel. Suddenly the Crucified spoke: "Thou hast written well of Me, Thomas; what reward wilt thou have for thy labors?" "None other than Thyself, O Lord," was the Saint's prompt reply.

Whenever he was urged to finish the Summa he said: "I can do no more." In the middle of the tract on Penance he had put aside his pen. To Reginald he said: "I can do no more. Such secrets have been communicated to me, that all I have written and taught seem to me to be only like a handful of straw." The Summa was the last thing he wrote; it represents the fruits of his fully matured genius and is his great gift to the Church.

Just before Christmas Thomas went to pay his last visit to his sister, the Countess of San Severino. He stayed with her a week, but during that time he had only one long conversation with her. His abstraction was constant and his raptures so frequent that Reginald had to feed him like a child. Such burning desire for the eternal mansion is fatal. There is something peculiarly unearthly, touching, and awe-inspiring about this spectacle of the Angel of the Schools fainting away from the sheer intensity of his longing to be dissolved and to be with Christ.

But he was obedient even unto death. Pope Gregory X summoned him to attend the General Council of Lyons, which was to open on the first day of May. Accordingly the holy Doctor left Naples on January 28, 1274, accompanied by the ever-faithful Reginald and another friar. By order of the Pope he took with him his treatise, "Against the Errors of the Greeks." On the way he was constantly lost in contemplation, and, as the little party descended from Terracina by the Borgo Nuovo highway, he struck his head so violently against a fallen tree that he lay stunned for some time. From that moment Reginald never left his side. To distract his mind from the pain he was in, Reginald said: "Master, you are going to the Council on behalf of our Order and the kingdom of Naples." Thomas answered quietly: "May God grant me the grace to see this great good." "Furthermore," continued his friend, "they will make you a Cardinal, like Friar Bonaventure, for the good of the two Orders." To which the Saint promptly replied: "There is no other state in which I can be more useful to the Order than that in which I am now. I shall never change it." His strength failing, Reginald procured a mule, upon which the Saint rode to visit his niece, the Countess Francesca de Ceccano at Maenza Castle. Here he became extremely ill, and was able to say Mass only twice during his stay of five days. The Abbot of Fossa-Nuova paid him a visit. His niece, his brethren, and the Abbot did everything they could for him. One morning he felt slightly better and announced his intention of proceeding onward to the Council. Reginald earnestly begged him to remain where he could have every care and attention, but in vain. So once more he mounted the mule, accompanied by his brethren, the Abbot and some of his Cistercian monks. But he soon saw that he could not go much further, and begged hospitality from the Abbot. "If the Lord wishes to call me," he said, "it is better that I should be found in a monastery than in the house of seculars." So after seven weary miles the party came to the Abbey. It was the 10th of February, 1274. They carried him first to the church, where he paid his last visit to the Blessed Sacrament. Then, at the earnest request of the Abbot, they carried him to that prelate's own apartment. As they bore him through the cloister they heard him say: "This is my rest forever and ever: here will I dwell, for I have chosen it." (Ps. 131, v. 14.) The good monks, true to their traditions, lavished every attention upon him, even cutting and carrying the wood for his fire. "Whence comes this honor to me," he cried, in his distress of humility, "whence comes it that the servants of God should serve a man like me?" The report of his illness spread abroad, many Dominicans and other religious from Rome and Naples, prelates and nobility, hurried to the Abbey to bid farewell to him whom they venerated and loved so much. Among the friars of his Order came his younger brother Rayner, afterwards Archbishop of Messina.

The Cistercians, wishing to have the last words of his teaching as a memento, begged him to dictate an exposition of the Canticle of Canticles. "Give me the spirit of Saint Bernard, and I will do so," he said. Touched by their pleadings, he assented. This commentary is his second exposition of the Canticle, and is entitled, "Sonet Vox Tua." At the eleventh verse of the seventh chapter, "Come, my beloved, let us go forth into the fields," he fell into a swoon. When he revived he made a confession of his whole life to Reginald and received Extreme Unction. The Abbot brought him Holy Viaticum, and, as he lay supported in Reginald's arms, he made his last profession of faith: "If in this world there be any knowledge of this mystery keener than that of faith, I wish now to use it to affirm that I believe in the Real Presence of Jesus Christ in this Sacrament, truly God and truly man, the Son of God, the Son of the Virgin Mary. This I believe and hold for true and certain." After receiving the Sacred Host he said in a clear voice, "I receive Thee, the price of my redemption, for whom I have studied, watched, preached, and taught. I have never wilfully said anything against Thee, nor am I obstinate in my own opinions. If I have spoken wrongly of this Sacrament, I leave all to the correction of the Holy Roman Church, in whose communion I now pass from this life."

Reginald was in tears and could not believe that his holy friend would die so young. But Thomas consoled him: "My son, do not trouble yourself about me. I might have made further progress in learning, and have made my learning more profitable to others, but God has shown me, that if, without any merit of mine, He has given me more grace and light than other doctors who lived a long time, it is because He wished to shorten my exile, and to take me the sooner to Himself, out of pure mercy. If you love me truly, be content and comforted, for my own peace is perfect." After this last farewell to the friend who had always clung to him so faithfully, the Angelic Doctor began to recite his great hymn, "Adoro Te Devote Latens Deitas." And when he had finished, he gently fell asleep, to awake in the white radiance of the Divine Presence. This was the 7th of March, 1274, in the forty-ninth year of his age.

His death was miraculously revealed to many holy men, among them Master Albert of Cologne, who said with tears in his eyes: "My son in Christ, Thomas of Aquino, the light of the Church, is dead, as God has revealed to me. He was the world's flower and glory, and has rendered superfluous the writings of the Doctors who shall come after him." Friar Albert of Brescia saw in a vision Saint Augustine of Hippo and Thomas of Aquin. "Thomas is my equal in glory," said the Saint, "but surpasses me by the aureola of virginity."

The Angelic Doctor's glory was revealed by very many miracles, ninety-six of which were duly attested, and submitted as evidence for his canonization. While his body yet lay in the Abbey Choir, the subprior, John of Ferentino, who was totally blind, placed his eyes against the Saint's and immediately regained his sight.

The Requiem Mass was sung by the Franciscan Bishop of Terracina. Reginald of Piperno delivered the funeral discourse, with sobs and tears revealing the great holiness of his dead friend and master. At the conclusion he protested that he only left the body until further word should come from the Master General. Then the holy remains were buried in the Abbey Church under the high altar. The Pope and Cardinals at the Council of Lyons were profoundly grieved to hear of the Saint's death, and by order of the Supreme Pontiff the treatise, "Against the Errors of the Greeks," was sent on to Lyons.

In 1318 the solemn process of canonization was begun, promoted by Robert, King of Sicily, and supported by the petitions of the hierarchy, clergy, the universities, and the Order of Preachers. The process was completed by three Dominican Cardinals, Nicholas Aubertin, Nicholas de Freauville, and William de Godieu. The canonization took place in Avignon on July 18, 1323. In the presence of Pope John XXII, the Cardinals, a great many Archbishops and Bishops, King Robert and Queen Mary of Sicily, many princes, nobility, and ambassadors, the Bull of canonization was read. Then the Pope proceeded to the Cathedral, where he sang the first Mass in honor of the Saint. In his fervent eulogy the Pope cried out: "His doctrine was not other than miraculous. He has enlightened the Church more than all other Doctors, and more profit can be gained in a single year by the study of his works, than by devoting a lifetime to that of other theologians. He has wrought as many miracles as he has written articles." And since that day more than eighty Popes have vied with one another in extolling the sanctity and learning of the Angel of the Schools.

Not few were the translations of the relics, until finally Pope Urban VI, a Benedictine, gave them back to the Dominicans. In 1369 they were placed in the Dominican Church in Toulouse. During the French Revolution, the treasure was transferred to an obscure corner of Saint Sernin's Church. In 1878 the sacred relics were judicially verified by the Archbishop of Toulouse and then enclosed in a beautiful sarcophagus of gold and silver.

Pope Pius V proclaimed Saint Thomas Doctor of the Church in 1567. At the Councils of Trent and the Vatican the "Summa" was placed beside the Bible on the altar. On August 4, 1879, Pope Leo XIII published his Encyclical "Æterni Patris," which is one great defense and eulogy of the Angelical's teaching. On the Feast of Saint Dominic, 1880, the great Leo again issued a Brief. "In virtue of our supreme authority, for the glory of Almighty God, and the honor of the Angelic Doctor, for the advancement of learning and the common welfare of human society, we declare the Angelic Doctor, Saint Thomas Aquinas, Patron of all Universities, Academies, Colleges, and Catholic Schools: and we desire that he should be venerated as such by all."

BIBLIOGRAPHY

"Acta Sanctorum" contains the life by Tocco (cf. Mar. 7).

"Bullarium Ordinis Prædicatorum."

Conway, P.: "Saint Thomas Aquinas," London, 1911.

DRANE, A. T.: "Christian Schools and Scholars," London, 1881.

English Dominicans, "The Summa Theologica of Saint Thomas literally translated." London and New York. Begun 1911 and still in progress.

KENNEDY, D. J.: "The Summa Theologica of Saint Thomas." Catholic University Bulletin, Vol. XV, No. 4.

"Specimen Pages from the Summa," Vol. XVI, No. 8.

"Saint Thomas and Medieval Philosophy," New York, 1919.

MANDONNET, P.: "Des écrits authentiques de S. Thomas d'Aquin." Fribourg, 1910.

DE WULF, tr. COFFEY: "Scholasticism Old and New," Dublin, 1907.

Catholic Encyclopedia, Articles on Saint Thomas and on Saint Bonaventure.

PERRIER: "Revival of Scholastic Philosophy," New York, 1909.

"Opera Omnia S. Thomæ," Rome, 1570; Venice, 1594; Antwerp, 1612; Paris, 1660; Venice, 1775; Parma, 1852–69; Rome, Leonine Edition, begun 1882 and still in progress.

Saint Raymond of Pennafort

THE THIRTEENTH is called the greatest of centuries. Divine Mercy was singularly manifested to the world at the end of the twelfth and the beginning of the thirteenth centuries. God called into existence the Order of Friar Preachers to stem the tidal wave of heresy, which at that time threatened Europe with spiritual and social ruin. To this Order in its infancy God gave many illustrious men, who have been the leaders and exemplars in every line of Christian endeavor for the past seven hundred years.

It was in 1175 that Raymond first saw the light of day in his father's castle of Pennafort, a few miles from the city of Barcelona, in Catalonia. The castle stood on a rocky cliff overlooking the River Monjos. A Dominican priory, built in 1601 on the site of the castle, still remains, but, excepting one tower, the castle has disappeared. Raymond's parents were of royal blood, descendants of the Counts of Barcelona and allied to the race of the Kings of Aragon. Their piety and devotion prompted them to procure for the boy Raymond an education worthy of his noble rank and of the holy aspirations which he had manifested at a very tender age.

His early youth was devoted to practices of Christian piety, and very soon his studies demonstrated the brilliancy of his mind. Catholic parents in those heroic days were accustomed to dedicate one or more of their sons to God's service in some monastery or cathedral, leaving them full liberty, when they became of age, to embrace the ecclesiastical state or to return to the world. Thus did

Saint Raymond of Pennafort

the Church obtain ministers, trained from youth in the ecclesiastical spirit and solidly developed in virtue. So it was that Raymond's parents, inspired by faith, offered him to God in his earliest years, and sent him to Barcelona to be educated with other children in the cathedral school.

In the deserted monastery of Saint Dominic at Pennafort are still preserved two paintings. One represents Saint Raymond as a child of six or seven years of age listening attentively to the pious exhortations of his mother and father. The other painting shows the boy of twelve clothed in clerical garb. He is receiving the paternal blessing as his mother stands aside weeping for joy. His guardian angel in the garb of a traveler touches him on the shoulder, apparently urging his departure. In the background is seen a servant with a horse prepared for the journey. The scene portrayed is evidently Raymond's departure from his father's castle for the studious cloisters of the cathedral of Barcelona.

At that time Barcelona was distinguished for a highly developed intellectual spirit. When Raymond arrived there to continue his studies, which were begun at home, he found flourishing schools handsomely provided with the best equipment of the period. He entered these schools with a genius capable of receiving and assimilating the best they could offer. He possessed one of those rare and blessed personalities to which nature seems to have refused nothing. A few years of study perfected him in every branch of knowledge, lifted him beyond the reach of his fellow-students and soon placed him among the ranks of the masters.

So rapid was his progress in the sciences that, in 1196, when only twenty years old, he began to teach the liberal arts in Barcelona. Every day students flocked around the chair of the new professor, whose charity was such that his lectures were free of charge. His holy life edified all who were so happy as to know him, and his exemplary piety was as eloquent as his teaching. Highly accomplished in many things Saint Raymond had a special preference for the study of law. We shall see how in the course of his life this was providential, and how marvelously fruitful it was for the Church. There is a record of a decision submitted by Raymond to the Bishop of Barcelona regarding a dispute between two canons in 1204. It was an early indication of his aptitude for canon law.

Having discovered his talents and put them in service first in his fatherland, the saintly Raymond was inspired with the desire to perfect himself in learning, to assume again the rôle of disciple, and go abroad to seek more suitable masters. Convinced that the best masters were to be found in the celebrated University of Bologna he set out for Italy. At this time he was about thirty-five years of age. This was in the tenth year of the thirteenth century in which he was destined to pass seventy-five years of his life. His name was already celebrated in Spain; his departure for Bologna was the beginning of a period of still greater renown.

His journey from Barcelona was not uneventful. He set out with another cleric, Peter Ruber, who likewise later became a Dominican. Passing Briançon in Catalonia the two travelers witnessed a miracle which took place in a chapel dedicated to the Blessed Virgin at Elbeza. There arrived about the same time a young man in a frightful state of suffering. His enemies had attacked him, cut off his hands, and gouged out his eyes. Raymond saw the young man's eyes and hands miraculously restored to him at the altar of the Holy Mother of God. Devotion to Mary was already deep-rooted in his heart, and this miracle served to increase his confidence and love for her whose mercy he was destined to proclaim to the world.

In the University of Bologna Raymond continued his former plan of life, devoting his time to prayer and study, not neglecting works of charity toward the poor. After six years of serious application to the study of law, civil and ecclesiastical, he was honored not only with the degree of doctor in these sciences, but also with the chair of professor in the university. Bologna in a short time saw what Barcelona had seen, students attending in unprecedented crowds the lectures of the brilliant stranger. His lectures, as usual, were free to all. The Senate of Bologna, learning of his generosity, voted a large sum to him annually to induce him to remain in the city. Raymond accepted the money, but only that he might increase the abundant alms he distributed to the poor. The talents and virtues of the pious Doctor made him one of the most beautiful ornaments of the famous university. He taught there for three years, until 1219.

About this time the Bishop of Barcelona, Baranger de Palon, came to visit Pope Honorius. Returning to his see he passed through Bologna, where he desired to secure some Dominicans for his diocese. He found the city resounding with the praises of the new Order of Preachers, and of Raymond, a professor from his own diocese. After considerable persuasion the Bishop succeeded in obtaining from the Holy Patriarch, Saint Dominic, some of the friars whom he comfortably established in the magnificent Church and Convent of Saint Catherine the Martyr. This gem of architecture stood a monument to Dominican activity until it was destroyed by the barbarous revolutionists in 1835.

Having accomplished part of his mission in Bologna, the Bishop now directed his attention to the more difficult task of reclaiming Raymond of Pennafort for his diocese. The professor, long accustomed to sanctify his work by charity, was not anxious to leave the country where he had labored so usefully. The Bishop earnestly represented to him the needs of the Church in Barcelona, his particular obligation to serve the land of his birth, and what seemed to be the will of God in the matter. The supplications and zeal of the pious prelate, his character and the justice of the cause he pleaded added force to his reasons. He obtained Raymond's consent, to the extreme regret of the University and the Senate of Bologna, who appreciated their treasure and regarded him as their own. It is said that the pleadings of the Bishop of Barcelona were supported by a command from Pope Honorius III, obliging

Raymond to repair immediately to Spain to undertake the education of the young king, James I of Aragon. The renown of the celebrated canonist had already attracted the attention of the Holy See.

The scene of the Saint's life now shifts back to Barcelona where the devout people are celebrating a triple jubilee: upon the safe return of their Bishop from Rome, the arrival of the Friar Preachers in their midst, and the recovery of their learned Saint Raymond of Pennafort.

The Bishop made Raymond a canon and archdeacon of the Cathedral of Barcelona. By his innocence of life and his exact observance he became the model of his associates. His new sources of revenue merely augmented his liberality toward the poor. New honors only made him more humble, and caused him to lead a more retired life. His ardent devotion to the Blessed Virgin, the Mother of God, inspired him to secure from the Bishop a more solemn celebration of the Feast of the Annunciation. A good portion of his revenues was devoted to this purpose. The devotion spread and Mary was soon glorified by the zeal of her pious servant throughout the kingdoms of Aragon and Castile. His tender piety, exemplary modesty, and boundless charity attracted the admiration and devotion of all. His virtues contributed more to the reform of the Cathedral Chapter than all the authority exercised by the Bishop.

But the desire to lead a more perfect life, penitential and hidden from the eyes of the world, determined him to change his state. When he taught in Bologna he witnessed the noble virtues of Saint Dominic, and the miracles with which God approved his work. At that time the entire University was attracted by the preaching of Blessed Reginald, Prior of the Dominicans at Bologna. Now he looked with pleasure and longing upon the angelic lives of the Dominican Friars recently established near Barcelona. Answering the voice of God calling him to the cloister to prepare him for the Apostolate, he resolved to become the imitator and brother of those whom he had admired. Consequently, on Good Friday, April 1,

1222, he applied for and was invested with the white habit of Saint Dominic, a few months after the death of the Holy Founder, with whom Saint Raymond was in all probability acquainted in Bologna.

This was the first favor with which Mary had rewarded his zeal for her glory. He considered it the greatest event in his life. Is not a religious vocation the greatest grace one could desire in life? His example induced many learned clerics and nobles to receive the Dominican habit; their vocation and talents added a new luster to the Order throughout Catalonia. Saint Raymond was already forty-seven years old, but he immediately took his place as the youngest novice, eager to embrace every means to advance in the practice of all the Christian virtues. The new state of life meant for him a renewal of fervor in the school of perfection.

We find some charming details of the religious life of Father Raymond as a Dominican in the Convent of Strict Observance at Barcelona. He was frequently aroused from his sleep by an angel in time to assist at the midnight office of matins. In the recitation of the Divine Office, either in choir with the community or privately, he manifested the same ardent devotion, always faithfully observing the minutest details prescribed by the rubrics. He spent every spare moment before the Blessed Sacrament in prayer. Visiting each altar of the church, he would prostrate himself before it, and would frequently chastise his body with disciplines, with so great a contrition for his sins that his groaning could be heard by the entire community. Over and above the long, strict, and frequent fasts of the Order, Saint Raymond had a personal rule of self-denial which was remarkable. Of food and drink he took only what was absolutely necessary, and except on Sundays he took but one meal a day. In recreation he was a bond of union among the brethren, pious and edifying in his conversation, the champion and defender of the absent. Before Mass each morning he went to confession, and he offered the Holy Sacrifice with an intense devotion. A column of fire descended from heaven one day when he said Mass. It enveloped his head and shoulders and lasted from the Consecration until he had consumed the Host. If anything prevented his saying Mass he felt unhappy the whole day.

Nor did he spend his whole time in prayer and contemplation. Great Doctor that he was, he applied himself assiduously to the study of Holy Scripture to prepare himself for the apostolate of preaching, and he did not disdain to attend the lectures given in his convent by professors of less renown than himself. When asked for advice on obscure points of law or difficulties of conscience, instead of giving his own opinion immediately he would diligently search authorized works to see if his private opinion was warranted by authority. But when he had reached a conclusion based on sound reasons and supported by the standard authors he rendered his decision with such firmness and confidence, that those who consulted him felt safe in following his advice.

When the holy man received the habit he begged his superiors to impose a severe penance on him so that he might expiate the sins of his youth. Complying with this request Father Suero Gomez, Provincial of Spain, commanded him to make a collection of cases of conscience for the guidance of confessors. He executed this obedience with the same precision which characterized all his work. He set to work without a model, for it was the first work of its kind; he collected all sorts of difficulties and solved them by the authority of Holy Scripture and Canon Law or the writings of the Fathers and the decrees of the Popes. The result was the precious volumes which are known even to this day as the "Summa of Saint Raymond."

He possessed a prodigious zeal for the salvation of souls. To his already fruitful occupation of writing he soon added the other functions of the apostolic life, and accomplished them with the success which we expect from such an intellectual giant. The instruction of infidels by preaching the Word of God, recalling sinners to repentance and reconciling them to God in the tribunal of confession, consoling the afflicted, procuring alms for the poor, laboring ceaselessly for the conversion of heretics, Jews, and Moors, interceding with kings and princes for the glory of the Church and the interests of the people: such were the occupations of Saint Raymond of Pennafort from the day of his religious profession until the day of his death, a period of over fifty years.

What he was not able to accomplish himself he often effected through the ministry of those who had chosen him as a guide on the road to heaven. Among these penitents there were two of a very particularly distinguished character, James I, King of Aragon, and the illustrious Saint Peter of Nolasco, later with Saint Raymond the co-founder of the Order of Mercy. We shall soon see the salutary influence which Saint Raymond exercised over the royal authority for the propagation and defense of the Faith, and his co-operation with Saint Peter in the practice of works of mercy and the redemption of captives.

For several centuries the Moors, all zealous Mohammedans, had held possession of many Spanish provinces, exercising a tyrannical dominion over the territory which they conquered. They made frequent invasions upon the lands of the Christians, pillaged and burned their homes, and reduced them to a cruel slavery. The perilous situation of the faithful thus exposed to lose their faith and salvation, after being deprived of their freedom, made a lively appeal to those inflamed with fraternal charity. Saint Raymond was especially affected, and he had the consolation to find the same sentiments of compassion and zeal in the heart of his penitent Saint Peter Nolasco. He was a Frenchman belonging to one of the first families of Languedoc. Saddened by the ravages of the heresy, he left his native land for Spain and enrolled himself under the banner of Simon de Montfort. The latter appointed him tutor in the court of King Peter of Aragon to educate the young James I. He lived a holy life at the court, devoting much time to prayer, study, and penance. Struck with pity for the poor Christians who were captured by the Moors, he decided to devote his whole fortune to their ransom.

Saint Peter and Saint Raymond were animated with the same desire to deliver, or at least to aid, these captives who were otherwise often helpless and sometimes forgotten. The former generously sacrificed his comfort and means, and undertook dangerous voyages to release some of them from slavery. The latter contributed with his prayers, advice, and the abundant alms which he solicited from the wealthy for this work of charity. Their efforts were crowned with success. But they wished to make the work enduring, so they redoubled their mortifications and prayers. God blessed the work, heard their prayers, and inspired both of them to found a new religious order especially devoted to the redemption of captives.

It was the Mother of God who appeared to Peter in a vision to give him the divine commission to found the new order. Hastening to consult his spiritual director, his joy was increased when he learned that Raymond, too, had received the same command from the Blessed Virgin. Together they proceeded to enlist the aid of King James, and their joy and surprise was complete when they discovered that he had likewise received the same command from the same heavenly messenger. Saint Peter soon gathered around him a number of willing and enthusiastic disciples and the Order was solemnly instituted August 10, 1223, in the Cathedral of Barcelona, before the Bishop and in the presence of King James, his entire court, and the city magistrates. Saint Raymond of Pennafort invested Peter with the habit of the new Order, and compiled its rule based on the rule of Saint Augustine and the Dominican Constitutions. Pope Gregory IX, in 1235, formally approved the new institution under the name of "The Order of Our Lady of Mercy for the Redemption of Captives."

Thus came into existence the Order of Mercy, a glorious and blessed offspring of the Dominican family, partaker in a way of its fulness of life and vigorous youth. It was Saint Raymond whom God chose instead of Saint Dominic, who died several years before, to be the father of this posterity. It was Raymond who organized its government, prepared its first saintly Superior General, Peter Nolasco, and secured from King James its first monastery.

In 1229 Pope Gregory IX, who two years previously had succeeded Honorius III in the Chair of Peter, sent as legate to Spain John of Abbeyville, Benedictine Abbot of Besançon and Cardinal of Santa Sabina, to enforce the observance of some decrees of the Lateran Council, to preach a crusade against the Moors, and to investigate the validity of the marriage of King James of Aragon with Eleanor of Castile. The legate assembled a Council at Tarragona which the king attended, accompanied by Saint Raymond. It was on this occasion that the Cardinal, recognizing the talents and virtues of Raymond of Pennafort, wished to attach him to his legation to preach the crusade against the Moors of Spain. The Holy Friar Preacher accepted the task and went before the legate, preaching the crusade with such wisdom, zeal, and charity that he laid the foundations for the final glorious triumph which heaven subsequently accorded the Christian armies. First he had to overcome the vice and corruption rampant among the faithful themselves. He brought the people to realize that, in order to triumph over their cruel enemies, they had first to conquer themselves and their evil passions, to forget their internal jealousies and enmities, and to purify themselves of those terrible vices which led them away from God, shut them out of heaven and exposed them to everlasting perdition.

Saint Raymond everywhere met with pronounced success. The force of his preaching and example soon produced a general reformation in the morals of the people. After his strenuous preaching, he spent hours in the confessional reconciling sinners with God. As the legate followed after Raymond he found the people well disposed to receive the indulgence of the Crusade and the Papal Benediction. Amidst all his labors our Saint inflicted upon himself the most severe mortifications. He journeyed on foot, and observed with a scrupulous exactness the abstinences and fasts, never permitting himself the slightest relaxation from the rigorous observance of his rule. The precious fruits of a zeal so pure, and a conduct so regular, evoked the generous applause and co-operation of the faithful, and the sincere esteem and admiration of the Cardinal Legate.

When the Cardinal was about to return to Rome, he believed it was his duty to present to the Pope a subject so capable of being employed in the most important affairs of the Church. John of Abbeyville frankly acknowledged the great influence which Raymond exerted toward the success of the mission, and hoped to be able to induce him to make the journey to Rome. But he had counted too much upon the docility of his dear friend. Raymond's zeal in labor was equaled only by his humility in shrinking from honors. The Cardinal's proposal was rejected, and this was perhaps the first time that these two men disagreed.

John returned to Rome alone in September, 1229; but hardly had he arrived at the Holy See when he related to Pope Gregory IX, the wonderful work of Raymond of Pennafort, his rare talents and his heroic virtues. The legate had no difficulty in persuading the Holy Father to accede to his desire. Consequently Raymond soon received a papal brief summoning him to Rome, November 30, 1229. It was neither a request nor an invitation, but an order in the presence of which Raymond knew nothing but obedience. The Holy Friar had already begun to occupy himself with the construction of the celebrated convent and church of Saint Catherine Martyr at Barcelona; he had resumed all the labors of his former ministry, but at the command of the Pope he set out immediately for Rome.

Pope Gregory soon discovered that Raymond's worth had not been exaggerated. He made him his own confessor and Grand Penitentiary of the Roman Church. Besides, as Chaplain of the Pope, he was called upon to deliberate with the Holy Father on the most important legal cases of the Church. It was a very important office which today is confided only to a Cardinal.

In his office of Penitentiary Saint Raymond was invested by the Pope with extraordinary powers to examine and judge, to bind and to loose, to absolve and condemn those who, sometimes guilty of most horrible crimes, flocked to the Holy See as to the source of all mercy. His success was phenomenal, for which reason he is often represented in art with a key in his hand, a characteristic sign of his dignity as Grand Penitentiary. Raymond's charity made him especially attentive to the pleading of cases for the poor. He thus earned for himself the endearing title "Father of the Poor." He imposed upon the Pope the penance to expedite all matters relating to the poor, to graciously hear the just pleas of those who were without protection and to act promptly upon the affairs of widows and orphans.

Amidst the distracting environment of the Papal Court Saint Raymond continually longed for the solitude of his cell, and for the Dominican life of contemplation and preaching. But the more he desired this the more difficult seemed its attainment. In calling Raymond to Rome Gregory IX intended to utilize the Saintly Friar's knowledge of law. Consequently the Pope decided to employ Raymond's talents in rearranging and codifying the canons or laws of the Church. The holy canonist applied himself to this task with such diligence and success that it was completed in less than three years, and in 1234 was approved by the Holy Father, who commanded that this work of Saint Raymond should alone be considered authoritative and used in the schools. In compiling this work, Raymond had to rewrite and condense decrees that Popes and Councils had been multiplying for centuries, and which were contained in some twelve or fourteen collections already existing. Many of the decrees in the collections were but repetitions of ones previously issued, many contradicted what had already been issued, many on account of their great length led to endless confusion, while still others had never been embodied in any collection and were of uncertain origin. This work, comprising five books, has been known to this day as the Decretals, and so manifested Raymond's genius, learning, and sound judgment, that it alone would suffice to place him first among canonists of all times, and Patron of Canon Law. The General Chapter of Dominican Provincials celebrated at Viterbo May 21, 1904, commissioned the Master General of the Order to procure diligently from the Holy See the elevation of Saint Raymond to the rank of Doctor of the Church.

As a public acknowledgment of his talents and the services Raymond of Pennafort had rendered the Church, Gregory IX nominated him to the Metropolitan Archbishopric of Tarragona. With tears in his eyes and ill with grief, Raymond begged his release so earnestly that the Holy Father reluctantly revoked the appointment, but at the same time commanded Raymond to choose a successor to the See. The humble friar recommended for the office a virtuous diocesan ecclesiastic, William de Mongriú of Gerona.

Saint Raymond was now sixty years old. The five years he spent in Rome serving the Church in the discharge of most responsible and fatiguing duties, without ever diminishing his penances and austerities, so seriously impaired his health that the papal physicians agreed that only the climate of his native Spain could sustain his life. The Pope, when notified, exclaimed, "I would rather have him separated from me and living than to see him before me dead or reduced to inactivity." So Gregory consented, but on condition that he retain the office of Grand Penitentiary. At Raymond's departure for Barcelona in 1235 the attendants at the papal court said of him, "This man goes away as he came, just as poor, just as modest as when he arrived."

The journey home from Rome was uneventful until Saint Raymond landed at Tossa, a small Spanish port, about thirty-six miles from Barcelona. He was accompanied by four other Dominicans, who thus became witnesses of a remarkable miracle, the first attributed to the intercession of Saint Raymond. A peasant called Barcolo, working in the harvest field, was suddenly struck with apoplexy and deprived of his speech, becoming quite insensible. Saint Raymond, seeing him, was moved to compassion and urged the spectators to join him in praying that the poor man might regain his senses sufficiently to make his confession before he died. After several moments spent in prayer the Saint arose, approached the man, and called to him in a loud voice, "Barcolo! Do you wish to confess?" The dying man opened his eyes and distinctly replied, "Yes, I do, and have much desired it." After the bystanders withdrew, Raymond heard his confession and prepared him for death. The malady returned immediately and the man died quietly and calmly amidst universal gratitude to God for the grace He had granted this poor peasant in answer to Saint Raymond's prayers.

Another miraculous grace granted to his merits, evidently about this time, is also found in the Papal Bull of his canonization by Clement VIII. A certain lay-brother, named Martin, before his conversion had led a very licentious life. The remembrance of the sins of his youth frequently raised most annoying images of unlawful pleasures in his mind. One day assisting at Saint Raymond's Mass he prayed fervently to God to deliver him from these temptations. At the Consecration he saw in the Host a most beautiful child enveloped in light, and at the same moment all the evil desires vanished never to return. Another lay brother, called Benedict, had suffered continual headache for more than two years and could not bear the least noise. At his request Saint Raymond placed his hands on the brother's head, whereupon the headache ceased at once and forever. A lady named Elisende Eymerich had long been afflicted with a quartan fever. Saint Raymond, accompanied by Brother William Pons, visited the woman, who confidently asked the Saint to cure her. In his humility Raymond pretended not to hear her, but she persisted until he gave way and miraculously granted her request.

Other miracles attributed to his intercession later in life and repeated after his death increase our devotion for Saint Raymond and prompt us to seek his patronage. Many were cured of various infirmities by merely touching his garments. A young girl named Burgeta, whose face was deformed from infancy, was entirely cured after the best efforts of skilled physicians had failed. Her face was covered with Raymond's cloak and her deformity immediately vanished. In a similar manner she was later cured of a headache. Her nephew was also relieved of a fever by the application of the same garment. It happened in Barcelona that a certain devout woman, who received Holy Communion frequently, would become very ill every time she communicated. Saint Raymond, upon being consulted, asked if she had been baptized. It was discovered that she had been incorrectly baptized when in danger of death. She was then baptized correctly and thereafter experienced the sweetest satisfaction in receiving her Eucharistic God.

Saint Raymond's return to Barcelona did not pass unnoticed. On the contrary, hardly had the news of his arrival been announced when visitors and penitents flocked around the Holy Friar from all sides. Seeking repose and solitude, he found instead the same occupations which had kept him busy in Rome, due to the fact that even in Spain he exercised the office of Pope's Penitentiary. Nevertheless, the surroundings of his beloved convent in his native land soon restored his health. He continued with a new fervor the special austerities which he added to those of his rule. His vigils were long, and his prayer as well as his abstinence almost continuous. He engaged himself again in preaching and caring for souls and for the needs of every one who had recourse to his counsel and to his charity. Urged by the Bishops of Spain, Raymond wrote a treatise on diocesan visitations; in answer to the request of several merchants he composed another work on the lawfulness of certain business practices. He also assisted at two celebrated national assemblies; at Monçon, in 1236, and at Tarragona the following year.

Saint Raymond found that his office of Grand Penitentiary absorbed too much of his time, and wrote to Pope Gregory IX to be released from his duties, alleging as a reason that the facility with which he could be approached diminished the respect due to the Holy See. But to preserve and increase the brotherly love which existed between the Franciscan and Dominican Orders, he asked to be allowed to continue as Penitentiary for these two Orders. Raymond obtained his request; but Gregory IX and his successors continued to consult him on most important matters and to confide to him the absolution of certain penitents. At Barcelona, as at Rome, Saint Raymond of Pennafort remained a man of confidence with the Sovereign Pontiffs.

It was in this relative calm that Saint Raymond was surprised by his election as Master General of the Dominican Order. The sad news of the death by shipwreck of Blessed Jordan of Saxony, the immediate successor of Saint Dominic in the government of the Order, having become known, the brethren were assembled at Bologna, May 24, 1238, for the election of a father and ruler, and to hold a General Chapter. It was the day after Pentecost that the electors went into conclave. A miracle marked the occasion of the election. While the election was being held behind closed doors, the community, prostrate in prayer, gathered about the tomb of our Holy Father Saint Dominic. Suddenly one of the brethren in a vision beheld the electors come forth from the chapter house, and going to the church they proceeded to erect a marble column. The vision was very soon interrupted when the electors did come forth to proclaim Brother Raymond of Pennafort elected unanimously to the Master Generalship of the Order. Saint Raymond was indeed a marble column raised for the support of the Church.

We now turn in loving admiration to the Master General elect in his quiet retreat at Barcelona. Saint Raymond was not present at the Chapter. The fathers, knowing well his modesty and unfeigned humility, feared greatly that he would decline the honor. They therefore sent a deputation to Barcelona to announce his election to him and to beg him to accept the office. They were Hugh of Saint Cher, Provincial of France, afterward Cardinal and well known for his commentaries on Holy Scripture; Pontius de Sparra, Provincial of Provence; Philip, Provincial of Syria; Stephen, Provincial of Lombardy, and several others. The unexpected news was an unpleasant surprise to the humble Saint, and his embarrassment was extreme. He was of a mind to refuse the honor and thus prevent a great scandal within the Order, as he said. But finally, submitting to the will of God, he accepted the office as a penance, resolved to return at the first opportunity to his former life of solitude, without doing violence to his own conscience or that of his brethren.

The entire Order looked with hope and expectation to the sagacity of the holy man of God in his government of the Order. During the strenuous labors of the generalship and the visitations of the various provinces, which he made on foot, the new General never ceased to observe the rigorous fasts, long vigils, and other penitential practices. Walking faithfully in the footsteps of Saint Dominic, always united to God, he was ever vigilant for the conduct of his subjects, and did all in his power to promote them in the perfection of their state. His corrections, ever tempered by prudence and sweetness, the love of regular observance which he inspired less by word than by example, and the zeal for the salvation of souls with which he seemed animated, proved him to be the perfect imitator of his predecessor, and the model of those who were to succeed him. He strove to instil the spirit of prayer, solitude, and study especially of Holy Scripture. He had the pleasure of receiving many gifted subjects into the Order, and established a number of missions among the infidels.

In order to be able always to keep the foreign missions supplied with a sufficient number of men, and to promote and foster the zeal of those who were laboring for the salvation of souls by the ministry of preaching, the Holy General requested two favors of Gregory IX. In the first request, which he did not obtain, Saint Raymond asked that members of the Order should not be obliged to accept the office of Bishop. In a brief, dated October 25, 1239, His

Holiness replied to Raymond that he deemed it expedient to name several members of the Order to the episcopacy. But he granted the second request, namely, that members of the Order should not be called upon either by papal legates, bishops, or the Holy See itself to discharge various apostolic commissions, which, without obliging them to separate themselves from the Order, nevertheless tended to distract them from the exercises of prayer, study, and preaching. In spite of this, the successors of Gregory IX continued to honor even Raymond with many important commissions.

Saint Raymond, while Master General, published a new edition of the Constitutions of the Order and divided them as we have them today into two parts: the first explaining the interior life of the brethren, the second outlining their external conduct. His work cleared up many obscurities and doubts; it was immediately received and authorized by three General Chapters. It was his chief work as Master General. It won for Saint Raymond the title of author of the Dominican Constitutions. The General Chapter assembled in Corias, Spain, 1920, appointed a committee of five to recodify the Constitutions of the Order in accordance with the legislation of the New Code of Canon Law. The revisors are commanded to preserve as far as possible in the very words of Saint Raymond of Pennafort those of his constitutions which still remain in force.

In the Chapter which Raymond convened at Paris on the Feast of Pentecost, May 15, 1239, he proposed and had approved a decree whereby the Order was obliged to accept the voluntary resignation of a superior when he had just cause to resign. In the Chapter which he convened at Bologna the following year, June 3, he demanded the right to make use of this same privilege, to resign the generalship. His age, then 65, and his infirmities seemed sufficient reason for his resignation. His retirement from office occasioned extreme regret throughout the entire Order. According to some historians, the definitors who accepted his resignation were all deprived of their offices in the General Chapter of 1242.

Freed from the burden of government Saint Raymond returned to Barcelona. Although he was already sixty-five years old, he lived thirty-five years longer, persevering in the holy and penitential life he had led from his youth. His old age was as fruitful in labors as was his vigorous youth. Given more than ever to all the exercises of a perfect religious, and to the functions of the apostolic life, he was always to be found occupied with writing, preaching, hearing confessions, or setting at ease those who came to him with their doubts and difficulties.

He took advantage of his comparative leisure now to launch several projects which were intended to save the souls and preserve the integrity of the Faith of the Christians of Spain, and to announce the truths of our holy religion to the Moors, Jews, and others. At his suggestion the Kings of Castile and Aragon founded two monasteries with colleges attached to them, for the study of Hebrew and Arabic, one at Murcia, the other at Tunis. To the latter a number of Dominican Fathers were sent to labor for the conversion of the misguided people. Against these unbelievers Raymond enlisted the aid of Saint Thomas Aquinas, who, in answer to the request, composed his immortal work, the "Summa Contra Gentiles." This book, published in 1263, was powerfully instrumental in crushing the errors of the times, and it has always been considered as one of the most remarkable works of the Angelic Doctor. The effect of this work combined with the strenuous apostolic labors of Saint Raymond himself was so great that a few years later Raymond was able to notify the Holy Father of the conversion of ten thousand infidels.

The Bishops of Spain, consulting Saint Raymond of Pennafort in all matters of religion, merely imitated the conduct of five or six Sovereign Pontiffs who seemed to vie with each other in the esteem in which they held this great man and in the confidence which they reposed in his advice. Popes Gregory IX, Innocent IV, Alexander IV, Urban IV, Clement IV, and Gregory X gave him offices which appeared to belong to none but themselves, such as the nomination of bishops, examination of the causes of prelates (with power to depose, absolve, or excommunicate them) and to dispense from irregularities.

It is impossible to estimate the value of the services which Raymond rendered to his country and to his King. James I of Aragon always consulted Saint Raymond in every important affair of State. Toward the end of his life Raymond accompanied the King on a journey to Majorca to obtain the conversion of the Moors of that island. James possessed the qualities of a great monarch. Respected by the people, whose happiness he ardently promoted, he loved his religion and protected the Church. Leader in peace as in war, intrepid in the greatest danger, wise in counsel, James I was considered a very accomplished prince. In a word, he was master of everything but his own evil passion. Lust had enslaved him and he took the miserable partner of his crime to Majorca with him on this occasion. Saint Raymond boldly reproved him several times, and bade him to forsake his sin. But when he saw that all his remonstrances were useless, he told the King that he could not remain attached to the royal suite as if approving such a dreadful scandal.

Consequently, Raymond began to look for passage back to Spain. It was impossible for him to procure a vessel, because the mariners had been forbidden under penalty of death to transport him from the island. When he learned this, Raymond said to his companion, a Dominican Father, "You will see that the King of Heaven will confound the wickedness of this earthly King and provide me with a ship." Having spoken thus, he went to the seashore, took off his cappa, or black cloak, and spread part of it on the water, while he fastened the other part to his staff, like a sail to a miniature mast. Then he fearlessly knelt down on that part which floated on the water, and invited his companion to do likewise; but the timid Father declined. Making the sign of the cross Raymond pushed off from land and quickly sailed away on his cappa. The Saint sailed along even more rapidly than on board the swiftest vessel, making the voyage of one hundred and eighty miles from Majorca to Barcelona in six hours. On reaching shore he stepped on land amidst the shouts of the crowds which had collected when they saw him coming. He gathered together his cappa and put it around his shoulders; it was as dry as if it had never touched the water. As he approached his convent the doors were locked, but suddenly the people saw him transported noiselessly and without any sign of his passage to the inside of the cloister. The news of this miracle brought King James to his senses. He sincerely repented and gave up his vicious life. The friendship of Raymond returned to James with the return of his virtue. To commemorate this astounding miracle a tower and chapel were built on the spot where the Saint landed.

Artists often represent Saint Raymond of Pennafort as he appeared in this miraculous voyage sailing peacefully across the sea on his cappa. It is well to compare it with his journey to his heavenly reward which followed soon afterward. This long, holy, and fruitful life must have its end. Raymond realized this and so began to prepare himself for death. He increased the rigor of his fasting and the austerity of his habits until his life became one long infirmity. As he became weaker in body his soul became the more ardent for the things of God. In spite of his weakness he still longed to preach for the conversion of sinners.

Although the holy man of God had so often pleaded with the Sovereign Pontiffs not to burden him with offices, nevertheless we see Gregory X employing him in a work of charity which it was difficult for Raymond to refuse. It was a commission to settle a dispute which had arisen between his dearest friends, the Franciscans and the Mercedarians. The commission was dated August 13, 1274, and his happy departure from this life occurred in the beginning of the following year.

The first news of Saint Raymond's last illness alarmed the faithful and drew to his death-bed all the royalty of the kingdoms of Spain. King Alphonse of Castile, his wife with their children, and Emmanuel his brother; King James of Aragon and his entire court, all visited him to recommend themselves to his prayers and to obtain his blessing. Fortified by the sacraments Saint Raymond calmly and sweetly died January 6, 1275, on the Feast of the Epiphany in the hundredth year of his age.

His funeral was attended by the Kings of Aragon and Castile with their entire courts, many prelates, and the clergy, and all the people of Barcelona. He was buried in the Dominican Church of Saint Catherine the Martyr in that city. The extraordinary honors, which at his death and funeral rendered testimony to the brilliancy of his virtues were but the prelude to the cult which was to follow his memory. It is impossible to describe here the great number and varied character of the miracles which set the seal on his sanctity and made his tomb a glorious object of pilgrimage.

After Saint Raymond's death, the King of Aragon and his successors urged his canonization, for which the voice of the people clamored. Pope Paul V beatified our Saint, and finally, after long delays and various procedures, he was canonized amidst great splendor by Pope Clement VIII, in 1601. The Feast of Saint Raymond was at first celebrated January 7, but later by a bull of Clement X was transferred to the 23d of January. Previous to the canonization his relics were twice translated. In 1596, by order of the Pope, the holy remains were translated to a magnificent tomb; again, three years later, a second translation was made in the presence of King Philip and Queen Marguerite of Spain. To satisfy the devotion of the clergy and the piety of the people of Barcelona a third translation was celebrated at Barcelona with great solemnity during the year of his canonization.

BIBLIOGRAPHY

BALME ET PABAN: Raymundiana, I and II, 1898–1901.

MORTIER: Histoire des Maîtres Généraux de l'Ordre des Frères Prêcheurs, I, Paris, 1903.

TOURON: Les Hommes illustres de l'ordre de Saint Dominique, I, 1743.

Année Dominicaine, 23 Janvier, Ed. Jevain.

FRANÇOIS PENIA: Vita S. Raymundi. Romæ, 1601.

Bollandistes, Acta Sanctorum, Januarii.

Bullarium Ordinis, V, 580.

ÉCHARD: Scriptores Ord. Præd., I, p. 106.

ANALECTA: Sacri Ord. Fr. Præd., 1904.

Acta Capituli Generalis, 1920.

Saint Agnes of Montepulciano

HE PRIMARY OBJECT of the Order of Preachers is to preach the Word of God and to save souls. Saint Dominic also instilled into his first daughters this apostolic spirit; so much so that by common consent they came to be known as Sisters Preacheresses. To accomplish the salvation of souls through the medium of prayer and penance has ever been regarded by the sisters as a primary duty. They are to stand, Moses-like, on the mountain top with arms uplifted in supplication to aid those who fare forth on the apostolate to combat heresy and vice. The Friar Preacher, obliged to go out into the wide world to preach the Word of God to those who sit in darkness and in the shadow of death, is often deprived of the shelter of his convent and the strength of the regular life. In order to preserve the fulness of the interior spirit, without which no great or lasting good can be effected, he has need of assistance. At times even men of prayer feel burdened by their many cares and cry out for help. We have an example of this in the case of Blessed Jordan of Saxony. Writing to Blessed Diana, he says: "You must exhort your sisters to supply for my deficiencies." And again: "Exhort the sisters to beseech Jesus Christ, the Son of God, to lend my voice the power of His, that I may honor Him, and bring forth fruit." Such, then, is the apostolate of Saint Dominic's cloistered daughters. We shall see how this sublime calling was illustrated in the life of Saint Agnes of Montepulciano, the chief glory of the Second Order of Saint Dominic.

Saint Agnes of Montepulciano

Saint Agnes was born in the year 1268, in the town of Graciano Vecchio, about three miles distant from Montepulciano, in Italy. Historians have neglected to chronicle the precise day and month of her birth. The annalists, however, state that on a certain day of the year 1268 a brilliant light from a number of burning candles had miraculously appeared and was seen streaming from the windows of Lawrence de Segni's house. Those who witnessed the phenomenon learned that the wonderful radiance had flooded the room where Agnes was born.

The youth of this child was adorned with traits that gave assuring promise of her future sanctity. She possessed qualities of mind and heart well adapted to receive the seeds of virtue. Her father's household presented excellent models of goodness. Before she seemed old enough to receive instruction as to how to pray, she had made great progress in prayer. At a very early age she assiduously repeated the Our Father and the Hail Mary. Whilst thus engaged, her exterior gave signs of that calm interior devotion which she felt toward the God of her heart. Coupled with this love of prayer, she early manifested a predilection for solitude. Thus she often retired to a secluded spot in her father's garden whither she would repair to satisfy her piety. Her dearest wish and constant petition was to be allowed to consecrate herself to God in the religious state. She anxiously sought to ascertain the will of her parents in this matter, but they gently spoke to her of delay, telling her that a child of five or six years could not expect to take such an important step. Despite this, Agnes felt confident that God would discover to her a means of following the call of heaven. Since there was no convent in Graciano Vecchio, she earnestly entreated her parents to go frequently to Montepulciano, or to move thither in order to satisfy her longing desire.

The turbulent state of Montepulciano, rather than a desire to turn away Agnes' mind from her design, prevented her parents from thinking of removing to that town. The fire of discord and the ardent spirit of national strife had been kindled in Montepulciano, which acted like principles of destruction in the policy of the smaller States into which Italy was divided. Lawrence de Segni, however, permitted his daughter to make occasional excursions to Montepulciano. On one of these, when Agnes was probably in her ninth year, a peculiar incident occurred. The old accounts report that the holy virgin, on this occasion, while near the gates of the city, in company with some women, was suddenly attacked by a large flock of crows that came from a neighboring hill on which stood a house of prostitution. These crows attacked her with their beaks and claws and could hardly be driven away. It is believed that the evil spirits, foreseeing that Agnes would in time expel them from that abode of infamy, made use of these crows to disturb her. The chroniclers assert that Agnes herself put forth this event before her parents as a means of overcoming their reluctance in permitting her to forsake the world.

As soon as the pious maiden had received her father's approval, she went without delay to a convent in Montepulciano of the sisterhood vulgarly called Del Sacco—that is, of sackcloth. This name had been given them because the habits they wore were made of the coarsest material. Agnes was now in the ninth year of her age. She was received by the sisters with the greatest joy. In a place like the convent Del Sacco, where virtuous lives were common, the daughter of de Segni became an object of special admiration. She gave herself up to prayer, meditation, silence, and fasting. Humility and obedience were practiced by her in a remarkable manner. Grace worked within her and crowned her at this tender age with the glorious fruits of holiness usually to be looked for in a subject of more mature years. Agnes realized the frailties of human nature and at the same time recognized the wonderful gifts bestowed on her. For these she never failed to render thanks to God. She resolved to profit by them so as to merit further graces.

At this time a religious woman of singular prudence was deputed by the Bishop of Arezzo to make a visitation of the convent.

She determined to investigate the truth of what she heard regarding the spirit and the virtues of Agnes. She found the merits of the young virgin far greater than she had anticipated. She congratulated Agnes and predicted that she would become the glory and the ornament of her institute. Seeing that this praise pained the humble religious, she called the mistress of novices aside and said to her with irresistible conviction: "Have a solicitous care in regard to this child. By supernatural revelation I assure you that as Agnes, the Virgin and Martyr, is hailed by the faithful as Saint Agnes, so also shall this child illustrate the Church by the same name."

After this prediction, God made known the holiness of his servant in many ways. Her prayers became so fervent and even rapturous that frequently she was raised from the ground in ecstasy. On a certain occasion, in the presence of several sisters, the holy virgin was engaged in prayer before an image of the Crucified, which hung high on the wall. Such was the vehemence of the transports of love that prompted her to draw near to the holy rood, that she was suddenly raised by a supernatural power as high as the crucifix, where she was able, suspended in midair, to express her intense affection and to satisfy her devotion in loving embrace of the sacred image. When the ecstasy was finished she placidly descended.

At the early age of fourteen, Agnes was placed in charge of the temporalities of the community in the capacity of procuratrix. The fact of her being placed in this position gives us a clear insight into her character. Young as she was, she was eminently fitted for the task of providing for the needs of the sisters with the greatest care. With tender heart, thoughtful mind, and liberal hand, she administered to the wants of the community. Agnes faithfully discharged the duties of her office without in the least diminishing her devotional exercises. During this time supernatural favors were not wanting to the servant of God. One of her favorite exercises of piety was a tender devotion to the Mother of God. In reward for her love, the most Holy Virgin appeared to her surrounded by celestial brightness. Our Blessed Lady spoke to her most affectionately. At the same time she gave Agnes three small stones of extraordinary beauty, telling her that she should one day build a church in her honor, reminding her to place her confidence as to this undertaking in the protection of the three Divine Persons, indicated by the number of the stones. We shall see later how Agnes fulfilled her commission.

Heaven decided that Agnes was to leave her cherished cloister in order that others might benefit by her wise guidance and shining example. The inhabitants of Proceno, a small village in the district of Orvieto, wished to erect a convent in their city and decided upon obtaining one of the sisters of the Convent Del Sacco who should guide the religious in the path of perfection. Some of the principal men of the place were accordingly sent to Montepulciano on this mission. Their request was considered suitable and just, and, after deliberating as to the person best fitted for this post, it was decided that Sister Margaret, the mistress of novices, should be sent. She did not object to undertaking this new charge, but she protested at the same time, probably inspired from above, that she would be unequal to her new task unless Agnes were permitted to accompany her. The sisters were loath to part with the treasure of their convent, but in order to carry out their decision they were at length obliged to allow her to depart.

When Margaret and Agnes arrived at Proceno they found a good number of young women gathered there, who had retired to a common dwelling in order to attend to the work of their sanctification. The community soon increased to such a number as to make an enlargement of the convent necessary. Strict observance was, after a short time, introduced and the sisters made rapid strides in perfection. Needless to say, Agnes was a model of every virtue to her coreligious. In fact, many were led to turn their backs upon the world and its allurements when they heard of the fame of Agnes' sanctity.

It was before long decided that Agnes should be placed at the head of the community as Abbess. All the sisters agreed upon her as the most fit person to rule the destinies of the community. This was, however, kept secret from her until the Holy See, by confirming their choice, would make refusal on her part impossible. Furthermore, an appeal to Rome was almost, if not absolutely, imperative, as Agnes was but fifteen years of age. Canon Law had not decided upon any fixed age for the superiors of religious, though it was generally understood that the Church would disapprove of one so young undertaking the guidance of a religious institute. Therefore, the application might have failed had not the matter been taken up by Federigo, Bishop of Ostia, who, by convincing Pope Martin IV of the extraordinary holiness of Agnes, succeeded in obtaining the ratification and benediction of the Vicar of Christ upon the choice of the sisters.

An extraordinary occurrence took place when the Bishop, Francis de Monaldeschi, came to the convent to consecrate the holy virgin and to install her as Abbess. When the prelate entered the church accompanied by the clergy, he found the pavement and the altars, especially the high altar, covered as it were by snow, with pure white particles in the shape of crosses. Writers of the Saint's life refer to these particles as "manna." The Bishop went through the sacred function, visibly affected by the tenderness and piety with which this prodigy, and the profound humility and modesty of Agnes inspired him. This shower of manna, Blessed Raymond of Capua tells us, was frequently sent by heaven upon Agnes whilst she was at prayer. Flowers of the most sweet perfume were also miraculously strewn upon the place where she knelt.

In the midst of all these wonders the spouse of Christ was exceedingly humble and unostentatious. Although she moderated the desires of her heart by the profoundest contempt of self, she had been inflamed for some time with an intense longing to see and adore Jesus face to face. She had prayed for this favor for a long time. At length on the eve of the Assumption, the most Holy Mary appeared to her in a radiant aspect, holding in her arms the blessed Fruit of her womb, Jesus. The consolation of Agnes was not limited to sight alone, but the Mother of God deigned to give the Divine Infant into her embrace. The holy virgin took the Holy Child into her arms and prolonged her loving communings with the God of her heart, until, with loving reluctance, she restored Him to Mary's arms. Before He was taken from her, she took a small cross of strange workmanship which hung around the neck of the Infant Jesus, and kept it as a memorial of the favor she had received. Agnes kept this vision secret from all except her confessor.

Our Saint bore an admirably tender devotion to the Holy Eucharist. On the days when she received Jesus in the Sacrament of His love, she redoubled her fervor. Heaven was to lavish on her many extraordinary favors. Blessed Raymond of Capua tells us that on ten consecutive Sundays she was miraculously fed on the Bread from Heaven by the hands of an angel.

Agnes was also singularly attached to the devotion of the Passion of Christ. She would spend hours in contemplation of the sacred mysteries of the Saviour's sufferings and His death. In spirit, she would visit over and over again the scenes of the way of the Cross. The Man of Sorrows rewarded her compassion in a wonderful manner. One night, as she was pouring forth her sighs of affectionate devotion over the blood-stained figure of the Crucified, an angel appeared to her and pressed a clod of earth into her hand which was enriched with traces of the blood shed by Christ on Calvary. The angel also gave her a fragment of the vessel in which Jesus was washed in His infancy.

In proportion as Agnes became the recipient of heavenly favors she strove to conceal her heavenly predilection from men. But, in spite of all her efforts, her holiness was known to all. People came to her in great numbers to ask her to pray in their behalf. Agnes complied with their pious requests and obtained from God the answer to their petitions. The worth of her confidence was proven by miracles. Twice the bread of the convent was multiplied at her prayer. Again, two empty jars of oil were miraculously replenished. At another time, when funds failed the community, money was found in the possession of the procurator which was supplied by divine intervention.

Though the religious were struck by these singular attestations of the sanctity of their superioress, they were even more in admiration of her heroic virtue. This holy virgin submitted herself to the most severe mortifications. During fifteen years she fasted on bread and water. Her night's rest was taken on the bare ground. She resorted to all means of crucifying her flesh. She even scourged herself to blood at times. All these penances, however, were not governed by her own whims, but were always undergone with strict regard to her confessor's advice.

God repeatedly employed the Saint as an instrument of His glory. On a certain occasion a possessed person was freed from his tormentor when Agnes drew near to him. A benefactor of the convent, who seemingly led a virtuous life, was apprised of the terrible state of his soul by Agnes, who knew of his misdeeds through supernatural revelation. Through her advice and prayers he was brought to sincere repentance after having made sacrilegious confessions for many years. After his death, Agnes received assurance by an interior illumination that his soul was safe with God eternally.

We have seen how our Saint chastised her body with severe penitential practices. At length her tortured body gave way and she was prostrated on a bed of sickness. She suffered with the greatest calmness and with perfect resignation. She once fell into a state of extreme languor, which was accompanied by fatal symptoms. At last it was ordered that she should eat some meat, that was especially prepared for her, to restore her strength. Agnes did not resist the order, but merely raised her eyes to heaven and uttered a brief prayer. At the moment when she prepared to eat the meat, it was changed into fish by an unseen power. He Who at the marriage of Cana in Galilee changed water into wine now changed this meat into fish, that His beloved servant might have the satisfaction of observing, even in the time of illness, the severe laws of abstinence that she had framed for herself. After Agnes had displayed a wonderful patience in all her suffering, her health partially returned.

At a later date, the Saint was consoled by a beautiful vision, in which she seemed to be admitted to contemplate the glory of the heavenly country. She was not really raised to behold that light which forms the happiness of the inhabitants of heaven, but the incomprehensible joys of the eternal kingdom were presented to her, as it were, by allegory. The attention of Agnes was especially fixed on the throne of the Mother of God, who was clothed with the sun and surrounded by ineffable beauty and glory. A choir of celestial spirits sang the praises of their Queen in melodies of the sweetest sound. Heaven resounded with their gladsome voices, and, with the exception of the triple Sanctus to the Most High, there was nothing in the whole court of heaven which sounded more jubilant and triumphant. At the close of this celestial vision, Agnes frequently recited or sung a devout Latin hymn in honor of our Lady which she learned from the angels on that occasion. The content of the hymn relates entirely to the seven joys of the Blessed Virgin which she experienced in regard to the Incarnation and life of her Divine Son.

Upon Agnes' restoration to health, she resumed all her devotional practices which she had previously outlined for herself. She ruled her community with great prudence. She was most careful to prevent idleness and dissipation in her community, but at the same time she took into consideration the natural dispositions of the sisters. Gentle and obliging, our Saint ever felt the greatest compassion for the weaknesses and the wants of her charges. Instead of considering them as burdens entrusted to her care, she regarded them as her support and her crown. Whether weak or virtuous, she ever looked upon them as her children whom she must bring up for Christ Jesus.

Regarding her own tendency toward perfection and sanctity, little need be said. Her progress in the science of the Saints was constant. Frequent acts of piety and the continual practice of virtue kept all her thoughts resolutely centered upon God under every circumstance. Her desire of living entirely hidden in Christ would have led her to conceal all those intimate communings with the Master had not obedience obliged her at times to make them known for the edification of others.

Twenty years had now elapsed since Agnes left Montepulciano. So great had her reputation for holiness become that the citizens of that locality often requested her to return to their midst so that they might benefit by her wise counsel and salutary example. To their entreaties she turned a deaf ear, saying that she was accomplishing the will of God at Proceno and that it was not fitting to her calling to make such a journey. These objections only led the citizens to redouble their entreaties, in which they were joined by the community of which Agnes had formerly been a member. It must be remembered that the laws of enclosure were not then in force. At last Agnes yielded to their pious wishes. Her reception at Montepulciano was the occasion of an unusual demonstration of joy and satisfaction. During her short stay there, she exercised an apostolate, the fruits of which gladdened her in later years. She exhorted those who came to hear her to the fear of God, to concord and to works of justice. Her lightest word was prized and much good was effected by her visit. She was urged to remain at Montepulciano, but, mindful of her promise to her community, she soon returned to their midst.

Some months had elapsed since the return of Agnes to Proceno. During that time she continuously thought that the designs of the Most High were that she should be the instrument of salvation to many souls in another place than Proceno. True, she had ever regarded her retreat at Proceno as a place she was never again destined to leave, but she was prepared to follow the will of God with the greatest alacrity, once she was convinced that the finger of God pointed elsewhere. The house of infamy that she had seen in Montepulciano many years before, returned to her memory again and again. Great was her affliction at the thought that no one undertook to purge that place of its vicious character. An interior voice was urging her on to undertake the task of destroying the dominion of Satan in the abode of disrepute and to establish the service of Christ there. During this time of uncertainty as to what was the will of heaven in this matter, she prayed most fervently that it would be revealed to her. Her prayer was finally granted.

The answer to her petition came about in this manner. It so happened that the Saint seemed to be standing on the shore of a vast ocean, with its waves raging and foaming under a heavily clouded sky. The tempest was suddenly calmed and the wind became still. Agnes then descried three ships approaching the shore. At the helm of each stood a person of dignified bearing. She recognized them as Saint Augustine, Saint Francis of Assisi, and Saint Dominic. Each of the three Saints pressingly invited her to enter his boat. Agnes was kept in reverential doubt as to which invitation she should heed, until Saint Dominic said: "The Lord has disposed that she should embark on my boat." As the vision vanished, an angel descended from above and unfolded its meaning to her. "The life of mortals," said the blessed spirit, "on this low region of earth, is precisely a sea agitated by a violent storm. Fly, therefore, from its perils, and leave those who serve the world to be shipwrecked. You have already separated yourself from it, by following part of the rule of Saint Francis with the religious of Sacco, and embracing part of that of Saint Augustine here in Proceno. But God further wills that you should return to your country, and consecrate yourself to the Institute of His servant Dominic, and build a monastery in that very place, where, as you well know, incontinence now reigns. This building is the work the Mother of God told you to undertake, and for which she gave you three stones, which are still in your keeping." After having said this the angel disappeared, leaving Agnes overjoyed at what she had seen and heard.

Early in the year 1306 Agnes returned to Montepulciano. Having arrived there, she made the utmost exertion to purchase the place pointed out to her so wonderfully. Armed with a boundless confidence in Divine Providence, she overcame every obstacle. Through the generosity of some relatives and friends she was enabled to buy the desired location. Having obtained from Monsignor Ildebrandino, Bishop of Arezzo, permission to build a church and convent, she set about earnestly to have the ill-famed building demolished to make room for the house of God. The Bishop of Arezzo entrusted the laying of the first stone to Father Bonaventura Forteguerri, prior of the Servite monastery in Montepulciano.

The church was completed at the same time as the convent and was called Santa Maria Novella. The convent was built, according to Agnes' design, in poorest style. Her purpose in doing this was to present her foundation to the world as a school of humility, retirement, and detachment, a visible sign that "the glory of the King's daughter is within."

Many young women assembled around Agnes offered within those walls the acceptable sacrifice of their whole beings. Father Forteguerri, acting for the Bishop of Arezzo, received their religious vows, to bind them still more to this manner of life, though they did not bind themselves to any particular institute.

It was necessary at this juncture to choose one who should be entrusted with the spiritual welfare of the community. Father Forteguerri left the choice of a superior in the hands of the religious, who unanimously elected Agnes to this position. A peculiar custom of the time was then carried out. As soon as the Bishop was informed of the election, though it gave him great satisfaction, he ordered the rector of the church of Saint Bernard at Montepulciano, to publish this election to the people, in order to ascertain whether they had any objections to the choice. Needless to say, general approbation was expressed and the Bishop sent Father Forteguerri to install Agnes as superior of Santa Maria Novella.

Mindful of the injunctions of heaven in regard to her foundation, Agnes assembled the community and announced to them her intention of introducing and establishing in the convent the Rule and Constitutions of the Order of Saint Dominic. She also expressed the desire that all should unite to put on the habit and submit to the rule of this Order. After a few days of especially fervent prayer, all made known their wish that Santa Maria Novella should become a Dominican convent. This action was seconded by the Bishop and the approbation of Rome was obtained.

The spiritual advantages which the introduction of a fixed rule introduced proved the propriety and the wisdom of Agnes' plan. The Saint then set about most zealously to see that every prescription of the rule be carried out. With all the tenderness she manifested to her spiritual daughters, we are told that she was exact even to strictness in maintaining the observance of the rule, saying that the most minute points are of incalculable importance, since, in a system composed of closely connected parts, the smallest cannot be disjoined from the rest without altering the whole.

The life which Agnes led in the practice of every virtue steeled her against any adversity that might transpire to disturb the tranquillity that reigned at Santa Maria Novella. Yet God, Who had lavished on her so many favors, was now to send her a trial to prove her virtue and her trust in Divine Providence. When it was least to be expected, a great part of the walls of the church and convent collapsed. Their poor construction gave no evidence that they would last for a long time, yet no one would have suspected that they would crumble in the short space of four or five years. This untoward occurrence greatly grieved Agnes, but she consoled herself by remembering that no one had perished. Her greatest solace was her unflinching resignation to the will of the Most High, Who, she was convinced, would provide the means of rebuilding the sacred edifice.

In a public meeting held on April 6, 1311, Guglielmo del Pecora, a prominent citizen of Montepulciano, made known to his fellow-citizens the plight of the sisters and declared it a public duty to lend them assistance. By generous response to his appeals, the church and convent were rebuilt on a handsomer and more substantial scale. A pious and rich woman, in particular, contributed a large sum of money left her by her father to be devoted to charity. Doubting as to how to dispose of the legacy in the best possible way, she was enlightened in a dream which was repeated on three occasions. She dreamed that she saw a ladder, on which many angels ascended and descended, whose top rested on the clouds. The base rested on the hill where Agnes had raised her humble edifice. This ladder unexpectedly fell. The good woman consulted a holy person who interpreted the dream as symbolic of the accident which befell Santa Maria Novella. Accordingly she gave the money left by her father to Agnes to defray the expenses of rebuilding her convent.

It now seemed that nothing was left to the spouse of Christ but to end her days in the peaceful shelter of her convent in close communion with God. After a time, however, she felt inspired to undertake a pilgrimage to Rome in order to see the many trophies of our holy religion preserved there, as well as to obtain definite approval of her work at Montepulciano. She confided her plan to her spiritual director, who approved of her pious intentions.

Agnes' visit was accomplished during the sad and troublesome period when Rome was abandoned by its Chief Pastor, for Clement V, formerly Archbishop of Bordeaux, had sought the greater ease and freedom of Avignon, where the Popes resided for seventy years. Monsignor Arnaldo, Bishop of Sabina, who was Cardinal Legate of the Pope, granted her every request. During her stay in the Eternal City Agnes observed a rigorous retirement. Many illustrious persons sought to obtain the benefit of her wise counsel. Agnes was not puffed up over this nor was she led to place her confidence in the protection of the great, as she had long before learned to place her trust in God alone. The Saint also visited the tombs of the Martyrs to venerate their relics. She wished to obtain some relics of the Princes of the Apostles, for whom she had a singular veneration, but humility prevented her from asking for them from those who could easily have granted her request. However, when she went to pay a final visit to the tombs of Saints Peter and Paul, two small pieces of cloth were laid in her hands. It was at the same time revealed to her that they were fragments from the garments of these Holy Apostles.

Agnes returned to Montepulciano filled with fresh eagerness to make further progress in the school of perfection. The gifts which she received from above were accepted by her with the greatest profit to her soul. All her spiritual favors were scrupulously confided to him who stood in the place of God in her regard. The gift of faith implanted in her soul, strengthened by love, was so intense that she realized to the fullest degree that God is the Highest Good and that separation from Him is the greatest evil. In Him she placed all her hope. To these supernatural qualities she added filial fear, which is a portion of that anxiety natural to an affectionate heart. She, however, gloried not in the possession of these gifts as if she had them of her own merits, but she referred all with the deepest gratitude to their Author. She renewed her protestations of love and devotion constantly to her Divine Spouse and sometimes felt her whole being ravished to such sublime heights that she had reason to doubt whether her nature was being changed or whether she still existed in the flesh. It was this same ardor which one day prompted the Apostle Paul to exclaim, "I live, now not I, but Christ liveth in me" (Gal. ii, 20).

When Agnes went to Montepulciano to undertake the foundation of Santa Maria Novella, she left behind her at Proceno the little cross which she took from the Infant Jesus when He appeared to her. The Saint was desirous of having this precious memento of her spiritual transports on that occasion. The nuns at Proceno, who were greatly grieved at her departure from them, absolutely refused to give up the treasure. Agnes sent a letter to them reminding them that it was in accordance with the will of God that she left them. At the same time she urgently pressed her request to restore the cross which she so justly prized. Their intention of keeping the cross was frustrated, for they discovered one day that it had left its reliquary where it had reposed and returned to Agnes' keeping. The Saint then wrote to inform the sisters that what they had refused her was granted miraculously in answer to a single prayer.

Meanwhile Agnes continued to govern her community with her wonted prudence. In the practice of virtue she ever set the example for the nuns to follow. She ever chose the most difficult and the most laborious methods in the exercise of good works. There were unceasing demands on her charity. Those of timid consciences never sought her counsel without obtaining solace and advice in their perplexities. The devil, ever on the alert to throw obstacles in the pathway of perfection, beset the convent with all manner of strange noises, especially during the night. Agnes had recourse to prayer to set at naught the machinations of the evil one, whereupon the disturbance ceased. The fame of Agnes' power over the spirits of darkness was soon noised abroad and shortly we find a possessed person being brought to her for deliverance from the tormentor. A quiet word of command from the Saint, her hand gently laid upon his head while she traced the sign of salvation upon his forehead, reciting the Athanasian Creed as she did so, and the sufferer was freed.

Another instance of the wonderful power of the servant of God was manifested in the case of one of the sisters who had become totally blind. Being disconsolate as a result, this religious had recourse to the Saint. The holy virgin said to her: "If you will promise God never more to shed a tear from those eyes for whatever temporal misfortune may happen to you, and to consecrate all your affections to Him, weaned from all earthly care, I promise you on His part the consolation of recovering the perfect use of your eyes." When the sister did as she was bidden, Agnes made the sign of the Cross on her sightless eyes and she was cured.

By similar wonders did the Most High glorify His servant. One day she was informed by the sisters that there was no bread in the convent larder, nor had they the means to buy any. The Saint listened calmly to their words. When they had finished, she said with a smile: "Nothing is impossible to God." Thereupon, an unknown person brought a few small loaves to the sisters. These were insufficient for their needs, but when Agnes blessed the loaves they multiplied so that they had more than enough.

Thus the wonderful life of our Saint went on. She daily made rapid strides in heroic sanctity, drawing ever closer to her Master. She was, however, to pass through various stages of suffering which were to increase her reputation for holiness and to prepare for her a crown of unfading luster. She was miraculously warned of these impending afflictions. One Sunday morning, whilst the Saint was at prayer, an angel appeared to her and said: "Follow me for I have to show thee a great mystery." Agnes followed the angel without delay. The messenger of God led her to the convent garden and stopped under an olive tree. He then gave her a cup filled with a most bitter liquid, which he commanded her to drink to the very dregs. "This," said he, "will make thee in some degree like the Redeemer of the human race, who in the Garden of Gethsemane did not disdain for thy salvation to accept a cup of immense sorrow from the hand of His Heavenly Father, and to submit voluntarily to inexplicable sufferings." This vision was repeated on nine following Sundays.

Agnes was not slow to fathom the signification of these presages. It would be difficult to describe with what alacrity of mind and with what fervor she prepared for the afflictions that were to come upon her. Anxious to resemble Christ most closely she besought her Spouse to send a heavy trial, but to give her the all-powerful assistance of His grace to aid her in becoming a victim of love. Accordingly, she spent hours before her crucifix to study Christ in His bitter Passion that she might suffer with Him conformably to His own example.

Ere long Agnes' strength failed very greatly and she was soon reduced to such a weak state that she thought that death was near. Her courage and patience enabled her to endure her sufferings for some time without the knowledge of others. Her countenance bore the same placid expression as usual. She observed faithfully every religious duty and continued her customary mortifications. At last, however, her illness made such progress that she was obliged to seek the aid of a physician. Acting upon his advice, she went to the baths of Chianciano. Though the Saint was convinced that the remainder of her life was to be passed in suffering, she, nevertheless, submitted to the will of others in every prescription made to restore her health. When the illness constantly grew worse, she was the only one who did not manifest any alarm. She was accompanied to Chianciano by several sisters and a priest of the Order of Saint Dominic.

Agnes' stay at this place was the occasion of several miracles. Once when she entered the waters, a shower of "manna" in cruciform particles fell and covered the waters and the adjacent ground. At the same time a new spring gushed forth near the baths, which was soon found to have healing properties. It came to be known as Saint Agnes' Spring. Many other wonderful works were wrought at Chianciano. The power of Agnes' prayers gained for her universal esteem. Her touch instantly cured a child who had received a serious wound in the knee. Her blessing changed water into wine. But the greatest of the miracles worked through her instrumentality is that which we are now to relate. A little child was playing at the edge of the baths and fell by accident into the water. As there was no one about, the child was drowned. Its dead body was afterward discovered floating on the surface of the water. Agnes was moved to compassion by the grief of the child's mother. Taking the corpse into her arms, she retired to a solitary spot and prayed for a long time. Then she returned to the crowd which had gathered in expectation of what was going to transpire. Agnes laid the body of the child at the feet of its mother. Then, taking its hand, she raised it from the ground alive and well and restored it to its mother. These miracles were regarded by all as signs of God's predilection for His servant. Agnes profited by the favorable dispositions of the people to promote the glory of God and to instil in the people a horror of sin and its consequences. At the same time she impressed upon their minds the necessity of looking to God for solace in their afflictions and for help in combating their evil inclinations.

Agnes had now spent some months at Chianciano, when it was perceived that it was futile to look for any improvement in her health. She accordingly returned to Montepulciano. She had constantly longed during her absence for the day when she would be able to return to her beloved Santa Maria Novella to await in holy expectation the day when she would be dissolved and be united with Christ. Looking upon herself as an unprofitable servant, she offered herself to God as a victim of infinite imperfection. Accordingly she besought heaven to send her the most painful trials that she might glorify God and offer Him satisfaction for the many insults heaped upon His Divine Majesty. She constantly meditated on the Saviour's bitter Passion and offered up her pains in union with His. She never tired weeping for the sins of men and longed to become a barrier to stop men in their wicked course at the cost of any imaginable torment. She was filled with the greatest transports of love when she approached the Holy Sacraments. It was sufficient to cast a glance upon her countenance to be convinced that she lived but for God in Whom was her strength.

The light of prophecy enjoyed by the servant of God was another indication of her favor in the sight of the Lord. She knew everything that passed interiorly in the souls of her spiritual charges. She profited by this knowledge to make corrections wherever needed, but she did this in such an amiable manner that none were ever rendered uncomfortable at the thought that their failings were known to her. She prophesied the future to many people, and her predictions were always verified. When the peace of the country was threatened by the rising discords between some of the powerful families, she called the nuns together and urged them to pray with her before an image of the Mother of God. While they petitioned Mary to avert the evil that was to befall their country, the face of the image of our Lady changed color, grew pale, frowned, and at last broke into tears like one suffering from terror and grief. The sisters were motionless with fear, but Agnes reassured them, saying that they should have recourse to God to appease His just anger. The Saint must have felt doubly sad as a result of this prophecy, for she was filled with the deepest love for her neighbor and it pained her to bequeath such predictions to her countrymen as her life was drawing to a close.

Worn out at length by long labors and by illness, Agnes was obliged to remain in bed. The servant of God was never known to have been more joyful than when she realized that her life was despaired of. She knew that she was soon to obtain the crown of all her good works, that she was in a brief space of time to be numbered among those who follow the Lamb whithersoever He goeth. She poured forth most fervent acts of faith, hope, and love. She then received the last Sacraments in the holiest dispositions. When she saw that the religious gathered about her wept disconsolately at the thought that she was about to be taken from them, she addressed to them these words: "What! do you not love me enough to rejoice when you see that I am soon to go to God, Who is the only end for which all creatures were made?" When they answered that they were sorrowful because they were before long to be deprived of so faithful a guide, she rejoined: "Do not be afraid of losing my assistance; I shall be your mother, your companion, and your sister, whenever in your wants you call on me to be so." Then there was a pause. Suddenly Agnes cast her eyes aloft, her countenance beamed with heavenly peace, and she said most joyfully: "I go to Him Who is my only Hope." So saying, her angelic soul fled to the sweet embrace of Jesus, the Spouse of Virgins. She died in the forty-ninth year of her age, on Tuesday night, the 20th of April, in the year of grace 1317.

At the moment of Agnes' death, many of the little children of Montepulciano, who were asleep, for it was midnight, woke up, calling out, "Holy Sister Agnes is dead." A woman, who was suffering from an abscess on her arm, was amazed to see our Saint enter her room, bright with the radiance of heaven. The Saint told the woman that she would be cured by going to the convent on the morrow and touching her body.

Heaven, which had set its mark of approval on the holy actions of Agnes during her life, attested her sanctity by many miracles after her death. The height of glory to which Saint Agnes attained in her heavenly home is far above our comprehension, yet we can, notwithstanding, relate a fact which will open a field of pious meditation. Saint Catherine of Siena assures us that one day when she was rapt in spirit she beheld Saint Agnes in glory seated on a lofty throne of beauteous light, and an empty throne near her, which was reserved for a soul of equal merit. When Saint Catherine humbly besought the Lord to reveal to her for whom the vacant throne was intended she was informed that it was to be occupied by herself. This vision increased the devotion of our Seraphic Mother for Saint Agnes. In a letter addressed to the Prioress at Montepulciano, she tells how our Lord once spoke to her about Saint Agnes when she was engaged in writing her treatise on Divine Providence. "Sometimes," He said, "I provide for My servants' wants, as thou knowest of that sweet Virgin Saint, Agnes. From her childhood to the end she served Me with true humility and firm hope, for she never thought with doubt about herself or her household. With living faith she began, in her poverty, to build the monastery of Saint Mary's. She never thought 'How can I do this?' but she worked with My providence, and made it a holy place. And I, in return, supported her and eighteen virgins whom she had collected for Me, even when they were left without bread to sustain life. And if thou dost ask Me, 'Why didst Thou keep her in such want, for Thou hast told me that Thou dost never fail Thy servants who hope in Thee?' I reply that I permitted this necessity that those less perfect should, by the miracle that followed, have reason to make their foundation in the light of faith. I can give to a few herbs such a quality that the human body will be better supported by them than by their usual nourishment; and this thou knowest, for thou hast experienced it thyself. And I also provide by multiplying, for when Agnes cast the eyes of her mind on Me, saying 'My Lord and Father, hast Thou made me take these daughters out of their fathers' houses to perish with hunger? Provide, O Lord! for their necessities,' I did so, and I gave her so much virtue in breaking the bread I sent, that all were more than satisfied."

Saint Catherine's admiration for the Saint did not end with her writing about her. She herself went to Montepulciano to venerate her body. When she was in prayer before the holy remains, as she bent down to kiss the foot of the Saint, Agnes prevented her from stooping by raising her foot. On another occasion, when Saint Catherine visited the body, a shower of "manna" fell from heaven, which covered them both.

Saint Agnes of Montepulciano was enrolled in the catalogue of the Saints by Pope Benedict XIII, a son of Saint Dominic, on the 12th of May, 1726. Her feast is observed on the 20th of April. The life of Saint Agnes was written by Blessed Raymond of Capua, O. P., who became confessor to the community at Montepulciano some fifty years after her death.

In "Dominican Contemplatives" we find the following comparison drawn between Saint Agnes and our Holy Father, Saint

Dominic: "She first lived under the rule of Saint Augustine and did not find her final vocation until shortly before her death. She possessed that wonderful serenity which so characterized her Blessed Father, so that merely to look at her restored peace to troubled souls. Like him she had a special power over evil spirits; at her prayer, as at his, God deigned to send food by the hand of angels; she had his zeal for souls, his spirit of penance and prayer, and his supernatural tenderness for his spiritual children. Like him she ended her work for God in the prime of life, worn out by labor and penance, and consumed by a burning thirst to drink of the torrent of living waters."

BIBLIOGRAPHY

Acta Sanctorum, April, II, 789. Parisiis et Romæ, 1865.

Bullarium Ordinis Prædicatorum, Vol. V, 526–577. Romæ, 1733.

Saint Agnes of Montepulciano. Oratorian Fathers. London and New York, 1852.

GERTRUDE, S. M.: Loreto. St. Agnes of Montepulciano. London, 1900.

Année Dominicaine, Vol. IV. Sainte Agnès de Montepulciano. Lyons, 1889.

DYSON, FR. THOMAS AUSTIN: St Agnes of Montepulciano. New York, 1893.

TAURISANO, P. INNOCENTIUS, O. P.: Catalogus Hagiographicus Ordinis Prædicatorum. Romæ, 1918.

Short Lives of the Dominican Saints. Edited by Fr. John Procter, O. P., S. T. L. New York, 1901.

A Dominican of Carisbrooke, "Dominican Contemplatives." London, 1919.

Saint Catherine of Siena

(1347–1380)

IN THE CENTRAL PART of Italy, on the undulating expanses of Tuscany, lies the ancient town Siena, in medieval public documents entitled *Civitas Virginis*—the City of the Virgin. Though now fairly forgotten, on account of the more thriving cities that surround it, the firmly constructed walls and ramparts, the many civic monuments and buildings, and the beautiful gothic cathedral proclaim an era in its history of comparatively great political power and prosperity. In 1339, imbued with that progressive spirit inaugurated a century before and impelled by laudable pride that sprang from past achievement, the enthusiastic population seized upon a wonderful plan that should immortalize its name. It was the Commune's purpose so to enlarge the *Duomo* that the present nave, which measures 292 feet, should form the transept of a new and more lofty edifice, a design that, if realized, would have presented a magnificent structure, the proportions of which would far exceed any cathedral built before and even after that time, with the exception of Saint Peter's Basilica, in Rome. The pestilence of 1348 compelled the craftsmen to interrupt the work most auspiciously begun, and with cessation from labor the monumental project was abandoned.

Such is but one instance of the progressiveness of the most medieval of Italian cities. Posterity, however, remembers the ancient town not so much for its former material prosperity as for its spiritual good fortune of having given to the Church saints and

Saint Catherine of Siena

holy Popes. And to none of these illustrious children, perhaps, is the city's devotedness so demonstrative and yet so sincere as to her who, at the very time the vast projected temple failed, was reared by God a resplendent Temple of the Holy Ghost, whose saintly renown has carried Siena's name to the furthermost parts of the earth.

In that section of *the Virgin's City* called the Fontebranda, on the old narrow street Oca that leads to the convent of the Friar Preachers, the traveler catches sight of a humble dwelling—part of which is now converted into a chapel—bearing the inscription: "The House of the Spouse of Christ, Catherine." Formerly this house was called the Fullonica, and was the home and workshop of Giacomo (James) di Benincasa, surnamed the dyer, whose occupation was the preparation of colors employed in dying wool. After losing his parents and having by his industry acquired a competency, this man married a young girl of sweet disposition and lovable character, named Lapa Piaganti, the daughter of a local poet. The couple dwelt peaceably together, enjoyed a considerable fortune and "belonged," says Edmund Gardner, "to the lower middle-class faction of tradesmen and petty notaries, known as *the Party of the Twelve*, which between one revolution and another ruled the Republic of Siena from 1355 to 1368." God blessed their union by granting them twenty-five children. Giacomo was a just and religious father, who by good example led his family in the practice of very exalted virtue. Lapa, on the contrary, though a woman of devout nature, a good housewife, and gentle mother, had a tinge of worldliness in her character that later caused unnecessary trials to herself and to her youngest child.

On the 25th of March, 1347, Lapa became the mother of two delicate girls, and not being able to nourish both she confided one to the care of a friend. When the infants were baptized the mother's choice was called Catherine and the other Jane. Little Jane died a few days afterward. On the death of her tiny child, Lapa consoled herself by bestowing the most exceptional care on the twin sister, whom she frequently acknowledged she loved more tenderly than all the others.

From her earliest years Catherine received a training that befitted a child of God. Her mother instructed her in the rudiments of faith and took her to the Church of San Dominico, where she saw the mysteries enacted before her wide-open eyes. From the time she could walk it was with difficulty her mother could keep her at home, for neighbors and relatives found so much delight in her sweet company, in her childlike yet prudent conversations, that they were ever desirous of having little *Euphrosyne*—for so they were wont to call her—in their midst. Whether they were aware of the Greek signification of the name, which means joy or satisfaction, is unknown. At all events the epithet was no misnomer. As soon as one conversed with her all sadness of heart was dispelled; and it is also said that Catherine early in life, with a zeal for the salvation of souls, had resolved to enter the Order of Friar Preachers, dressed as a man, in emulation of Saint Euphrosyne, who, disguised in the garb of a monk, passed many years in a monastery. Catherine was likewise endeared to little children. When scarcely five years old, in ascending and descending the flight of stairs in her father's house, she was accustomed to genuflect on each step the while she recited the *Hail Mary*. Such pious practices, far from estranging her tiny girl companions, drew them to herself and made them love her all the more. Some even desired to imitate her example; leaving their play in the cobbled streets they would go to some remote quarter in order to undergo small austerities and say the *Our Father* and *Hail Mary* as often as she prescribed to them.

During childhood God frequently showed approval of this holy conduct by granting in various ways wonderful tokens of His special love. One day the future Saint, then six years old, and her brother Stephen, a year or two her elder, after a visit to their married sister Bonaventura, were returning homeward by the valley known as the *Valle Piatta*, when suddenly she beheld against the gable of the Dominican church a magnificent throne occupied by our Lord clothed in pontifical vestments and crowned with a tiara. At His side were Saints Peter and Paul and John, the Beloved Disciple. Gazing on this entrancing scene, she stood fixed in contemplation. Stephen had walked on, thinking she followed. When he perceived her absence, he called out to her, but she gave no heed, for Jesus, smiling upon her with benign tenderness, was raising His hand in benediction. At length her brother walked back, and, pulling her somewhat roughly by the hand, asked her why she tarried. Catherine, awaking as from a dream, said to him: "If thou didst see what I see, thou wouldst not disturb me." Her eyes instantly sought the vision, but it had vanished. She wept long and bitterly, reproaching herself for having lowered her eyes. From that moment, it seems, *Euphrosyne* ceased to be a child: denying all amusements common to children, diminishing the quantity of her food, disciplining her feeble body, and increasing her prayers and meditations, she strove to conform her every action to the manifest will of God.

About this time the Holy Spirit, without employing any human means, taught her the lives of many saints. She was most forcibly drawn to the mode of life pursued by the Fathers of the Desert; and, like Saint Teresa of Jesus, in the sixteenth century, who, at the age of seven, left her home with her little brother for the country of the Moors in quest of the martyr's crown, so Catherine, urged on by desire for the solitude and the living, daily martyrdoms of the holy eremites, one morning, taking a loaf of bread, set out very early in search of the desert. She went out at the gates of Siena for the first time in her life. She proceeded in the direction away from the city, and, as the distances from one habitation to another grew rougher and further between, she thought she was verily approaching the wilderness. Having discovered a natural grotto formed of shelving rock, which to her fancy became a hermit's cell, she entered to pray.

Hardly had she begun her prayer when she was elevated to the vault of the cavern. Suspended thus in mid-air, she remained till the afternoon, when an interior voice bade her return to the Fullonica, since the Almighty had greater things in store for her. She was far from the city walls, and, fearing lest her departure should cause anxiety to her parents, she commended herself to God, and in one moment found herself in the Fontebranda, in the vicinity of her home. Many similar incidents occurred in childhood. Often angels bore her to the top of the staircase with such rapidity as to frighten the mother.

These manifestations of the love of our Saviour caused the heart of the holy child to grow with so intense love for Him and His Immaculate Mother that all human solicitude in life, as compared with a preoccupation in things divine, was as dross is in a crucible of gold. And, in order to live in total conformity to the will of Jesus, her little heart now longed for a life of absolute purity, which the Holy Ghost had instructed her to admire in the saints as the most acceptable of human oblations. She frequently begged the Queen of Virgins to ask her Son the grace of ever remaining pure in body and soul, and ardently and constantly implored that she might see the best way clear to its fulfillment. These persevering prayers were not unanswered.

Catherine was seven when she made the vow of perpetual virginity. Heavenly prudence at length bade her no longer stifle the lofty emotions of a soul enlivened and drawn by the gentle movements of divine grace. One day, kneeling alone in prayer, she invoked the Blessed Virgin and concluded her petition with a voluntary offering of her whole being to Mary's Divine Son: "I promise thy Son and I promise thee," she said, "never to accept any other spouse and to preserve myself to the best of my ability pure and unspotted." This vow the young child sincerely cherished, and the sequel of this narrative will show with what sacred fidelity and holy pertinacity she kept it.

After this entire consecration of herself to God, although the next few years were spent, for the most part, in the quiet of the family circle, yet they were years of extreme spiritual fruitfulness; for, saintly as she was, Catherine took yet greater and more rapid strides on the upward path leading to perfection. Her visits to the Church of San Dominico became more frequent and more prolonged. And though she often suffered most keenly in body, still her soul, during this period, enjoyed deep, interior peace. As the lily in its sheath naturally buds and blossoms, nurtured by the elements, so this lily of chastity, planted in religious soil, watered by the dews of heavenly mercy, embraced by the atmosphere of divine grace, bathed in the sunshine of celestial love, was supernaturally predestined to traverse the stages of spiritual development; and as, in the order of nature, storms, bleak days, days of drought come on, it seems, to retard the natural growth of the flowers, so, too, in the order of grace, holy souls are sometimes subjected to persecutions, temptations, and seasons of dryness to hinder, it would seem, but really to promote, their spiritual growth in the garden of God's kingdom on earth. Catherine's budded virtue of soul was now blossoming, as she was about to suffer many and diverse trials.

Living in a clime where the physical endowments of the tender sex very quickly arrive at their maturity, while Catherine's heart was expanding in love, her body, also, took on a somewhat firmer mold, and from her countenance shone forth the beauty of her soul. She had attained the age of twelve; and according to custom, like other unwedded girls of that time, she never left her home without an escort. Lapa took great pains in dressing and adorning her hair and in attiring her in richly colored gowns, after a fashion calculated to win for her a worthy husband. The Saint divined the reason of her mother's solicitude and submitted very reluctantly to what was so contrary to her wish and nature. This grieved Lapa very much; for, acting in complete ignorance of the secret vow of virginity and, of a consequence, not understanding the pure and upright motives of her daughter's opposition, she deemed it but maiden shyness or a foolish whim. Being determined on her course of action, she summoned to her aid Bonaventura, whom she knew Catherine loved very dearly, confident that Bonaventura should overcome her sister's repugnances. In this the mother was not deceived. Through the solicitations of the married daughter the innocent girl gave more time and attention to her attire and adornment. Bonaventura, however, died suddenly, and it became known to Catherine that her sister's soul was suffering in Purgatory. She was so struck by the vanity of her own conduct that she resolved never again to render her appearance attractive to others. And although never for a moment, as later she declared, did she entertain as much as a thought of renouncing her vow, yet this little breach of divine trust, perhaps the greatest failing of her whole life, affected her so profoundly that she considered it a matter for repeated confession. From this time dates the life-long devotion to Saint Mary Magdalen, whom she took for her spiritual mother, whom she imitated in deeds of penance, and whose intercession she continually implored for the grace of a most perfect contrition.

The death of the eldest daughter made the parents and relations even more determined to find a husband for the youngest child. But she avoided the society of men and proved in every way the inflexibility of her resolution, never to give to a mortal her heart that had once been accepted by the divinely Betrothed. They tried every means to shake her will. Lapa, very ingeniously, hit upon a new device. She besought a Dominican father to speak with her daughter in order to procure her consent. The friar did so, but found her absolutely firm. And instead of contending with her, this religious advised her to cut off her hair, in this manner proving the constancy of her resolve. Catherine received the counsel as from above and immediately executed it. She then covered her head with a veil and hurried back to her small tasks. Lapa, however, soon noticed the change in her appearance, and snatching the scarf from her head, shorn of its abundant and beautiful tresses, shrieked at the top of her voice. The entire household was aroused and in unison gave way to violent anger.

This occurrence was made the occasion of more vehement persecutions. With one accord it was decided that the servant should be dismissed and that all the menial work should devolve upon Catherine, in order to deprive her of every opportunity of communing with God, for they rightly suspected that this was the secret of her constancy. To this severe treatment they added contempt, and multiplied such reproaches as were most painful to her sensitive nature; and then they would suggest that the panacea for all her ills, her disgrace as well as their own, lay in her reach did she but choose to marry. But the little maiden remained calm, and the constant attacks served only to strengthen her courage and augment her patience. Deprived of her own room, she erected a cell in her soul, and every act of drudgery she turned into a prayer. Moreover, she adopted a plan of looking upon her father as representing our Master; her mother, our Blessed Lady; her brothers and other members of the family, the apostles and disciples; and served them with so great joy as to astonish them all.

Giacomo, who all along entertained misgivings as regards his daughter's procedure, began to understand daily more and more that she was doing the will of God and not pursuing the passing fancies of a capricious maiden. One day, when Catherine was kneeling in Stephen's room, her father saw a white dove perched upon her head, which upon his entrance flew out at the window. He inquired what dove it was. "My father," replied the Saint, "I saw no dove nor any other bird." Giacomo was filled with wonder. He withdrew in silence, puzzled in mind as to the meaning of the mysterious dove. The constancy of her devotions, and the meekness and cheerfulness she displayed in bearing the opprobrium heaped upon her, at last won the admiration of her brothers, who owned they were foiled. Thereafter her burdens lightened and were soon to be lifted away.

One night, not long after the events just recorded, Catherine, kneeling by her lowly cot, was gazing up at the wondrous firmament, when suddenly the heavens became inhabited with the founder-saints of various Orders. One by one they approached and beckoned her to follow; but none seemed to attract her until the great and holy Patriarch, with a dazzling white lily in his hand, advanced and presented the habit of the Sisters of Penance, saying to her: "Daughter, be of good heart, fear no obstacle, excite your courage, for the happy day will come when you shall be clothed in the pious habit you desire." Thereupon she wept with joy; and on the following day, when the family was assembled, she told them in simple and forceful language of her consecration to God in holy virginity. Her words, so full of pathos, touched their hearts, and they wept abundant tears. Giacomo was the first to recover himself and forbade them any longer to molest her or oppose her wishes, declaring her free to follow the divine behests. Catherine thanked them all, and blessed God that she was again at liberty to serve Him.

The Saint now selected a small, dark room in the remote part of the house where she might torment her body at will and worship her Lord in silent contemplation. It is said that her food, at this period, consisted of uncooked herbs and a morsel of bread. She delighted in eating the most unsavory food, whereas slightly sweetened victuals or the mere odor of meat would sicken her stomach. The wine, which earlier in life she had always diluted with water, now, in her fifteenth year, she refused entirely. The quantity of food was insufficient, and her stomach became incapable of properly performing its functions, so that finally she remained without bodily nourishment almost continuously. She wore a hair shirt next her skin, which later she exchanged for an iron chain. A few planks sufficed for a bed, with no covering besides the clothes that she wore. In the beginning she extended her vigils till the matin bell called the Dominicans to the Divine Office at midnight, which as time went on she gradually lengthened, often giving the whole night to prayer and meditation. When Lapa discovered her daughter was lying on rough boards, she would call her to her own bedchamber to sleep with her. In obedience, Catherine would respond, but would lie at the edge of the couch until her mother fell asleep, when she would return to her solitude. Sometimes the poor woman, finding her child in her cell, her body, torn and swollen by the cruel scourge, literally covered with streams of blood, would stand aghast: "Alas! alas! my daughter, what dost thou? Wilt thou kill thyself?" and as one gone mad she would run about the house, uttering piercing cries. When the neighbors witnessed these horrible lacerations, they knew not whom to pity more, the anguished mother or the innocent child, who for sinners' sake endured such terrible expiation.

Catherine never for a moment relinquished the fond hope of belonging to the great Order of Saint Dominic. While, on the one hand, she rejoiced in suffering the most excruciating self-torture, on the other hand, her heart could not bear the least misery she beheld in the lives of others. Touched to the quick by the spiritual deformity of persons living in the state of sin, she felt a burning zeal for the salvation of souls. She desired, therefore, the day of her reception to be at hand, that she might imitate the apostolic charity of the glorious Founder. But Lapa had not lost hope of dissuading her child both from the extreme austerities of her life and from this holy design. In obedience to her earthly mother's wish, Catherine one day accompanied her to the public baths. Lapa in this way strove to distract her daughter from her grewsome macerations. Catherine, however, betook herself unobserved to that quarter where the vapors and boiling sulphurous waters could sear her mangled flesh, by these means forestalling, as she said, in this life all the pains of Purgatory or Hell which she might deserve in the next. Her mother, baffled, felt constrained to ask her admittance to the Sisterhood. Twice the sisters refused, each time adding that only widows of mature age, who wished to consecrate their lives to God, were admitted; for inasmuch as they had no cloister each member was required to be able to govern herself at home. It so happened, however, that Catherine fell ill of the smallpox and, her life being despaired of, the heart-broken mother nursed her with tenderest care and trembled at the thought of her death. Mindful of the promise made by Saint Dominic and assured that her lamentable plight should prevail, the stricken postulant importuned her mother to plead once more her cause, saying that she would die if frustrated in this holy vocation. Touched at the mother's grief, the sisters answered: "If thy daughter be not too fair, we shall receive her." So they followed the distressed woman to the house where the child lay on her sick bed, and owing to the horrible eruptions they discerned not the comeliness of her features. Further, they were so impressed by the wisdom of her utterances that they no longer demurred, but, to Catherine's exceeding great joy, decided that upon recovery she might enter their ranks.

Saint Catherine speedily recovered her health, and at sixteen, much to the chagrin of her mother, donned the white-and-black garb of the Mantellati, as the Tertiaries of Saint Dominic were then called. She did not, however, pronounce the three vows of religion, as is often erroneously supposed; she promised obedience to the father-director and to the prioress, practiced her private vow of chastity, and lived an existence of abject poverty, often begging God to render to her parents the blessing, which later actually befell them, of becoming very poor, that they might enter more easily into the Kingdom of Heaven. Then for three long years she withdrew into the solitude of her dark, small chamber, where she underwent every form of mortification imaginable, spoke long and familiarly with God, and laid the deep and solid foundations of that edifice of holiness that was soon to astonish the world. Her cell, which, during this period, she never abandoned except to go to church, and where she kept a rigorous silence never broken unless it were in confession, our Lord frequently visited, and remained for long with His beloved daughter, chanting with her the psalms of the Divine Office. Here it was He miraculously taught her to read. Having striven for several weeks to learn the alphabet, she finally besought God to enable her to read if it were His divine will. Scarcely had she begun her petition when Jesus answered it; and from that time she could read with ease difficult manuscripts, and acquired an admirable knowledge of the Scriptures, especially of the New Testament writings. Later, Christ also miraculously taught her to write. Catherine feared lest her many visions might sometimes be the delusions of the spirit of darkness, her Betrothed therefore instructed her how to distinguish between divine visitations and demoniacal illusions. Many and diverse were the sublime revelations vouchsafed her, as recorded in her many biographies. The following beautiful doctrine of exalted humility is an example: "Thou art who is not," said Jesus to her one day, "I am He who am; if thy soul is deeply penetrated with this truth, the enemy cannot deceive thee and thou wilt avoid all his snares; thou wilt never consent to do anything against My commandments, and thou wilt acquire, without difficulty, grace, truth, and peace."

But while God was actively bestowing such an abundance of His heavenly bounty on the young novice in her self-chosen, stern novitiate, as a preparation for her after apostolate, He was likewise fitting her, in quite another and passive manner, by permitting Satan to assail her soul. Between one celestial favor and another long intervals of spiritual dryness would sometimes intervene, periods during which the evil one was very busy and the Saint felt miserably alone. Christ had told her to choose to have trials and afflictions and to endure them not only with patience, but to embrace them with delight, for, if she would acquire fortitude, she must imitate Him, who, as the Apostle says, ran with joy to the cruel and ignominious death of Mount Calvary. The devils attacked her on every side, yet most frequently on that where lay her greatest strength—her purity of soul—knowing that, did she fail in this, she would become an easier victim. They pictured to her imagination the most degrading scenes, suggested the most abominable of deeds; they assumed the appearance of persons who pitied her in her ruthless self-abnegations, while questioning the usefulness of them; and, failing to vanquish her by reasoning, they adopted a new method of attack, by pursuing her under the guise and shape of phantoms most loathsome, with hellish screams inviting her to partake of their abominations. The poor, struggling, valiant girl, driven almost to despair, augmented her vigils so far as to deprive herself of all sleep and courageously drew the iron chain around her body, causing the blood to flow that her soul might remain pure. One of the most severe temptations Catherine had to undergo lasted for several days. Her soul was plunged into a profound melancholy because our Lord—Who often appeared when the horrible spectres became almost insupportable—this time seemed to abandon her without relief, visible or invisible. Catherine, having returned from church, where the infernal obsessions tormented her less, recalled that God had indicated the means of obtaining fortitude. The words, "If thou wilt acquire fortitude, thou must imitate Me," rang in her ears, and she resolved, after the manner of Christ in the desert, to bear with holy courage the dreadful temptation of the impure spirits. "Then," says Blessed Raymond, "one evil spirit, more malicious than the others, said to her: 'Poor miserable soul, what art thou about to undertake? Canst thou pass thy whole life in this state? We will torment thee to death unless thou dost obey us.'" Catherine answered: "I have chosen sufferings for my consolation; not only will it not be difficult for me, but delightful, to undergo similar afflictions, and even greater ones, for the love of my Jesus, and as long as His Majesty wills!" Instantaneously the prince of darkness and his legions fled, and the Prince of Light appeared to her as when He hung on the Cross, and consoled her with loving words. "Lord, where wert Thou when my heart was so tormented?" "Daughter," came the reply, "I was in the midst of thy heart!"

After many other celestial visitations, Catherine underwent the mystical experience known as the spiritual espousals. This took place probably during the Carnival of 1366, during one of those festivities celebrated in Siena, as in many places the world over, at the approach of the holy season of Lent. It was very likely on the Mardi Gras or Shrove Tuesday festival, which Blessed Raymond calls "a foolish adieu to the viands which the Church is on the eve of prohibiting," that Catherine withdrew into her cell to keep strict fast and prayer in reparation for the sins of those who in bacchanalian routs and festive revelry offended the Saviour. While she knelt in prayer beseeching God to grant her a perfect faith that nothing should be able to sever the betrothment between Jesus and herself, Christ appeared and said: "Because thou hast shunned the vanities of the world and forbidden pleasure, and hast fixed on Me alone all the desires of thy heart, I intend, whilst thy family are rejoicing in profane feasts and festivals, to celebrate the wedding which is to unite Me to thy soul. I am going, according to My promise, to espouse thee in faith." And whilst He was yet speaking there appeared His glorious Mother, Saint John the Evangelist, Saint Paul, Saint Dominic, and the prophet David. Then, amid tunes of unearthly sweetness played by the Royal Psalmist, the Mother of God approached, and taking the right hand of Catherine presented it to her Son. Jesus condescended with love and placed upon her finger a golden ring, set with four precious stones, in the center of which sparkled a large diamond. Then the Bridegroom spoke again: "I thy Creator and Redeemer, espouse thee in faith and thou shalt preserve it pure, until we celebrate together in heaven the eternal nuptials of the Lamb. Daughter, now act courageously; accomplish without fear the works that My Providence will confide to thee." The vision vanished, but the mystic ring was ever visible to her, though invisible to everybody else.

Mysticism may be defined as the union of the soul with its God in contemplation and love. Nothing can permanently satisfy the noblest longings of the soul but the Infinite Goodness, because the

Infinite Goodness alone is perfect and absolute truth, and truth is the proper food of the intellect. The mystic saints were those, who by special grace, with wings of the spirit, unburdened of the desires of the flesh, have soared to the heights in contemplating the Absolute Truth, toward Whom every adult, human soul in grace, at least in some degree, is drawn in contemplation. Such a mystic saint was the glorious Catherine. And although her soul had at this period passed, for the most part, through the purgative and illuminative ways into the unitive state of the spiritual life, still at the command of her Spouse she came out into the public gaze, to be an instrument in the hands of God of most abundant good. Clothed in the habit of a Sister of Penance; her spirit penetrated with the spirit of Saint Dominic, who left as a heritage to his followers, contemplation, mortification, and the apostolic life; proved in the fires of temptation; inundated by heavenly favors—the saintly daughter of the Sienese dyer, after her mystical alliance, was gradually introduced to the active ministry.

A short time after this spiritual marriage, Jesus came one day into Saint Catherine's seclusion and bade her go down to join the family at table. She was at first thunderstruck at this announcement and, begging our Lord to allow her to remain with Him, pleaded inability to eat. But Jesus remained firm. He reminded her of her zeal for souls in youth and of the reasons why she assumed the habit of the Mantellati. Then Catherine said: "Lord, not my will but Thine be done, I am only darkness and Thou art all light; I am nothingness and Thou art; I am ignorance and Thou art the Wisdom of the Father; but, Lord, suffer me to inquire how I shall execute Thy commands—my sex presents an obstacle, for women have no authority over men, and propriety interdicts frequent relations with them." Our Lord answered that all things are possible with God. She, therefore, rejoined her family and began to devote herself anew to the duties of the household. Her Spouse did not desert her and she was ever intimately in communication with Him despite external employments. The mere thought of God would frequently cause her body to be raised into an ecstasy. Sometimes she was lifted above the earth, and the extremities of her body became cold, contracted, and insensible. When her mother Lapa saw her for the first time in such a state—for these raptures occurred more and more frequently in public—she was so taken aback and alarmed at the stiffness and the contraction of her limbs, that she hurried to her, and by force attempted to straighten the neck which had become somewhat awry. When Catherine came to her senses she declared that her neck was all but broken. Several times when rapt in ecstasy her body was found on burning coals into which she had fallen or perhaps the devil had cast her, but never to the hurt of any member.

Saint Catherine now worked at home; the next step she took was also to employ herself for the welfare of her neighbor. The holy Tertiary strictly observed the three evangelical counsels and would not dispose of what belonged to others without their consent. She, therefore, approached her father and asked his permission to give to the poor. Giacomo willingly consented. As a little apostle she quickly sought out the needy in the Fontebranda, bestowing on them, according to their need, corn, wine, and oil. If there were some in the neighborhood, as sometimes happens, who were ashamed to solicit aid, Catherine would arise early and before dawn secretly bestow of her plenty. Nothing could deter her from these works of charity. At times she would rise from her sick, miserable couch and, weakened in body, would crawl or drag herself to some forlorn hovel to give succor to an unfortunate and starving widow and her infants. Twice our Lord appeared to her in the guise of a destitute man, once asking alms, at another time demanding clothing. Catherine always ready to alleviate the indigent, in the first instance, gave all that she then had, a little crucifix of silver, and, in the second instance, went so far as to give Him all the clothing she could find in the house. Each time, during her vigils, Christ appeared, showed her the crucifix studded with precious jewels and the garments richly embroidered with pearls: "Thou didst give these to Me and on the day of Judgment I shall restore them to thee, such as they are, in the presence of men and angels; for what thou hast done for Me shall never be forgotten."

Saint Catherine's charity was often accompanied by miracles. It happened, for example, that the Saint, who was accustomed to proffer the best when administering to the poor, drew daily from a certain hogshead wine of exceptional quality. The quantity in the cask would ordinarily have supplied her family for about twenty days. Another cask, actually in use, having spoiled, the family had recourse to this very one from which Catherine was continually drawing. Notwithstanding the great quantity used the amount of wine suffered no diminution, and was so superior that it was remarked by all. This continued for a long time, and all began to wonder. Months passed and still no change. At length, the vintage time at hand, the vintners, coming to this barrel, brought vessels wherein to pour its contents that it might be opened and cleansed to receive new wine. They filled the vessels, but the wine continued to flow. The director of the vintage, growing impatient at what he thought to be stupidity, ordered the workmen to open the cask at once. To their amazement they found it perfectly dry. On many other occasions her labors were sustained and blessed by miraculous intervention. Several wonders are recorded which the Servant of God wrought over inanimate objects, such as broken earthenware, utensils, and even flowers, of which she was most fond. On one occasion, while in the house of Alessia, a young widow, who had left her house to occupy one near Catherine's to be able to commune more frequently with her she so sincerely loved, the Saint made most excellent bread out of flour spoiled by humidity. All the bread previously baked was of a sour and bitter taste. When the bread was distributed among the poor it was found to be so plenteous that there ever remained a great quantity in the pantry.

Catherine later said that the Blessed Virgin herself appeared to her and helped in kneading the dough. Toward the end of her life, when at Rome with sixteen spiritual companions, it chanced that one day bread nearly failed them. Catherine commanded them to eat the little they had at hand, and, although there was not a sufficient amount for four persons, all ate heartily, and afterward there still remained a copious quantity on the table. This same prodigy of the multiplication of loaves occurred at different times.

In her apostleship amongst the poverty stricken, Catherine's charity seemed to know no bounds. As far as lay in her power she sought the alleviation of all their needs, and her heart went out to them with sincerest sympathy; but for the sick and suffering she cherished so great a tenderness and commiseration, that her conduct in dealing with them is almost incredible, especially when we reflect on the humility, the patience, the meekness with which she succored those who returned evil for good. Among the many sick poor in Siena there was one woman named Thecca, who on account of her extreme need was forced to betake herself to a public hospital. This woman was covered with leprosy, and the stench which arose from the dead and ulcerous portions of her flesh became so offensive as to be almost insupportable, and there was none who would take care of her. Moreover, the accommodations at the hospital were inadequate, and it was deemed necessary to remove her outside the city walls. When Catherine heard this, she visited and kissed the leprous woman; and after banishment, according to her promise, came morning and evening to the woman's hut to sweep and cleanse and to supply her with the necessaries of life. All this only inspired the heart of Thecca to arrogance and ingratitude. Occasionally Catherine was a little late or did something not in conformity with the old woman's wishes. The old woman would then chide her benefactress with scurrilous words. Everybody was in admiration of this heroic charity, except Lapa, who feared her child should contract the loathsome malady. Catherine's fingers actually became infected; but Thecca died soon afterward, and directly she had washed, clothed, and buried the corpse, the leprosy disappeared.

About this time there lived in Siena a Sister of Penance, called Andréa, who was stricken with a cancer of the breast. One day, while washing and changing the linens, Saint Catherine was almost overcome by the suffocating odor. Perceiving this weakness the Saint reproached herself and stooping down she applied her mouth to the ulcer until she was conscious of having overcome her disgust and triumphed over her natural revolt. This conduct, no doubt, astonishes one; but when we are told that this very woman suspected the maiden's purity and calumniated her before the Sisterhood, we begin to realize the heroism of Catherine's charity. Lapa, convinced of her daughter's innocence, threatened her with disinheritance if she approached the wretched woman again. Catherine, however, pleaded with her mother till she granted her leave to return. Andréa finally repented; and calling together the sisters retracted the scandal she had caused. Some days afterward, while bathing the open wound, Catherine's stomach bounded with nausea. Filled with holy anger against herself, she said: "Thou shalt swallow what inspires thee with such horror." Then collecting the water that flowed from the ulcer, she went aside and drank it. She later confessed she never drank a potion so sweet and agreeable. As a reward for this victory over the devil and over her lower nature, God, in vision, gave her to drink of the blood that flowed from Christ's Sacred Side. After this she found it almost impossible to take the insignificant amount of food to which she was accustomed.

During the remaining years of her earthly pilgrimage, the Servant of God worked many wonders both for the corporal and spiritual well-being of her neighbor. Some she delivered from the tyranny of the devil. The cures wrought over sickness and plague and serious physical injuries are too long to dwell on in this short sketch. About the year 1368, however, the Saint's father Giacomo died. Catherine prayed for his immediate entrance into Heaven. This God granted her; but when his soul ascended heavenward, immediately she experienced an acute pain in her side which remained the rest of her life. Her mother also grew seriously ill at this time and lay at the point of death. She besought her daughter to intercede for her life. God promised the favor, but added that the time would come when she would sigh for death. Lapa lived to an extreme old age, and died in her eighty-ninth year, but in many privations, trials, and afflictions, as Catherine had told her on the part of God. But it was most of all for the conversion of sinners that the Saint worked unceasingly. Nothing could daunt her courage: she followed sinners to their most hidden haunts, often asking admittance into the prison, with burning words begging and exhorting their return to God. Several criminals she assisted in their last moments. At one time she accompanied a young man condemned to death at the block, whose soul she saw purified and consigned to eternal happiness. Alice Meynell very beautifully pictures this scene in one of her poems:

"She prayed, she preached him innocent;
She gave him to the Sacrificed;
On her courageous breast he leant,
The breast where beat the heart of Christ.

"He left it for the block, with cries
Of victory on his severed breath.
That crimson head she clasped, her eyes
Blind with the splendor of his death."

It was about this time also that God showed her the spiritual deformity of the soul of a certain Sister of Penance, named Palmerina, who was living in very heinous sin. The little Apostle of the Wayward prayed indefatigably for her conversion. When on her death-bed, God relented and showed mercy. Palmerina was converted, confessed her grievous faults aloud, and, having received the

Sacrament with signs of profound sorrow and sincere love, expired. Later God showed His servant the state of this soul in glory. "If I have exhibited this soul to thee," said our Divine Saviour, "it is to awaken in thee a more inflamed desire of promoting the salvation of souls, in proportion to the grace I have given thee." Catherine thanked her Spouse and intreated Him in the future to show her the beauty of all the souls who might have relations with her, that she would be the more devoted to their salvation. God granted this request, and more; ever afterward she saw not only the beauty, but also the ugliness of souls. The efficacy of this grace was such that she perceived more distinctly the state of the soul than that of the body, not only of persons present, but even of persons at a great distance, who at any time were to become an object of her tender and special solicitude.

The gift of prophecy and spiritual insight Catherine possessed in an almost incredible degree. She saw men's most secret thoughts. Sometimes she revealed vice to very hardened sinners, that they might omit nothing in their confession. Later in her many journeys when coming in contact with persons who to all outward appearances seemed men of respectable demeanor, she would say: "Let us confess our crimes and then we may go on with our dealings." At one time Friar Thomas, her first confessor, and another religious were overtaken at a great distance from Siena by a band of highwaymen. The robbers were about to take their lives, when Thomas had recourse to his spiritual daughter. The very same moment Catherine, perceiving the danger threatening her ghostly father and his companion, prayed for their escape. Taking but a little money from the friars, the bandits gave them their release. Later, in the year 1375, when the greater portion of the cities and lands belonging to the Holy See revolted against the Sovereign Pontiff, Gregory XI, Blessed Raymond expressed his sincere grief to his spiritual daughter. Catherine said to him: "Now laymen behave thus; but ere long you will find that the clergy will also render themselves culpable.

When the Holy Father will attempt to reform their morals, the ecclesiastics will offer the spectacle of a grievous scandal to the whole Church; they will ravage and divide it as though they were heretics." This prediction, which evidently refers to *the Great Western Schism*, was soon to be verified.

It was most likely about the year 1370 that our Lord made known to Saint Catherine that thenceforth her life would be filled with such amazing prodigies that ignorant and sensual men would refuse to believe them. "I will diffuse in thy soul such an abundance of grace that thy body will experience its effects and will live no longer except in an extraordinary manner." This extraordinary manner of life, to which our Lord had reference, was her miraculous existence; for from this time till her death, ten years later, Catherine lived on practically no food save the Blessed Sacrament. The vital functions of her body became so modified that food was barely necessary; nourishment caused her serious suffering, sometimes almost precipitating death. Relatives and friends called this favor from God a snare of Satan, and even Friar Thomas commanded her to take food daily, and advised her to give heed to no vision telling her to the contrary. The Saint ate, according to her confessor's commands, but was reduced to such a state that fears were entertained for her life. Sending for Friar Thomas, she proposed him this dilemma: "Father, if, through excessive fasting, I was in danger of death, would you not prohibit my fasting, so as to prevent me from committing suicide?" "Without doubt," replied her confessor. "If, therefore," she resumed, "you see that I am killing myself by taking nourishment, why do you not forbid me, as you would forbid me to fast, if the fast produced a similar result?" Friar Thomas told her that thenceforth she should act according to the inspirations of the Holy Ghost. From the beginning of Lent until the Feast of the Ascension the Saint took no food save the Eucharist. On Ascension Day she partook of a little bread and vegetables; then, recommencing this marvelous manner of life, she interrupted her fast only at long intervals. Thin and nerve-broken and physically shattered as she was, always suffering intense pain, continually persecuted—even by friars of her own Order and by her sisters in religion—still all contemporaries bear witness to the strength and gayety of her soul and to her extraordinary personal charm. The frequent receptions of the Body of her Lord was the secret of this vitality. Many persons, among whom were some religious, murmured at this procedure, and Friar Thomas went so far as sometimes to deprive her of this grace. Blessed Raymond later defended her conduct in this matter by offering proofs from the Scriptures, from the practice of the Church, from the Fathers and Doctors, particularly from the Angelic Doctor, to the effect that frequent and even daily Communion is not only profitable, but most praiseworthy also, if the recipient in the state of grace approach the Sacred Banquet with great devotion and reverence. Catherine would often sigh for the Bread of Angels. "Father, I am hungry," she would say; "for the love of God, feed my soul." For this reason the Holy Father, Gregory XI, by a special bull gave her permission to have a priest and a portable altar, so that she could everywhere and always hear Mass and receive Holy Communion. One day, while Blessed Raymond was saying Mass, the Divine Spouse took a particle of the Sacred Host from the corporal and bore it to Saint Catherine, who was kneeling at the rear of the church, as had also happened in the case of little Blessed Imelda. Often after the reception of her Eucharistic King she was transported into ecstasies and God would reveal to her the *arcana Dei*—the hidden things of God.

The heavenly visions and colloquies at this period of Catherine's life were so numerous and so prolonged that Blessed Raymond tells us, were he to recount them all, time rather than materials should fail him. Friar Thomas di Fonte, her first confessor, wrote four books containing these admirable apparitions and revelations, which unfortunately have been lost. It was about this time that Catherine's Celestial Bridegroom exchanged hearts with her, and seemed to introduce her soul into His Sacred Side. Often the saints would appear to converse familiarly with her, especially Saint Agnes of Montepulciano. During the summer of 1370 she received a series of special manifestations of divine mysteries, which culminated in a long ecstasy, in which she was shown Hell, Purgatory, and Heaven, and heard the voice of her Divine Spouse commanding her to return to life in order to show those who offend His Majesty what glory they lose and what shame and suffering they endure who live and die in a state of sin. Saint Catherine was greatly confused at the thought of returning again to life. But our Lord then added these words: "Daughter, the salvation of many souls demands it; thou shalt no longer live as thou hast done; henceforth thou must renounce thy cell continually and pass through the city, in order to save souls. I will always attend thee; I will conduct thee and reconduct thee; I will confide to thee the honor of My Holy Name, and thou shalt teach My doctrine to the lowly and to the great, to laymen, priests, and monks; I will impart to thee speech and wisdom which none can resist; I will place thee in the presence of Pontiffs and the rulers both of the Church and of the State, so as to confound, in My way and by this means, the arrogance of the mighty."

While the humble Tertiary was carrying on her mission of charity, some time during the years 1366–1368—that is, from the time of her mystical espousals until the dissolution of the popular government called *The Twelve*—a terrible revolution had broken out in Siena. *The Party of the Twelve*, then in power, bore a hatred toward the nobles, who in turn detested their rule and plotted their overthrow. The Servant of God at this time brought about a reconciliation between the factions, by no means an easy task for a young woman, unschooled in diplomacy, who, although of no party, was notwithstanding a commoner by birth. Like reconciliations and social readjustments, effected on her part, were not of uncommon occurrence. "One of her first triumphs," says a biographer, "was the reconciliation of the Maconi with the Tolomei and Rinaldini, three families of the Sienese nobility." Stephen Maconi, a member of the first-named family, became a devoted disciple and private secretary to the Saint, and upon her death, according to her holy wish, entered the monastery, later becoming the General of the Carthusians.

Immediately after the mystical death, Saint Catherine entered very extensively the public life of the world and began to gather followers round her, both men and women, who formed a wonderful spiritual fellowship, united to her by the bonds of purest love. With these companions she went about *the Virgin's City* everywhere doing good. Soon the news of her sanctity spread abroad. Multitudes flocked to Siena to hear her words of counsel and be converted from their sins. In 1374 Blessed Raymond was given to Catherine as confessor by the Mother of God. In the September of this year the plague broke out in Siena and worked direst havoc. Raymond, who was animated with charity, did not allow the inhabitants to be deprived of his ministry; and Catherine was the angel of the plague-stricken, curing many who were at the point of death. During this time the Servant of God went to Pisa, having been called thither by many of the citizens, but above all by the sisters of a certain convent. Blessed Raymond and several other Dominicans accompanied her so as to hear the confessions of those that were moved by her fervent words. The Sovereign Pontiff granted to the priests that went along on her journeys the right to absolve in all reserved cases. At Pisa, as everywhere she visited, they witnessed many marvelous cures. Returning to Siena, her confessor was at last stricken down by the disease and was about to die a victim of his charity. His spiritual daughter, however, was watching over him, and, foreseeing the great services he would one day render the Church, obtained the restoration of his health, upon which he immediately returned to his sick. When the epidemic had diminished, he made a pilgrimage to the tomb of Saint Agnes of Montepulciano, whose life he had written, and it was on this occasion that a heavenly manna came down on him and Saint Catherine, who had taken part in the excursion. In 1375 Raymond left Siena, with a letter from Catherine, to persuade the English brigand, John Hawkwood, to cease his pillaging raids and to defend the Holy See with his troopers. "Brother Raymond, my father and my son, comes to you," read the opening lines. "Have faith in what he tells you, for he is a faithful servant of God, and will only advise you for the Divine honor and for the salvation and glory of your soul." Hawkwood promised and held his word. On the 15th of April, the same year, Catherine and Raymond were at Pisa, and it was on that occasion that our Lord favored His Servant with the stigmata, but upon her request the marks did not appear outwardly in her body while she lived.

The year 1375 brings us to that period in the life of Benincasa's saintly daughter for which the world knows her best. But before we write of her as one of the leaders of reform in the Church at this dark period of its history, it will be well to give a notion of one of the means she employed in effecting this reform. This medium was her copious correspondence.

The correspondence of the Saint still extant embraces a collection of nearly 400 letters. We are told that she could dictate three different letters at once to her three secretaries, and that her correspondents included kings and princes and rulers of republics, leaders of armies, and private citizens alike. Her letters to Popes Gregory XI and Urban VI are sometimes almost dictatorial; but she was their most loyal daughter and poured wise counsel into their ears. It is quite impossible in a few words to give an adequate idea of the matter and manner of these letters. Some are valuable documents to the historian, while others, especially those written to private persons, men and women in the cloister or in the world, are either like practical discourses of advice and guidance to the devout, or, again, like short exquisite treatises on the mystical life for the privileged souls of God. They are written in the Tuscan dialect and, with her series of "Prayers" and the "Dialogue," rank among the classics of the Italian language.

Pope Clement V, elected in 1305, was crowned at Lyons. Clement never saw Rome, and, after visiting several French cities, chose Avignon as his residence. Thus it was that in 1309 the Roman Court was transferred to France, an event which proved very disastrous to the interests of the Holy See and to the welfare of Italy. The Papacy, except for a short interim, remained in the little rock-perched town for nearly seventy consecutive years and became politically a mere vassal of France, for which reason this epoch of Church history has become commonly known as *the Babylonian Captivity*. Rome, during the absence of the Popes, had fallen into ruins and was often the scene of terrible strife and bloodshed, while many cities of the Italian peninsula were frequently in open revolt with the common Father of Christendom. Historians have, as a rule, drawn too lurid a portrait of each of the seven French Pontiffs; but that they lived in luxury and were too much fettered by the power of France, sometimes adopting its policy, greatly prejudicial to the common weal of other nations, cannot be denied. It was in view of this and the deplorable state of affairs in the Eternal City, caused by tyrants, such as Cola di Rienzi, that, shortly after the election of Clement VI, fourth in the Avignon line, a deputation headed by Stephen Colonna and the poet Petrarch supported a petition for the restoration of the Popes to their proper residence. After two months of hesitation the Holy Father replied that the times were not propitious. The sixth Pope, Urban V, returned to Rome at the request of Charles IV, Petrarch, and Saint Bridget, in 1367, but soon became homesick for his fair Provence. In vain did the holy Swedish princess, Bridget, threaten Urban with the wrath of God and early death if he returned. In vain the Roman senate besought him to remain. After three years the successor of Peter bade farewell to the shrine of the Prince of the Apostles, and during the September of 1370 entered again the Papal Palace at Avignon. He swore upon illness to come back to Rome, but died in December of the same year. Pope Gregory XI followed him in the Pontificate.

Pope Gregory, upon his election, had appointed legates as rulers in the Papal States and as representatives in the various republics of the peninsula. These were for the most part foreigners, and as such universally hated. The black plague of 1374 was followed by a dire famine in Tuscany, and owing to the misgovernment of Papal officials it was with the greatest difficulty that corn might be procured from the States of the Church. The city of Florence, together with eighty others, defied the Pope. Led astray by certain factions and incensed by the atrocities of the Papal Nuncio, the populace of Florence flayed him alive in the streets, and actually buried him before life was extinct. Nor did the maddened mob stop at this. They desecrated churches and massacred priests. Moreover, sixty strongholds belonging to the Church fell into the hands of the Florentines. Gregory XI replied by excommunicating the authors of these violent acts and placing the city under an interdict. The Florentines for the most part disregarded these measures and formally declared war on the Pope. Saint Catherine was then at Pisa, using every effort to keep the city in peace, for the Pope had commissioned her to secure the neutrality of Pisa, Lucca, and Siena. Hearing of the breach between Florence and the Papacy, she immediately dispatched letters to the Pontiff, asking his indulgence, to which he responded by sending viceroys to the Republic with propositions of peace; but the upshot of all the negotiations, on this occasion, was a state of affairs worse than before. Finally, however, some of the better disposed citizens sought a competent mediator to reconcile them with the Church. But who were they to choose?

Casting about for one whose mediation at the Papal Court might bring a lasting peace, a great number of the Florentine nobility besought Saint Catherine of Siena, whose sanctity shone throughout all Italy, to accompany her confessor on this urgent mission. It was no new thing for her to be called upon to reconcile enemies, so she threw her whole soul into this proposal, for it meant the healing of the wounds of the Church. Blessed Raymond went to Avignon in March, 1376, to predispose minds for peace. Catherine arrived there as the ambassador of the Florentines, either in April or June of the same year, and was received by the Pope with the greatest honor. She speedily obtained from the Sovereign Pontiff the grant of a general armistice for the Florentine people, but, owing to a few seditious members in the constantly changing government, who influenced the populace to freshened revolts, negotiations again fell through.

Although the primary purpose of Catherine's journey to Provence had been thwarted, nevertheless the Church derived great benefit on account of her presence there. In all her conferences with His Holiness, the Saint spoke in the Tuscan tongue, and, as Gregory was a Frenchman by birth, Raymond translated her words into the Latin. This he also did when Catherine addressed the Pope by letter, which was frequently her custom, to avoid appearing in the splendid palace and to escape the opposition of many of the Cardinals. She implored the Holy Father to leave Avignon, urging his departure as the best means of procuring peace with Florence and of ending the incessant turmoil through the entire peninsula. This latter was, previous to her mission from the Florentines, a subject of her correspondence with the irresolute Pope. Gregory, though highly cultured, was yet deplorably lacking in those qualities which go to make up the equipment of a supreme ruler and chief pastor of Christendom. Easily influenced by false advisers, a slave to family affections, practically controlled by the French king, though he felt the inestimable value of the Seraphic Virgin's counsels and the inevitable cogency of her reasonings, and was touched by the irresistible power of her sanctity, still he lingered. And Catherine, finding him vacillating in his resolve, dictated letter after letter, each growing in insistence. Finally, she sent Blessed Raymond to consult with the Pope, and wrote a still more urgent missive: "I tell you, on behalf of Christ crucified, it befits you to achieve three chief things through your power." These three things were the reform of the clergy, the crusade against the Turks, and the return to Rome. In an earlier letter she had urged: "Have a care for spiritual things alone, for good shepherds, good rulers in your cities, since on account of bad shepherds and rulers you have encountered rebellion. ... Up, then, Father, and no more negligence. Raise the gonfalon of the most Holy Cross, for with the fragrance of the Cross you shall win peace. I beg you to summon those who have rebelled against you to a holy peace, so that all warfare may be turned against the infidels." In the former of these letters quoted from Catherine continues: "Do you uproot in the garden of Holy Church the malodorous flowers, full of impurity and avarice, swollen with pride—that is, the bad priests and rulers who poison and rot that garden. Ah me! you our Governor, do you use your power to pluck out those flowers. Throw them away, that they may have no rule. Insist that they study to rule themselves in holy and good life. Plant in this garden fragrant flowers, priests and rulers who are true servants of Jesus Christ, and care for nothing but the honor of God and the salvation of souls, and are fathers of the poor. ... But reflect, sweet Father, that you could not do this easily unless you accomplished the other two things which precede the completion of this—that is, your return to Rome and the uplifting of the standard of the most Holy Cross. ... I tell you come, come, come, and do not wait for time, since time does not wait for you." No artifices were spared by most of the Cardinals, the power of France, and the enemies of the Church to deter the Pope from his design. The humble daughter of the Sienese dyer at length prevailed: in spite of the opposition of the French king and almost the entire Sacred College, Gregory XI overcame by her help all the obstacles set in his way. It is even said that when Gregory's aged father threw himself across the palace gateway, declaring that the Pope should depart only if he passed over his body, Gregory stepped calmly over the prostrate form and passed out of Avignon, thus ending that veritable Babylonish captivity, the seventy years' exile of the Papacy.

On September 13th, 1376, the Holy See bade a lasting farewell to Avignon. Catherine began her journey homeward at the same time as Gregory; but while the Holy Father set out to sea at Marseilles, she and her companions took the land route. The Saint stopped at Toulon, Varazze—the birthplace of Blessed James of Voragine—and Genoa. In these places, as in all the intermediary villages, the inhabitants desired to see her. Several miracles are recorded as having happened at this time. At Toulon she cured a deformed infant. At Varazze, upon Catherine's advice, the inhabitants made a vow to build a church dedicated to the most Holy Trinity if they were delivered from the plague, which favor was granted them. It was in the same town that the Servant of God received certain heavenly instructions concerning the value of indulgences, which Raymond wrote down in his own hand; and here also on the feast of Saint Francis of Assisi she predicted that a few years thence Raymond would translate her body from one tomb to another. Here, too, God revealed to His daughter that He had granted her confessor the remission of all his sins. The Saint was delayed at Genoa for some weeks on account of the illness of one of her companions; and there Gregory arrived on October 18th, having suffered shipwreck off the coast of Tuscany. The Pope remained ten days, often having interviews with Catherine and Raymond, to receive from both the encouragement and information concerning people and events, of which he stood in need. Then the Pontiff regained his galleys to continue his way to Corneto, where he arrived on December 6th. Ascending the Tiber on January 15th, 1377, he disembarked at Saint Paul's on the 17th, and on the 18th, the feast of the Chair of Saint Peter at Rome, made his triumphal entry into the Capital of Christendom, amid the joyful acclamation of the multitude.

This much Catherine had wrought; and, having returned to Siena, she spent the greater part of 1377 in effecting a marvelous religious revival in the country districts of her own beloved Republic. Early in 1378 Gregory sent for Catherine to come to Rome, thence to go to Florence to treat of peace. Unfortunately, says Gardner, "through the factious conduct of her Florentine associates, she became involved in the internal politics of the city, and during a popular tumult (22d June, 1378) an attempt was made upon her life." Catherine was much disappointed at her escape, for she always desired one day to cull, according to her own expression, the ruddy rose of martyrdom. Nevertheless she remained in the territory of the Republic, perhaps at Vallombrosa, until the revolution known as *the Tumult of the Ciompi* was ended, and peace was at last concluded with the new Pope, Urban VI. Gregory XI, being surrounded by discontented French Cardinals, who constantly urged retreat to Avignon, had failed to establish either peace or reform in his dominions, and had died on the 27th of March, 1378.

After the peace of Florence with the Holy See was concluded, Catherine instantly returned to Siena and passed a few months of comparative seclusion dictating her *Dialogue* or Treatise on Divine Providence. She told her secretaries to be present during her ecstasies and to record whatever she might dictate. Thus in a short time a book was composed in the form of colloquies between a soul and God, treating of the whole spiritual life. Edmund Gardner calls this work "the mystical counterpart in prose of Dante's *Divina Commedia*."

In the meantime the Great Schism was dividing the Church. Urban VI was lawfully elected on the 9th of April, 1378, and was duly crowned, recognized, and acclaimed as legitimate Pope and successor of Saint Peter. Wishing, however, during the first days of his Pontificate, to restore to the Roman Church the beauty of ancient days, he commenced a reform of abuses so drastic that many were disappointed by the nature of his government. Catherine now pleaded moderation, and in her first letter to Urban told him to "act with benevolence and a tranquil heart, and for the love of Jesus to restrain a little those too-quick movements with which nature" inspired him. Instead of striving to conciliate the French Cardinals, the Pontiff covered them with reproaches and accusations and denounced their vices; and, while he alienated them by his severity, he took no heed of Catherine's advice to create new Cardinals to counterbalance their influence. Suffice it here to say, that all but one of the Cardinals who had elected Urban went to Fondi, and, declaring Urban deposed, elected there in his stead Robert of Geneva, on the 20th September, 1378, who took the name of Clement VII, and soon went to Avignon.

From the first Saint Catherine adhered to the true Pope, Urban VI, who in November, 1378, summoned her to Rome, where she spent for the most part the two remaining years of her life, laboring her utmost for the deliverance of the mystical Body of Christ. She wrote letters everywhere in behalf of the Roman claimant, Pope Urban. Writing to the three Italian Cardinals, who joined the French members of the Sacred College, she exclaims: "You have deserted the light and gone into darkness; the truth, and joined you to a lie; . . . before Christ on earth began to sting you, you confessed Him and reverenced Him. . . . But this last fruit that you bear, which brings forth death, shows what kind of trees you are, and that your tree is planted in the earth of pride, which springs from the self-love that robs you of the light of reason." In another letter she writes: "You have turned to flight, like cowardly knights. . . . It is you who have taught me not to believe you. . . . Whoever is not for the truth is against the truth. Whoever at Fondi was not for Christ on earth, for Pope Urban, was against him. I tell you, you have done ill, you and the antipope; and I repeat that it is a member of the devil who has been elected." Several times she took it upon herself to send Blessed Raymond on an embassy to Charles the V, King of France, whom she desired to turn away from the Schism. Upon Urban's wish she and her sister in saintliness, Catherine of Sweden, daughter of Saint Bridget, were to proceed together to rally the crafty Queen Jane of Naples to the Roman obedience. Saint Catherine of Sweden, however, did not like to undertake the voyage. Raymond, therefore, spoke with the Pontiff, who concluded it would be imprudent to permit them to go. Saint Catherine of Siena, however, wrote letters to Jane, but these remained unanswered and without result. Some nations went over bodily to the obedience of the antipope, Clement VII. England, under Richard II, who strove to ascertain the real facts concerning the conclave which elected Urban, never swerved from the Roman obedience. Having arrived at an inevitable conclusion as to the validity of Urban's election, Richard wrote to Peter, King of Arragon, who, with Wenceslaus, Emperor of Bohemia, decided in the true Pope's favor. It is well established, though unfortunately the letter is lost, that Catherine wrote to the King of England at the beginning of the Schism, and it is quite probable that her missive was the reason of his faithfulness. In December, 1378, Raymond embarked at Ostia on an embassy from the Pope to King Charles V of France. Thither Catherine accompanied him. Raymond did not reach the French court, and the French king remained a firm supporter of the dissentient Cardinals and Clement VII. Before the ship slipped cable, Catherine addressed her confessor in the following words: "My son, all is over; you will never see me again in this world." Then, kneeling down on the beach, she made the sign of the Cross over the departing vessel, a scene which recalled the last farewell, in the same port of Ostia, between Saint Monica and Saint Augustine. The Saint returned to Rome, working indefatigably for the Church, and her last political enterprise, practically accomplished from her death-bed, was the reconciliation of the Roman Republic with Pope Urban VI.

The Seraphic Virgin's strength rapidly became consumed, and she died what may be described as a martyr's death, having offered her life to her Divine Bridegroom, for the sins of the world. "Be assured," she wrote to Pope Urban, "that if I die the sole cause of my death is the zeal which consumes me for the Holy Church." In the end it seemed to her that the responsibility of this distraught condition of Christendom rested on her shoulders. From Sexagesima Sunday until the Sunday before the Ascension she suffered most excruciating pain, both in soul and body. Lying on planks, it appeared she was already in her coffin, and it was only when the Holy Eucharist was brought to her that her body seemed again enkindled with life. Shortly before her death she gave instructions to her spiritual companions, who with deepest sorrow were watching the approach of her last moments. On the 29th of April, the feast of Saint Peter Martyr, in the year of the birth of Saint Bernardine of Siena, 1380, she passed to her Divine Spouse.

Saint Catherine was buried in Rome. The pious mutilation of her body took place in 1385, at the time of its translation by the Master General of the Dominican Order, Blessed Raymond. The head was borne to Siena, where today it is inclosed in a reliquary in Saint Dominic's Church, and is rightly considered the town's most precious treasure. Small portions of her body were sent to enrich the convents and churches in which her memory is honored, while the greater part of her holy remains rests at Rome, in the Church of the Minerva.

Many miracles were worked by the Saint's intercession after her death, and in 1461 she was canonized by Pope Pius II. Her principal feast is celebrated on the 30th of April. In our own times she has been proclaimed Patroness of the Eternal City. The Catholic world rightly finds in Seraphic Saint Catherine a heroine to match the hero Seraphic Saint Francis of Assisi; both were souls at the topmost summits of divine faith and love, who, notwithstanding their rigid asceticism and unique mysticism, have won by their strong and fascinating personalities the unstinted admiration of even the less Christian world.

BIBLIOGRAPHY

RAYMOND OF CAPUA, BLESSED: "Life of St. Catherine of Siena." Translated from the French by the Ladies of the Sacred Heart. (Philadelphia, 1859.) (New York, reprint.)

DRANE, A. T.: "The History of St. Catherine of Siena and Her Companions." (London, 1887.)

GARDNER, E. G.: "St. Catherine of Siena." (London and New York, 1907.)

ANTONY, C. M.: "Saint Catherine of Siena, Her Life and Times." (London, 1915.)

THOROLD, A.: "The Dialogue of St. Catherine of Siena." (London, 1898.)

SCUDDER, V. D.: "Saint Catherine of Siena as Seen in Her Letters." (London, New York, 1905.)

Saint Vincent Ferrer

"OMING EVENTS cast their shadows before," is an old saying. In the case of Saint Vincent Ferrer the truth of the proverb seems to have been brought out in a striking manner. We recall the calm and solemn style in which the Evangelists tell of the birth of our Saviour; how, consciously or unconsciously we know not, they create the atmosphere of tranquillity and peace that was to be so characteristic of the Prince of Peace. The leading characters in the wondrous scene that was to be enacted at Bethlehem had so long lived in the silent repose of innocence they seemed not to notice that mankind had finally layed aside its weapons, but went quietly to the City of David to be enrolled. In contrast to this idyllic calm is the commotion that went before the birth of Saint Vincent Ferrer.

Strange to say, his mother felt not the pains that are inseparably connected with pregnancy, but enjoyed a continual and indescribable gladness. The father dreamed that a Dominican announced to him that his son to be would one day enter the Order of Preachers. A poor woman when giving thanks for an alms astounded the mother of the Saint by crying out, "O! happy mother, it is an angel that you bear, and one day he will give me my sight." A wonderful saying, and prophetic! General interest became so aroused that at the birth of the child the City Council decided that the magistrates should act as sponsors.

Thus heralded and thus attended upon, Saint Vincent Ferrer, the second son and fourth child of William Ferrer and Constance Miguel, was born into the world at Valencia, in Spain, on the 23d

Saint Vincent Ferrer

of January, 1350. He was baptized the same day in the Church of Saint Stephen. After much wrangling about a name, the parish priest settled the dispute by calling him after Saint Vincent Martyr.

The Ferrer family was of English origin. A hundred years before, some of them took part in the conquest of Valencia and had been ennobled for their service. But our Saint did not belong to the branch that had been raised to the nobility. He was a commoner.

The young Vincent was watched over by a solicitous mother, who could never forget under what extraordinary circumstances God had given her this precious child. He grew up in innocence, and at once his mind began to turn to God, of whom he never tired hearing in sermons and instructions. At school he outclassed all his companions, as is evidenced by the fact that he began his classical course when eight years old. He finished his philosophy and took up theology when he was but fourteen.

Surely a brilliant career in the ecclesiastical life was open to this young man. His parents procured beneficies for him, but to no avail. God had destined him for the Dominican Order, and obedient to a call he heard while listening to a sermon, the future glory of the Church in Spain and the prince of preachers knocked at the door of the priory in Valencia and humbly asked admission. On the feast of Saint Agatha, February 5, 1367, he received the white habit. Vincent was then in his eighteenth year.

In the religious life none other than the great Master of the Order could do for his model, and he set himself to follow faithfully in the footsteps of his Holy Father, Saint Dominic. While yet a simple novice, his penances were of the most rigorous type. Satan besought him to cease the senseless persecution of his body and hedged his life around with trying temptations and spiritual assaults. But the supreme test of his sincerity came when his crying and disconsolate mother begged him to leave the cloister and serve God in the secular ranks. Truly this was a severe trial. The young novice was too affectionate to see in his fond parent anything like a worldly ambition, as he was too candid with God to be able to forget the resolution he had made to leave the world to follow Him whose standard was the daily cross of the religious life. He was torn between love of parent and love of God, but the latter was the stronger. Severe as was the temptation and greatly as it grieved Vincent, he gently but firmly refused to take off the habit.

After solemn profession, February 6, 1368, he studied at Tarragona and two years later was appointed Lector of Philosophy by the chapter held in Valencia. After a time he continued his course in Scripture and Hebrew at Barcelona. It was here that the Saint, while yet a deacon, made a remarkable public prophecy, when in the course of a sermon he told a starving people that by nightfall long-looked-for relief would arrive. Though he was severely censured for this statement, his words came true. After a year's work at Toulouse he was ordained to the priesthood by Clement VII in 1379.

Having been elected Prior of Valencia toward the end of the same year he began eagerly to support the cause of the antipope. His position in the affair made him very unpopular with the city magistrates; so, to avoid any strife, Saint Vincent resigned his office. From then on till he was called to Avignon by Peter de Luna, who had succeeded Clement VII as Benedict XIII, his time was taken up with giving lectures in philosophy and theology and in preaching Lenten and Advent courses in the foremost pulpits of the land.

In 1395 Benedict XIII called Saint Vincent to Avignon. Even then the Spanish Dominican was known far and wide. The ability with which he held the Chair of Theology in the Cathedral of Valencia; the excellence of his lectures; the astounding influence of his various Lenten courses, all these had made him a conspicuous figure among many prominent members of the Order in his native country. Furthermore, he showed the comprehensiveness of his sympathy and the universality of his genius in the manner in which he handled the uprisings against the Jews in Valencia in 1391 and later on in Toledo. About this time, too, he was made confessor to Queen Yolande, the wife of King John I, the woman he cured of curiosity in an amusing manner when, prying around to watch the Saint at his prayers, he was seen by all others, but was invisible to her who was inquisitive even to disobedience. Commanded to follow the Court, he obeyed, though it was understood that he was not to be hindered in preaching the Word of God. His eloquence was electrical. Whenever he spoke enthusiasm knew no bounds, and an impressionable people went to excess endeavoring to show their gratitude. It was not uncommon that bolder ones among the throng would crowd about the friar and cut pieces from his habit with which they worked miracles without number. But then, even as now, "place and greatness had millions of false eyes stuck upon it, and volumes of report ran with these false and most contrarious quests upon its doings." The great preacher was accused of heresy and summoned before the Inquisition. Benedict XIII, who knew Saint Vincent too well, would not tolerate this insult to his friend and at once ordered the proceedings closed and called the eloquent Dominican to Avignon, as has been said, in 1395.

Peter de Luna, who followed Clement VII in the false papacy of Avignon, was, as historians have shown, no true Pope. It may be of interest, however, to look a little more closely at de Luna, as he played a rather important part in Saint Vincent's life.

Antipope Benedict XIII was of noble birth, rich, talented, and of severe life. These, coupled with the gifts of fortitude and prudence, made him a favorite with Pope Gregory, the immediate predecessor of Urban VI, in whose time the schism began. Paradoxical, as it may seem, it was the existence of these great qualities in de Luna that made Saint Vincent's position at the Court so trying. In the capacity of Confessor and Chaplain to the Pope, Apostolic Penitentiary, and some say Master of the Sacred Palace, he certainly found enough to engage all his attention. But add to this the fact that Peter de Luna was quite an extraordinary man with talents that commanded respect, and abilities that were recognized; with prudence that savored of cunning diplomacy, if not rank duplicity; with fortitude that lapsed into rashness, and still was known for the rigor of his life, and we have a combination that might easily have puzzled even a saint. Brother Vincent was often called into consultation, and at an early date he discovered that he had a very untractable penitent on his hands, yet one he felt sure was Pope and one therefore who should be obeyed, difficult though as that task undoubtedly was. Benedict's actions during the schism show how greatly grieved Saint Vincent must have been, and how fearful he must have felt for the welfare of Mother Church.

To all appearances Peter de Luna was sincere in his efforts to end the schism when Clement was at Avignon, but a most remarkable change took place when he had the same power in his own hands. He always said that he desired the reunion of the Church, but his every action gave his words the lie. He became so stubborn that even an united Christendom at the Council of Constance could not move him.

In all good faith, Saint Vincent was a staunch defender of this man and Benedict fully realized early in his career as antipope what prestige was given his claims and his government by the active support of the influential Dominican. But it appears that when engaged in the calling as Messenger of the Judgment, the Saint did not directly busy himself about the details of the schism. Instead he was pointing out the only sure way the rupture could be healed and that was by a complete reversion to God and to the spirit of the Gospel. Saint Vincent was held in such high regard that he did not need to engage in constant striving to strengthen the cause of Avignon. Spain was friendly to the antipope, and it became doubly so when he espoused the same party. Toward the end, when the schism had spent itself, a universal reversion to Rome was taking place, and Spain inevitably would have followed suit. But, as even contemporaries admit, it was due to Saint Vincent's prompt action that a great portion of the Avignon support did not prolong the division when it became possible at Constance to end it. In 1415 King Ferdinand asked Saint Vincent to decide the case. The latter used all his influence and all his eloquence to persuade Benedict to resign, but he labored in vain. Then, after due consideration and prayer, he replied, saying that since Benedict was stubbornly resisting a necessary union and was giving grave public scandal, obedience should be withdrawn from him. Ferdinand and the assembly of bishops representing the Avignon allegiance confirmed this as has all subsequent history. The Saint preached on January 6, 1416, to 10,000 persons and read the withdrawal of obedience from Benedict. This was the death-knell of the latter's power and the signal for a solemn Te Deum and universal rejoicing at Constance, because then the peace of the Church was assured. "Without you," wrote the famous Gerson to Master Vincent, "this could not have taken place."

It has been a matter of concern to many that saints should have been on opposite sides during the schism. It should be remembered that the times were abnormal, but more important is it to keep in mind that saints are human. Salembier says, "Christendom was quickly divided into two almost equal parties. Everywhere the faithful faced the anxious problem, Where is the true Pope? . . . The conflict of rival passions and the novelty of the situation rendered understanding difficult and unanimity impossible. As a general thing scholars adopted the opinion of their country." He might have added that the holy men and women of the time acted in the same fashion.

But what did the call to Avignon mean to the Saint? It meant, first of all, that a thorough-going religious was torn away from his community and his "heaven," as he always called his cell. It meant that a close student and man of thought was suddenly thrown into a whirlpool of excitement and business at a time when affairs were very far from normal. That Saint Vincent was not a dismal failure in these circumstances, we think it can be said in truth, was due to his Dominican training for reasons upon which it will be advisable to dwell in another portion of this paper.

Though the Saint was coping successfully with the difficulties and labors concomitant with his high position at Court, the strain was too great for the body that had been treated so unmercifully to bring it into perfect subjection to his will. He fell seriously ill and, in fact, all hope for his recovery had been abandoned. In the time of trial and physical prostration God vouchsafed to give him a most unusual calling. "Nearly fifteen years ago," Saint Vincent wrote in 1412, "a religious who was dangerously ill asked God to restore him to health that he might preach His Word. And, as he prayed, Saint Dominic and Saint Francis appeared to him, kneeling and praying with him. At their prayer our Blessed Lord appeared to the sick religious, and, touching him familiarly with His All Holy Hand, made known to him in an interior manner, but very clearly, that it was his mission to go forth and preach to men even as the two saints present had done. At the touch of that Divine Hand the religious rose up healed of his sickness." Needless to say, he was relating the story of his own cure, which occurred on October 3, 1398. Ever prompt in his obedience, the Confessor to the Pope at once asked to be dismissed from Avignon, that he might take up his mission. Benedict, however, perhaps because he may have been a little skeptical of Master Vincent's story, but certainly because he needed the help of this man, found means to delay his departure. Some time later our Lord appeared again and commanded him to take up his apostolic work. Thereupon this chosen one of God renewed his suit with the Pope, who finally gave his consent to the departure of his valued counselor.

Saint Vincent Ferrer was forty-nine years old when he took up the duties that were to engage all his time and strength for twenty long years. Contemporaries tell us that he was of medium height, with a high forehead and fair hair. His color, though he was a Spaniard, was pale.

He left Avignon late in the year 1399, armed with all the power and authority Benedict could give him. The first record we have of him in his new capacity is that of a sermon preached on December 24, in the Dominican Church, before the Bishop and magistrates of Carpentras. From there he journeyed in February, 1400, to Arles. During the space of almost two years he confined his activities to Aix and the surrounding country, including Dauphine, Savoy, and the Alpine valleys. Later he visited the Grande Chartreuse, where Boniface, his brother, was General of the Order, and of these men an annalist naïvely remarks, "that God worked wonders by means of these two brothers. Those who were converted by the preaching of one brother received the religious habit from the other."

"Those who were converted by the preaching of one brother" were even at this time scarcely within reckoning. The wonderful preacher did not spare himself in carrying out the mandate of Heaven. His days were spent in seeking out sinners, exhorting and persuading them to leave their evil ways, healing the sick, and settling the difficulties of thousands who sought his aid. As some one has said, "Every step was a miracle." This had one very great effect. A man who spoke as never man spoke before, who stirred up and brought around time-hardened sinners, who probed every moral malady to its cause that he might render effectual assistance, who lavished gifts, temporal and spiritual, with a munificent hand, and one who astounded more than half the Continent with prodigious manifestations of supernatural power—such a one could not travel about unaccompanied by a joyous and awe-struck band in those wonderful days, when Faith was young and fresh. And so the "Company" of Saint Vincent has become famous in history.

This Company was made up of priests, among whom were always some Dominicans, who stayed with the Master all the time and who were necessary for the confessions after the sermons, and to carry out the liturgy as the Saint desired. Then there were what might be called the penitents or, rather, converts. Some of these joined the Saint early in his career and remained till his death, but a great portion only followed to the border line of their province, while many others were left behind by the leader to begin works such as monasteries, hospitals, and bridges, or to continue others that had been begun under his supervision. Finally, were those that stayed with the Saint continually and who composed the main group of those who took part in the procession held daily at nightfall. These are called the Flagellantes, from the practice they had adopted of scourging themselves as the band wended its way through the city. These pilgrims generally wore the Dominican colors, black and white. Thrown in with these were men of every profession and state in life, skilled and unskilled hands, inexperienced young men and men gray with age. The mere mentioning of the elements that made up this Company of Saint Vincent is interesting; but we are forced to smile at the word Company and to open our eyes in astonishment upon learning that the number of the followers of the Saint reached as high as ten thousand at a time. What an impossibility in our days of superculture and superscience, but how characteristic of the ages of Faith! And to the greater glory of the Dominican leader it can be said that, despite the almost countless numbers that followed him for so many years, not a case of scandal or immorality or a single record of riotousness or outbreak can be found in the thousands of documents that exist concerning the Saint and his Company. Truly this is a remarkable fact, most significant of the powerful influence exercised by the Legate of Christ.

The Saint and his band went through the same exercises practically every day. Among the many remarkable things in Saint Vincent's life surely the routine amid all the traveling is not the least noteworthy. He rose every morning at 2 o'clock to recite Matins and Lauds chorally. After this he said the Psalter and read the Holy Scriptures. In summer at 6 and in winter at 7 o'clock he sang Mass, accompanied by the priests, who rendered the parts prescribed for the day, assisted by a portable organ when nothing better could be found. Immediately after Mass he preached, his discourse generally lasting about three hours. He abstained from all food till 1 o'clock and then only partook of a frugal meal. After that began his work among the poor and the sick, the rich and the strong and among those that needed any kind of help. He made use of the afternoons to visit the monasteries or convents that might chance to be in the town. At dusk was held the procession, and very frequently a bell was rung to call all those who had any infirmity from which they sought relief. Then it was that the flood-gates of grace were opened, and miracles were so numerous they became well-nigh commonplace.

After Saint Vincent left the Grande Chartreuse the records trace clearly his labors in northern Italy. It was at Alexandria he made the prophecy concerning Saint Bernardine of Siena, to the effect that the young man would one day enter the Order of Saint Francis, and that he would become a Saint and be canonized before Vincent himself. Continuing his journeys, he covered practically all of Piedmont, where a grateful people still have many a shrine to the lovable Spanish Friar. In 1403 he preached in Savoy, Switzerland, and Lyons. Embarking at some southern port unknown to us, Saint Vincent sailed for Flanders, in which country we first find the custom of ringing a bell for the sick to be brought to the Thaumaturgus.

God sent Saint Vincent as a very special messenger and he was commissioned to preach "in season and out of season." He followed out all his instructions, but he has made it difficult for any one to follow in the wake of his travels up and down and across the Continent. Père Fages, the authority on Saint Vincent, has done this perhaps as well as the work will ever be handled; but in a short paper such as this, it will be impossible to mark each stopping place in the endless quest for souls.

Suffice it to say that the great Dominican traveled the length and breadth of Spain, covered almost all of France, journeyed extensively in Italy, and penetrated far into Brittany and Normandy, though he never visited England or Ireland, as some have said. Perhaps a more useful work will have been accomplished if, instead of tracing Saint Vincent through the records of twenty long years of restless activity, we can give a more personal and detailed picture of a man who is too often looked upon with wonder only and too often entirely forgotten in the glamour of his miracles.

Beyond all shadow of doubt, Saint Vincent Ferrer received graces from God of the most extraordinary nature. In accordance with the plans of an omniscient Providence, God conferred special helps and virtues on the Saint when he was chosen to play so important a rôle in a time when the Church was in the disabling grasp of the schism. But we are apt to forget, looking at the matter from this angle only, that though God can use any instrument, He most frequently uses those that are best fitted for any particular work. We are liable, in other words, to get away from the human element that is in every saint, no matter to what unscalable heights he or she may have been raised by God. To lose sight of the human side of Saint Vincent's life is to fail in the understanding of a career the like of which has never been seen since the days of the Apostles.

The glorious son of Valencia, as we have pointed out, was extraordinarily endowed. The success of his early studies, the excellence of the works, "De Suppositionibus Dialecticis," "De Natura Universalis," and "De Schismo," show clearly a quick, clever, penetrating mind. Saint Vincent can receive little credit for ability gratuitously given, but he must be praised because he did not allow natural endowments to furnish him with specious arguments against the feverish pursuit of greater knowledge, as so often happens with men naturally brilliant. When a student, he sought to perfect all the faculties of his mind and soul by alternating study with prayer and prayer with study. Note carefully the studies in which our Saint was expert and it will explain a great many of his successes in later life. He was a Professor of Philosophy, a Lector of Theology, and was proficient in Scripture, Hebrew, and Arabic. Now his entire life as a preacher was spent treating with out-and-out heretics and unbelievers, such as relapsed Jews, unconverted Jews, and Moors; settling disputes between Catholic parties that were well versed in theology, and with the common people, who were hungering and thirsting after the solid food of the Gospel that had been so long denied them.

The Jews in Saint Vincent's time were by no means a negligible quantity, as they never will be so while creation lasts. They were rich and powerful and had all the means of pursuing the higher studies. History tells us that they did this. No man with a superficial knowledge of Biblical lore, a hazy notion of philosophy, or a bare smattering of Hebrew could argue day in and day out with rabbis, convince them of error, and change their synagogues into churches, as Saint Vincent did. No one with indefinite or undefinable ideas about inspiration or prophecy, or with a vague idea of the philosophy of history, or with a most elementary knowledge of Arabic could meet in endless discussion with the intellectually brilliant Moors and replace their Khoran with the Bible. Yet Saint Vincent did this. According to Jewish testimony, he converted over 200,000 of their belief to Christianity, and in the heart of Islamism in Spain, in romantic Alhambra, he converted 8,000 Moors. He would have brought them all to Christ had not slaves of Mohammed threatened revolution, and Master Vincent was asked to leave the city by the ruler, who was not at all unfavorably disposed toward him.

The great point is this, that Saint Vincent was ready when God called him. He was fitted out by his thorough Dominican training with all the panoply necessary for a successful war against ignorance, and he was armed for the moral struggle by habits deep rooted in the religious life. There is no need to have recourse to the supernatural in a great portion of the life of Saint Vincent, as we have more than enough palpable facts to show that much of his glory was achieved by the sweat of his brow. His career certainly was stamped with the supernatural; but this is almost incomprehensible if we do not take into account the human element of his achievements.

Still there is another feature that must be brought out, it seems, before one can truly analyze this wonderful life. Père Lacordaire says somewhere that "the first condition of a great life is a great ambition." The ambition of the Thaumaturgus of the Middle Ages was God-given. Saint Vincent was the Angel of the Apocalypse and he knew it. His sublime ambition was given in the angelic character of his vocation, but the fact that he realized this was the determination of his entire life, after the vision at Avignon. It will be recalled that before his birth the poor woman at Valencia surprised the mother of the Saint with the declaration that the child she bore was an angel. Saint Vincent must have known this; and though the expression could easily have been interpreted to mean the boy was to be of exceptional sanctity, still it appears to be a more specific prophecy in the light of the child's subsequent actions. That the Saint considered himself the Angel of the Apocalypse is certain beyond all possibility of doubt, and to prove his own statement to that effect he worked a miracle that to those present was nothing less than terrible.

In 1412, at Salamanca, he was preaching in an open place on account of the great concourse of people. In the course of the sermon he told his listeners that he was the angel spoken of by Saint John the Evangelist. Such a startling statement, we are ready to believe, caused comment in the crowd. By chance a corpse was being taken to a church near by and Saint Vincent called the pall-bearers to bring the remains to him. Then, before that immense throng, among whom were members of the Inquisition, he commanded the dead woman to come back to life and testify whether he spoke the truth or not. To the astonishment of all, the woman corroborated his contention and immediately fell back dead. Evidently the Legate of Christ was convinced of his calling. Benedict XIII allowed him the title he substantiated so fully; the Bull of canonization calls him the "angel flying through the heavens," and the Church has incorporated the expression in the lessons read on his feast. Again, another chosen one of God, Saint Louis Bertrand, calls him by the same unusual title. Many of Saint Vincent's actions can hardly be explained if we pass lightly over this determining factor, that he was, and he knew he was, the angel spoken of by the Evangelist.

Granted, then, that he was the Angel of the Apocalypse, what follows? In the first place, it made him what might be called a terrible in distinction to the more gentle and suave of the Saints. Acting in his capacity as a messenger of the Judgment, he created an atmosphere of fear and terror. When that resonant voice rang out like penetrating blasts from a silver trumpet, or when he cried out in stentorian tones that reached to a distance that was in itself miraculous, for sinners to repent, men, women, and children fell on their faces and cried aloud for mercy. Himself consumed with zeal, he inflamed a people that had grown old and cold in sin; with all the fiery eloquence of an ancient prophet, he pitilessly lashed the iniquity of a sinful generation. The effect was so great at times that the eloquence was stopped by the very outburst it created. Frequently in his sermons he was forced to stop to allow a terrified audience give vent to its feeling of dread and horror before he could proceed with his exhortation.

Again this calling accounts for the fact that the Saint gave frequent punishment. His terrible words and deeds were the means necessary to recall a people to its God. In the course of time he became a sort of privileged character, for men saw in him something of more than human authority. An example of this is the position he held at a discussion for a successor to the throne of Aragon. This kingdom had become without a ruler upon the deaths of Martin the Elder and Martin the Younger. At once six claimants sprang up, demanding the right of succession. The parliaments of Valencia, Catalonia, and Aragon called upon our Saint to take part in the deliberations. Nine judges were chosen, Saint Vincent being the eighth. The examination of the claims of the contestants took about thirty days. After that they proceeded to elect a king and a successor to the throne of Aragon. Though the great Dominican was second last on the list of arbiters, he voted first and gave his support to Ferdinand, the Infante of Castile. A majority voted in the same manner. The glorious deeds of Ferdinand justified the choice of Saint Vincent, and despite the grumbling and criticism of none too well disposed historians of the compromise of Caspe, the glorious Son of Valencia has merited the additional title of Pater Patriæ.

Let it not be understood, however, from what has been said above about the severe character of the Saint's mission, that he was heartless. He was nothing of the kind. He worked thousands of miracles, and most of them sprang from love and human sympathy. We must distinguish with Saint Vincent between his hate for sin and his love of the sinner, between his call to the sinner and his treatment of the same.

The Thaumaturgus of Europe was given most extraordinary gifts by God, but out of the many we shall enumerate but three.

As was said, Saint Vincent traveled over the larger portion of the Continent in obedience to his special vocation. One would naturally suppose, then, that he was conversant with no less than five or six languages. But the Saint used none other than his own Valencian dialect. Nevertheless, he was understood by all who heard him, as was his pious Brother in religion, Saint Louis, when he preached to the aborigines of America.

Saint Vincent likewise had the gift of prophecy. He foretold the coming of succor to the starving people of Barcelona; the canonization of Saint Bernardine of Siena, with the explicit detail that it would precede his own; the raising to the Papacy of Alphonsus Borgia, adding that this man would officially call him a Saint, and a list of others too long to be mentioned here. But the Saint has become famous for his prophecies concerning the end of the world and the Judgment and has raised a never-ending discussion as to their meaning and their non-fulfillment. He spoke almost always on these two subjects and was wont to exclaim again and again, "Cito, bene cito et valde breviter," "Soon, very soon, and within a short time," will come that frightful Day of Reckoning. Saint Vincent passed away in 1419 and the globe has not passed through the crucible of destruction he so frequently and dogmatically presaged. Was he a monumental impostor, or was he carried away by zeal to the realms of exaggeration?

To answer these questions it may be well to consider for a moment prophecy itself. Prophecy, in a strict sense, is the foreknowledge and foretelling of future events. The knowledge must come from God and must be expressed by the prophet in sign or in word. The one foretelling may have perfect or imperfect illumination of the mind. It is perfect when not only the thing revealed is known, but also the source of revelation—that is, when it is known for certain that God has spoken; it is imperfect when the source of revelation is not certainly known. As far as the object of the prophecy is concerned, there are three kinds, namely, prophecy of denunciation, of foreknowledge, and predestination. We shall content ourselves with dealing at length with the second of these, as it appears that Saint Vincent's predictions of the Dies Iræ fall under that category.

We have prophecy of foreknowledge "when God reveals future events which depend upon created free will and which He sees present from eternity." Of such a nature was Jonah's prophecy when he said positively, "Yet forty days, and Nineveh shall be destroyed." Nineveh repented and God spared the men of that city. And of such a nature, too, it is reasonable to hold, was Saint Vincent's prediction of the Judgment.

It may be objected immediately that the conversion of Nineveh was a future contingent thing, pure and simple, and that no parallel can be instituted between that and the Judgment, which must come necessarily, as it lies in the very nature of God, in the nature of man, and in the laws of good and evil. The fact that the Judgment is wrapped up in the three things mentioned is true; but the time, the exact date of the Final Call, certainly can be looked upon as a future contingency in so far as we are concerned. That we are to die is as true as Truth itself, but when we shall die is a contingency. But to say that God could not have placed a condition that was happily fulfilled by the preaching of Saint Vincent seems to derogate from the omnipotence of the Deity. By way of supplementary argument, we have the bold contention of Saint Antoninus that it was due to the wonderful preaching of our Saint that the destruction of the world was postponed.

What God did not do was to specify the exact time the destruction of the world and the final call to men was to take place. God has never done this. Saint Vincent himself never stated the certain date when all this was to take place, but maintained only that what was to come was coming in a very short time. We must study prophecy again for an explanation of this.

In the first place, "there is no suspension of the sense activities when anything is presented to the mind of the prophet through impressions of the senses, nor is it necessary when the mind is immediately enlightened that activities of the senses should be suspended." In fewer words, Saint Vincent was influenced by the state of the world at the time he received his illumination. The schism was on; prelates were giving much time to procuring benefices and to the pursuit of pleasure; priests neglected their people because the bishops first neglected them; monks and friars had little or no idea of discipline; universities, grown large with royal favor, were assuming unwarranted authority; heresy was thriving on the unhealthy air of ecclesiastical division, and finally Jews were being converted by the thousands. Little wonder was it that Saint Vincent may have thought the world was fast coming to the cataclysm so long ago foretold by Our Divine Saviour, as certainly any number of the things that were to precede it were taking place.

Nevertheless, there is yet another theory on which the Valencian Saint may be defended, and it is by no means the poorest argument in his favor. In the Epistle of Saint John (xii: 31) we read, "Now is the judgment of the world; now shall the prince of this world be cast out." And in the Apocalypse are the words, "The hour of His judgment is come." Finally, omitting other quotations, Saint Matthew says (xxiv: 34), "This generation shall not pass till all these things be done." Saint Vincent, then, was scriptural at any rate, and he never said anything stronger than the texts given. If exegetes think they can explain to their own satisfaction and without compromising the authors of the passages quoted, it should not be difficult to understand Saint Vincent, as he said identically the same thing. If he spoke of the particular judgment that is the lot of every one after death, he was correct. If he spoke of the General Judgment, we can still maintain that his words were true in so far as the Gospels are true, and that he did not err until it can be proved that God never made the destruction of the world at his time a condition of Saint Vincent's preaching. But, no matter what the explanation may be of the non-fulfillment of his words, Saint Vincent certainly had direct illumination from God, and no sane man will or can condemn him as an impostor, for, apart from all that has been said, he can be justified by what we know is the conditional prophetic threat. In other words, if people then had not repented his words would never have given rise to controversy; there would have been an end.

The last special gift of the Saint to be mentioned is that of miracles. After that of the Angel of the Apocalypse, there is no name more fitting the great Dominican than that of the Thaumaturgus. From the cradle to the grave his life was an unbroken chain of miracles. When yet in his swaddling clothes he cried out to his bewildered parent, "Carry me in procession and the drought will cease," and thus started a career of wonders that ended only with the last blessing of the Bretons with the promise that they should enjoy his intercession in Heaven—a blessing that has been miraculous—for, despite the universal decadence about them and in spite of the fiercest and most insidious onslaughts of heresy, these people have held fast to the faith so well taught them by Saint Vincent.

The Acta Sanctorum inform us of 873 miracles performed by the Saint. Though the number is eloquent of the power of this man of God, it by no means covers all his wonderful deeds. In 1412, when he told his audience he was the Angel seen by Saint John, he added that "God had wrought in His mercy, through him, a miserable sinner, three thousand miracles." Master Vincent lived seven years after this, and the greatest of his miracles were not prior to 1412. God is wonderful in His saints; still, perhaps one of the most astounding things read of these elect of Christ is the wholesale manner in which Saint Vincent performed miracles. Did not document after document solemnly assert the fact, we could scarcely believe that any one called together every evening with a bell the lame and the weak, the sick, and the dying, and restored them all to health and happiness! Saint Vincent has that distinction.

The Bollandists cite seventy persons as being delivered from diabolical possession; Saint Antoninus says that twenty-eight were raised from the dead, but he falls far short of the true number. Further enumeration would be useless. All the woes and afflictions of mankind, every species of physical distress and disease, moral maladies and death, all were set right by our Saint.

But, despite the glory with which God enhanced him, despite the honors conferred by popes and princes; despite the universal acclaim of the populace, Saint Vincent was an humble friar and he never lost sight of that fact. Now the ground plan of the life of every religious is determined at profession. This is especially true of a friar preacher, who in the formula of profession makes explicit mention of only one vow, namely, of Obedience. No matter what the superstructure may be or what may accrue to the spiritual edifice by way of accidental perfections, the entire building must be grounded in perfect submission of the will. In the final analysis, perfection of Obedience seems to be the reason why Saint Vincent Ferrer became the great figure of his age and such a bright light among so many luminaries in the Church.

His entrance into the Dominican Order was in obedience to a call by God; his progress in the novitiate can only be explained by a whole-hearted response to the injunction of striving for perfection; his success as a superior was due to his co-operation with his subjects and a filial devotion to the constitutions, and the unparalleled results of his labors as the Legate of Christ were due entirely to the perfect manner in which he answered his vocation. Perfect in his obedience in small things and perfect in his obedience in great things, he was perfect in all things.

It is unnecessary to catalogue all the virtues and spiritual endowments of this wonderful athlete of God, because if he was perfect in obedience he was perfect in all the other virtues. The Angelic Doctor tells us that there is an intimate connection between all the acquired moral virtues; so much so that if a person is perfect in one he will be perfect in all the others, as a necessary consequence. Brother Vincent was perfect in his obedience, and hence he is a Saint—and a Saint that lived every word of what he wrote in the beautiful book, the "Treatise on the Spiritual Life."

The last day of the Saint's life was not far distant. Spent with labor, worn out with incessant journeys, broken down with physical ailments, consumed by the flame of his unquenchable zeal, the Wonder-worker of Europe was soon to pass away. In 1417 Saint Colette, after communing with God in an ecstasy, told Saint Vincent that within two years God would call him to his eternal rest and reward. The certain knowledge of his approaching dissolution acted but as a spur on the then old man of sixty-eight winters. Numerous as are the records of the Saint during the last years of his work, it is still impossible to follow him in that last anxious hunt for souls. Every day of the last two years was taken up trying to complete the work he knew he must soon leave forever.

About this time the close friends of Saint Vincent had become alarmed at the condition of his health and made preparations to bring the Saint back to Spain to die. Finding that he could not refuse their request that he set out, it was decided to leave Vannes during the night and to depart from Brittany unknown to the inhabitants. The next morning the company found itself still before the gates of the city and at once saw something preternatural in the occurrence. Smilingly Vincent informed them it was God's will that he die in Brittany, as had been foretold by Saint Colette. However, another attempt, this time by boat, was made to reach Spain, but the Saint became so sick at the beginning of the voyage the ship was forced to return to the landing still known as Port Saint Vincent. He returned to Vannes amid the acclamations of the enthusiastic people, never again to depart.

Kind and solicitous hands sought to restore the aged man and to preserve the life of him whose every moment was a benefaction and whose every breath a benediction. For the first time in forty years, he used a bed and consented to take off the hair shirt he always wore; but to the end he refused to partake of meat or any dainties.

His last day had come. Feeling himself slowly but surely sinking, he asked that the Passion be read and that the Penitential Psalms be recited. At the approach of death the great man trembled. He who had preached judgment for so many years was next to be called, and he feared. But little wonder was it that he trembled, as none had meditated so long on the deep meaning of dissolution; none had pondered so deeply on the infinite justice of God, and none knew so well the heinousness of sin. His terror lasted but a moment. Fear could not long coexist with the ardent charity of Saint Vincent's heart. Full to overflowing as it was with the love of God, it could not contain dread, and as the Litany of the Saints was ended he gazed fondly on his crucifix, smiled sweetly with the rapture of Heaven, and passed away. Venerable with seventy years, he died on April 5, 1419. The great Preacher was silent; the Legate of Christ was giving his final account; the Wonder-worker ceased his ministrations in the flesh and the Angel of the Apocalypse joined forever the shining army that ever cries, "Holy, holy, holy!" As his soul took its flight to Heaven, white butterflies flew into the room and circled about the remains, while an indescribably sweet odor gave fresh evidence of the fragrance of his virtuous life.

On Friday of the same week the remains were placed in the choir of the Cathedral of Vannes by the Bishop of the city. The greater part of the relics have remained in the possession of the city, despite the petitions of princes and of the entire Dominican Order. The miracles wrought at his tomb rival those he performed when alive.

The process of his canonization was commenced at once. In 1451 the official inquiry into his life and virtues was formally opened by a Bull of Nicholas V. In June, 1455, one of Saint Vincent's prophecies was fulfilled, when Alphonsus Borgia, then Calixtus III, declared that on the 29th of the month he would solemnly canonize the Valencian Friar. This he did, though it was Pius II who published the Bull, on October 1, 1458.

The beautiful office in his honor was composed by Martial Auribelli, then Master General of the Order. The author has perpetuated his name by means of the acrostic running through the hymn for Vespers and the antiphons for Matins and Lauds.

Great men live and great men die, but great thoughts and great inspirations are everlasting. After five hundred years, Saint Vincent is still influencing the world and carrying on his all-embracing apostolate. The memory of this Saint, perhaps one of the most wonderful the world has ever seen, must be always fresh and inspiring. A perfect son of a perfect father, Saint Vincent and Saint Dominic stand close together in Paradise.

BIBLIOGRAPHY

Acta SS., April I, 475.

Anal. Boll. XII, 324; XIV, 71.

Bullarium, O. P. Index, 836.

PÈRE FAGES, O. P.: Histoire de Saint Vincent Ferrier.

FR. STANISLAUS HOGAN, O. P.: St. Vincent Ferrer, O. P. Longmans, Green, 1911.

MIGUEL: Portentosa vida y milagros de San Vicente Ferrer. Madrid, 1856.

Quetif=Échard. Script. Ord. Præd., I. Paris, 1719.

CHABAS: Estudio sobre los sermones valencianos de San Vicente Ferrer. Mad., 1903.

HELLER: Vin. Ferrer nach seinem Leben und Wirken. Berlin, 1830.

ALLIES: Three Catholic Reformers of the 15th Century. London, 1879.

Turon IV, 1.

P. TAURISANO, O. P.: Catologus Hagiographicus, O. P. Romæ, 1918.

P. TAURISANO, O. P.: Hierarchia, O. P., 43.

Catholic Encyclopedia: Saint Vincent Ferrer, Western Schism.

Saint Antoninus

LL THE DOMINICAN saints seem to have an easy and natural facility in breaking free from every secondary interest to bring themselves face to face with the most immediate need of the Church. With a vision that is purified by devotion to Truth, they clearly see how the evil can be remedied. Then they set to work, doggedly but cheerfully, to brighten the menacing sky. There was no odious heresy for Antoninus to combat. The master minds of the two previous centuries had won over philosophy to the defense of the Faith. Great preachers had just spread abroad their temporary benefits. Now there must come the steadying influence of example and direction.

During the Schism of the West, people for the most part held to the Faith; but they lost respect for the Church and the sacred character of her institutions. Like children of a divorced mother who had squandered her affections, they grew wayward and intractable. The ordinary man, the cleric, and the religious must be made to understand the importance of living up to their respective Christian obligations. Such was the task that our Saint saw before him.

Florence was the scene of the greatest labors of Saint Antoninus. There he was born, toward the end of March, 1389. His father, Niccolo Pierozzi, was a notary public and had been at three different times chosen proconsul of the art—a distinction which gave him the first rank after the priors of the commune in all public ceremonies. From him Antoninus inherited a methodic and

Saint Antoninus

painstaking devotion to work. Of his mother, Madonna Tommassa di Cenni di Nuccio, scarcely anything is known. She was Niccolo's second wife, and died when the Saint was only six years old.

This loss and other burdens encumbered his early years. He was a pale and sickly boy and the doctors thought he would die young, of consumption. At school he showed little enthusiasm for the ordinary pranks of youth. His whole attitude was stamped with unusual reserve and gravity. Tradition emphasizes his religious bent by picturing him in long hours of prayer before the miraculous Crucifix in the Church of Or San Michele, and one of his boyish delights was to watch the Dominicans in procession at Santa Maria Novella.

More powerful, however, than the lure of the ceremonies was the attraction of one friar in particular, Blessed John Dominici. This man, whom history may one day acknowledge as the individual who, more than any other, was responsible for the Council of Constance and the ending of the Schism of the West, had a remarkable career. With no other extraordinary talents except that of undying perseverance, he was admitted to the Order after repeated refusals. Though Santa Maria Novella was then the nursery for many of the Church's bishops, he surpassed all his associates both in learning and sanctity. While professor at Pisa he came under the influence of Saint Catherine and was henceforth one of the most ardent supporters of the movement of reform. When he was recalled to teach Sacred Scripture at Santa Maria Novella, he found time to do much preaching. He soon acquired the reputation of being one of the greatest pulpit orators of the day.

How deeply our Saint was affected by these discourses is recorded in his own words: "It was the preaching of Dominici that led me to the religious life." The story of the interview between these two illustrious sons of Saint Dominic has become famous. John Dominici's idea of reform had taken on a very practical shape. He saw the futility of attempting to change the lives of men settled in their easy-going habits. He intended to start with a community of men who were trained in austerity from their youth. While negotiating for the erection of a convent at Fiesole, he opened a novitiate house in Cortona. When Antoninus presented himself with the hope of joining this new community, Dominici felt constrained to refuse him admittance. His weak-looking body seemed unfitted for the rigors of strict religious discipline. Yet he could not entirely discourage the eager youth. He told him that if he would return at the end of the year, having committed to memory the whole of the Decretal of Gratian, he would be accepted. The Decretal of Gratian was the nearest approach to an official code of canon law that the times had to offer. Difficult though the condition was, Antoninus successfully fulfilled it.

The Saint finished his year of probation at Cortona in February, 1406. After waiting a few months for the profession of three other novices, he accompanied them to Fiesole at Pentecost. The new convent was not yet ready for occupancy; so the little band stayed for a time with the Hermits of Saint Jerome and later went to the Abbey of Saint Bartholomew. Bishop Altoviti, a Dominican, celebrated Mass in a temporary chapel on Saint Dominic's Day. On the 4th of September they moved into the infirmary, which was the first part of the edifice to be finished. By the 29th of the month each friar had his own cell and regular observance began.

Dominici was determined that, above all, his followers were to be men of sanctity. To this end he gave them a lengthy talk every day. In November he was suddenly called away to Rome. Henceforth, as Cardinal of Ragusa, his services were wholly given over to the Roman Pontiff. Though deprived of their leader, the community continued to thrive. During the three months of intimate companionship, Antoninus absorbed the spirit of his master, and no amount of hardships was able to thwart the great purpose that was then firmly planted in his soul. To be sure, these ardent beginnings foretokened great achievements. And it must have rejoiced the heart of Antoninus when, in the year 1407, the renowned Fra Angelico and his brother, Bendetto, joined the community, increasing its membership to sixteen. Still, like every uplifting movement within the Church, this project of Dominici's had its period of trial.

In June, 1409, the Council of Pisa elected a third claimant to the throne of Peter, who took the name Alexander V. This attempt to settle the disturbance of the Church only made matters worse. It spelt disaster for the new Dominican foundation. In consequence of their refusal to acknowledge the authority of the antipope, the friars were dispersed by order of the bishop. Some of them went to Cortona, while the others found refuge with the Dominican Bishop of Folgino, Frederico Frezzi. It was not until eight years later that they were able to return to their convent.

Antoninus was among those who went to Folgino. There, under very difficult circumstances, he lived the life of a true religious and made a serious study of the questions of the hour. With his companions, he was convinced that the Roman Pontiff, Gregory XII, was the real Pope. He saw how the schism had engendered a widespread disregard of the laws of the Church. The ordinary man, the cleric, and the religious must be impressed with the sacredness of their respective obligations. Musing on thoughts such as these, he patiently bore the anxieties of his exile. After a pestilence at Folgino in 1413, he and two others were the only survivors of the original group who settled in that place. It is believed that shortly before this event he was ordained priest. From 1413 to 1421 he was at Cortona. As he was prior there when the schism came to an end, in November, 1417, he could not accompany the friars who returned to Fiesole. However, at the expiration of his term he was elected prior of the convent at Fiesole.

The history of Saint Antoninus up to this point is constructed from facts that are meager and often conflicting; yet it is certain that he was a youth who, in the face of overwhelming trials, had forged ahead bravely in the pursuit of a grand ideal; for he had triumphed over the sorrow from the death of his mother in childhood, over the distress of his ever-present bodily infirmities, over the pain inflicted on his noble soul by the sad state of the Church, and in the struggles of his heroic community. We may form some idea of how trying it was for them to persevere when we read that it was practically impossible for them to keep up their studies with any regularity. The Saint tells us that, but for a few lessons in dialectic, he had to be his own teacher. But to follow the example of Dominici was a goal worthy of every sacrifice.

He is thirty years of age now, as the curtain rises on the stage of his longed-for toils. The schism has gone and is forgotten. Only its scars remain. The proud city of his birth, by a strange exception, has avoided war for the past decade. Everything seems to favor the sudden appearance of a great reformer. Yet Antoninus did not rush upon the scene. His faith lay in the slower but steadier course of spreading a love for strict observance within the cloister.

John Dominici had encountered serious opposition from those who thought that to establish within the Order of Preachers a distinct group of communities, under separate jurisdiction, would mean the destruction of that unity which had long been cherished as one of the finest heritages of the Order. However, a vicar general for the observants was again appointed after the Council of Constance. And at the General Chapter, held at Metz in 1421, it was decreed that at least one house of strict observance should be established within a year in every province of the Order. The letter of the Master General, sent out at this time, recognized that there was much room for reform. The new vicar of the observants needed missionaries to help him in his work. In Antoninus he found his best colaborer.

In 1424 he went as visitator to the Convent of Saint Peter Martyr at Naples, where he was soon elected prior, which office he held until 1430. Not only did he help the community in a spiritual way, but he also completely renovated the church and convent. Here also, for the first time, his influence directly touched the public. His reputation for holiness spread among the people, as he threw himself eagerly into the work of bringing them back to a faithful observance of their religious duties. The theme he was to develop so extensively in his moral theology, and that already governed his intercourse with others, was this: As happiness cannot be found on this earth, in purgatory, or in hell, it follows that man should make ready to find it in heaven by conforming his life here below to the requirements of the moral law and in seeking in the sacrament of penance peace of conscience. He dedicated a little book to a nobleman of the city which was written for the instruction of the faithful, especially with regard to the sacrament of penance. He was also the director of many souls, some of whom were in correspondence with him till the end of his life.

In 1430 we find him prior of the Convent of the Minerva in Rome. The sacred remains of Saint Catherine reposed in the adjoining church and were already the object of veneration; but they were in a rather inconspicuous corner. Antoninus had the body exhumed, put into a marble casket, and moved to an honorable setting, in the Chapel of the Rosary. As an indication that he was, even at this time, regarded as a man of learning and of judgment, we are told that he acted as one of the judges of the rote, a tribunal which then, in addition to all ecclesiastical cases, had to deal also with the civil processes of the Pontifical States.

The Florentines were not slow to recognize the attractive holiness of the friars of Fiesole; they were eager to see them established in their city. Cosimo dei Medici had just been recalled from exile and was steadily advancing toward complete control of the government. Whether his motives were, at bottom, praiseworthy is a question. At any rate, he joined the others in requesting from Rome the necessary authorization for the transfer of the Church and Convent of Saint Mark's to the Dominicans of the reform.

The Sylvestrians who held this foundation had fallen into disfavor. By a Bull, dated January 21, 1436, the Dominicans were given the property, while the Sylvestrians were to take over the Church of Saint George-beyond-the-Arno, where a few friars from Fiesole had settled the previous year.

The formal entry of Antoninus's brothers into their new home was carried out very pompously; yet they found the edifice anything but desirable. The ground about the place was marshy, the walls of the convent were falling down, and the cells almost uninhabitable. Several of the community soon died of fever.

Just when he first came there, we do not know, but in May, 1437, Antoninus was at Saint Mark's. On the 28th of the month he was officially appointed Vicar General of all the strict observance houses in Italy. It was due to his tact that the proffered assistance of Cosimo began immediately to effect a wonderful architectural transformation in the old Saint Mark's. Twenty cells were built in what was formerly the refectory and work was started on the church.

After traveling about in the interests of reform, Antoninus returned to Florence in January, 1439, as Prior of Saint Mark's. Together with Fiesole, it then formed but one community. A close friendship had now developed between Antoninus and Cosimo, and it was largely through the Saint's direction that the wealth of this potentate was kept from less worthy purposes and found its way into those enduring and uplifting monuments of art which have ever been the glory of Florence. Cosimo came to Saint Mark's every day for Mass, and he had his cell in the convent, where he often talked over the affairs of his soul with his saintly friend. He saw to it that the friars wanted for nothing. He supplied the necessities for their sacristy and even set up their famous library.

In Saint Mark's the renowned architect for Cosimo's Via Larga, Michelozzo Michelozzi, is said to have reached his ideal of grace. But more than by its architectural grandeur has Saint Mark's claimed the veneration of subsequent centuries through the paintings of Fra Angelico. The praises of this divine painter are widely sung, but rarely is it said that Saint Antoninus was the author of the heavenly conceptions that Fra Angelico so delicately fixed in lasting color. As it was the Saint's great prepossession to lead people away from their busy absorption in matters of earthly interest, his influence on art was to inspire in the artist the power to carry men's thoughts deftly into the pure realms of celestial peace. Thus was the medieval symbolism saved, amid the destructive influences of the Renaissance.

Saint Mark's without Saint Antoninus is inconceivable. Whatever hold this hallowed pile had upon the exuberant Florentines of the fifteenth century in preventing them from running entirely away from God was due to his influence. He constantly raised the souls of his brothers to the heights of spirituality that Dominici had built up in his own heart. In spite of all the gifts showered upon the community, Antoninus rigidly lived up to Saint Dominic's idea of poverty. If anything was received beyond what was needed for immediate necessities, it was forthwith given to the poor. The younger friars were especially the object of his fatherly care. He was broad enough to allow them to read profane authors, and secured for their instruction the best teachers the Order could provide. His own humility was itself a wonderful lesson. The meanest tasks in the community he reserved to himself. Love for the cloister and for his cell was one of his remarkable characteristics. In spite of his many cares, he found time every day for serious study.

One of his charitable schemes that shows the wide range of his mind was the association known as the "Buonomini of San Martino." At the time there were hundreds of people of the better class who had been reduced to poverty by the repressions of their successful political rivals. There seemed to be something entirely incongruous for one brought up in an atmosphere of comfort and culture to be suddenly forced to beg. The merciful heart of

Antoninus appreciated their embarrassing distress and tactfully contrived a way to help them without hurting their traditional pride. He called together twelve prominent citizens and formed them into a confraternity whose object was to collect money and provisions for secret distribution to these unfortunates. They had certain pious exercises to perform and their protection was confided to Saint Martin. Here again the Saint insisted on the law of poverty. Under no conditions was the society to acquire a reserve. If a legacy were left to them, it must be entirely disposed of at once. The benefits of this organization were incalculable. It supplied money, food, and furniture; it provided for the education of children, gave doweries for marriages, and paid off heavy debts. As a lasting remembrance to the wisdom of its founder, it has continued in existence down to the present day.

Another very practical engagement of his at this time was the supervision of four societies that brought together the children for instruction in Christian doctrine on Sundays. Here is an early instance of the Sunday School. He also introduced another salutary practice among the citizens. While at Fiesole he had admired a custom of the early Church which the Blessed Carlo di Monte Granello, Superior of the Hermits of Saint Jerome, had revived. The laity came to church on the eve of each great feast and spent the night in prayer. In collaboration with Carlo, Antoninus founded in Florence four confraternities to keep up this practice. They also have survived until our day.

With that overmastering trend of his mind toward the practical, he saw the necessity of a theological treatise which would help the pastor and the preacher in their dealings with the people. The application of the principles of Saint Thomas to the actual problems of every-day life had not been made in one work. To attempt such a work in the midst of his many other labors was a great undertaking; but it was what the Church needed and he would not shrink from the task. During his term as Prior of Saint Mark's he finished the first two parts of his Moral Theology. His opinion was often sought in problems of theology by priests and prelates. A Dominican of Lombardy sent him a list of sixty-nine questions in liturgy and morals to be solved.

By the year 1444 both convents had so largely increased in membership that it became necessary to have a separate prior for Fiesole. This office was confided to Fra Bendetto. Antoninus relinquished the reins of government and departed on an apostolic mission. But in a short time he returned, to give to the city of his birth an example of devotion and real service which she has cherished as one of her dearest memories.

In August, 1445, Bartolomeo Zabarella, the Archbishop of Florence, died. On account of the disturbances then prevailing in Italy, it was of the utmost importance that the Pope, Eugenius IV, should have in the center of Tuscany a devoted and reliable prelate, on whom he could count to support the Holy See both in its spiritual and temporal affairs. The Florentines recommended five candidates, and there were others under consideration. For nine months the Pontiff hesitated to make a choice.

At this time Fra Angelico was at Rome painting frescoes in the Chapel of the Blessed Sacrament. The Pope often came there to talk with him. When, one day, he explained how difficult it was for him to decide who should be the next Archbishop of Florence, Fra Angelico proposed the name of Antoninus. It was like a flash of light from heaven to Eugenius. The very next morning he called a consistory and nominated Antoninus. This was about the 1st of January, 1446.

On the ninth of the month the Bull of nomination was sent out, and, needless to say, the Republic showed complete satisfaction with the appointment. Antoninus was on his way to Naples with a lay-brother when the news was brought to him. Instead of rejoicing at the announcement, he was exceedingly alarmed. He wanted to run off and hide himself, and even thought of escaping to Sardinia.

A nephew prevented such a step and succeeded in conducting him to Siena. Antoninus wrote immediately to the Pope, begging him not to lay such a burden on his weak shoulders. The reply was an order for him to go directly to Fiesole. This much he could not refuse.

For a month he continued to use every available means to induce the Pontiff to change his mind. The Florentines came out each day to pay him homage and they endeavored to persuade him of the immense good his acceptance would mean for their city. Yet he was not convinced. He himself wrote to Rome and got others to write. Finally the Pope had Cardinal Capranica inform Antoninus in rather forceful terms that he must accept the office. As the will of God now seemed clearly against his own attitude, he held out no longer. Calling together a large number of priests, abbots, prelates, and leading citizens, and voicing again his belief that he was unfitted for the dignity, after praying in tears with those around him, he made his acceptance.

On March 12, 1446, he was consecrated at Fiesole by the Dominican Lorenzo Giacomini, Bishop of Achaia. The next day he made his entry into Florence. He set aside the fine vestments and the richly caparisoned horse which custom demanded on such an occasion, and, though the solemnity could not be entirely done away with, he eliminated everything that savored of worldly pomp. Clothed in the plain Dominican habit, he came down from Fiesole at daybreak and said Mass in the little Church of Saint Gallo, near the gate of the city. After that he was met by his guards, the canons and clergy, and signory. An immense crowd followed the procession as it moved toward the Church of San Pietro Maggiore, where the symbolic marriage of the Bishop to his diocese took place. The rest of the way to the cathedral he went barefoot. After the Mass and solemn Te Deum he gave an audience to the principal men of the city.

The great ambition of his life to labor for the general betterment of the Church was now offered wide opportunity for realization.

Florence certainly presented instances in abundance of every difficulty and abuse—the sores he had dedicated his life to heal. The ill effects of the schism lingered on, and it required a strong hand to wipe them away. Laxity was rampant; not a few of his priests had been driven to the wall by Jewish money-lenders. Hundreds of his flock were without any sense of their religious obligations, and in the country districts he had to contend with horrible ignorance and superstition.

His first act was to clean out his own house. All predatory inmates of the episcopal palace were dismissed, and its luxurious atmosphere was supplanted by an air of monastic poverty. The walls became bare, the furniture scant and poor, the meals frugal. Like the great Bishop of Hippo, he believed in setting the example of an austere life for the benefit of his clergy. He even insisted on reading in the refectory and would allow no mistake to go uncorrected.

His round of daily occupations left no time for leisure. He rose early in the morning and gave the first hours of the day to study and to the writing of his Moral Theology. At 9 o'clock he said Mass. The rest of the morning was usually taken up by visitors, who came to him with their complaints and difficulties. Nobody was neglected. The door of the house was always open and admitted the meanest pauper to the same cheerful reception accorded dignitaries.

His incessant and personal visitations of religious institutes was productive of lasting good. The canons were neglecting the office at the cathedral. That condition was remedied by the Bishop's attendance at Matins every midnight. Neither fatigue nor bad weather ever prevented him from keeping up this practice. Priests who wore fine clothes and played cards were severely punished. On his visitations he would go over the registers carefully to make certain that the church lacked nothing that was needed for sacred ceremonies. He made pastors produce the records to show that they were lawfully holding their benefices. Some priests were so ignorant that they could not administer baptism or give absolution. Many had even sold their breviaries. He enjoined residence on those who were accustomed to take prolonged vacations. Threats, privation of benefices, suspensions, imprisonments, and even corporal punishments were wielded, as the occasion required. It was one of his principal comforts when he came to die to know that he was leaving his diocese restored to order and his clergy disciplined and dutiful.

One church that was used for unholy purposes was closed up altogether and converted into a library for the Cathedral Chapter. Another that was falling to ruin, though in the hands of an upright, if impoverished, pastor, was placed under the patronage of a wealthy Florentine, who rebuilt and endowed it. Many other churches the Saint also rebuilt. However, it was not elegance of adornment he sought. "I leave that to my successors," is his observation on the matter. But he did want the dignity of the churches respected and the ceremonies carried out strictly according to the liturgy and in a respectful fashion. Many stories are told of his efforts to put a stop to all unseemly conduct in church. Once he left the sacristy of the cathedral and with his cincture drove out a young bride whose youthful admirers were creating quite a disturbance.

The Pope frequently commissioned him to look into the affairs of monasteries which normally lay outside his jurisdiction. Many were the reforms he instituted. He was also delegated judge and commissary apostolic for matters of usury, then presenting some very embarrassing questions.

Though he did much preaching, there are few of his sermons extant and their plan was invariably the same. First a certain vice was described; this was followed by a description of the motives for conversion; lastly he proposed the remedy, the sacraments of the Church.

An outstanding characteristic of our Saint's life was the courage he manifested in carrying out his conscientious convictions. This was especially evidenced when objections were made to his disposition of certain benefices which formerly were conferred directly from Rome, but over which he had received authority to act. He was relentless in enforcing the law of the Church, no matter whose were the interests involved. Two of his clergy were arrested for a public offense, but the police, instead of bringing them secretly before the Archbishop, as they should have done, humiliated them publicly by leading them handcuffed through the streets, amid the shouts and jibes of the amused throng. The Archbishop, in order to safeguard the honor of the priesthood, excommunicated the officers who were responsible for the affair.

He was really rigorous when there was need for it, and the episcopal prison was the scene of many sound whippings. Naturally complaints were carried to Rome, but Nicholas V knew the character of our Saint well and would never allow an appeal from his decisions in cases that concerned the morals of his clergy. His severity must not be taken for cruelty. His heart fairly overflowed with tenderness. Suffering of any kind roused his sympathy, and he was so responsive to the cries of the poor that he gave away everything he possibly could. He even stripped his residence of its scant furniture and turned over his flower garden to the raising of vegetables for the poor. Even in the midst of his episcopal occupations his interest in religious and monastic life was sustained.

Two communities of Third Order Dominican nuns and one Benedictine convent under his direction reached a high degree of sanctity. His interest in Saint Mark's never died. A cell there was kept ready for him, if he should ever choose to return to it. He found work for his brothers to do, such as painting miniatures and copying manuscripts. The convents at Pistoa and Cortona received much material aid from him. He took upon himself the upkeep of more than one monastery.

Not only was he quick to help the sudden misfortunes of individuals, but he was also the leading figure in organizing and carrying out a system of relief when public calamities were visited upon the city. Toward the end of the year 1448 came one of those periodic pestilences that wrought such widespread destruction of human life during the fifteenth century. People were streaming away in crowds to the healthier villages of the Apennines. Parents left their children, and children deserted their helpless elders. Death called many who were deprived of the last sacraments and Christian burial. Every day the holy Archbishop might be seen leading a donkey through the streets bearing food and medicine to the afflicted. He enlisted the aid of the young men of the city in this work and called in brother Dominicans from Lombardy to help those of Fiesole, Santa Maria Novella, and Saint Mark's, who were already overburdened with their ministrations to the starving and the dying. Antoninus practically ruled the city in those days; so when the signory allotted three thousand florins to carry on the work of relief the money was all turned into his hands for distribution.

The same vehement charity he again exhibited after the earthquake of September, 1453. And during the summer of 1456 his natural serenity and patience were severely tested in trying to quell the exorbitant superstition of those who looked upon the famous comet of Saint Sixtus as an omen of destruction. On the 22d of August a great tornado rooted up trees, killed some fifty persons, and destroyed the crops. This meant famine for Florence. Industry was held up and a financial panic was imminent. In this crisis Antoninus was charged with the gigantic task of restoring order. Toward the end of the year when the Arno overflowed its banks and the pestilence reappeared, after he had exhausted every other means, he did not hesitate to beg assistance from the Pope and to request him to suspend the tithe for the crusade.

In quieter times as well, whenever there was any prudent need for it, he came prominently before the attention of the public. Shortly after the election of Nicholas V he was called to a conference with the new Pontiff. All Rome respected him then as a great canonist and a man of holy life, and only through his own strong objections was he prevented from becoming a Cardinal. When Calixtus III succeeded Nicholas, it was Antoninus who was commissioned to head the Florentine Embassy to the Papal Court. His speech on this occasion, explaining the duties of the Pope and the necessity of a crusade, was highly praised, and again he had to seek escape from the burden of the cardinalate. When Pius II ascended the throne a similar commission fell to him. Though feeble and really sick at the time, he made a profound impression on the Pope, and his exhortations were largely responsible for the persistence with which that energetic Pontiff labored to block the advancing forces of Islam. Pius hoped for much assistance from the holy Archbishop and made him one of the college of reform.

He was often sent away as the Republic's representative to courts less exalted than that of Rome. The dignity of receiving distinguished visitors to Florence was usually given to him. But in every such instance his absolute aloofness from pride or worldliness was very apparent. It emphasized the fact that these public engagements went counter to his secret inclinations, and were participated in only from a sense of civic devotion. For, if duty seemed clearly to require it, he would not hesitate to make his presence conspicuous in circumstances that were naturally undesirable. Thus he frequently broke in upon the assembled signory and called to their attention matters wherein they had obviously exceeded their lawful powers. He generally gained his point, as when he championed the ancient liberties of the people.

During the entire century the question of taxation was perhaps the most bothersome thing in Florentine politics. Even sliding scale and progressive income taxes figured in their experiments. But whenever ecclesiastical property or the clergy became involved the Archbishop would insist on his own rights and the rights of the Church.

In 1434 Eugenius IV yielded to the signory and allowed the Republic to take a tithe of sixteen thousand florins from the

Church revenues. Difficulties were, of course, encountered, and complaints were sent to Rome accusing the collectors of fraud. The Pope ordered Antoninus to investigate the matter and to convict and excommunicate the offenders. Here the Archbishop's wonderful prudence showed itself. He first convinced the Pontiff that the procedure he recommended would only aggravate the difficulty. Then he took upon himself the burden of collecting the tax, and so relieved his clergy of the embarrassment the fiscal agents had been causing them.

When it came to his notice that the signory and the colleges were violating their oaths in regard to the manner of voting prescribed by statute, he could not stand by and see the spirit of liberty trampled upon and the way opened for all sorts of perjuries. He posted on the door of the cathedral a proclamation, written in his own hand, denouncing the lack of respect shown to the oath and imposing excommunication on each offender, insisting that it was his duty as Bishop to remind those who sat in the Council, just as well as the common people, of the things which pertained to their eternal salvation. Five delegates were chosen to call on the Archbishop and remonstrate. Antoninus received them with sweet and courteous words. But when they saw he was not prepared to yield to their views they threatened to deprive him of his office. Here is his remarkable answer: "Oh, in the name of God, I beg you to do so, and I shall be forever obliged to you, for you will remove a great burden from my shoulders. I shall go back to Saint Mark's, to a mean cell, the key to which I always carry with me, and there in holy peace shall I end my days. A greater joy I could not desire nor better appreciate." At that the delegates withdrew. It must be observed that he always interfered as Bishop and never assumed the exaggerated rôle of political reformer, as did Savonarola some years later.

This reply to the offended politicians reveals, perhaps better than anything else, the real sanctity of his character. It bids us look into the more intimate workings of his soul, to search for the source of that extraordinary sweetness and evenness of temper which he preserved in the face of every threat and danger. Like every other great Dominican, we find that he was eminently a man of prayer. He used to say that he would never have been able to bear the burden of his charge were it not for the consolation that he experienced in his communings with God. We have already observed that he went to the cathedral at midnight to chant Matins. But in addition to the Canonical Office he recited every day the Seven Penitential Psalms and the Office of the Blessed Virgin. Twice a week he said the Office of the Dead, and, on the principal feasts of the Church, the whole Psalter.

We read also that he was accustomed to fast quite severely and to flagellate his weak body. He would spend hours in his little chapel before the Blessed Sacrament; and there his secretary sometimes saw him in ecstasy. Thus we may believe the statement that he allowed himself only two or three hours of the night for sleep.

When he expressed delight at the thought of being able to return again to Saint Mark's he was thoroughly sincere. To labor for reform as an ordinary Dominican friar had been his only ambition. His life in the episcopate was, fundamentally, what it had been before his elevation to that dignity. His observance of poverty and the other monastic austerities was never abandoned. As he passed by in the street he could not be distinguished by his dress from any other Dominican. And so it happened that, after his death, he was generally spoken of as "The Archbishop Antoninus, who always went about as a simple religious of the Order of Saint Dominic."

Although it never entered his mind to aspire to any fame as a writer, the Saint's "Spiritual Letters" have been declared a real contribution to Italian literature. They show that he had nothing in common with the Humanists; nor did he respect the extravagant ambitions of their adversaries. His work appeals to those who look for simplicity and purity of the language. "Antoninus merits the reputation of an elegant writer," is the opinion of a careful student of these letters. He was one of the first ascetic writers to treat piety as something blithe and smiling, and in a way that would render it attractive to everybody. In the wisdom of his advice and even in expression of thought has he been recognized as the forerunner of Saint Francis de Sales.

The little book, entitled the "Confessionale," which he wrote when he was prior at Naples, though not referred to as having any particular literary merit, was extensively used as a guide to the spiritual life in Italy, France, and Germany. As early as 1492 it appeared in a Spanish translation. It is not improbable that Saint Teresa got from it the idea she carries through all her writings, of treating the soul as a garden. She says she read about it in some author whose name she could not remember. Another work on the spiritual life, the "Opera a Ben Vivere," that is attributed to him, was published in 1858.

In the domain of history he gave expression to an essentially Catholic ideal. His "Chronicles" were written for the express purpose of holding up as examples of virtue the famous characters of past ages. It was a sort of supplement to his Moral Theology. Since he accepted as true much that modern scientific investigation would not credit, his history is, for the most part, of little value now. Still in the treatment of contemporaneous events he stands unsurpassed.

The "Summa Moralis," comprising four huge volumes, is his greatest bequest to posterity. For two hundred years it remained the standard Moral Theology. Down to the year 1741 it had gone through twenty-six editions. And even today its authority is not infrequently resorted to. In the famous decree "Quam Singulari" of Pope Pius X, Saint Antoninus is cited as favoring the practice of allowing children who have reached the age of reason to receive Holy Communion.

His study of the intricate questions that arise through economic and social relations has in recent years received much attention. It is surprising to find that he had a solution for many problems that we are accustomed to think quite new. For instance, he insisted on a living wage, and would allow the State to fix the prices of those commodities which everybody needed. He understood the workings of credit and practically accepted the modern theory of the productivity of money. In short, he analyzed every possible difficulty that might arise among the men of his time, whether it had to do with politics or industry. The principles that should govern all human transactions and dominate every relation between capital and labor he held forth with characteristic energy.

By discussing in detail the various sins then prevalent, he has left a complete record of the morals of his time. The work, furthermore, is a veritable storehouse for sermon matter. Frequently, after giving the doctrine on a certain point, he states it again, but clothed in a style suitable for preaching. The original manuscript volumes are now at Saint Mark's in the cell said to have been occupied by the Saint.

In the year 1838 a movement was set on foot to have Saint Antoninus declared a Doctor of the Church. Just why it failed to succeed is not known. Perhaps his writings were not characterized by that originality and durability such an honor seems to require. Too often he simply gives the opinions of previous masters rather than judging for himself. However, it was not for posterity that he wrote. His great aim was to attack each particular evil that flourished in his immediate surroundings, to root out all the vices and abolish all the abuses that formed the peculiar heartache of the Church in his day.

Captivated in his youth by the ideal of Saint Catherine as he saw it living in the person of Blessed John Dominici, he shaped his whole career to realize that dream. Conscientious and precise in everything he did, with a zeal that was moderated by sound common sense, combining all the qualities of a perfect administrator with a most compassionate heart, he certainly had a powerful influence in checking the rising tide of paganism and irreligion.

He seemed to understand that the effect of his work would be limited; but by his example and by his intimate control over the hearts of certain courageous souls he hoped to inaugurate a movement that would, in due time, restore the former grandeur of God's Church. And if his great aims did not live after him and accomplish, in an orderly way, what the Reformation bungled so horribly, the reason is to be sought in the providence of God, for his work, according to the natural sequence of things, should have had a greater success.

On the first of May, 1459, the faithful followers of the good Archbishop were not in the mood to join in the elaborate fête which the gay Florentines were then staging. Their saintly idol was in his last agony. For some days an ugly fever had completely mastered his worn-out frame. For his comfort he was taken out to a villa near the gate of Saint Gallo; but he knew it was the end. "God has appointed seventy as the number of our years," he said. He was just entering on his seventieth year. At twilight on that first day of May the last sacraments were administered and his brothers from Saint Mark's, standing round, began Matins. From time to time during the office his feeble voice would utter, "Servire Deo regnare est" and "Laudate Dominum de cælis." In the early hours of the following morning, after one last kiss upon the image of his Crucified Saviour, his eager soul departed.

Pope Pius II, who was in the city, commissioned Cardinal Peter Barbo to take charge of the funeral. He himself put on mourning garments and, together with the attending prelates, escorted the corpse to the cathedral. After the service it was taken to Saint Mark's, and there for eight days was exposed for the devotion of the crowds, mostly his beloved poor, that poured in from the mountain villages. His own request to be buried in the Church of Saint Mark's was complied with.

In the episcopal palace could be found no works of art and no costly furniture. What little money he could lay claim to at his death was left to the poor. There were not even any books belonging to him; but on his table lay an unfinished manuscript, "A Dialogue of Saint Gregory," to testify that he ceased his labors only with his last illness.

Several miracles were recorded during his lifetime. However, they were as nothing in comparison to the hundreds of cures worked at his shrine. The Church officially announced his sanctity to the world on the 31st of May, 1523. And Florence perpetuated the memory of her distinguished son by placing his Statue in the center of her exclusive hall of fame.

BIBLIOGRAPHY

BEDE JARRETT, O. P.: S. Antonino and Mediæval Economics. St. Louis, B. Herder, 1914.

RAOUL MORCAY: Saint Antonin. Paris, J. Gabalda, 1914.

P. MANDONNET, O. P.: Article, "Antonin," in the Dictionnaire de Theologie Catholique, Vol. I. Paris, 1909.

MORTIER, O. P.: Maîtres Généraux de l'Ordre des Frères Prêcheurs, Vol. III. Rome, 1907; Vol. IV, Paris, 1909.

Année Dominicaine, Mai 2. Lyons, 1891.

TOURON, O. P.: Histoire des Hommes illustres de l'Ordre de S. Dominique, Vol. III. Paris, 1746.

ÉCHARD, O. P.: Scriptores Ordinis Prædicatorum, Vol. I. Paris, 1719.

Bollandists Acta Sanctorum, Vol. XIV, Tom. I. Paris and Rome, 1886.

FRANCESCO DA CASTIGLIONE: Vita Beati Antonini. Florence, 1680.

VESPASIANO DA BISTICCI: Vite di Uomini illustri del secolo XV. Bologna, 1892.

ROBERTO UBALDINI: Vita di S. Antonino. Florence, 1519.

V. MAINARD: Vita et Officium ac Missa S. Antonini. Rome, 1525.

FROSINO LAPINI: Vita di S. Antonino. Florence, 1569.

SILVANO RAZZI: Vita, Miracoli e Traslazione di S. Antonino. Florence, 1589.

DOMENICO MACCARANI: Vita di S. Antonino. Florence, 1876.

Saint Pius the Fifth

"REJOICE, O happy children of Dominic, and burn torches in honor of Pius the Fifth! Be glad, O Mother Church, so long weeping at the River of Babylon! Let all the heavenly hosts exult, and reduplicate our festive Alleluia to Pius." Thus begins the Vespers of Saint Pius and it sounds the dominant note of his entire office. Well indeed might the family of Saint Dominic rejoice, that family which has given to the Church so many eminent canonists, profound philosophers, learned theologians, and saints, for in Pius the Fifth all these qualities in a high degree were uniquely combined, and, moreover, he is honored by the universal Church as Pope and Saint. The Church has good cause also to honor him as her valiant defender, for he came to her in the time of her great tribulation and distress, and proved himself to be her stalwart and faithful son. All of Christendom owes a debt of gratitude to this saintly "Father of Nations," who, stern in the path of righteousness, yet lowly in his deep submissive reverence for the mandates of God, has done so much to strengthen the Christian religion and to extend the Kingdom of God upon the earth.

It is proverbial that at all times, when the Church was passing through periods of storm and stress, God raised up mighty and valiant leaders to guide her safely over the troubled waters into the harbor of peace and calm. So, in the beginning of the sixteenth century, one of the most trying through which the Church Militant has had to pass, Almighty God sent a new Moses, not only to deliver His Church from the bondage of political

Saint Pius V

entanglements into which human ambition had betrayed her, but also to save European civilization from being supplanted by Asiatic fanaticism.

The family of the Ghislieri, once richly-endowed but having become impoverished by the civil wars, which in the fifteenth century had desolated Lombardy, came to hide their poverty in Bosco, a small town in northern Italy. There on the 17th of January, usually a chill and gloomy month in southern Europe, Dominica Augeria, wife of Paul Ghislieri, gave birth to a boy whom they called Michael. This child is the subject of our story. Little is known of Dominica, the boy's mother, beyond the fact that she instilled into the heart of her son a fervent spirit of piety toward God and a very tender devotion to His Blessed Mother, virtues which characterized his life as a Dominican, as a Cardinal, and as Vicar of Christ. And, although wealth was no longer the portion of the Ghislieri, their only possessions being a tiny dwelling, a little vineyard, and a small flock of sheep, yet a better inheritance descended on the future Saint—an inheritance of piety, resignation, and steadfast endeavor to fulfill the adorable Will of God by daily labor.

Michael was a gentle and serious child, peacefully happy in his quiet way, and never boisterous in his amusements. As he advanced in years he found his greatest pleasure in reading, and when at school he was pointed out as a boy of unusual talent and application. But Paul Ghislieri was too poor to indulge ambition for his son. Instead of being allowed to continue his studies, Michael must be taught a trade whereby he might aid his father in earning a livelihood for the family. Thus spoke both the parents, and their little son listened with sinking heart, for another voice had already sounded in his ears, and his daily prayer was for strength and opportunity to follow it. He was longing, as only the chosen of God can long, to consecrate himself to Christ. At this time the boy was twelve years old, tall for his age, slight of build, with fine, clear-cut features, and luminous eyes full of intelligence, honesty, and enthusiasm. And just as plans were being completed for his entering a new life in the world, strangely and unexpectedly, the door of the sanctuary was thrown open for him.

There was no seminary nor monastery near Bosco, and consequently no priest nor religious to give him a helping hand. However, one day, when returning from school, Michael met two Dominican Friars, who chanced to be passing through the village. Seizing the opportunity for which he had so long waited, he timidly accosted them, told them with great respect, yet with earnestness, the secret desire of his heart, and begged them to take him to their convent. They questioned him closely and were so impressed by his simple candor and innocence, and by the premature wisdom of his questions and answers, that they agreed to receive him as a pupil, with a view to testing his vocation. This unexpected fulfillment of his cherished hopes seemed to Michael an answer to his prayers, and his heart overflowed with gratitude. He asked to be allowed a few minutes' delay in which to make known to his parents his secret desires and the opportunity offered for their realization. This granted, he hurried home, and, in a rather excited frame of mind, opened his heart to his father and mother and begged leave to go. They were not a little astonished at their son's eagerness, but, having had long noted the signs of a vocation which were so abundantly evident in him, they were not altogether unprepared to make the sacrifice. They willingly consented, thanking God for their son's vocation, and expressing the wish to see him clothed in the habit of Saint Dominic. Again the boy's heart bounded for gladness, and, bidding his parents a hasty good-bye, he ran back to his new friends. They were traveling on foot and had a great distance to go, so the poor little fellow would scarcely have been able to keep up with them had he not taken hold of the cloak of one of the Fathers; with this help he followed them to their convent at Voghera, a town in Lombardy.

From the day he entered the priory he was serenely happy in his new surroundings, and applied himself to the duties of his calling with an eagerness that excited both the admiration of his superiors and the emulation of his fellow-novices. His probation was of short duration, for he was soon sent to the priory of Vigevano to make his novitiate. There the novices regarded him as one who had advanced far in the science of the saints. He was habitually silent and recollected, always prudent, docile, and humble, and jealously observant of rules and regulations. In May, 1520, he received the Dominican habit, and a year later made his religious profession. The next seven years were spent in the study of philosophy and theology at the Convents of Fermo, Pavia, Ravenna, and Raggio. He studied as the saints have always studied, with continual elevation of mind to the Throne of Light, frequently interrupting his work to pour forth his soul in fervent prayer. He had no sooner finished his studies than he was appointed professor of theology, and his first direction to his class was this: "The most powerful aid we can bring to this study is the practice of earnest prayer. The more closely the mind is united to God, the richer will be the stores of light that follow its researches."

In his twenty-fifth year he was ordained to the priesthood, and although he had not seen his parents since leaving Bosco, some twelve years before, he dreaded even then yielding so much to nature as a visit home, and it was only in obedience to his superiors that he was constrained to visit them. So he set out to say his first Mass in the old parish church of his native village, where it had been his custom to pray at his mother's side. He arrived at Bosco only to find that the town had been burned to the ground some months before by the French troops of Francis I on their way to Pavia. All the inhabitants had fled. Such was his home-coming. Hearing that his family and friends had taken refuge in the village of Sesodia, some miles away, he sought and found them there, and in the parish church of that village, surrounded by his own people, he celebrated his first solemn Mass.

During the next fifteen years Father Ghislieri held various offices in the Order. He was successively elected prior of the Convents of Vigevano, Soncino, and Alba. One point which he emphasized in his conferences to his religious subjects was the one on which Saint Dominic himself laid so much stress—that is, that they should take great care to preserve intact the religious spirit while mixing with the world for the salvation of souls. "As salt," he said, "is quickly converted again into its first element, water, when the former is mixed with the latter, so religious, who 'are the salt of the earth' withdrawn by God from the waters of the world, are but too easily absorbed once more into their native element, with all its vices and its temptations, if they return to it without sufficient and just cause."

In works of charity he was indefatigable, often taking in the interests of charity, long and tiresome journeys, invariably traveling on foot and carrying his bag on his shoulders. He was always ready to give comfort, help, or advice to the weak and suffering, as though he had learned by experience to enter into every trial, and knew the most efficacious soothing for every sorrow. In 1543 he was summoned to the Provincial Chapter at Parma, and there he refuted the errors of the Lutherans in a masterly thesis dealing with many points of false doctrine. In consequence of this defense he was sought as a confessor by several persons of note, who needed especially enlightened direction. Among them was the Governor of Milan. This entailed a frequent journey of twenty miles, which the Saint made on foot, and so poorly clad that he must often have suffered extremely from the piercing cold and heavy rains of winter.

When in 1543 the heresy of Luther was beginning to make its way into the hitherto unperverted regions of the South, spreading the poison of falsehood through the inborn piety of the Italians, prompt measures of defense became necessary. The cardinals of the Holy Office in Rome, remembering the brilliant defense of the truth by Father Ghislieri at the Dominican Chapter of Parma, and relying on his reputation for prudence and firmness, sent him to Coma in the capacity of Inquisitor. No other inducement would have drawn him from his retreat, but this was a powerful one. He was called to a post of danger, of difficulties, and of thankless labor; for second only to the hatred which the innovators attached to the Office of the Supreme Pontiff was that which they associated with the Office of Inquisitor, and yet he accepted the charge in the hope that his efforts might prevent the plague of heresy from spreading among the children of God.

There are some who, while admiring Saint Pius's administration as Pope, accuse him of undue rigor and intolerance as Inquisitor. But if they will follow him faithfully through his disagreeable and arduous tasks, they will soon acknowledge their mistake. Instead of finding him overbearing and intolerant they will find him going about humbly, prayerfully, and patiently from city to city and from hamlet to hamlet, examining the faithful, arguing with the heretics, testing, judging, and reproving with all kindliness, but yet with apostolic firmness. The threats of wealthy and influential opponents hindered not the man of God in his work. On one occasion he was cited before a civil tribunal as a disturber of the peace. And although warned that assassins lay in wait for him on the road, he went, nevertheless, and as he stood before the judge, his serene unruffled gaze meeting the angry eyes of his accusers, the magistrate, as if speechless with rage at the tranquil indifference of the champion of truth, rose and, glaring furiously at the friar, left the court in haste. It is true that he did use stringent means for the suppression of new doctrines and not infrequently was instrumental in having severe punishments imposed upon obstinate heretics. But to form a proper appreciation of his actions we must judge them in the light of the conditions which then prevailed. Most of the governments were still Catholic, and in consequence any violation of her laws or any attempt to sully the purity of her doctrine was regarded not only as an offense against the Church, but also as an offense against the State. Whatever tended to undermine obedience to the Church was regarded as subversive of the peace and prosperity of the State. Hence it was that the Inquisitor by pronouncing a person a heretic rendered him subject to the penalties imposed for violation of the laws of the State. If these penalties were too severe, the blame is to be laid at the door, not of the Inquisitor, but of the State which had established them. The age of which we speak was one of force and violence, and the sanction which was then attached to all laws was more severe than that which is attached to them at the present day. Consequently if we view the conduct of Saint Pius in the light and spirit of the age in which he lived, we can find no sufficient reason for the harsh criticisms which have been made against him, as well as against many others who held the office of Inquisitor. Two instances will suffice to give an idea of his methods.

One of the most mischievous publications of the sectaries had been sent to a merchant at Coma for distribution among the inhabitants. Father Ghislieri, in virtue of his office, seized the books and refused them to the merchant who claimed them as his property. The merchant had friends in the Cathedral Chapter and appealed to the Vicar Capitular for redress; his appeal was successful, and the Inquisitor, in order to warn the faithful of the false doctrine contained in the consignment of books, and also to put them on their guard against the disseminators of evil, at once excommunicated all parties concerned. He was assailed by the mob with stones, and when threatened to be thrown into a well he calmly answered, "That shall be as God wills." The Governor of Milan summoned him to answer for his conduct and threatened him with imprisonment, but the servant of God had procured a mule and was far on his way to Rome before the Governor found means to carry out his threat. An incident in connection with this journey of the Saint is worthy of note. Father Ghislieri, travel-soiled and exhausted, reached the Eternal City late Christmas eve, 1515, and quite naturally enough went directly to his own monastery of Santa Sabina for lodgings. No notice of his coming had been given, and the prior not knowing the Saint, and distrusting the account of the poverty-marked wayfarer, asked: "What is the reason of your visit? Will you present yourself to the Cardinals in the hope of being elected Pope?" "I have come," answered the future Pontiff, "in the interests of the Church. I shall go home again as soon as I have been directed how to act. I ask only a few days' hospitality for myself and my poor worn-out mule." He was assigned a room next to that which had been occupied by Saint Dominic. Both rooms are now venerated as household sanctuaries. His case having been reported to the Cardinals of the Holy Office, they approved of his action, and with full confidence sent him back to his perilous and difficult charge. In returning he was advised to lay aside his Dominican habit and travel in secular disguise, since his life was in danger, but he refused, saying: "I accepted death with my commission, I can never die in a holier cause."

A certain Jew, who had become a Catholic while still a boy, had entered the Order of Friars Minor, and became a popular preacher. In course of time his discourses became tainted with heresy and the young friar was imprisoned. He, however, retracted, was released and returned to his Order. But being a second time convicted of heresy he was more obstinate, and there seemed to be no hope of his escaping death by fire, the penalty for a relapsed heretic. Father Ghislieri when walking through the prison was struck by the profound misery of the young Franciscan; he spoke to him kindly, begging him to confide in him as a friend. After long persuasion the young man told his name and history, but refused to renounce his error. The Inquisitor doubled his prayers, every day offered the Holy Sacrifice of the Mass for his conversion, and daily visited him, speaking to him with tenderness and sympathy. At last the persistency of the Saint prevailed. The prisoner, bursting into tears, expressed the wish to repent and to prove his sincerity by a life of penance. Saint Pius hastened to the Pope and sought and obtained his pardon. The prisoner made full abjuration of his heresy, confessed to his preserver, and received absolution. The Inquisitor next undertook to provide for the future of his penitent, who refused to return to the Order he had so shamefully disgraced. He received him into the Order of Preachers, clothing him with one of his own habits and adopting him as his spiritual son. This young friar later became the celebrated Biblical scholar Sixtus of Siena. Such were the methods used by Father Ghislieri, the Inquisitor, in his difficult and delicate task, with the result that he did perhaps more than any one else to check the tide of heresy and to keep Lutheranism from taking root in Italy.

In 1555 Cardinal Caraffa ascended the Papal Throne, as Paul IV, and one of his first acts was to appoint Father Ghislieri Bishop of Nepi and Sutri, near Rome. Tears were not common with Father Ghislieri, but at this news they flowed freely, while he implored the Holy Father to choose another prelate and let him go back to his convent, "to live and die as a Dominican." The Pope merely silenced the appeal with an express command to accept the charge; and when later on as Bishop he begged to resign his diocese, the Holy Father answered: "I will bind you with so strong a chain that even after my death you will never be free to return to your cloister."

This was a clear indication of the next step, and shortly afterward Bishop Ghislieri was peremptorily ordered to accept, without offering any opposition, the dignity of the Cardinalate. It was characteristic of the Bishop that he remained silent when urged to offer the customary thanks for the honor received. He was not grateful for the promotion and would not express gratitude when he did not feel it. It fell, then, to the members of the Sacred College to thank the Holy Father for giving them so worthy a colleague.

For his Titular Church he chose the Dominican Church Santa Maria sopra Minerva. He also wished to be called Cardinal Alessandrino instead of Ghislieri, as the former name had been given to him by the Father Provincial on the happy day of his religious profession, and it seemed like a last link to the Order from which he had been so reluctantly separated. Though Cardinal, he still wore the Dominican habit, observed the fasts and other austerities of the Dominican Rule, and lived in the simplicity which characterized his former life. When employing servants he would say to them: "If you come to me, remember you will not live as they do, in Cardinals' palaces. My household is like a monastery, and you must be prepared to live like lay-brothers." Yet he was kind and indulgent to the members of his household.

On the accession of Pius IV, December, 1559, Cardinal Alessandrino (Ghislieri) was confirmed in the Office of Supreme Inquisitor, to which office he was appointed by Paul IV, and appointed to the See of Mandovi. There he restored the purity of faith and discipline so gravely impaired by the wars of Piedmont. Frequently called to Rome for consultation, he displayed the same zeal and adherence to principle which had characterized his other activities. There he offered unceasing opposition to the appointment of Ferdinand de Medici, then only thirteen years old, as a member of the Sacred College, declaring that the Church needed not children, but men of mature years to sustain her reputation for wisdom and virtue. It was also due in great measure to his decided stand that the endeavors of Maximilian II, Emperor of Germany, to abolish ecclesiastical celibacy were defeated.

Pius IV died December 9, 1565, and on December 26th a conclave was opened for the election of his successor. Never was the choice of a Sovereign Pontiff of more vital importance. A man of no ordinary ability was required to meet the exigencies of the time and to carry out with firmness and discretion the discipline and regulations of the Council of Trent. Happily the most influential person in the conclave was the great and saintly Archbishop of Milan, Cardinal Charles Borromeo. He placed the name of Cardinal Alessandrino as a man capable of fulfilling the office, and after a little balloting his nominee received the number of votes necessary for election. Cardinal Borromeo and two other Cardinals were delegated to make known to the Pope-elect the choice of the conclave. They anticipated his objections, and carrying him from his cell bore him in their arms to the chapel, where he received the homage of the assembled Cardinals. "Pronounce your acceptance, Most Holy Father," commanded Cardinal Borromeo, "in the name of the Church." But the answer was more startling than words, for the strong, self-controlled Cardinal Alessandrino burst into tears, and his whole form shook with sobs while he repeated the words, "I cannot; I am not worthy." It was long before they could calm him, long before the ring could be placed upon his finger and before he could be prevailed upon to pronounce the word "Acceptamus." "We accept." Prudence, learning, and sanctity ascended the throne in the person of Pius V. When the report had reached his ears that the Romans dreaded the inflexible severity of the new Sovereign, he exclaimed: "Ah! so they think I shall rule them with an iron sway. God grant me the grace to so act that they may grieve more for my death than for my election." And so indeed it came to pass, for all classes from the highest to the lowest, even those who had little expected such thoughtful generosity, learned to love the great Pontiff for his unobtrusive benevolence.

It was indeed a dreary and woeful scene on which the Chief Shepherd's eye looked down from his watch-tower on the seven hills. Rome lay desolate under the curse of her children's sins. Usury, assassination, and immorality in a multitude of forms everywhere disgraced the Papal Domains. The scepter of the Holy Roman Empire was held by the weak and vacillating Emperor Maximilian II. In France, the wily Queen Regent, Catherine de Medici, had been intriguing with the rapidly increasing Huguenot party, in spite of its avowedly anarchistic and anti-Catholic tenets. The throne of Spain was filled by Phillip II, who unquestionably had the welfare of religion at heart, but was swayed by ambitions, personal and national, which too often injured its interests. Sebastian, King of Portugal, had not yet completed his fourteenth year. Elizabeth ruled in England, and had already severed it from the unity of Christendom. Such was the state of affairs in the wide family of which Pius V had now become father.

Divine Providence, however, had provided for him a corps of saints as co-workers. Saint Phillip Neri went daily through the streets winning thousands by the sweetness of his charity, and preaching everywhere frequent communion and continual prayer as the great means of spiritual regeneration. Saint Charles Borromeo, the model of Christian pastors, co-operated intimately with the Pontiff, in whose elevation he had been the principal instrument. Saint Francis Borgia was General of the Society of Jesus, which had lately been founded, and whose founder, Saint Ignatius, had just passed from this life. Saint Stanislaus Kostka was on the threshold of his saintly life, and was soon succeeded by Saint Aloysius. In Spain, Saint John of God and Saint John of the Cross were laboring for the restoration of primitive fervor, and Saint Theresa had just laid the foundation for a marvelous reform. In this reform she was aided by Saint Peter of Alcantara, who died two years before the accession of Saint Pius.

The first public measure of the new Pope indicated what was to be the spirit of his reign. The money which at the installation of Pontiffs had been scattered amid the populace in the streets was carefully distributed among those in greatest need and whose weakness or modesty would have prevented them from gaining anything in the general scramble. The thousand crowns usually spent on a banquet to the Cardinals and Ambassadors present at the coronation were sent as an alms to hospitals and to the poorest convents of the city. "For I know," said the Pope, "that God will not call me to account for suppressing a feast for the wealthy, but He may punish me severely if I neglect His poor."

It was soon manifest also that the general reform contemplated by the Pope was to begin with the reformation of his own court and capital. He began his reign with exceptional fasts and prayer, by commending himself to the suffrages of the various religious communities, and by publishing a jubilee to draw down upon himself and the Church all the graces so urgently needed at that critical time. He then assembled all the members of his household, made known to them what he expected of each according to his rank, and laid down special rules for their conduct. He fixed a certain time for evening prayers, at which he himself never failed to be present. He wore his Dominican habit under his pontifical vestments and slept upon the same hard pallet which he had used in his cell. Not only were the ordinary fasts of the Church observed in his household, but such was the frugality of his table that its daily cost did not exceed a *testone*, or about thirty-two cents of our money. Instead of armorial bearings, the following verse was engraved on his seal: "O that my ways were directed to keep Thy Commandments." A crucifix stood always on his table, at the foot of which were inscribed these words: "God forbid that I should glory save in the cross of our Lord Jesus Christ."

In a consistory held expressly for the purpose he addressed a fatherly exhortation to the Cardinals and Prelates, in which he explained to them the surest way to appease the wrath of God and to stay the progress of heretics and infidels was that each should begin by setting in order his own conscience and his own house. "It is to you," he said, "that Jesus Christ addresses these words, 'You are the Light of the world; you are the Salt of the earth.' Therefore enlighten the people by the purity of your lives and by the brilliancy of your holiness! God does not ask from you mere ordinary virtue, but downright perfection!"

A very annoying source of evil was the intercourse of Christian families with the Jews. The crafty Jews took advantage of the simple credulity of the Christians. Practicing under a fake science of astrology, they introduced among them various kinds of immorality, while at the same time they ruined their fortunes by usury. The new Pope, therefore, banished all Jews from every part of the territories of the Church, except the Jewish merchants at Rome and Ancona, where their presence was necessary for keeping up the commerce of the Levant. But even in these places they were confined to separate quarters of the city as a precaution against their evil influences.

The assassinations and robberies daily committed in his domains did not escape the vigilant eye of the new Sovereign. By an agreement made with the viceroys of Naples and Tuscany, it was enacted that bandits should be seized and executed wherever they should be found, without distinction of territory. By these prompt measures the Ecclesiastical States were soon freed from this scourge. He exhorted unceasingly all magistrates and rulers to justice, and enacted many laws for the improvement of public morals, which were enforced with so much vigor that within less than a year the whole aspect of affairs in the Papal States had changed.

The next care of Saint Pius was to procure the recognition of the disciplinary decrees of the Council of Trent by all Catholic nations. A few of them, among which Portugal, the Republic of Venice, and the Catholic cantons of Switzerland were honorably distinguished, yielded instant obedience. But France and Germany temporized and hesitated, and even Phillip imposed certain restrictions upon the publications of the decrees in Spain, Flanders, and in the Italian States. The Pope's pen was constantly in hand directing nuncios, explaining the Church's canons, and reasoning with and exhorting Ambassadors. He also used his growing influence with the Bishops to hasten the establishing of diocesan seminaries, for hitherto the universities had been the only educational centers for ecclesiastics. From the Papal treasury he defrayed the expenses of students who were unable to educate themselves for the priesthood.

In September, 1566, the Catechism of the Council of Trent was issued. The new edition of the Breviary, revised by the Saint, was published in July, 1568, and the revised Missal two years later. By a special decree, those orders which could show a rite of their own in existence for more than two hundred years, approved by the Holy See, were permitted to retain it. Thus the Benedictines, Carthusians, Cistercians, Carmelites, and Dominicans kept their ancient office and Mass. Church music received much attention. Being solicitous that the Real Presence in the churches should be hailed with the homage of sacred music, he ordered the old Gregorian plain chant to be restored in its simplicity, and appointed Palestrina master of the orchestra in the Papal Chapel.

To appreciate his world-wide political activities in the interests of humanity it would be necessary to study carefully the eighty volumes of the Pope's correspondence preserved in the Vatican.

Saint Pius, as Supreme Pontiff, religiously kept the resolution he had made when Cardinal, never to make his own exaltation a means of advancing his family. He was, however, prevailed upon to entrust the administration of temporal affairs to his great nephew, Michael Bonnelli, who was chosen, not on account of his relationship, but for his admirable fitness to fulfill the office. He made him steward of the ecclesiastical domains, and at the same time issued a solemn decree forbidding all alienation of those domains. The Cardinals were bound by oath, from which they were never to seek absolution nor accept a dispensation, to resist with all their power any infringement of this decree in future.

We now come to an incident in the life of Saint Pius which portrays his character in a new light. We have seen how inflexible he could be when called upon to defend the truth against the insidious attacks of heretics and how much energy he displayed in combating the moral and social evils of his time. But in his dealings with Elizabeth, the Apostate Queen of England, we are given a striking example of his forbearance and prudence, and also of his tenderness toward the oppressed of that unhappy realm. When Saint Pius ascended the Papal throne Elizabeth had for seven years been trying to uproot the Catholic faith within her domains. But still he withheld his hand, watching the tragedy deepen, as the unhappy nation accepted in sullen resentment the new religion forced upon it by fear and violence, until in 1570 he issued a Bull of excommunication and deposition against the Queen, separating her from the communion of the faithful, and absolving her subjects from their allegiance.

It will be remembered that Elizabeth's title was but a parliamentary one, since she was the illegitimate daughter of Henry VIII and Anne Boleyn, born during the lifetime of the true queen, and that subsequently, on Henry's marriage with Jane Seymour, she had been declared illegitimate by act of Parliament at her father's command. Nevertheless she had taken the oath of Catholic sovereigns and promised to rule as a Catholic queen. Ten days after the coronation ceremonies she began to legislate against Papal authority in England. Through Parliament she enacted laws whereby the reigning sovereign became the head of the Church in England—"Supreme Governor in all ecclesiastical and spiritual things as well as temporal." Mass was prohibited, Catholic Bishops deposed, imprisoned, or exiled. Before the first year of Elizabeth's reign was over the acts of Queen Mary and Cardinal Pole had "vanished like smoke," and before ten years had passed the Penal Laws were in full force. The words "Traitor" and "Catholic" had become synonymous, and priests were hanged, drawn, and quartered for celebrating Mass. Protestantism, "by law established," had become the national religion. Elizabeth had by her conduct proclaimed herself the determined adversary of the Catholic cause in England, and had, moreover, supported rebels against the Catholic sovereigns on the Continent. Pope Pius made every possible overture for a reconciliation. He had offered to legitimize her and to recognize her claim to the allegiance of her subjects, but all efforts were futile. She would do nothing more than ridicule the generous character of the Saint. Elizabeth was warned of the steps the Pope would take if the present state of affairs continued, but the warning fell on irresponsive ears.

In 1568 Queen Mary Stuart, Elizabeth's cousin, was driven from Scotland by the disloyalty of her subjects and sought refuge in England. There, in defiance of all justice and decency, she was thrown into prison, and from that time till her execution, in 1587, she was the victim of plots, intrigues, and slander. Pope Pius had long taken a paternal interest in the widowed Queen, who had turned to him in her anguish, and with full confidence in his fatherly pity made known to him the treacherous and unnatural treatment which she was receiving from the cruel and ambitious Elizabeth. The Pontiff's letters to the broken-hearted Mary Stuart are gems of rare and warm manifestations of sanctified tenderness. He granted her the privilege of receiving Holy Communion from her own hands, sending her a golden pyx containing consecrated hosts, and he appealed continually to the great Catholic powers to come to the rescue of the captive Queen, but all efforts were fruitless.

In October, 1569, an uprising took place in the North. Its primary object was the release of Mary Stuart, but to have prominently put forward this idea would have been equivalent to signing her death warrant; consequently the proclamation merely stated that the Catholics had taken up arms in defense of the true religion. The insurrection failed miserably and was followed by severe punishment. More than eight hundred northern Catholics perished at the hands of the executioners.

A Bull of excommunication had been prepared for some time, but Pius deferred its promulgation, hoping that Elizabeth would relent. At length, when the intelligence arrived of the failure of the insurrection and of the cruelties perpetrated by Elizabeth on the insurrectionists, he deemed the time ripe for striking a decisive blow. He signed the Bull on the 25th of February, 1570, and ordered its promulgation. Three months later a copy of it was nailed to the door of the residence of the Protestant Bishop of London by John Felton, a Catholic. He was captured and put on the rack in the hope of forcing him to make known the name of the person from whom he received his commission. Upon his persistent refusal, he was subjected to other indignities and was finally hanged in Saint Paul's churchyard August 8th. He has since been beatified.

Though Elizabeth professed to despise the sentence pronounced by the Pope, it is clear that she did not like it. She thought it was connected with some plan of foreign invasion or domestic treason, declared it to be an insult to European sovereigns, and induced Maximilian II, of the Holy Roman Empire, to endeavor to have it withdrawn. To the solicitations of the Emperor the Pope answered by asking whether Elizabeth deemed the sentence valid or invalid. If valid, why did she not seek a reconciliation with the Holy See? If invalid, why did she wish it revoked? The abusive language and revengeful threats of Elizabeth were unable to alter the Pope's decision, and the sentence remained unwithdrawn.

That the Bull, as regards the deposition, failed in its effect, is not due to Pius, but to those temporal rulers who, nominally Catholic, passed it over in silence, ignoring it for motives of self-interest instead of uniting with the Holy See in enforcing it upon England. Temporal weapons were the only ones feared by Elizabeth, and the knowledge that the great powers of Europe stood prepared to support the Holy Father in his sentence against her would speedily have brought her to her knees, and certainly have changed the course of English history.

Spain also contributed much to the ever-accumulating anxieties of the Supreme Pontiff. There the Inquisition had become a secular tribunal, deriving its authority from the King, and its judgments were often far different from what they would have been had the Church guided its proceedings. The odium of many of its acts fell on religion, and not infrequently was it imperative on Rome to clear up the mistake.

The Pope tried to persuade Charles IX of France to use the sword only in the interests of peace, and also to exercise the virtues of regal justice and mercy, virtues which are so important in a ruling monarch at all times, but especially when the wild passions of men are let loose, as was the case during the Huguenot uprising. Unfortunately the influence of Catherine de Medici proved fatal to the great good which should have resulted had the Pope's instructions been followed; yet there can be no doubt that, were it not for the unwearied exertions of the Supreme Pontiff, turbulence and irreligion would have had a far more demoralizing influence.

Saint Pius devoted also much time to America, then but recently discovered. His great care there was to aid those devoted bands of missionaries, Benedictines, Jesuits, Franciscans, and Dominicans, who were wearing out their lives in conflicts with ignorance and vice on the very frontiers of Christendom. The natives listened eagerly to the voice of the missionaries who preached the Christian faith to them, but when they saw the evil lives of many Christians they concluded that a religion which produced such evil results could never have come from heaven. Thus the noble efforts of the missionaries were thwarted by the cruelty and wickedness of European Christians. Bartholomeo de Las Casas, an eminent Dominican missionary of the South, complained bitterly that the vices of the European settlers greatly hindered the spread of Christianity among the natives, and begged the Pope to use his influence with the temporal rulers that they should restrain the guilty. Hence the Pontiff wrote the Catholic sovereigns of Europe, emploring them to reign as vice-gerents of the King of kings and to encourage the propagation of the Catholic faith in their new western dominions.

From the internal wounds of Christendom the watchful eye of its Father turned to the dangers which threatened it from without. In the far East, Solyman the Magnificent, Sultan of the Turks, was carefully watching every movement of his Christian neighbors. He hailed with exceeding satisfaction the appearance of Luther, whom he took to be a new prophet sent at the prayer of Mahomet to be an aid toward the subjugation of Christendom by the Mussulman armies. It is difficult in these days, when the Mussulman Empire lies an inert mass at the threshold of Christendom, to realize the terror of its name in the days of Pius V. Then the Mediterranean was covered with its fleets, Greece and Hungary were under its dominion, and the conquest of Malta and Cyprus were the only obstacles to its advance upon Italy.

The Knights of Malta heroically guarded the outposts assigned to them as a barrier against the inroads of the fanatical Turks. They were truly chivalrous champions of God, men after the heart of Saint Pius. But the day came when it was clear that the gallant force was so weakened by the toll it had paid to the ferocity of its assailants that the next attack of the enemy would crush these valiant defenders of Catholic peace. A massacre of the garrison would surely follow the surrender of Malta, and without prompt succor the island could not hold out. The Grand Master of the Order, John de la Valette, sent word to the Pope, explaining the situation, and asking whether or not he should abandon the island and retreat to Sicily while there was yet time. "No," came the answer from Pius V; "remain at your glorious post. Willingly would I hasten to die, God permitting, at your side. As duty binds us here, we will call on Christendom to take our place in this God-crowned warfare, and while we open the spiritual treasures of the Church with liberal hand to your auxiliaries, we shall also afford you all the temporal help in our power, praying the Divine Omnipotence to guard you." By means of the money and troops sent by the Pope the danger was averted for the time being.

Under Selim II, however, the progress of the Turks became more alarming than ever. They had taken Cyprus with the active co-operation of the Greek population of the island, and were massacring the Latin nobility and clergy. Yet the Saint found it impossible to move Christendom to its own defense. In 1570 he sent

Cardinal legates to every court, excepting England, to preach a crusade, to beg for ships, men, and money. Every court but Spain returned an excuse. At length by dint of effort he succeeded in forming a league between Spain, Venice, and the Holy See. Don John of Austria was appointed Commander-in-Chief. Saint Pius assured him that "if relying on divine grace, rather than on human help, he attacked the enemy, God would not be wanting to His own cause." He enjoined the officers to look to the good conduct of their troops; to suppress swearing, gaming, riot, and plunder, and thereby to render themselves deserving of victory. A fast of three days was proclaimed for the success of the enterprise, and the Rosary was to be recited every day on board the ships. All the men went to confession, received Holy Communion, and took advantage of the plentiful indulgences which the Pope attached to the expedition. The Forty Hours' Exposition of the Blessed Sacrament was ordered in all the churches of Rome, during which the Rosary was to be recited aloud. A universal jubilee also was published to draw down God's blessing on the Christian army.

On the afternoon of October 7, 1571, the Christian fleet, consisting of 210 vessels, met and engaged, in one of the decisive battles of the world, the Ottoman fleet, numbering about 300 ships, under command of Ali Pasha. During the night preceding the battle and all through the day itself the aged Pontiff, aged and broken in health as he was, passed in fasting and prayer; thus, like another Moses, he prayed while the armies of God fought. All through the city the monasteries and colleges were also in prayer. As the evening advanced, and he was in anxious consultation with some officials of the Papal Court, he suddenly paused and began to pray. His serious emaciated countenance, lined with care and responsibility, grew flushed with the fervor of his petition. Then rising he went to the window that overlooked the Campagna and gazed silently across the blue distance. All at once his countenance lit up with an expression of joy and a murmur of thanksgiving parted his lips;

then, turning to his attendants, he said: "This is no time for business; go, return thanks to the Lord God. In this very hour our fleet has engaged the Turks and is victorious." He then dismissed his attendants, and threw himself upon his knees, while tears of gratitude for so signal a victory coursed down his cheeks. The date and hour of this prophecy were carefully noted by the Cardinals, and it proved to be the decisive moment in which the Christian fleet triumphed over the Turks in the Bay of Lepanto.

It was near the end of October before Contarini, the messenger from the fleet, reached Rome with tidings of the victory. He arrived at midnight and was immediately admitted into the presence of the Pope. When the Saint heard all the particulars of the glorious and complete victory he fell on his knees, crying out in the fulness of his heart: "He hath regarded the prayer of the humble and He hath not despised their petition. Let these things be written unto another generation, and the people to be created shall praise the Lord."

Upward of thirty thousand Turks lost their lives in the battle, ten thousand were made prisoners, and almost their whole fleet was taken, while fifteen thousand Christian prisoners were liberated. The Crusaders lost seven thousand five hundred men. This was the turning point of Turkish invasion of Europe. They lost prestige and self-confidence, and from then onward their power gradually declined.

In memory of this unparalleled victory, and in gratitude to our Blessed Lady for her powerful intercession in behalf of the Christian forces, Saint Pius inserted the words, "Auxilium Christianorum, ora pro nobis," "Help of Christians, pray for us," in her Litanies, and ordered that thenceforward the commemorative feast of Our Lady of Victories should be observed on the anniversary of the battle, October 7th. Pope Gregory XIII changed the title of the feast to that of Our Lady of the Rosary, and appointed the first Sunday of October (Rosary Sunday) for its celebration.

When one considers the immense amount of work that fell to Saint Pius as Pope, he is naturally led to inquire what time could he possibly give to the care of his own soul. Engaged unceasingly in attending to the wants of others, or to the affairs of State, it would seem that he could give but little time to private devotion. But such, indeed, was not the case. The early hours of the day were given to prayer and meditation. He celebrated Mass very early in the morning, and with such fervor as to greatly edify all who assisted at it. After Mass he spent a long time in thanksgiving and meditation, often becoming so absorbed in God that his attendants were obliged to pull him by his habit when they had occasion to speak to him. Every day he studied the Scriptures, and read some portion of the Life of Saint Dominic, or of some other Saint, preferably of the Dominican Order. His devotion to the Rosary was very great. He recited it unfailingly each day, and published decrees confirming the privileges granted to the Rosary Confraternity. The following is a quotation taken from one of these decrees: "Inspired, as is believed, by the Holy Spirit, the Blessed Dominic, Founder of the Order of Friar Preachers, on an occasion similar to this in which we now find ourselves, at a time when heresy blinded a great number of souls, turning his eyes toward heaven, where the Blessed Virgin reigns, conceived a very easy way, within the reach of all, to propitiate the Mother of God by the recitation of her Rosary or Psalter. We ourselves also turn to that mountain whence cometh our help in the midst of our sorrows, and we tenderly exhort all the faithful disciples of Jesus Christ, in the Name of the Lord, to follow this example."

He prayed fervently for the dead, and often declared that he had received marvelous assistance in his greatest needs through that devotion. At times when troubles accumulated he loved to ponder on the spirit of the Martyrs of Rome, toward whom he was especially devoted. It is told of him, that once, when asked by a stranger for some relic to take back home, the Pope bade him take a handful of the dry earth at his feet. The stranger, not wishing to offend the Pontiff by refusing the proffered gift, did as he was bidden, and found to his astonishment that it stained his scarf with blood. The Saint then informed him that the ground upon which he stood had been saturated with the blood of Martyrs.

Early in the day he began to grant audiences to those who had business with him, and frequently they were so numerous that it was late in the evening before he could dismiss the last one. To gain time he sometimes admitted ambassadors and men of important affairs during his meals. It was not uncommon to see early in the morning groups of strangers, or even ecclesiastics, wending their way by torchlight through the narrow streets of Rome to the Vatican in order to secure an audience with the Pope. He gave one day each month exclusively to the poor, whom he received with such kindness, and listened so patiently to all they had to say, that when he could not grant what they asked they could see it was a great grief to him to refuse their petitions.

Throughout his whole life, Saint Pius was remarkable for his austerity, and toward the end of his career became more and more self-denying. He suffered extremely from gravel, but offered the pain as a penance for his sins and firmly refused all remedies, from which his modesty shrank. When suffering the tortures of this painful malady he would invariably slowly drag himself to kneel before his crucifix and repeat the prayer: "Lord increase my pains, but increase also my patience." He could never be prevailed upon to take the nourishing food recommended by his physicians. His repast consisted of eggs and wild chicory or some other bitter herb, and he forbade all seasoning of it. On fasting days he did not consider this austerity severe enough, but ate only once, and limited the number of glasses of water he drank.

He listened humbly to reproofs given by ill-tempered subjects, and afterward thanked them for the service they had rendered. He one day pardoned a libertine who had lampooned him, saying: "My friend, I would have punished you if you had insulted the Pope, but since you attacked only Michael Ghislieri, go in peace." It was his humility that made him wish to abdicate. But when he announced his intention of doing so and of retiring to the Dominican monastery at Bosco, his native village, to end his life in prayer and meditation, his spiritual adviser and the Cardinals overcame his resolutions by representing to him that God had entrusted to him the guidance of His Church, and that it was his duty not to abandon it. He little loved the honors which his exalted dignity merited for him, regarding all such things as painful thorns, useful only in so far as they warned him of the peril in which he was placed. He often declared that he had not a single moment of peace since becoming Pope; also that he was worthy of compassion. He bitterly repented having accepted a charge he considered so far above his abilities.

Six months after the Battle of Lepanto Pius V lay on his deathbed. He had been suffering uncomplainingly for years, but at this stage of his life his painful malady increased rapidly. At the beginning of Lent he, although his weakness was very great, began to fast as though he were in sound health. His attendants, wishing to keep him alive, mixed gravy with the vegetables he ate, but as soon as he tasted the flavor of meat he said: "Would you wish me, during the short time I have to live, to break the laws which I have always kept and God has given me the grace to keep for fifty-three years?"

March, 1572, found him failing fast, and many times he had to deny himself the consolation of saying Mass. On such occasions Holy Communion was brought to him by his nephew, Cardinal Alessandrino, an heir alike to his name and virtues, and for hours afterward he would remain in a transport of love, from which he could be recalled only with difficulty.

Public audiences having been suspended, in order to allow him to spend the days yet left to him in preparing for eternity, the report spread abroad that he was dead, and consequently the city was filled with mourning and lamentations. The Pope was deeply moved on hearing of the grief of his children. He felt that his first words as their Sovereign had been a true prophecy, and that his people would mourn for him as their friend and father rather than as their ruler, and wished to give them his pontifical blessing once more. Hence on Easter Sunday, conquering the mortal weakness that was creeping over him, he robed himself in full pontificals, had himself carried to the balcony above the entrance to Saint Peter's, and there solemnly blessed the assembled crowds. A deputation of the clergy and Roman nobles then waited on him to offer congratulations on his supposed recovery, but the Saint quickly told them of his real state. "My children," he said, "I have no longer any business to transact except with God. The account which I shall soon have to render to Him of all the deeds and words of my life requires me to employ all the powers of my soul to prepare for it."

To the consternation of his friends, and contrary to the advice of his physicians, he insisted on paying a farewell visit to the seven Basilicas of Rome and to the Scala Sancta. He set out on foot, upheld by the arms of his assistants. More than once he halted as though the agony of death were mastering him, but, murmuring feebly, "He who can do all things will finish the work He has begun," continued his journey, thus following his "Via Crucis" to the end.

On his return to the Vatican, he was told that a number of English Catholics had come to seek shelter at Rome from the persecution of the tyrant Elizabeth. He desired to see them, made anxious inquiries concerning the state of Catholics in England, and charged his nephew to supply all their wants. As they left the room he was heard to say: "My God, Thou knowest that I have ever been ready to shed my blood for the salvation of that nation."

On the 30th of April he announced that his hours were numbered, and asked the Bishop of Segia to administer to him the Sacrament of Extreme Unction, and from that time on the little strength that remained to him ebbed swiftly away. Once, when every one present believed him to have passed away, he revived, and with an animation wonderful in a dying man said to the bystanders: "If you love my mortal life, full of so many miseries, you ought much more to love that unchangeable and blessed life which by the grace of God I hope soon to enjoy in heaven. You know well that the greatest wish of my life has been to conserve in its purity the deposit of faith, to overthrow the empire of the infidels, and to extend the Kingdom of God upon earth. But my sins and crimes have proved obstacles to the attainment of my wishes. I adore the depths of the judgments of God and acknowledge myself to be His unprofitable steward. It only remains for me to recommend to you, with all my soul, that same Church which God committed to my care. Do your utmost to elect a successor full of zeal for the glory of God, who will be attached to no other interest in the world, and who will seek nothing but the welfare of Christianity."

When he had uttered these words a little incident occurred which shows the delicate perfection of his chastity. In the movement of his arms one of them became bare. This wounded his natural purity, and he quickly tried to cover it again with the sleeve of his woolen tunic.

He died on the first day of May, 1572. His feast is celebrated on May 5th. The heroic virtues which he practiced throughout his eventful career, and the miracles wrought during his lifetime and through his intercession after death, merited for him a place in the calendar of Saints. He is known and venerated as Saint Pius the Fifth, the last of the canonized Popes.

BIBLIOGRAPHY

Acta Sanctorum, Bollandists, May 1st.

L'Année Dominicaine, St. Pius. Lyons, 1891.

FALLOUX: Histoire de S. Pie V. Paris, 1844.

ANTONY, C. M.: Saint Pius V. New York, Longmans, 1911.

WILBERFORCE, O. P., B. W.: Saint Pius V. London, C. T. S.

ANONYMOUS: Life of St. Pius and Other Saints of the Order. New York, 1887.

DE MONTOR, ARTRAND: History of the Popes. New York, 1867.

LINGARD: History of England, Vol. VI.

HALLAM: Europe in the Middle Ages.

LEE, D. D., Rev. F. G.: The Church under Queen Elizabeth. London, 1880.

St. Pius V, the Father of Christendom. Dublin Review, LIX, October, 1886.

Saint John of Cologne

"God is wonderful in His Saints" (Ps. lxvii, 36). These words of the Psalmist find their fullest verification in the life of Saint John of Cologne, who by his life, sufferings, and death was to show forth the wonderful works of God. Hence he merited to the greatest extent those sublime titles bestowed on him by Pope Pius IX in the Bull of Canonization of the Martyrs of Gorcum. In this document our Martyr is hailed as "Most brave athlete of Christ," "Honor of the Dominican Family," "Splendor of parish priests," "Ornament of the Sacerdotal State," and "New glory of the Catholic Church." Thus were also fulfilled in him, in a remarkable manner, the prophetic words of the Magnificat Antiphon for the feast of All Saints of the Order of Preachers, "He that is mighty hath done great things to the Order; He hath received Dominic His Servant, blessed him and his seed forever."

Judged according to worldly standards, our Saint is but a beaten martyr, done to an ignominious death. But how different is the judgment of the Church. More than three hundred years have elapsed since his martyrdom and he is honored as a glorious champion of Jesus Christ; and his death, regarded by the world as "utter destruction," is declared by the Church as "precious in the sight of the Lord." In Dominican martyrology, the name of Saint John of Cologne is written in letters of gold and he takes his place, by the side of the heroic Saint Peter of Verona, at the head of that legion of martyrs of the Order of Preachers who have dyed their white habits red with their life's blood. "This is the true brotherhood, which

Saint John of Cologne

could never be vanquished in conflict. By shedding their blood they have followed the Lord, and by spurning princely honors they have attained the kingdom of heaven."

Saint John was, furthermore, to shed additional luster on the Order of Preachers by becoming the "Martyr of the Blessed Sacrament and of the Primacy of the Roman Pontiff." Profound devotion to the most Holy Eucharist and unwavering loyalty to the Apostolic See have ever been cherished by the Order as most noble traditions. Faithful to this heritage, our Saint laid down his life in defense of the two crucial doctrines, "the rocks of scandal," upon which the so-called Reformers were making shipwreck of their faith, namely, the dogmas of the Real Presence of Christ in the Blessed Sacrament and of the Primacy of the Pope.

As the "Splendor of parish priests," Saint John stands out pre-eminently among the saints of our Order as the shining example of the friar preacher laboring in the parishes for the salvation of souls. In watching over the flock entrusted to his care, our Saint set about with the utmost zeal to pattern his life after that of the Divine Shepherd. Like the Master, he went about doing good, never flagging, never faltering, never failing in the work of saving souls. When the "wolves" came to catch and scatter his sheep, this intrepid Son of Saint Dominic stood by and defended the sheep of his flock until he was captured and imprisoned. Then he proved himself to be indeed like the Good Shepherd by laying down his life for his flock.

The few facts that have come down to us regarding the life of Saint John of Cologne are soon told. He was born in Germany. The exact time and place of his birth, however, are unknown. At an early age he entered the Order of Preachers in the famous Convent of the Holy Cross, in Cologne, which belongs to the German Province. The school connected with this convent was renowned throughout the Middle Ages for its profound learning, and ranked with the great universities of Paris, Bologna, and Oxford.

It harbored within its walls at various times, as teachers, scholars, or theologians, many of the most shining lights in the history of the Order. Among these were Saint Thomas Aquinas, Blessed Albert the Great, Blessed Ambrose Sansedonius, Blessed Henry Suso, and the famous mystic, John Tauler.

Two qualities that should distinguish every friar preacher were remarkably evident in Saint John, namely, learning and sanctity. For twenty years he labored most zealously as pastor of the parish in the village of Hoornaer, near Gorcum, in Holland. What remains of our Saint's history shall be recounted when he enters the company of the holy martyrs of Gorcum to become one of their number and to share in their triumph and glory.

Before giving a detailed account of the acts of these martyrs, it is necessary to know something of the conditions of the times and the state of Holland and Belgium in the latter half of the sixteenth century. The inhabitants of these countries were at that time in rebellion against the dominion of Spain. Calvinism was professed by a great portion of the population, and the Protestant leaders, profiting by the people's natural hostility to Spain, a staunch Catholic power, strove to impress upon them that to be loyal to their country they must belong to the Protestant party, since the Catholics must necessarily be amicable to Spain and enemies of the fatherland.

Charles V of Spain, who was aware of the seditious and anarchical character of the so-called Reform, had introduced the Spanish Inquisition into the Netherlands to check the inroads of heresy, but he could not stem the torrent. Error can hardly be suppressed by force when it meets no opposition in conscience and when it has already gained part of the people. The severity of Charles succeeded, however, in keeping the Dissenters from forming a faction powerful enough to menace the security of the Church or the State.

When Philip II succeeded to the throne, three thousand soldiers, who were able to hold the rebels in check, were recalled upon protest of the people. The Protestants, who resented the fact that the most important offices in the State were filled exclusively by Spaniards, placed themselves under the united leadership of the Prince of Orange, the Count of Egmont, and the Count of Hoorne. William, Prince of Orange, the recognized champion, drew up a petition which was signed not only by a large number of Protestants, but also by many Catholics, protesting against the Inquisition. They demanded its suppression and asked that all measures enacted against heretics should be revoked.

Not obtaining all that they desired, the Protestants rose simultaneously all over the country. In this uprising they were aided by many disaffected Calvinists who had returned from France. The work of pillage and destruction was carried on everywhere; churches, monasteries, convents, and even hospitals were given up to the merciless Reformers. They ruined the magnificent cathedral of Antwerp, the pride of the country. In Flanders alone four hundred churches were sacked. This formidable rebellion was at length suppressed and the government was placed in the hands of the stern Duke of Alva.

The Duke, with an army of select troops, entered Brussels on August 22, 1567, and quickly brought the leaders of the revolt to condign punishment. He had quelled the rebellion, but had not rooted it out of the land, for its numerous ramifications were only waiting another opportunity to spring into life again. The Prince of Orange, who had escaped punishment for his treason by a voluntary exile, was raising troops and conspiring with the Calvinists and the court of France, then under Huguenot influence. He was advised to build a fleet and to attack the northern provinces, where the heretics existed in great numbers.

A fleet of about forty sail had been fitted out under the direction of the ferocious Lumnaye, Count de la Marck. The Gueux, or Watergeuzen (Sea-beggars), made their way across the North Sea and along the coast of Flanders. This was in the spring of 1572. Adverse winds drove them on the Isle of Voorn, at the mouth of the

Meuse. The port of Brielle was captured on April 1st, the same year. They pillaged churches and religious houses about the city, broke images and all that bore marks of the Catholic Church. The town was fortified by the Gueux, for whom it became a place of refuge and afterward the nucleus for insurrection. Dortrecht and other towns of the locality also fell into their hands. Three months after the occupation of Brielle, Marin Brant, a man of considerable military talent, who had previously been a dike-digger and later a pirate under the Count de la Marck, ascended the Meuse as far as Gorcum.

Gorcum, originally Gorinchen, is a little town in Holland. It is situated in the midst of a fertile country, about twenty miles from Dortrecht. At the time of Brant's approach the town was in a very poor state of defense. In fact, the only place considered safe at all was a citadel built on the town walls, at the foot of which flowed the Meuse. When the town was attacked the inhabitants hoped that it would hold out until assistance could be obtained from the neighboring cities, still loyal to the throne of Spain. The Protestants of Gorcum had, however, sent messengers to Dortrecht, which had just been captured, to attack the town suddenly. Accordingly, on the morning of June 25th, thirteen vessels carrying soldiers were sighted coming up the river from Dortrecht. They sailed almost to the very walls of the city, their appearance causing great joy to the Calvinists, but sorrow and dismay to the Catholics.

In the town of Gorcum there was a monastery of Franciscan Recollects. When the town was approached by the invaders these religious took refuge in the citadel. A number of the most influential citizens also fled thither. They were later joined by the learned parish priest of Gorcum, Leonard Vechel, of Bois-le-Duc, and also his assistant, Nicholas Janssen, surnamed Poppel, of Welde, in Belgium; Godfrey van Duynen, of Gorcum, who performed his sacerdotal offices in his native city; and John Lenartz, of Oisterwijk, an Augustinian, who was director of a convent of nuns of the Order of Saint Augustine, in Gorcum.

Father Leonard Vechel and Father Nicholas Poppel had done all in their power to animate the courage of the citizens. They visited the magistrates, made a tour of the walls, and harangued the soldiery, but, as the enemy had proclaimed toleration for Catholicism, the citizens failed to see their danger.

The refugees had scarcely reached the fortress when the Gueux were secretly introduced into the town by their partisans. They were under the leadership of Brant. As soon as he found himself in possession of the town, he assembled the inhabitants, proposed that they vow eternal hatred to the Duke of Alva and to the Spanish conquerors of the country, and that they swear allegiance to the Prince of Orange. All present consented with loud cries of "Long live the Gueux!" Brant then convoked the town council and made arrangements to complete his successes.

The Gueux then proceeded to besiege the citadel. The place was poorly fortified and the aid expected by the inmates had not arrived. The soldiers of the enemy greatly outnumbered those in the fortress. Consequently the besiegers soon found themselves masters of the situation. The citadel was surrendered on the condition, which was accepted by Brant, that every person within, whether of the clergy or of the laity, should be allowed to go free and unharmed; but all the property was to be turned over to the conquerors.

During the parley preceding the surrender the ecclesiastics prepared for the worst. They confessed to each other and then heard the confessions of the rest. Father Nicholas Poppel had brought with him the adorable Sacrament and all were enabled to communicate. When the Gueux entered, the Catholics found to their profound sorrow how many of their fellow-citizens, even of those who had been reputed among the best, had gone over to the enemy. The mob carried with them many articles plundered from the village churches, and now they came to demand the treasures that they thought had been carried into the citadel by the religious. Brant then commanded all the inmates of the fortress to go to the upper story. Then the Gueux surrounded them, exclaiming, "Open your purses!" "Turn out your pockets!" After they had searched them and found that they had been disappointed in their calculations, they treated their prisoners, especially the clergy, with great cruelty. The injuries heaped upon them can well be imagined. Crowds of curious spectators came to the prison to gaze upon them and wantonly to insult them. "We have them at last," they cried, "these shaven pates, supporters of the Papacy and Spanish despotism!" The captives, however, remained silent, rejoicing thus to suffer in imitation of the Master.

After a day elapsed, spent in mingled fear and hope, the names of the prisoners were called, and all except the priests and religious were set at liberty, but only after having paid large ransoms. The aged priest, Godfrey van Duynen, was also permitted to leave; but upon reaching the drawbridge one of the heretics asked the soldiers who accompanied him whither they were taking him. "He is allowed to go because he is a fool," answered the soldiers. "Fool!" rejoined the citizens. "He has wits enough to make his God in the Mass, and enough head to be hung." Upon this they jeeringly led him back to prison.

On the following Friday, though faint with hunger, the holy men refused to partake of the meat set before them in mockery of their religion. The soldiers, having surfeited on the food and drink found in the castle, were just in condition to vent their fury to the fullest extent upon their prisoners. They resolved to call them in turn, to ascertain "the state of their purses."

The parish priest, Father Leonard Vechel, was the first summoned. He still had a little money, which he promptly turned over to them. Godfrey van Duynen was called next. "Show us your treasures," they demanded. The priest responded that he had none. "Possible!" said the soldiers. "You are half fool; it is not to you that valuables would be given, but rather to this old confessor of nuns."

They meant Father Theodore van der Eem, chaplain to the Sisters of Saint Agnes. Holding a pistol to his heart, they demanded his treasures. But upon his earnest reiterations that he knew of none, they proceeded to question Father Nicholas Poppel. When he also declared that he had nothing, they blasphemingly cried, "At least give us the God which you made in the Mass. You, who have often railed against us in the pulpit, what do you think now, in the face of this pistol?" With the courage of a martyr, he replied, "I believe in the Real Presence of my God in the Sacramental species. If that is a reason why I should die, then kill me. I should be happy to die at the end of the confession of faith you desire from me." Casting himself upon his knees, he exclaimed, "Into Thy hands, O Lord, I commend my spirit." But his time had not yet come. A soldier snatched the cord of Saint Francis from one of the friars and twisted it around Father Poppel's neck. Fastening one end to the prison door and pulling the other, they violently raised him from the floor repeatedly. They continued their questions regarding his possessions. He could only answer by gesture that he had none. At last they left him half dead. The cord left a mark around his neck which remained distinctly visible until his death.

The Franciscans were next called upon. They answered that they possessed nothing of the goods of this world, since the Rule of Saint Francis forbade them to have anything of their own. Thinking that the younger religious would betray the place where the supposed hoard lay, they ill-treated them in various ways. One of them, overcome by pain, answered with tears in his eyes that the Father Guardian was intrusted with the goods of the community. Upon hearing this they laid hands upon the Vicar, Father Jerome of Weert; but the Superior, Father Nicholas Pieck, quickly presented himself, not wishing to have the crown of martyrdom thus wrested from him. They fell upon him at once and tossed him backward and then forward, demanding the imaginary riches of the friars. He replied that all that he had brought with him, the sacred vessels, were already in their hands. They then asked for the alms that the religious received by begging. When told that nothing remained of them, they called Father Nicholas a liar. But he answered not a word. He was then subjected to the same barbarous treatment that had been meted out to Father Poppel, but with added ferocity. When the cord broke and he fell apparently lifeless to the ground, the heretics applied burning torches to his mouth and ears, thrust them into his nostrils and mouth, scorching his tongue and palate. They ended by rudely kicking him, and then left him for dead upon the prison floor.

After the departure of the soldiers the religious crowded about their saintly confrère and looked reverently at his wounds. They were surprised to hear a sigh escape from him. They raised him and washed his bleeding neck and burnt face. At last he spoke: "I hoped that my good Master would have received me into His bosom; but His holy will be done." The next morning the soldiery returned with hatchets to hack his body to pieces. Finding that he was still alive, they cried: "He does not want to die, this shaven pate! His soul cleaves to his stomach, but we know how to bring it out." Then they kicked him and beat him with their fists, taking care, however, not to endanger his life again.

For ten days all the martyrs were subjected to this kind of fiendish cruelty. When one band of soldiers was satisfied with torturing them, another arrived to take their place. In fact, when any citizens came to visit the prison they, in concert with the soldiery, devised new methods of barbarity. One of them forced the martyrs to puff out their cheeks and then dealt them stinging blows in the face, so that the blood spurted from their mouths, noses, and ears. They did not even spare the feeble Willehad, who was decrepit from extreme old age and who merely exclaimed at every blow that he received, "Thanks be to God." At other times the soldiers amused themselves by kneeling before the priests, making mock confessions, and whispering into their ears all kinds of nonsense and abomination.

Saint John of Cologne

It was during these days of sorrow and anguish that Saint John of Cologne was brought prisoner into the citadel to partake of the sufferings of the heroic band and to win the crown of martyrdom. When this intrepid son of Saint Dominic heard of the imprisonment of the Gorcum clergy, he lost no time in obtaining the consent of his superiors to minister to the wants of the incarcerated priests and religious and also to extend his pastoral care to their flocks. With the permission of his superiors, our Saint clad himself in secular attire as a measure of prudence to avoid detection. In this guise he would travel from Hoornaer to Gorcum. Entering the prison "as a lamb among wolves," he would bring solace and spiritual succor to the martyrs of Christ. Thus he became in very fact "the Angel of the Lord of Hosts." After having performed his acts of heroism in their midst, he would go about among the faithful and bring to them the consolations of their holy religion. The saintly friar preacher was especially zealous in the administration of the sacraments, particularly the Sacrament of Baptism. But after a time his coming and going were noticed. On one occasion, when Saint John was suddenly called from his parish in Hoornaer to Gorcum to baptize an infant, just as he was about to perform this sacred function, he was arrested by one of the Gueux and imprisoned with the other martyrs in the citadel. They charged him with being a traitor and alleged that in visiting the city he had hostile designs; but the real reason for the seizure of his person was that, like the rest of the noble company, he was a priest and a friar, faithful to the religion of Jesus Christ.

After a time news of the harsh treatment of Saint John and his companions began to excite pity among many of the citizens, and attempts were made to liberate them by the payment of ransoms. The case of the imprisoned religious was even mooted in the council of the town, and one senator had daring enough to recall to the mind of Brant the terms of capitulation. Feigning surprise, Brant cast the blame upon his superiors and said that he was awaiting orders from them. All these things made the heretics apprehensive lest their prey should escape them, and they resolved to hasten the execution of their prisoners. They communicated with the Count de la Marck, who was at Brielle planning a maritime insurrection. Lumnaye ordered that all those detained in the fortress should be immediately sent to him.

Saint John of Cologne and his holy associates were suddenly awakened at midnight of the 5th of July, stripped almost naked, and taken aboard a large ship. The vessel left Gorcum at 1 o'clock and arrived at Dortrecht at 9 in the morning. Here the captives were exposed to the idle curiosity and cruel taunts of a Calvinistic mob.

The ship again set sail in the afternoon, and, after another night, they landed at Brielle on the morning of July 7th. The Count de la Marck was still in bed when told of their arrival. He immediately arose, mounted his horse, and hastened to the shore. He ordered the heroic band to march as if in solemn procession and to make the round of the gallows three times, walking backward. He then commanded them to proceed toward the town. The young Franciscan, Henry, was made to take up a banner that had been plundered from one of the churches and to precede the martyrs as standard-bearer. The others followed. The soldiers rode on either side of the line, carrying branches of trees, with which they whipped their prisoners. The Count himself rode at the rear of the company and with a large whip mercilessly lashed them as they proceeded on their way. Amidst all their grief and pain, Lumnaye ordered them to sing. They obeyed, and surely the white-robed army of martyrs on high must have taken up the strain, as they intoned the "Salve Regina" and other canticles in honor of her who is invoked as the "Queen of Martyrs." They were singing the majestic "Te Deum" as they entered Brielle.

The whole town was astir to meet them; but with what a reception! Some of the fanatic rabble cast stones at them, while others threw dirty water into their faces, mockingly exclaiming, "Asperges me Domine." Thus they advanced, pale and haggard, already more or less disfigured by the traces of violence, one of them sixty, another seventy, and a third eighty years old—a spectacle to men and angels. Our Saint and his companions were finally ordered to halt in front of a gibbet in the principal square of the town. Around this they were commanded to walk a number of times, and then to kneel and to chant the Litany of the Saints. When they came to the end of the petitions, there was a dead silence. "Oremus! Oremus!" cried the crowd. "Let some one sing the Oremus, for it shall be the last that we shall hear in this country!" Then Godfrey van Duynen, the oldest priest, sang the prayers in a loud, clear voice, to which the others responded "Amen."

At last they were led to prison, where they were joined by some unexpected companions, two priests who had been there some time and two others who were brought in about an hour later. They were the parish priests, Adrian of Maasdam and Andrew Wouters of Heynoord, and two Premonstratensian Fathers, Adrian Janssen and James Lacops, from the parish of Monster.

The prison of Brielle contained three rooms, one built above the other. The lowest of these was uninhabitable, as all kinds of filth and waste matter were thrown into it from the two higher stories. Conditions in this bottom room can better be imagined than described; yet in this fetid hole, that never received the least ray of light, John of Cologne and his companions were placed.

At about 3 o'clock in the afternoon they received a little food. The evening of the 7th of July and the following morning were taken up by discussions with the heretical ministers in the presence of Lumnaye. The generous soldiers of Christ sustained their belief firmly and with dignity. They bore witness particularly to the Dogma of the Real Presence of Christ in the Eucharist, and to that of the Supremacy of the Roman Pontiff. Their noble defense of their religion only brought upon them maledictions and outcries for their condemnation and death.

In the meantime a messenger arrived, bearing letters to the Count from Marin Brant, from the town council of Gorcum, and from the Prince of Orange. Brant's letter was a simple passport, written in his own hand, in which he assumed the title of Lord. This only served to increase Lumnaye's anger. The council of Gorcum, in its letter, reminded de la Marck of the terms of capitulation, that the lives of the prisoners should be spared. They bore witness to the good reputation of all the prisoners, certifying that they had never done anything but good toward their fellow-citizens, and ended by interceding in their behalf. The letter from the Prince of Orange was more decisive. He had written at the request of the council and ordered that the Gueux should refrain from further molesting priests and religious. These letters, however, produced no effect toward alleviating the persecution of the martyrs. The Count de la Marck was filled with fierce indignation when he read these messages and renewed his oath to kill all priests who fell into his hands.

As Lumnaye was retiring to rest that night, after one of his habitual orgies, he again read the letter of the Prince of Orange. Then it was for the first time that he perceived that Brant had sent him merely a copy of the letter, retaining the original. This lack of respect put the finishing stroke to his fury. He declared that he was master of the place, and with an oath affirmed that it was high time that this fact should be known. Accordingly, he at once issued orders to conduct his prisoners to the Convent of Saint Elizabeth at Ten Rugge, which had been sacked when the Count captured Brielle. There they were to be hanged. The saintly band were tied together, arm to arm, in couples. Soldiers surrounded them, some of them mounted and others on foot. In this manner they were led forth from their prison. A large crowd had gathered, though it was midnight when all this transpired.

On their way toward the old Augustinian monastery at Ten Rugge they confessed to each other and mutually encouraged one another for the final struggle. Adjoining this desecrated convent stood an old turf-shed which belonged to the friary. This, then, was to be the scene of their martyrdom. A stout beam ran from one wall to the other of this shed, and another beam projected part of the distance across. Upon these, in the small hours of the morning of July 9, 1572, Saint John of Cologne and his companions were to win their crowns.

When they arrived at this place they were stripped of their clothing. The Guardian of the Franciscans mounted the ladder first, after having embraced all his associates. He then addressed them in these words: "I show you the ladder to heaven. Follow me like valiant soldiers of Jesus Christ, that, having fought together, none may be wanting at the eternal triumph which awaits us on high." No sooner had he finished than the executioners fastened the noose about his neck and withdrew the support from under his feet.

Father Jerome of Weert was the second to be hanged. He ascended the ladder invoking the Mother of God and the Saints. A Calvinist minister placed himself directly before him on the other side of the ladder and said: "Do not invoke Holy Mary, or Saint Peter, or the Saints, but call upon God." The intrepid friar, to show his indignation and contempt at this blasphemy, put his foot through the rungs of the ladder and kicked the minister in the stomach, prostrating him on the floor. He then reprehended him for his impiety. The heretics thrust their pikes into his mouth to silence him. He then submitted cheerfully to be put to death. One by one the other martyrs made the supreme sacrifice. The Dominican, Saint John of Cologne, was among the last of the holy company to be hanged. He went to his death with the courage of a warrior of Jesus Christ, confident that he was soon to be admitted into the visible presence of Him to Whose sacramental presence he was bearing witness by laying down his life. "In the might of Thy arm, O Lord, scattering the proud, Thou hast regarded the humility of Thy servants; and behold all generations shall call them blessed."

The holy martyrs of Gorcum were nineteen in number, namely, Saint John of Cologne, of the Order of Preachers; Saint Nicholas Pieck of Gorcum, Saint Jerome of Weert, Saint Theodore van der Eem of Amersfoort, Saint Nicasius Janssen of Heeze, Saint Willehad of Denmark, Saint Godfrey of Mervel, Saint Anthony of Weert, Saint Anthony of Hoornaer, and Saint Francis de Roye, priests of the Order of Saint Francis; Saint Peter of Assche and Saint Cornelius of Wyk, lay-brothers of the same Order; Saint John Lenartz of Oisterwijk, of the Order of Saint Augustine; Saint James Lacops of Oudenaar and Saint Adrian Janssen of Hilverenbeek, of the Order of Premonstratensians; Saint Leonard Vechel of Bois-le-Duc, Saint Nicholas Poppel of Welde, Saint Godfrey van Duynen of Gorcum, and Saint Andrew Wouters of Heynoord, secular priests.

After the death of the martyrs, the soldiers shamefully mutilated their bodies. They cut off their noses, ears, and other members. Then, placing them on their pikes or binding them to their hats, they went to promenade the town. Some dissected the bodies and searched the entrails for the fat that was believed to be a remedy against certain maladies. When the day dawned crowds of people flocked to the old turf-shed to satisfy their curiosity, the soldiers exacting an entrance fee.

In the evening a pious Catholic paid a large sum for permission to bury the sacred remains of Saint John and his companions; but, going early the next day, he found that the magistrates had ordered the soldiers to bury them. They had dug two ditches, in one of which they placed fifteen of their victims and in the other the remaining four.

God made known the death of the holy company to Matthias Thoran, a pious citizen of Gorcum. This man was in the habit of rising every night to pray for the welfare of the State. While thus engaged, in the early morning of July 9th, he beheld in vision this blessed band, clad in white garments, having golden crowns upon their heads and resplendent with glory. When the day dawned he informed the other citizens. A similar favor was granted to another inhabitant of Gorcum, so that the martyrdom was known there long before the messenger arrived from Brielle with the announcement of their death.

Many miracles have been granted through the intercession of the Martyrs of Gorcum and the application of their relics. At the beginning of the eighteenth century a little fragrant flower sprang up on the scene of their triumph at Brielle. It grew rapidly and was of so unusual a form that it could not be classed with any known species of flower, as was attested by many learned botanists. Father Adrian Antony received a sprig of this plant, which he preserved in a small box. He opened it from time to time to look at the flowers, always finding them as fresh as if just plucked. Once he allowed eight or nine months to go by without looking at them. When he again opened the box in the presence of several friends he found that their number had increased to nineteen, the exact number of the martyrs. This miracle was duly attested at the time of its occurrence.

The Martyrs of Gorcum were beatified by Pope Clement X in 1675, and since that time have always been held in the highest veneration in the Netherlands. The greatest portion of their relics is preserved in the Church of the Franciscans at Brussels.

On January 6, 1865, Pius IX caused a decree to be read in his presence ordering the proceedings to be instituted for their solemn canonization. The preamble of this decree is worthy of attention. It reads: "Born of the blood of Jesus Christ and nourished with the blood of martyrs, the Catholic Church will be exposed to bloody persecutions until the end of the world. And it is not without a marvelous design of Divine Providence that the cause of these illustrious victims of the Calvinistic heresy of the sixteenth century is taken up and completed in these unhappy days, when heretics and false brothers are recommencing a war, an implacable war, against Jesus Christ, against His Holy Church, and against this Holy Apostolic See."

On June 29, 1867, amid the most solemn festivities commemorating the eighteenth centenary of the deaths of Saints Peter and Paul, at which a great concourse of cardinals and bishops from all parts of the world were present, Pius IX enrolled John of Cologne and his companions in the catalogue of the Saints. July 9th, the anniversary of their glorious victory, is the day set apart by the Church to honor the Martyrs of Gorcum.

The beautiful Office of Saint John of Cologne and Companions was composed on the occasion of their canonization. The Master General of the Order of Preachers, Father Alexander Vincent Jandel, collaborated in its composition and himself wrote the strophe of the hymn that is dedicated especially to Saint John of Cologne. The office commemorates their heroic deeds, their sufferings, their courage, and their virtues. Special stress is laid on the dogmas for which they especially suffered death, namely, the Real Presence of Christ in the Blessed Eucharist and the Primacy of the Roman Pontiff. "They overcame by the blood of the Lamb, and by the word of the testimony, and they loved not their lives unto death" (Apoc. xii, 11).

BIBLIOGRAPHY

Bullarium Ordinis Prædicatorum, VI, 318, 328. Romæ, 1734.

Bulla Canonizationis. Acta Capituli Generalis Ordinis Fratrum Prædicatorum. Romæ, 1868.

Acta Sanctorum, Julii, Tom. II, 736. Parisiis et Romæ, 1867.

Année Dominicaine, "Saint Jean de Cologne," Vol. VII. Lyons, 1895.

M. L'Abbé Patrice Chauvierre: Les Martyrs de Gorcum. Paris, 1867.

Hubert Meuffels, C. M.: Les Martyrs de Gorcum. Paris, 1908.

T. A. Dyson, O. P.: The Life of St. Pius V and Other Saints and Blessed of the Order of Friar Preachers. New York, 1897.

"The Martyrs of Gorcum." The Catholic World, Vol. VI (October, 1867.) New York, 1868.

L'Année Dominicaine, Juillet, 1889. "Saint Jean de Cologne." Paris, 1889.

Short Lives of the Dominican Saints. Edited by Fr. John Procter, O. P., S. T. L. New York, 1901.

Kirchenlexikon. Freiburg in Breisgau, 1888.

R. P. Mortier, O. P.: Histoire des Maîtres Généraux de l'Ordre des Frères Prêcheurs, Tome Cinquième. Paris, 1911.

Cormier, O. P.: Quinze Entretiens sur la Liturgie Dominicaine. Rome, 1913.

P. Mannes Rings, O. P.: Das Werk des Heiligen Dominikus. Dülmen i W., 1910.

P. Innocentius Taurisano, O. P.: Catalogus Hagiographicus Ordinis Prædicatorum. Romæ, 1918.

Saint Louis Bertrand

When in the year 1517 Martin Luther published in Wittenburg his famous theses, he flung into the face of God a virtual challenge to save His Church if He could. Prompt and adorable came the divine answer. Mindful of His promise to be with the Church all days, and wishing to point out to men the way of true reform, God raised up in Europe such a galaxy of saints as had never before since primitive Christianity graced a single century. Prominent among these true reformers whose sanctity was to leaven the world we find many whose direct mission seems to have been to counteract the evils wrought by the rebellious heretics. Saint Ignatius, Saint Cajetan, Saint Philip Neri, and Saint John of God were to found new religious institutes in the Church; Saint Theresa and Saint John of the Cross were to bring about the grand reform of Carmel; Saint Pius, the hammer of heretics, was predestined to the chair of Peter, while Saint Francis Xavier and Saint Louis Bertrand, working in fields afar, were to gather recruits among the heathens to fill the depleted ranks of Christendom.

In the careers of all these saints the direct action of Providence is plainly traceable, and in the life of Saint Louis especially is this the outstanding feature. It first manifests itself in the circumstances of his birth; for his father, a model Christian notary of Valencia, had determined on the death of his first wife to leave the world and enter the cloister. He was actually on the way to the Carthusian monastery of Porta Caeli to carry out his holy purpose when he was met by Saint Bruno and Saint Vincent Ferrer, who assured him

Saint Louis Bertrand

that it was God's will that he remain in the world and take again unto himself a wife. This he did, and the first fruit of his union with the pious Joan Exarch was the future Saint, Louis Bertrand.

Louis was born in Valencia, Spain, on the first day of January, 1526. On the same day he was taken to the parish church and baptized at the very font from which his illustrious kinsman, Saint Vincent Ferrer, had received the waters of regeneration. In his early childhood Louis began those practices of penance and devotion that were to characterize his entire life. At the age of eight years he recited daily the Office of the Blessed Virgin, toward whom throughout his varied life he bore the tenderest affection. He early steeped himself in habits of mortification and even in boyhood would have nothing but a rude plank for a bed. During this period, too, he planted in his soul the seeds of that wonderful love of neighbor that in after years was to bear him over the trackless seas to America. He took keen delight in making the rounds of the city hospitals, doing his feeble best to lighten the sufferings of the sick poor.

An interesting story detailing the Saint's fervor and spirit of sacrifice is preserved to us by one of his later novices and his first biographer, Father Vincent Antist. At the age of about fifteen years Louis determined to follow the example of Saint Alexis and Saint Roch and leave his comfortable home to embrace a pilgrim's life. He prepared quietly for his departure and left Valencia secretly early one morning in winter. His absence passed unnoticed till nightfall, when a letter from Louis brought to his parents the first news of his intention. His mother, already ill, was prostrated by the sorrowful tidings. His father in alarm immediately instituted a search and located Louis a few miles outside of Valencia. The knowledge of his parents' grief, and especially of his mother's critical state, moved the lad to abandon his design and return to serve God at home. Here he redoubled his zeal in charitable works and, collecting a band of fifteen pious youths to help him, he devoted most of his time to the service of the poor in the hospitals.

Louis soon found this work all too inadequate for his religious zeal. Although he had bowed to the will of God and given up all intention of becoming a pilgrim, he still longed to leave the world. The life in the cloister drew him strongly, and early associations, as well as his relationship with Saint Vincent Ferrer, directed him toward the Order of Friar Preachers. His application was received with joy by the Fathers, who knew well the worth of the humble postulant, and a date was set for his reception. Louis awaited the day with fervent impatience, happy beyond words that at last his desire was to be realized. But God saw fit to send him yet another bitter trial.

On the very day Louis was to have received the habit, his father, learning of his intention, went to the prior, and, pleading the poor health of his son, persuaded him not to admit Louis to the Order. Saddened by this sudden reversal, which in his deep humility he attributed to his own sinfulness, the boy returned home to take up again his work among the sick and the poor. But his heart stayed with the Dominicans, and to their priory he used often to steal, after the day's work, to tend the convent garden and spend a few happy hours in prayer. On several occasions he managed to elude the porter's vigilance and to conceal himself for the night in some dark nook of the choir. Here he would watch the brethren at midnight Matins and drink in the fervent exhortations of the prior at chapter.

Such perseverance could not be without its reward. Father Ferran was succeeded as prior by Father John Micon, who the day after his installation promised shortly to admit Louis to the habit. The date was set for August 26, 1544. The intervening time Louis spent in fervent preparation, carefully guarding his secret from his father lest he again prevent his design. The entire vigil of the happy day he passed in the presence of the Blessed Sacrament, and at last, on the morning appointed, he was clothed with the habit of Saint Dominic.

On learning of his son's reception, John Bertrand did everything in his power to persuade Louis to return to the world; or, if he must be a religious, to join the Carthusians or the Fathers of Saint Jerome. He pleaded especially ill health and lack of sufficient talent for the arduous, studious life of the Friar Preacher. To all his arguments Louis replied with respectful firmness, and when on one occasion Father Micon commanded him in the presence of his father to say truly if he was happy and felt equal to the penitential life, the novice answered that he would rather die than leave the convent and added the vow to live and die in the Order of his choice. Convinced at last of his son's vocation and moved by his evident happiness, John Bertrand withdrew all opposition and concorded fully with the wishes of his son.

In the novitiate Louis made rapid progress, treading surely the way of the saints. Especially assiduous was he in the practice of the virtues of obedience, piety, and humility. His love of the poor followed him within the cloister, and while now he had little to give, he gave that little unstintingly, daily setting aside the greater portion of his own food for their relief. Among his fellow-novices he was deeply loved and revered. Though naturally of a melancholic temperament, he forced himself in hours of recreation to triumph over nature and showed always to others a sweet and cheerful gentleness. And so at the end of a year we find all the members of the convent rejoicing that this young novice, whom they recognized as a saint, was bound to them as a brother by irrevocable vows.

His solemn profession, on August 27, 1545, spurred Louis on to a more intensely spiritual life; but it was at the same time the occasion of a severe trial. During the simple novitiate, with its entire year set aside solely for advance in the way of perfection, the young Saint had grown very close to the heart of God; and now, when as a professed novice he had often to turn from prayer and contemplation to the tedious round of study, he found the change irksome to his fervent soul. But here obedience and a deep realization of the ideal of his Order came to his aid, and he was quick to penetrate the thin disguise of piety and to see in this dislike for study a diabolical device to lure him from his chosen goal. And, this once realized, he applied himself so diligently to the work at his hand that, though gifted with no extraordinary powers of intellect, he achieved in his studies a more than mediocre success.

During his course of study he never abated his severe fasts and mortifications. At last his frail body could bear up no longer, and his superiors were obliged to order him to mitigate his penances and to retire for some months to the suburban Convent of Saint Matthew for the sake of his health. He went in ready obedience, but with the return of strength came back at once to Valencia to resume his studies and join in the regular observance of conventual life.

In 1547 his superiors judged Louis sufficiently advanced in his studies, and in October of that year he was raised to the priesthood, probably by the great Archbishop, Saint Thomas of Villanova. As hitherto he had been the model for the novices, the young priest now became the pattern for the older members of the community. His spiritual mind keenly realized the stupendous privileges ordination had conferred upon him. He never approached the altar without long and fervent preparation, and such was his humility that his soul, so wonderfully pure, seemed in his eyes laden with sin, so that from the very beginning of his priesthood he made it a rule to go to confession every morning before offering the adorable Sacrifice. At this time, too, knowing that his priestly duties would often prevent his presence at the choral office, he drew up a schedule for the private recitation of the divine office, to which his biographers assure us he adhered rigorously every day for the rest of his life.

It is not surprising that this model priest, when only twenty-three years of age, was sent with Father John Micon to open the new Convent of the Holy Cross, built for the Dominicans at

Lombay by the Count of Gandia, who afterward became Saint Francis Borgia. The mission was most welcome to Louis, who anticipated much profit to himself from this association with the holy priest who had clothed him with the habit. His stay at Lombay was, however, unexpectedly short; for two months later he was warned in a vision that his father lay dangerously ill, and, hastening to Valencia, he arrived just in time to assist at the bedside of his dying parent. Louis was detained in Valencia by his superiors and two years later was appointed Master of Novices.

For his new task our Saint was admirably fitted. His prudence, wisdom, rigorous zeal, and unbounded charity formed an ideal union of virtues in one entrusted with the training of young religious. With his novices he was very strict, but it was only because he realized the improbability of a lax, careless novice becoming later a fervent, zealous priest. This same realization prompted him to extreme carefulness in admitting postulants to the novitiate and to a ready acquiescence with any who expressed a desire to leave. Whenever it happened that a novice cast off the religious habit, Louis would call those who remained into the chapter-room and address to them the words of Christ, "Will you also go away?" But, with all his strictness, Louis mingled such a deal of gentle charity and kindly consideration that his subjects held him in the deepest love. Often he would give a novice a very light punishment for his offenses, and then, retiring to his cell, would balance the scales of justice by inflicting on himself a severe penance for the novice's faults. For the sick especially he had an almost motherly solicitude, even depriving himself of bed clothing on wintry nights to assure for them an abundance of warmth.

Together with the care of the novices was entrusted to Saint Louis the training of the lay-brothers. Holding in high esteem the important rôle filled by these humble religious in the Dominican scheme of life, he devoted the utmost care to their formation and instruction, teaching them everything that pertained to their state—Christian doctrine, the way to say the Rosary well, and an easy method of meditating with profit. To inspire them with love for their state, he used to point out to them how they could co-operate efficaciously in the labors of the Apostolate by their willing service and their prayers, and how well fitted they were for the contemplative phase of the Dominican ideal; "For," he used to say, "God is pleased to converse with the simple and humble of heart; and in the school of Mystic Theology, in which the Holy Spirit is the Master, devout aspirations are more profitable than arguments, sorrow of heart more than lofty speculations."

It will be remembered that during his own days as a novice our Saint was subjected to a temptation to neglect his studies for the pursuit of the spiritual life. So completely had he overcome this aversion and so deeply had he become imbued with the love of study characteristic of his Order, that strangely enough we find him after a few years seeking permission from the Master General to surrender his charge of the novices that he might apply himself to an intensive study of theology at the University of Salamanca, then at the crest of its rejuvenated glory. To the great grief of the entire community at Valencia, the permission was granted, and though Father Micon assured him that he was called to be Master of Novices and not Master of Theology, Louis persevered in his design and set out on foot for Salamanca.

On his way to the university he stopped to consult a religious famous for his prudence and sanctity, and as this man confirmed the judgment of Father Micon, Louis humbly gave up his cherished project and returned to Valencia to take up again the direction of the novices.

But such was the Saint's burning zeal that, since he could not combat the reformers as a militant theologian, he determined at least to mount the pulpit, there to contribute his share toward stemming the tide of heresy. For no office did he seem less fit. His voice was raucous, his memory treacherous, his carriage without grace. But the unction and inspiration of his fervent words so completely offset these natural defects that he was soon hailed throughout the neighborhood of Valencia as a second Saint Vincent Ferrer. Like his great patron, he, too, added miracles of healing and of prophecy to the miracle of his eloquence and gained for himself the title of the wonder-worker of his day.

About the year 1557 the pestilence broke out in Valencia, and as the novices were dispersed to safeguard their health, Louis was relieved of his post as novice master and sent as vicar to the Convent of Saint Anne at Albayda. During his three years in this convent he devoted himself almost entirely to the apostolic life. His preaching bore remarkable fruit; but the fiery zeal of his words stirred up against him many adversaries. In one of his sermons he had mercilessly flayed the vicious and scandalous lives of several Spanish noblemen. One of these, feeling in his guilty conscience that he was among those rebuked by the Saint, vowed summary vengeance on the preacher, and some days later, meeting Louis and his companion on the road, leveled his arquebuse against the man of God. With heroic faith in Providence, Louis calmly bade his *socius* to cast away all fear and in silent prayer he made the Sign of the Cross over the drawn weapon. Immediately the gun was transformed into a crucifix. The stupified nobleman threw himself to the ground in fear and, promising amendment of his life, received the Saint's full pardon. On account of this event Saint Louis is generally represented in art as bearing in one hand a crucifix, the lower part of which is formed from the stock of a gun.

Another miracle famous in the life of the Saint took place at Albayda. One day in midsummer the dried stubble in a neighboring field caught fire, and, fanned by a vigorous breeze, the flames swept rapidly toward the convent. In vain were all human means tried to arrest the fire; but at a simple Sign of the Cross made by Saint Louis the hungry flames subsided at the very confines of the threatened property.

These miracles spread Louis' fame for sanctity far and wide and led many holy persons to seek his guidance in their undertakings. Even the great Saint Theresa did not hesitate to consult him about her proposed Reform. We still have Louis' answer, characteristic in its brevity, humility, and confidence inspired by prayer: "I have received your letter; and, since the point on which you ask my advice has reference to the honor and glory of God, I thought it best first to pray for light on the subject. This will explain the delay of my answer. And now I say to you, in the name of our Lord Jesus Christ, Go on as you have commenced. The Lord will assist you; and in His Name I declare that in fifty years your reform will be one of the most useful and one of the most renowned in the Church of God." Saint Theresa derived great consolation from these prophetic words of the Saint, and, certain now of the will of God, wrought unceasingly and with full success at her cherished project.

For three years the pestilence raged in Valencia; but when, in 1560, it had finally spent its force, the novices were recalled and Louis was again placed at their head. But his apostolic zeal, fed by his recent active labors, now became a devouring flame that could not stay pent up within four cloister walls. The time had come for the Saint to begin his great work abroad. In a wonderful manner Providence pointed out to the friar his place in the divine plan, for it was from an impostor from South America then staying at the convent in Valencia under the guise of a religious, that Louis first learned of the work to be done among the pagan tribes of the new world and conceived a desire to give himself wholly to the foreign missions. Hardly had the Saint formed this new resolution when there arrived at Valencia two Dominicans bound for America and bearing with them letters from the Master General asking for volunteers to accompany them to the distant harvest fields. To the great grief of all his confrères, Louis' immediate offer of his services was accepted. Early in Lent, 1562, he bade farewell to his novices, and with his two companions started on his long and arduous journey.

The vessel on which they sailed had scarcely put out to sea when God chose to call attention to the sanctity of the missionary by a miracle. One of Louis' companions was so seriously injured by a cross-tree falling from the mast that his life was despaired of by the ship's physician. Motioning aside the doctor, Louis took the case in his own hands. He gently washed the wound with water and put the religious to bed. The following morning he touched with his own head that of the still unconscious friar. Immediately the gaping wound closed, leaving not even a scar, and the man rose, perfectly cured and totally unaware that he had been the victim of a serious accident. This incident argued well for the favors Louis could expect from Providence in his new field of labor.

The country for which the three friars were bound was by no means an untilled portion of the heavenly vineyard. From the days of the first explorers the white habit was a frequent sight in South America, and at the time of the Saint's arrival four provinces of the Order were flourishing there. The renowned Las Casas had already labored in the interests of the natives for half a century and was still living in the Convent of Valladolid when Louis started on his missionary career. To the heroic work of these pioneers and to the favorable impression they had made on the natives we can trace a good deal of our Saint's wonderful success as a missionary; for though it is true that the greater part of Louis' work was done among tribes unreached by his predecessors, yet many reports concerning the friars had come to these natives and disposed them favorably to receive the word when it was finally preached to them.

Saint Louis and his companions disembarked at Cartagena, a large seaport of Colombia, and at once repaired to the Convent of Saint Joseph, in that city, there to rest a while and recollect themselves before beginning their arduous work. Shortly afterward his superiors entrusted to Louis the evangelization of the vast country which today makes up the greater part of Colombia and western Venezuela. The most of this territory was extremely wild, as civilization had as yet scarcely penetrated beyond the towns bordering on the rivers and the sea. The outlying districts were inhabited by numerous Indian tribes, and among these especially Louis was to exercise his apostolate. In utter ignorance of their language and customs, he knew well that of himself he could accomplish but little among them, so with characteristic trust in Providence he left all to God, begging from Him the graces needed to aid in fulfilling his vocation. His trust did not go unrewarded. In answer to his prayer the gift of tongues was added to the gifts of prophecy and miracles he already possessed. Constantly during his stay in America these signs from Heaven were set as a seal upon his work, and they lend to his life an unearthly charm and wonder.

The very first of his conversions was thus accompanied by a miracle; for as Louis set out for Tubara, the scene of his earliest labors, he was met by an Indian bearing a sick child in his arms, who told the Saint that in the mountains a spirit had appeared to him, bidding him seek out the stranger, who would pour water on the head of his child and give to it everlasting life. Filled with new confidence by this manifest favor from Heaven, Louis proceeded to Tubara. His mission here was most successful, more than six thousand of the natives embracing the faith.

From Tubara he went on eastward to Cipacoa, where again he triumphed over the superstitious idolatry of the Indians and brought the entire tribe to the service of the true God. Everywhere the chief obstacle encountered by the Saint was the ingrained idolatry of the natives and their haunting fear of dire punishments sure to follow swiftly on the rejection of their pagan deities. The Saint's most effective means of overcoming this obstacle lay in the many miracles with which God was pleased to approve his work.

From Cipacoa Louis turned to the natives of Paluato, where his best efforts were apparently fruitless. Only two of his hearers received baptism. Leaving the inhabitants of Paluato in their obstinacy, Louis retraced his steps to the mountainous district of Santa

Martha, in the northeast section of Colombia. Here the word of the Apostle fell upon good ground and brought forth the rich harvest of fifteen thousand converts to the faith. But a still greater joy was in store for the Saint. At the end of this mission he was approached by nearly fifteen hundred Indians, who had come from afar to beg the grace of baptism. They were the tribe of Paluato, who, being miraculously apprised of the value of the grace they had previously scorned, had now crossed the mountains to seek it.

With such rich harvest to feed it, the zeal of the Saint grew indomitable. He next resolved to bear the cross to the Caribs, a cannibal tribe dwelling probably on one of the neighboring islands and as yet unvisited by any missionary. In going to them Louis was humanly certain of martyrdom, a prospect that served only to whet his zeal. He entered bravely into the work before him, and to show the impotence of the idols broke them before the terrified natives. His courage, however, far from eliciting the admiration of the natives, only aroused their hatred. The chiefs among them especially and the priests determined to be rid of him, and mixed for him accordingly a potion of their deadliest poison. On drinking it Louis fell into throes of agony and for five days lay at the very door of death. At last it seemed he was to gain the longed-for martyrdom. But God had other work for him. On the fifth day he was seen to vomit with the deadly drink a number of small vipers, symbolical of its virulence. The Caribs, cheated of their prey, made further attempts on the life of the Saint, but all were equally vain. At last they recognized the power of the God this stranger had come to preach, and in a body they forswore allegiance to their idols.

Other missions the Saint undertook, with like success, at Turvaco, Teneriffe, Mompos, in Panama, and on the islands of the Caribbean Sea, especially those of Saint Vincent and Saint Thomas. All were marked by the same stubborn superstition of the natives, the same calm contempt of death on the part of the Saint, and the same prodigal display of his miraculous power.

When we consider the rugged nature of the country, with its wild tropical forests, infested with venomous vipers and numerous beasts of prey, and the absolute lack of adequate transportation, forcing the Saint to travel on foot or in small, fragile boats, we cannot but wonder at the indefatigable zeal which led Louis to traverse these trackless domains unceasingly for more than seven years. And our wonder grows apace when we read that between missions he found sufficient time and energy to preach Lenten and Advent sermons to the Spanish settlers. In these sermons he retained the same fiery zeal that had characterized his preaching at Albayda during the first years of his active life. And here, too, in distant America, he found the same vices to rebuke, and flayed them in as uncompromising a manner.

The obstacles he met with among the Spaniards were more discouraging than any the Indians offered; for while the settlers whose vices Louis was forced to rebuke shrank indeed from mixing a poisonous drink to take his life, they did worse in trying to poison the Saint's reputation and influence. Twice they made foul attacks on his unimpeachable chastity—once by direct accusation and once by a hideous temptation. Under each of these trials the Saint bore himself with such steadfastness and uncomplaining patience that he not only disarmed all criticism, but even accomplished the conversion of his persecutors.

At last, however, Louis was disgusted with the actions of his unworthy countrymen, whose scandalous lives and flagrant maltreatment of the natives were constantly doing much to undermine and set at naught the work of the Fathers on the missions, and in the year 1569 he determined to return to Spain. It seems hardly likely that his motive was purely a human one. Throughout his life Louis lived in unbroken communion with God, Who on many occasions deigned to manifest His will to His servant, and it is altogether probable that in so important a matter as the abandonment of the missions Louis acted under direct inspiration from God.

Whatever may have been his motive, early in 1569 he applied for permission from the Master General to return to Spain. When this became known the distracted natives and his fellow-religious alike exerted every means to keep him among them. The Indians sought in vain to detain him by depriving him of every means of transportation, and the Fathers of the province resorted to the clever plan of electing him prior of the Convent at Santa Fe de Bogota, the present capital of Colombia. In humble obedience Louis set out to accept his new charge. Again Providence intervened. Though the other boats of the fleet with which he traveled finished a successful trip, that bearing the Saint was caught in such terrible storms that the voyage, ordinarily finished in three weeks, was not half completed in four. During this delay a letter from the Master General reached Louis, authorizing his return to Europe. Informing his local superiors of this permission, he turned back to Cartagena and took passage for Spain.

For seven and a half years the Saint had labored in the New World. The number of his converts we have no means of reckoning, but that his work was far-reaching and permanent is indicated by the staunch Catholicity of the natives of Colombia enduring from his day to ours.

On October 18, 1569, Louis again set foot on the soil of Spain. The following year he spent in retirement at the Convent of Valencia; but not for long was he to enjoy his beloved solitude, for the religious of the province, many of whom had passed their novitiate under his rare direction, sought for his kindly advice and prudent guidance in their active ministry. In the October of 1570 Louis was, accordingly, chosen prior of the Convent of Saint Onuphrius. On the expiration of his term of office, three years later, he was again appointed to the post of novice master, and from 1575 to 1578 he filled the office of prior in his mother convent at Valencia. To his new dignity of prior Louis brought the same rigor, prudence, kindliness, and supernatural insight into souls that had characterized his earlier career. Mindful of the scriptural promise that to those who seek first the Kingdom of Heaven all other things shall be added, he gave his best efforts to molding the spiritual character of his charges. And abundantly did he realize the fulfillment of the words of Christ, for never had the convents of Saint Onuphrius and of Valencia even such temporal prosperity as was theirs under his régime.

The brief interval as novice master between his two terms as prior was most welcome to the Saint, who gave himself up gladly to the quiet it afforded. The peace of the convent, contrasted with the ceaseless activity of his years in America, drew his spirit mightily, and for a time he seriously thought of entering the Order of Carthusians, that he might spend the evening of his life in unbroken solitude and contemplation. His zeal for souls, however, and his deep love for things Dominican proved cords too strong to be easily broken, and at last, after mature deliberation, seconded by the urgent advice of his intimate Franciscan friend, Blessed Nicholas Factor, he decided to remain with the Order of Preachers and spend himself in the active ministry for the souls of his neighbors.

From this time forth we find him coupling with his tasks as superior the arduous ministry of the Word. His preaching, attended always with miracle, prophecy, and supernatural insight into the hearts of his hearers, met everywhere with astounding success. It seemed as though Saint Vincent Ferrer had returned to earth and through the mouth of Saint Louis was again addressing the people of Spain.

On his mission tours Louis used to take with him several of the novices, to give them practical experience of the active life and to inflame in their hearts a love for the ministry of the Word. Strongly did he recommend to them sincerity in their preaching, bitterly flaying all manner of vain affectation. The result of his sermons he judged not by the applause they elicited, but by the genuine compunction and change of heart in the hearers. "If at your preaching," he used to tell the novices, "men lay aside enmities, forgive injuries, avoid occasions of sin and scandals, and reform their conduct, you may say that the seed has fallen on good ground. But to God alone give all the glory and acknowledge yourselves ever unprofitable servants." That his words and example bore rich fruit among the novices is shown by the large number of them who later preached with marked success in Spain and on the missions of the New World.

From the time of his American labors, Louis' health, which had ever been poor at best, constantly grew worse under the strain of preaching, till finally, in 1581, it broke down completely and he was forced to abandon the pulpit. The general anxiety concerning his condition changed to alarm when, some months beforehand, the Saint prophesied that he should die on the feast of Saint Dionysius. His prophecy was verified; for, after a lingering illness, he expired on the 9th of October, 1581. Miracles, which occurred with increasing frequency as his life drew to a close, crowded about his death-bed to attest his sanctity. A brilliant light leaped from his holy mouth, his entire body shone as pure crystal, and mysterious, heavenly music accompanied his soul on its flight to God. These miracles continued to multiply after his death. Countless sick were cured, lame healed, sinners restored to grace, and at least thirteen dead were brought back to life. His own body, too, was to attest his sanctity; for to this day, save for mutilations resulting from sacrilegious violation of the tomb in 1814, it remains practically incorrupt.

The Saint's wide reputation for holiness and his countless miracles in life and after death soon received the official sanction of the Church. On the 29th of June, 1608, he was declared Blessed by Pope Paul V, and on the 12th of April, 1671, Pope Clement X solemnly inscribed his name in the Catalogue of the Saints. October the tenth was set aside for the celebration of his feast. Additional honor was paid to him by the Holy See when, nineteen years later, Pope Alexander VIII declared Saint Louis patron of New Granada.

BIBLIOGRAPHY

WILBERFORCE: The Life of St. Lewis Bertrand. London, 1882.

TOURON: Histoire des Hommes Illustres de l'Ordre de Saint Dominique, IV, 485–526. Paris, 1747.

ROZE: Les Dominicains en Amérique, pp. 290–310. Paris, 1878.

BYRNE: Sketches of Illustrious Dominicans, pp. 1-95. Boston, 1884.

Acta Sanctorum. October, V.

Saint Catherine de Ricci

SAINT CATHERINE de Ricci was a mystic in the truest sense of the word. Her active life, spent almost entirely within convent walls, was as natural as that of any nun of today. Her contemplative life brought her into such close communion with God that she seemed to be more a creature of heaven than of earth. To fully appreciate the inner life of this Saint, one would need to study the science of mystical theology. The Christian mystic is gifted with a state of soul which cannot be produced by human effort or industry, even with the ordinary aid of Divine Grace.

A person favored by God with the mystic state is one raised to the higher forms of prayer, to the extraordinary heights of contemplation, and oftentimes receives private revelations and heavenly visions. The superior faculties of the mystic are engaged with the things that are above, not with the things of earth. It is a very real life that a mystic lives, but a hidden one; it is concealed by the bright cloud that hides the living God. It is a life more noble and exalted, more true and beneficial, than any merely natural life, but it is secret, invisible, and spiritual; it is a life of closest union with God by love. Saint Thomas tells us why the wonders of God are, for the most part, secret and veiled from the eyes of men: first, on account of their greatness; secondly, on account of their supreme dignity; thirdly, because the greater portion of men are unfit to receive them and too carnal-minded to understand them.

The biographer of a mystic would fain delve down into the depths of a soul and unveil the marvelous secrets hidden there; but,

Saint Catherine de Ricci

alas! he must rest content to narrate only those things in the life of his subject which appeal to the senses and are comprehensible to the human intellect. This is to leave untold that which is greatest in the life of Saint Catherine—her communings with God.

The Ricci family was a wealthy and influential one, being composed of bankers and politicians. Pierfrancesco, the father of our Saint, was one of the most prominent men of Florence, holding in continuous succession important offices of state. At the same time, in conjunction with his brother Federigo, he conducted a bank. In the Ricci family were to be found those contrasts common to the life history of all large households. A brother of the two illustrious men just mentioned made his name honored by his virtues as a Friar Preacher. A sister became so renowned for her wickedness that she was a source of much grief to her relations.

Pierfrancesco, in the year 1514, married a member of the House of Ricasoli. Her name was Catherine de Panzano, daughter of a Ridolfo, the last representative and sole heiress of a distinguished Italian family. Of this union, on April 23, 1522, the future Saint was born, and was baptized the next day with the name of Alessandra Lucrezia Romola (the name of Catherine being given her in religion). From a very early age she displayed natural piety, while the most notable characteristic virtue of her childhood was a sweet serenity of soul. Her knowledge of divine things was far in advance of her comprehension of earthly matters, and the love of God burnt brightly in her soul when as yet she gave no token of earthly affection. At the tender age of three, when children are usually so winsome and so seductive, so full of pranks and fun, this little maiden was often found in unfrequented parts of her father's house or in other solitary places recollected in prayer.

Alessandra had not completed her fifth year of life when her mother died. Pierfrancesco in due time took to himself a second wife, a woman of high birth. Her name was Fiametta Diaceto. She was a saintly person, free from all the faults of the traditional stepmother, and filled well the place of the deceased parent. By this second marriage the child Saint was given four brothers and five sisters. While still in the tender years of youth, death took from her a brother and a sister. Of the other three boys, the eldest entered the Dominican Order, another founded the famous "Ricci Bank" at Lyons, the third attained success as a statesman. The four girls all became members of the Third Order of Saint Dominic, having attached themselves at a very early age to the Monastery of Saint Vincent, at Prato. The spirit of religion, so manifest among her relatives, is a striking instance of the effect the wonderful graces of our Saint had on those brought into immediate contact with her.

At the age of seven this holy maiden, beloved of God and man, registered as a boarder in the Benedictine Convent of San Pietro de Monticelli. Her aunt, who was abbess, relates how the child spent hours each day, in prayer and meditation, before a large and affecting image of the crucifixion in the convent church. So deeply did the contemplation of the suffering Redeemer move her, that tears often bathed her little face. The good abbess fostered the spiritual tendencies of the child, hoping one day to receive her as a member of the Benedictine Community. In this she was disappointed, for, after two years at San Pietro's, Alessandra returned home.

The Benedictines conducted a school for educating girls of high rank. In teaching these young women to be fashionable, the nuns themselves imbibed much of the spirit of the world. In some respects they were regular and devout, but in other important practices of the rule they were woefully lax. Under the guidance of her stepmother, this young aspirant to the religious life sought to find a community in which the standard of conventual discipline was stricter than in the one she had left. She ended her quest by entering the Monastery of Saint Vincent of the Third Order of Saint Dominic, at Prato. Her biographer tells us that two lay-sisters from this convent came one day to beg at the villa of the Ricci family. Alessandra questioned them closely as to their manner of life and obtained her father's leave to go and spend ten days with the nuns on a visit. She was so delighted with what she saw that she implored to be allowed to remain among them.

Her father put many obstacles in the way to a happy consummation of his daughter's desire. Having been taken from the convent, she was confined at home by the irate parent. Added to the discouragement which these trials imposed upon her, a severe illness overtook the young maiden. Alessandra betook herself to prayer, asking the Lord to preserve her life in order that she might consecrate it to Him in religion. The Master appeared to her in a vision, accompanied by His Blessed Mother and the Virgin Martyrs, Saints Thecla and Cecilia. Having given her His blessing and cured her, He foretold the many sufferings of all kinds which awaited her in the religious life, but bade her be of good heart, for that He would always be with her. Touched by the miraculous cure, Pierfrancesco yielded a reluctant consent to her permanent enrollment among the members of the Dominican Community. On Whit Monday, May 18, 1535, she received the holy habit which her patron Saint Catherine of Siena had worn so honorably. Father Timothy de Ricci, her uncle, then confessor at the monastery, presided at the investiture. Her baptismal name was on this day changed for that of Catherine, either in remembrance of her departed mother or on account of her love and admiration for the renowned patroness of the Third Order of Saint Dominic.

He who had miraculously cured Alessandra de Ricci of a grave illness had also decreed that she, as Sister Catherine, should attain to the most sublime heights of sanctity, and for this reason He saw to it that she was firmly grounded in humility. The Master kept her in continual conversation with Himself, causing her to be completely abstracted from earthly things. Hence, despite her good intentions to be exteriorly as well as interiorly a perfect religious, she persistently failed in the outward observances of the rule. She seemed to have no capacity whatever for manual labor or the chant. At recreation she was apparently sleepy and morbid and gave the impression of being stupid, even in spiritual conversation. During this time of tribulation and humiliation the solidity of Sister Catherine's character shone forth. She bore the rebukes heaped upon her publicly and privately because of her seeming dullness, faithlessness, and disobedience with that serenity of soul which had been her winning virtue from childhood. She never opened her lips in self-defense and preserved unbroken the secret of what passed between her and her God. Not even to her confessor did she reveal the nature of the heavenly favors showered upon her. The community of Saint Vincent's was in a quandary as to what to do with a novice who apparently was not only a dullard, but showed no inclination to conform even to the simplest requirements of conventual discipline. The nuns, having taken counsel with Father Timothy de Ricci, finally decided to send her away. When Sister Catherine heard of this decision she began to storm heaven with prayers and to perform unheard-of penances. By these means she sought to appease the wrath of God and avert the calamity which threatened her fondest hopes and aspirations. Her confidence in God was well rewarded, for in an almost inexplicable way the religious were won over to her cause. She was approved by the chapter of the monastery for profession, and on the 24th of June, 1536, pronounced her solemn vows in the hands of her stepmother's brother, Father Angelo da Diacetto, who was then Prior of Saint Dominic's Convent, in Prato.

The higher Sister Catherine rose in perfection and the more abundant were the favors vouchsafed her by our Lord, the lower did she sink in the esteem of her fellow-religious. Even though she had been admitted to profession, she was still considered and treated as one lacking in mental acumen. A complication of diseases attacked the Saint some time during the year 1538. Unceasingly for two years she suffered excruciating pain. The doctors were baffled and left the ailment to take its course. Again her cure was the result of a miracle. This time Father Jerome Savonarola and his companions were the heavenly messengers sent to do the work of the Most High. The cultus of this great man had been constantly kept up at Saint Vincent's. Hence this apparition of their Patron was taken by the community as a signal proof of his sanctity and once more won for the recipient of the vision the good will of the religious. From this time forward the young ecstatic was obliged to reveal to her confessor all the supernatural favors she received from God. Several times afterward, when stricken by torturing maladies, Savonarola appeared to her and wrought a cure by his blessing.

Among the many extraordinary graces conferred upon Catherine at this time was the gift of a new heart, fashioned after that of the Holy Mother of God. She had prayed long and earnestly for this great boon, and on the Feast of Corpus Christi, 1541, her petition was answered. So complete was the change produced in the person of the good nun by this marvelous favor, that new blood seemed to course in her veins, while a mysterious ethereal atmosphere seemed to envelop her.

On the first Thursday of February, in the twentieth year of Sister Catherine's life, she experienced for the first time one of those mystical ecstasies which thenceforward became a weekly occurrence for a period of twelve years. During these ecstasies she conducted herself as a character in the great drama of Christ's Passion. The various scenes and acts of the unique divine tragedy were reproduced before her eyes. She was present at the parting of Jesus from Mary, and traversed the road from Bethany to Jerusalem in sacred companionship with her Divine Spouse. She found place within the cenacle; partook of the "Last Supper"; observed with wrapt attention the washing of the Apostles' feet, the institution of the Holy Eucharist, and heard with rapturous joy the sermon of our Lord. With the Divine Master she crossed the Brook Cedron to the Garden of Olives, and there saw Him in agony and prayer. As though witnessing a great panorama, the traitor and his band passed before her eyes. She beheld the giving of the treacherous kiss, the flight of the apostolic band, and the arrest of the Innocent Victim.

She found herself numbered among the motley crowd at the house of Annas; followed the throng to the court of Caiphas, thence to the tribunal of Pilate. A spectator at the trials by Herod and Pilate, she witnessed the scourging at the pillar, the crowning with thorns. To her the "Ecce Homo" was a reality and not a picture. She heard the death sentence, not as read from the written page, but pronounced by the living voice of Jewish madmen. With dolorous steps and mournful tears she accompanied Him to the doleful theater of His death. The excruciating torments suffered by the Master when His hands and feet were fastened to the tree of the cross were experienced by her. Three long hours she watched Him suffer ignominy, then death. The rapture concluded with her assisting at the bathing of the welts and sores of His virginal flesh when taken down from the cross.

This program, covering a period of twenty-eight hours, was gone through with fixed intervals between each phase, beginning at noon on Thursday and closing at 4 o'clock Friday afternoon, each week from the year 1542 to 1554. Although during these ecstasies the Saint endured every agony of the Master, her countenance always shone with a heavenly splendor. The reception of the Holy Eucharist alone interrupted this state of rapturous contemplation.

Sister Catherine and her fellow-religious were not without their misgivings as to the author of these amazing manifestations. They implored God by prayer and fasting that they be not made victims of a snare of the Evil One. The news of this weekly event spread to the four winds, and throngs desired admission to Saint Vincent's, seeking to see the wonders of which they had heard.

In pursuance of his duty, Father Francesco de Castiglione, Provincial of the Roman Dominican Province, came to Prato to make a personal investigation of the phenomena. He put the Saint through a severe examination, treating her as though she were a criminal. Catherine stood the test perfectly. The Provincial's decision, given to the ecstatic herself, was: "Take courage, my child, and be at peace. There is no delusion in your state. God himself is guiding you." Father Francesco Romeo made his report to Rome. At the time, Father Albert de las Casas was Master General of the Dominican Order; he did not doubt the Provincial's wisdom in making a favorable judgment in the case, but through devotion went to Saint Vincent's to see the holy nun.

After an interview with Catherine and a close observation of her during an ecstasy, he turned to his companions and said: "There is nothing to doubt about in this soul, but everything to revere." Despite the opinion of the two learned theologians, Pope Paul III was suspicious of some culpable motive in the community at Prato for attracting such a multitude of externs to their convent. He sent a commission, headed by Cardinal de Pucci, to Saint Vincent's to scrutinize carefully the rumored facts in the case and to make a formal report to him. This significant sentence is taken from the statement made by the commission to the Holy See: "In the grave state of things now prevalent in the Church, such numbers could not come together to witness such a spectacle but to the great advantage of true Christians and the confusion of heretics; for the extraordinary graces of which they themselves had just been witnesses constituted a most striking demonstration of the truth of the Catholic Faith." Many other prominent ecclesiastics came to make inquiries into the matter, but always with the same result.

As a further proof of the genuineness of the Saint's communings with God, Our Blessed Lady shortly after the first ecstasy revealed to her a canticle in honor of her Divine Son's Passion. This song, or lamentation, consists chiefly of prophetic verses taken from the Psalms. Father Francesco Romeo, when he succeeded Father de las Casas as Master General of the Order, commanded that

Saint Catherine's "Canticle of the Passion" should be placed among the regular devotions peculiar to Dominicans. Father Hyacinth Cormier, the late Master General, caused it to be incorporated in the Compline Book of the Order, since it should be said each Friday after that hour of the Divine Office.

On Easter Sunday, April 9, 1542, the risen Christ, resplendent with glory and carrying a brilliant cross, appeared to Catherine. The Divine Visitor, placing a ring upon the finger of the lowly Saint, addressed her in these words: "Receive, daughter, this ring, a pledge and token that thou art and ever shall be mine." On Friday of the same week, coming to the scene of the crucifixion in her ecstasy, she was moved by an extraordinary compassion for her suffering Spouse and offered to take His place on the cross. Simultaneously with her offer she felt the blow of the lance strike her breast and perceived her hands and feet to be pierced as if by nails. From that day until her death she bore in her body the sacred stigmata. The ring of her espousals and the wounds, like unto those which Christ received on Calvary, were always perceptible to the Saint, but less observable to others. Their presence on her body, however, has been authenticated sufficiently to satisfy the searching demands of the Church, as the Bull of Canonization by Benedict XIV clearly shows.

The last symbol of suffering borne in the Passion of her crucified Spouse was granted to her on Christmas Day, 1542. The Blessed Mother, accompanied by a host of heavenly spirits, appeared to Catherine bearing the Infant Jesus in her arms. The Holy Child was placed in the fond embrace of the lately espoused bride of Christ. Saint Thecla, one of the celestial multitude attending, placed before the favored nun three crowns—one of gold, one of silver, and one of thorns—and the Virgin Mary then bade her make a choice from among them. Catherine hesitated, because she feared the thorns would overtax her strength when added to the terrible torture of the stigmata. The Blessed Mother reproved the Saint for this weakness. With eyes bedimmed with tears of compunction, the humbled Dominicaness begged for the crown of thorns. This favor was bestowed upon her later by the Master Himself.

We will close these citations of the wonderful graces granted to so holy a woman of God by a brief reference to her miraculous crucifix. From this image of Himself crucified, the Redeemer often engaged her in conversation. The figure would hold its arms outstretched to her, and on one occasion detached itself from the wood, finding a place of rest in her arms. The miracles wrought through this remarkable symbol of the Christian religion have been verified, so as to place them beyond doubt, as have been all the other phenomena connected with the life of this notable woman.

Leaving the realms of the supernatural, into which the treatment of our subject's spiritual life drew us, we descend to earth that we might get a glimpse of the human element in her personality. Naturally the fame of the Saint of Prato spread to all parts of Italy. Throngs flocked to Saint Vincent's to see and converse with our prodigy of holiness. Some came through charity, others for it; some came for advice, others to give it, but the greater part came to implore her prayers, and to have the pleasure of hearing and seeing her. The numbers became so great as to become a source of annoyance to the community. Besides, Catherine, being of a retiring disposition, would rather spend days in the solemn quiet of her cell than a moment amid the distractions of public adulation.

At times it would take hours to withdraw her from some secret place of seclusion that she might pay her respects to some prince, princess, or other distinguished personage who had called to see her. To obviate this cause of frequent embarrassment, she was made subprioress by the community. One of the duties of this office was to assist the prioress in her intercourse with externs. As subprioress, the good nun never shrunk from the tasks the new charge imposed upon her. Her influence on souls was amazing, and soon she had a host of spiritual sons and daughters. Her dealings with these men and women demonstrated what a rare knowledge of human nature she possessed.

Another duty entrusted to her care was the direction of the newly professed sisters. She communicated to them that fervor and love for God which seemed to consume her own soul, but at the same time with tact and common sense she prevented them from going into excesses. She prayed God to lessen the number of her ecstasies, in order that she might give more time to the ministrations to which she was obligated. Her prayer was heard. Under her influence the community advanced, both spiritually and temporally, with seeming leaps and bounds.

It is not surprising, therefore, that in 1552 she was unanimously elected prioress—an office she would not accept until put under a formal precept of obedience. For thirty-six years she administered the affairs of her convent with such prudence and business skill as to put to shame some of our modern successful women financiers. It goes without saying that the spiritual concerns of the community were well directed during this period.

Despite the fact that Catherine was most severe with herself in all modes of mortification, she would permit none of her subjects to vary from the common rule in these matters. Her multitude of admirers numbered among them the most wealthy men of Florence. These contributed generously to the support of Saint Vincent's. She saw to it that her spiritual daughters lived comfortably, but always within the bounds of the rule and constitutions of the Order.

That the common life might be more perfectly observed and that she might lead the way in setting aside all that savored of individualism in both spiritual and temporal actions, she, in union with her religious companions, prayed unceasingly for two years that God would relieve her from the famous weekly raptures. This petition was granted. She also mitigated those practices of personal austerity which drew unwonted attention of externs to herself. During these later years of her life, however, she was granted from time to time the consolation of visions and visitors from the heavenly court. The Virgin Mary, Saints Dominic, Vincent Ferrer, Thomas Aquinas, and others of the celestial kingdom appeared to her, counseling her on affairs of importance. While losing none of her extraordinary holiness of life nor one iota of her influence over souls, her spiritual life as she advanced in years developed more and more into that most human form of sanctity, which consists in performing the ordinary duties of life extraordinarily well.

Saint Catherine's efforts to establish an exact observance of the rule was nowhere more marked than in the enforcing of the precepts of silence, conventual etiquette, and attendance at choral exercises. She punished herself severely for the slightest transgression of these rules of religious life. She was just as exacting with her subjects, not letting the slightest fault go unpunished. Her love of neighbor, however, was so great that the penances she imposed on others were always tempered by a Christlike tenderness and mercy.

Her first duty, after all had assembled in choir for an exercise, was to scan the stalls for a possible absentee. Finding a vacancy in choir, she would go immediately for the delinquent and escort her personally to her place. Nothing less than physical incapacity excused from common prayer. It was her practice to call each evening at the cells of those religious whom she had corrected during the day and say some kind word, showing her motherly affection for them. The outstanding characteristic of her régime as superior was an inexorable demand for, and the personal practice of, uniformity in the observance of the common life.

In her younger years our Saint had accentuated the contemplative phase of the spiritual life. Now, however, in her maturity she realized perfectly the ideal Dominican existence, which blends harmoniously the active with the contemplative life. She was filled with zeal for the salvation of souls, pursuing her apostolate by means of prayer and letter-writing. Her immediate family was the first object of her apostolic endeavors. Her father submitted to her direction as to a confessor, while the letters interchanged between her and her parents were most affectionate and redolent with the odor of sanctity.

As we have before mentioned, she was the oldest of five children of the same family, who had made their religious profession in, and continued to live long lives as members of, Saint Vincent's community. One brother entered the Dominican Order, in which he led an exemplary life. Her eldest brother was a wayward man, whose sense of duty to his loved ones seemed to vary with the seasons. He was continually getting into trouble, at which times he would become almost lovable to his saintly sister. As soon as she brought about the settlement of his difficulties, he would forget all about her until another storm began to brew on the horizon of his life. Catherine finally converted him from his evil ways, after he had advanced far into the age of manhood. She gave to her youngest brother all the care and affection usually lavished by a mother on a favorite son.

Outside her family circle and her own community, our Saint had an army of disciples, drawn from all classes and walks of life. Notable among these was the Grand Duchess Joanna of Austria, wife of Duke Francesco de Medici, who exulted in calling her by the name of mother. Philip Salviati, cousin of the Grand Duke Cosmo de Medici, was so attracted to Catherine as to build voluntarily for her a church at Saint Vincent's. To the Grand Duke this was the greatest proof of the Saint's miraculous powers, that she had made an almsgiver out of Salviati.

Buonaccorso Buonaccorsi, a renowned jurist, placed his professional services at her command in exchange for her services as director of the affairs of his soul. Cardinals, bishops, and priests were among her most ardent adherents. Worthy of mention among these were Cardinal Marcello Cervini, who afterward became Pope Marcellus II, and Father Vincenzo Giustana, once General of the Dominican Order. Cardinal Aldobrandini, who occupied the chair of Peter as Clement VIII, consulted her on many important and delicate matters of business. Pope Saint Pius V sent Cardinal Michael Bonelli to Prato in order to see the Saint and solicit the aid of her prayers for the success of his proposed league against the Turks.

The most admirable point connected with the holy nun's dealings with externs and the keynote of her correspondence is the good common sense displayed in checking those inclined to be spiritually erratic. To one who wanted to indulge in extraordinary periods of fasting she sent a basket of food with a note, saying: "We must not try to die, but to live and do good, in order to give glory and honor to God." To another who wanted direction in devotions she sent a rosary and information as to how to say it well.

A business man, trying to combine the austerities of a monk with a career in the mercantile world, counseled the Saint about his state. He was told in very plain language to choose one or the other mode of life. If his choice fell on being a man of affairs, then he must give up his severe penitential practices, so that he might preserve his health and serve his fellow-man.

Of all the multitude who sought the help and maternal care of Catherine, none were dearer to her than the poor. By her instructions, no beggar was to leave the convent door without being first relieved of his want, in so far as it was compatible with the resources of the community. She kneaded with her own hands the bread intended for the indigent.

Many of our Saint's wealthy disciples entrusted to her large sums of money to be distributed in alms, according as her prudence and charity should dictate. It was not an uncommon thing for her to draw on this fund in favor of deserving girls who desired to marry, but were in need of a dowry. The breadth of view she took of life and her insight into human nature was as great as her sanctity was perfect.

In so brief a sketch of Saint Catherine de Ricci's life it is not possible to give a detailed account of her miracles or record the circumstances of her many almost incredible conversions. We cite, however, an instance in which the spirit of prophecy, which she possessed, is manifested, since it reveals the close relation in which she stood with another illustrious saint of her time. A priest of Prato was attached to the house of Saint Charles Borromeo at Milan. Through the instrumentality of this good man a pious intercourse sprung up between the holy Cardinal and the Saint of Prato. The attaché of the Cardinal's court would always call to see Catherine when visiting his home town. On one occasion she gave him a picture of the "Ecce Homo" to bring to the renowned ecclesiastic of Milan, telling him to inform the Cardinal Archbishop not to regard so much the rudely executed likeness as Him whom it represented. Continuing her instructions, she said: "In a few days a horrible attempt will be made on the Cardinal's life, out of hatred for his zeal in the reformation of the Church, but our Divine Redeemer will deliver him by means of this picture." Only a brief space of time elapsed until this prophecy was fulfilled. Saint Charles, while occupied in his private chapel, was fired upon by a would-be assassin, but escaped uninjured. Out of gratitude for his miraculous preservation, the Cardinal had the little picture of the "Ecce Homo" placed in a precious frame and hung in a private study.

Saint Catherine also enjoyed a holy friendship with Saint Philip Neri, based on their mutual attachment to the memory of Savonarola. Though they never met in the flesh, they were favored with a miraculous meeting in spirit. Both saints have left us their testimony in proof of this fact.

As we have said, Saint Catherine was most solicitous about her disciples' austerities, exhorting them continually to be discreet. She punished her own flesh, however, to the limit of human endurance. One of the miracles of her life is that she lived so many years, sustained by the little food in which she permitted herself to indulge.

Counseled by Christ Himself to so act, she never ate meat, eggs, or any kind of food classed as the flesh of animals. One hour a week was all the sleep she would allow her weary body. She disciplined herself mercilessly each night with an iron chain, constantly wore a hair shirt, and seemed a genius in contriving new schemes for afflicting her tortured carnal self. She offered all her penances for her own sins, the sins of others, and the souls in Purgatory.

It is said that the souls of the dead, in the state of being purged from their sins, often appeared to her entreating her prayers in their behalf. As often as she recognized the presence of these spirits of the departed, she would kneel down and ask God to let her suffer in the stead of those laboring in the purgatorial flames.

At a late period in her life she was tormented by a most dreadful torture; for her whole body seemed a prey to a consuming fire. This condition continued for a space of forty days. We have the Saint's word for it, that by this affliction she atoned for the sins of a wayward prince for whom she had obtained a death-bed repentance. Heresy and crime, then so rampant throughout Europe, were a source of deep concern to her, and she offered the excruciating pains, which were seldom absent from her body, in expiation for these sins of men.

Catherine's devotions were typically Dominican. Next to her tender love and affection for Jesus in the Eucharist stood her deep attachment for the contemplation of His Passion. The Holy Mother of God held the next highest place in her heart to that of the Divine Son. Second only to these was her ardent love for the souls in Purgatory. Her prayer was ceaseless. In speaking of this exercise, she once said: "We must bring to prayer a great confidence that we shall be heard; for there are many graces which God inspires us to ask, and which we do not obtain by reason of our diffidence. When we desire to obtain a favor from Almighty God, we must go on asking for it till we get it; because He has determined the number of times we are to ask for it; and He will not grant our petition till that number is complete." The things of nature, the trees, flowers, rain, snow, etc., were constant sources of inspiration moving her to prayer and the praise of God.

A striking proof of Catherine's humility is given to us in the following incident related by her biographers. Certain members of the community at Saint Vincent's undertook to write a life of their saintly mother. All but what would have been the closing chapters was complete when the holy prioress was unintentionally informed about the matter. She was crushed by the thought that those things which she had done for the greater honor and glory of God should be set before the eyes of the world, bringing her into renown among men.

Secretly, while the community was in choir, she ransacked the house and confiscated all manuscripts. Taking them to the bake-shop, she said to the simple lay-sister in charge there: "Make haste, destroy all these papers quickly; woe to us if they were to be found in the convent." The obedience of the lay-sister was perfect. The Saint was enraptured with joy at seeing the record of her deeds go up in flames. As to obedience, the humble prioress would submit her will not only to equals, but even to inferiors, when this could be done without endangering discipline. Her patience in her endless sufferings and trials was a source of edification to all.

The day of January 23, 1590, had been spent by Sister Catherine in entertaining several of her near relatives. It was not until after a late repast in the evening that she detected that through neglect of self she had aggravated a chronic disease of which she was a victim. Racked for several days by the agony brought on by the complaint, she asked for a severe remedy to be administered to her—one which the doctors prescribed to be used only after all other applicable medicines had failed to bring the desired results. When this last remedy proved powerless to arrest the ravages of the ailment, the Great Saint of Prato surrendered herself to the divine "fiat."

Sending for each of the several branches of her community, she gave to them in turn a pious exhortation fitting to their respective progress in the religious life. Then, embracing fondly the miraculous crucifix, she gave herself up to ecstatic prayer. After two hours' preparation she rose from her bed in order that she might kneel to receive Holy Viaticum. Several more hours were spent in thanksgiving, after which the Sacrament of Extreme Unction was administered.

With amazing accuracy and keenness of mind, she arranged with a chosen few of her confidants for the administration of the temporal and spiritual affairs of the convent. The dominant note of her farewell conference with the community was that they should love God more and more, be regular in their observance of the rule, and, setting aside all discord, to love one another tenderly.

Her countenance seemed to glow with a heavenly light when, at 2 o'clock on the morning of February 2, 1590, she closed her eyes with her own hands and extended her arms in the shape of a cross, and thus passed to her eternal reward. At the same moment Saint Mary Magdalen de Pazzi went into ecstasy in her monastery at Florence and beheld the Holy Virgin of Prato enter into the Assembly of the Blessed in Heaven.

Her dead body seemed radiant and gave forth the fragrance of sweetest perfumes. Many beheld with extraordinary distinctness the bleeding marks of the sacred stigmata and the ring of her holy espousals. For two days Prato was thronged with sorrowful multitudes, who came to pay their respects to the remains of a true bride of Christ. The body, encased in a metal coffin, was placed to rest in a deep niche beneath a miraculous figure of our Holy Mother which adorned the wall of the nuns' private chapel.

It is not surprising that after her death innumerable miracles were worked through her intercession. On the 23d of November, 1732, Pope Clement XII celebrated her solemn beatification at Saint Peter's amidst the overwhelming rejoicing of the people of Florence, the Ricci family, and the Dominican Order. Benedict XIV, in the year 1746, enrolled the name of Blessed Catherine among the canonized in the Catalogue of Saints. The 13th of February, by pontifical appointment, is the day on which her feast is commemorated.

BIBLIOGRAPHY

F. M. CAPES: Saint Catherine de Ricci. London, 1905.

F. M. CAPES: Saint Catherine de Ricci. Cath. Encyc. (New York, 1908), III, p. 444.

Archives O. P.: Process of Canonization, Series X, 678–693. (Latin.)

RAZZI: The Life of the Reverend Mother, Sister Catherine de Ricci. Lucca, Busdrago, 1594. (Italian.)

FRA. FILIPPO GUIDI, O. P.: Life of St. C. de R. Fiorenza, 1622. (Italian.)

P. DOMENICO MARCHESI, O. P.: Life of St. C. de R. Rome, 1683. (Italian.)

ANONYMOUS: Brief Life. Rome, 1706. (Latin.)

ANONYMOUS: Brief Life. Rome, 1732, 1733, 1746. (Italian.)

FRA. DOMENICO M. SANDRINI, O. P.: Life of St. C. de R. Firenze, 1747. (Italian.)

Acts of the Saints (John Bolland and others). Paris, 2 Feb., I, 267. (L.)

ÉCHARD, O. P.: (Scriptores Ordinis Prædicatorum, Paris, 1719–21.) Vol. II, p. 991.

BULLARIUM, O. P.: Rome, 1729–1749; Index, 788, Vol. VIII.

BENEDICT XIV: On the Beatification of the Servants of God. Ed. III. Rome, 1747 (L.).

ALLIBERT: Vie de S. C. Lyon–Paris, 1846.

Année Dominicaine, II, 409. Lyons, 1883–1909.

P. HYACINTHE BAYONNE, O. P.: Vie. Paris, 1873.

P. TOMMASO G. TINTI, O. P.: Short Life. Firenze, 1890. (Italian.)

CESARE GUASTI: Letters of St Catherine. Firenze, 1890. (Italian.)

BENEDICT REICHERT, O. P.: Acts of the General Chapters, O. P., 1220–1840. Rome, 1894–1904, VI, 257; VII, 404; VIII, 172; IX, 108; 115, 116, 198 (L.).

Saint Rose of Lima

HE LIFE of Saint Rose of Lima appeals especially to Americans, for this servant of God was the first American pronounced a saint by the infallible voice of Holy Mother, the Church. Moreover, this charming girl-saint has been declared the Patroness of the New World. But, besides the local interest attaching to her life, Rose cannot fail to win our admiration and love, uniting, as she does, the intrepid fortitude of a soldier of Jesus Christ with the simplicity and winsomeness of a little child. We know that cowardice never found a place in the heart of this follower of the Crucified. She made no truce with the enemies of salvation, and yet at the same time she ever retained the guilelessness and meekness of her childhood. So forcibly did this maidenly gentleness impress the poetic mind of Father Faber that he deemed it her most striking characteristic.

Then, too, the life of this child of Saint Dominic should prove interesting to all, for hers was a humble, retired, and even commonplace life, filled with its round of duties and simple joys. In fact, it was a state of life not unlike that which falls to the lot of many of us unremarkable mortals. Unlike her patroness, the Seraph of Siena, it was not her glory to counsel the Vicar of Christ and to heal the heart-wound in the Church; nor was she destined to rule over a mighty people, like the saint-queen, Elizabeth of Hungary. Hers, rather, was the hidden, quiet, silent life of Nazareth. What needful lessons may not our proud and frivolous age learn from this humble and prudent American maiden!

Saint Rose of Lima

Saint Rose was born on April 20, 1586, in the royal city of Lima, Peru. Her parents were Gaspar and Maria de Flores, persons of very respectable lineage, though in rather straitened circumstances, due to reverse of fortune. The infant was not very robust, so it was baptized in its home, receiving the name of Isabel, which is the Spanish for Elizabeth. She received this name in honor of her aunt, Isabel Herera, who acted as her godmother. On Pentecost, which the Spaniards poetically style "the Easter of Roses," the little child was brought to the Church of San Sebastian to receive the solemn rites of the Church. The good priest who baptized her had a few years previously enjoyed the privilege of pouring the regenerating waters of baptism on the head of an infant who was destined by God to be raised to the altars of the Church, and whom we now venerate as Blessed Martin de Porres.

But how strange the name of Isabel sounds to us who are so familiar with the name of Rose! The beautiful story of this change of name is well worth recounting: One day, when the child was about three months old, her mother and some friends were sitting around the trundle-bed of the sleeping babe, gazing in admiration at her marvelous beauty, when a rose was seen to hover in the air above the child's head and descend to kiss the cheek of the little Saint. The mysterious rose then disappeared as it had come. There is no need to add that all were astonished and overjoyed at the miracle. Her mother pressed the child of predilection to her bosom and in her joy promised never again to call her except by the poetic name of "Rose."

Years afterwards, when the little girl was being confirmed by another saint—Turibius, the Archbishop of the city—he spontaneously gave her the same sweet name, thus manifesting that it was the Divine Will that she should be so named. Aptly, then, does the Church apply to her the words of Holy Writ: "Hear me, ye divine offspring, and bud forth as the rose planted by the brooks of waters."[1]

[1] Ecclus. xxxix, 17.

This remarkable infant, as the years passed, became the general favorite not only among the elder folks, but also among her brothers and sisters and other playmates; for, besides being a singularly pretty child, she was endowed with a very winsome way. Moreover, she was never given to selfishness and other petty faults so common among children. All who came in contact with her felt an indescribable awe inspired by the presence of this heavenly child.

Even when barely able to walk, little Rose manifested an intense love for our Divine Lord, and would delight in gazing upon a picture of the Redeemer of mankind with His Sacred Head crowned with thorns. It was also her custom to steal away from her games to some hidden corner of the playground to lisp her childish prayers. But God, who wished Rose to become a great saint, soon led her along the rugged pathway of suffering. Indeed, she was only three years of age when we find her courageously hiding a severely crushed thumb under her frock and bravely keeping back her tears lest she should startle her rather easily excited mother. Then, when the wound festered and it was necessary to call in a surgeon to remove the nail, the little heroine bore the sharp pain without the least sign of reluctance, and we have the testimony of the doctor that in all his years of practice he had never witnessed such heroic disregard for pain.

It was only shortly after this that the brave little tot was afflicted by a malignant abscess back of the ear, but though the pain was intensified by a mistaken remedy, so that a grievous inflammation set in, Rose refrained from groaning or even altering her position in bed, lest she should disturb her tired mother. When the terrible state of the sore was seen through the removal of the bandages, her horrified mother asked her why she had not cried out with pain, but the child merely replied: "Our Lord's Crown of Thorns was much worse."

But this patient child had her joys as well as sorrows. She enjoyed the tender love of her mother, who, though at times inclined to be irritable, nevertheless loved her daughter ardently. Besides, ten brothers and sisters were given her, and upon them she lavished the wealth of her affection. She never wearied of assisting them in their work and delighted to join in their play, cheerfully yielding her own desires and preferences to please them. Then, too, she was much sought after by the children of the neighborhood. In fact, it was while in the company of some girl friends that Rose received the call from on high to give herself unreservedly to the Spouse of all beauty. It happened in this wise: One day, when the children were gathered together in the garden, Rose, little child that she was, tried to persuade the girls to take the view that she did in a certain matter; but they would not heed her words of admonition and playfully threw some mud and dust at her, much to her annoyance, for she was always scrupulously neat. Her brother, Ferdinand, noticing her momentary vexation, exclaimed in the tones of a preacher: "Rose, a holy girl would not mind a little dirt on her head; she would know that fine hair is all vanity." These words, uttered at random and in jest, struck deep into the heart of the little Saint, and, realizing that they were the whisperings of the Divine Dove, she forthwith cut off all her beautiful tresses, and then and there vowed perpetual virginity to the Bridegroom of her soul. With all truth could this docile child cry out: "My heart is ready, O Lord; my heart is ready!"[2]

Saint Rose now began in earnest to follow in the footsteps of the glorious seraph, Catherine of Siena, whom she had chosen as her model in the following of the Crucified. It seems that the people of Lima had a tender devotion to this great Saint, and that Rose had learned of her wonderful life from her elders. Now, some months before the complete conversion narrated above, Maria de Flores decided to teach her daughter how to read, but after a few lessons she grew impatient and gave up the task. What, then, was her mother's surprise when one day little Rose came running in with a book to where she was seated, read a page of it for her, showed her a sample of her writing, and related how our Lord Himself

[2] Ps. lvi, 8.

had taught her. Then it was that Rose began to read the wonderful life-story of the Maid of Siena and to learn of the means that she had used to attain to such intimate union with God. As the child's knowledge of the Sienese Saint became fuller, the more did she wish to imitate her ways of holiness, and so when the sweet grace of true conversion flooded her heart, after the little incident recorded above, Rose, like Catherine, vowed perpetual virginity to God and resolved to spare no pains in modeling her life after Catherine's.

Shortly after Saint Rose had made her secret vow, her family removed to a place just outside Lima, called Guanta, where there were gold mines and mills. Though the location was noted for its beautiful scenery, it seems that the climate was rather damp and cold. Rose was attacked with a rheumatic fever, so that she was unable to move her limbs. Her mother thought to cure her by wrapping her in heavy furs, and gave her the injunction not to remove them on any account. The cure, however, proved worse than the affliction and caused a general suppuration of the skin. Rose obediently endured this purgatory for four days, when her mother was shocked to find her in such a state, and marveled at the wonderful Job-like patience of her young daughter.

Even from her tenderest years Rose had exhibited a self-control in matters of food and drink that was exceptional; she had the kindness to keep her fruits and sweetmeats for her little brothers and sisters. But now, when she was six years of age, she determined further to mortify her appetite by fasting on bread and water three times a week, namely, on Wednesdays, Fridays, and Saturdays. Moreover, she never partook of this frugal repast, if such a name it deserves, until evening, and she made sure that the bread was stale and the water tepid.

Although we do not know when this little heroine made her First Communion, it is certain that she was rather under the age when children were then accustomed to be admitted to the Sacred Banquet. What joy must have flooded her heart on that occasion we can better imagine than express. It surely must have been like that of Blessed Imelda, if we are to judge in the light of subsequent events, for one day after having received Holy Communion Rose beheld our Divine Lord, who told her that He was well pleased with her fastings, and that He would henceforward sustain her body as well as soul by the Bread of Life. This noble child then made a vow never to eat meat unless, of course, obliged to do so by obedience. Thus we see her further following the footsteps of Catherine of Siena.

When Rose's mother heard of the promise her daughter had made of never eating flesh meat, she was naturally surprised, for we must remember that Rose was of a delicate constitution and was almost chronically ailing. So her anxious mother in all good faith told her child that she must eat what was placed on the table. Rose obediently did so, but immediately her stomach refused to retain the food. Some time afterwards Rose was again taken ill, this time very dangerously so. When she was convalescing, the doctors ordered her to eat some very nourishing meat, that she might the more rapidly regain her strength. Our Saint meekly obeyed the prescription, but endured such tortures that, had the command not been recalled, death would undoubtedly have occurred.

"So it is that God," remarks one of her biographers,[3] "when He has marked out for His own all-wise purposes some special road to sanctification for a soul, interferes occasionally Himself in what may seem like trivial matters, to prevent interference on the part of creatures with the carrying out of His design. Whether the strength of a sick girl should or should not be restored by the eating of flesh meat might appear in itself a question not likely to have an important bearing on her future spiritual life; but her Maker has appointed strict abstinence from this particular food as the path by which Rose is to go to Him; and to preserve her obedience to His appointment intact, He thenceforth endows it with unwholesome qualities for her which it has not in its own nature."

[3] Capes, F. M.: Life of Saint Rose, p. 60.

When Rose was about fifteen or sixteen years of age her mother made her accompany her in paying visits of a social nature. Rose would have preferred to remain at home, working and praying, but her mother was insistent. She wished her attractive daughter to be a social favorite, and with this end in view she secured expensive clothes and ornaments for her. Nothing was further from Rose's thoughts, for she never forgot for an instant her youthful vow to our Saviour. So, when unable to escape these visits, she made it a point to mortify herself in some hidden way, so that she might not be guilty of vanity. Once, when she failed to do this and was putting on a pair of perfumed gloves, they so burned her hands with an unseen flame that they had to be quickly torn off. Ever afterward this saintly maiden performed her secret penances when on these visits of pleasure.

Finally, as these visits grew more frequent and protracted, for it seems that Maria de Flores was much addicted to this form of entertainment and that it was much in vogue in the city of Lima at that time, Saint Rose determined to see if she could not put an end to it. Accordingly she resolved to disfigure her lustrous eyes by rubbing pepper in them. We may imagine how angry her mother was when she found out what she had done. She told Rose that her eyesight might have been ruined; but the servant of God answered that she would much rather be blind than continue to use her eyes in beholding the vanities of the world! Thus she succeeded in escaping these displeasing visitings with their accompanying fine clothes.

For a while now our heroine had a little peace and was allowed to dress in the rough apparel of a working-woman; but her mother had not entirely relinquished the idea of securing an advantageous marriage for her beautiful daughter, and so when several offers were made for the hand of Rose, her mother did not fail to urge her to consider them. For a time the affair was deferred without a positive refusal on the part of our Saint, but things were brought to a climax when the mother of a very wealthy young man asked that Rose become her daughter. The whole family looked upon this offer as a blessing from Heaven, for thus their poverty would be relieved, and they could once more assume their proper social position. Rose had now to give a final and resolute refusal. She explained to her parents that she had irrevocably bound herself to our Lord by a vow of chastity and could never for a moment consider an earthly marriage. When they heard this, Rose became the object of insults and even blows, all the more painful to her tender and affectionate heart because they came from those she loved most dearly. She was charged with ingratitude and selfishness, and her brothers and sisters upbraided her with hard-heartedness for failing to assist the family in its straitened circumstances. Verily, Rose's most powerful enemies were those of her own household. It takes but little thought to realize what she must have undergone, torn, as she was, between the natural love for her father and mother and the supernatural love for the Lord of all. But this valiant girl never for a second wavered in her fidelity to her Beloved. Indeed,

> "Demons and all the might of hell
> Could never take this citadel.
> Alone, this gentle, high-born maid
> By worldly scorn was undismayed." [4]

We may be sure that the Infant Jesus consoled her in her sorrow, and gave her, while she was treated with disgrace, that peace which passeth all understanding. We do not know how long this period of trial lasted, but finally, when her parents saw that her decision was adamantine, they ceased persecuting her and permitted her to do as her conscience directed. Thus was settled the question of marriage and never more was she to be afflicted by their importunities in this regard.

But Rose's life up to this period was not wholly taken up with the struggle to keep her troth with the Child Jesus. She was always

[4] From Matin Hymn for Saint Rose's Feast.

busy about the house, helping all that she was able. She was ever ready to assist her brothers and sisters and also often succeeded in obtaining from their rather hot-tempered father forgiveness for their faults. Without preaching, Rose succeeded in inculcating in their innocent hearts many a lesson of goodness and truth. Her mother, whom she loved most dearly and who, despite her many faults, was a good mother, Rose helped in the management of their large household, for the family was never able to have more than one servant. This was a very religious woman, named Marianna, who did all she could to encourage the Saint in her endeavors to arrive at perfection. Rose, out of gratitude, lent a willing hand in the menial occupations which fell to the lot of the maid. It is a beautiful and inspiring picture, the noble girl cheerfully working side by side with the humble servant. It is a scene on which we would wish to dwell, for it is all too rare in this haughty age of ours. Rose, then, was a model girl—humble, obedient in everything that did not intrude between her and her Redeemer, and diligent in all her tasks.

Of these tasks two especially took up the time of Rose de Flores. She was an expert in needlework and spent many an hour embroidering with silks. It was well known in Lima that Rose was so deft with the needle that she could execute in a half hour what any other worker would require an hour for accomplishing. Moreover, so exquisite was the art with which she wrought the roses, lilies, and other flowers in her designs that it was whispered about that she had received the aid of angels. Indeed, in the light of the marvelous gifts vouchsafed from on high to this eager lover of the Crucified, this explanation was the only logical one.

Another duty that received Saint Rose's attention was the cultivating of flowers in her father's garden. Here, too, the special blessing of Heaven was manifested. Rose's flowers were of the rarest hues and perfumes and always brought the best prices at the flower market. It is even related that her plants often bloomed out of the regular season. Thus she helped to support the numerous household by her embroideries and bouquets. "It is but a little trade, certainly, but my heavenly Spouse's goodness makes the profits large," are the grateful words of the Saint.

"Why are there so few saints today? Because ours is an age of luxury, of self-seeking—an easy and effeminate age. Penance and mortifications are spectres that terrify us";[5] but to the mind of the heroine of Lima they presented no such aspect. She realized that "a saint must be essentially and necessarily a man or woman of penance"[6]—a victim on the altar of sacrifice. She knew that "self must abdicate if God is to reign."[7] Hence we have seen how Rose, even from her tenderest years, took to heart the words of the Man of Sorrows: "If any man will come after Me, let him deny himself and take up his cross daily and follow Me."[8]

But now, as the years passed by and Rose approached womanhood, she sought ever more and more to resemble her Divine Lover. Her food was the coarsest and most unpalatable that she could concoct. To the rough crusts that she allowed herself she added bitter herbs that she grew in the garden plot. Moreover, to deaden her sense of taste and to imitate Christ, who was given a draught of vinegar mingled with gall, Saint Rose daily rinsed her mouth with the gall of a sheep. In addition, this holy maid began to wear a hair shirt and to scourge her innocent body with a discipline of heavy-knotted cords. Several times in the day she applied this lash in memory of the Second Sorrowful Mystery.

But the severest struggle that Rose had to wage was to overcome sleep. Even as a little child, she was wont to creep out of her downy bed to sleep on the hard, cold floor, and now, as she approached her nineteenth year, she constructed a bed that would render the little sleep she took as uncomfortable as possible. It

[5] Proctor, Fr., O. P.: Introduction to Life of Saint Rose.

[6] Ibidem.

[7] Ibidem.

[8] Luke ix, 23.

consisted of an old box, in which she placed broken earthenware and gnarled pieces of wood, with a block for a pillow. Thus, by curtailing her sleep Rose found time for her many acts of devotion and service about the house. Nor must we think that after a long day of toil it was a pleasure for her to rest her weary body on this uninviting couch. True it is that she received great supernatural helps, but these perfect and do not destroy nature.

Indeed, one night when Rose was tempted to give up this rude resting place and was well-nigh overcome, our Lord appeared to her and said: "Remember, My child, that I was not content with merely lying on stone and wood; My feet and hands were pierced, and I bore unspeakable sufferings till the very moment when I gave up My spirit. Think of this, My child, when you are inclined to yield."

These penances would seem to be sufficient for even the most devoted ascetic, but Rose found still another way to liken herself to the Redeemer of mankind. We may recall how as a baby she was often found gazing with pity on a picture of the thorn-crowned Saviour that hung in her mother's room. Her holy ingenuity now devised a way in which to imitate that ignominious crowning with thorns which Christ suffered. She fashioned a circlet of some pliable metal and studded it with sharp points. Thus she was kept ever mindful of the pain that the Sacred Head endured for our salvation, and further copied her pattern, Catherine Benincasa, who preferred a crown of thorns to one of roses. In view, then, of these penitential exercises practiced by the First Flower of America, most appropriate are the words sung by Holy Mother Church in her honor:

> "With Christ, the dying Lord of all,
> On Calvary's gloomy height she mourns;
> She shares His stripes and bitter gall,
> And on her brow the piercing thorns." [9]

[9] From Vesper Hymn of Saint Rose's Feast.

Saint Rose had never any doubt as to her divine call to suffering and mortification. She had eagerly responded to the invitation of Holy Writ, "Be converted to Me with all your heart, in fasting, and in weeping, and in mourning."[10] Although naturally of delicate health, weak in body and physically feeble, she did not shrink from the awful share in Christ's Passion allotted to her. Now, however, she began to hear the further vocation to the religious life. Naturally her thoughts turned to the Order of the glorious patriarch, Saint Dominic, of whom Dante writes:

> "And I speak of him as the laborer,
> Whom Christ in His own garden chose to be
> His helpmate. Messenger, he seemed, and friend
> Fast knit to Christ; and the first love he showed
> Was after the first counsel that Christ gave. . . ."[11]

When it was noised abroad that the de Flores' saintly daughter was thinking of joining some religious organization, all the convents in Lima wished to secure such a treasure for themselves. The niece of Saint Turibius, the great Archbishop of the Royal City, was at this time founding a convent of the daughters of Saint Clare and earnestly begged Rose to help her in the foundation. The Augustinian Convent of the Incarnation also eagerly sought for Rose, and it seems that she finally decided to join this holy community. So she went to the Rosary altar of the Dominican church in order to bid Our Lady farewell; but, as she was about to leave the church, she found that she was unable to move from the spot, nor could the gigantic efforts of her brother, who had accompanied her, avail. Then the idea flashed across her mind that this was our Blessed Lady's method of showing her that she was to remain in the world as a Tertiary. No sooner had this devoted client of Mary made this decision than she was released by this mysterious force and permitted to return home. So she was

[10] Joel ii, 12.

[11] Paradiso, xii, 65–69.

admitted as a novice into the Third Order of Saint Dominic by her confessor, Father Velasquez, in the same Rosary chapel.

Rose was now in her twentieth year. But she was destined to be tried yet more in the fires of temptation. Indeed, Rose herself tells us: "I have bought the habit of our holy Father, Saint Dominic, with so many sighs and tears, with so many fasts and prayers, in order that I may lead a hidden life." She now became a prey to scruples and worries as to the perfection required of her as a Dominican; and, besides, her humility was greatly affected, for whenever she went out of the house people would stop and point her out as a living saint. Her sensitive soul recoiled at this publicity and made her fear for the purity of her intention.

Do we wonder, then, that when Don Gonzalez de Massa, a wealthy friend of her family, offered to provide a dowry for her if she would enter the Convent of the Carmelites, that Rose wavered in her purpose to become a Dominican and would have accepted this kind offer had not God, the Light of the World, shown her His Will in a way that could leave no room for doubt. While humbly praying for light and guidance, our Lord deigned to wrap her into ecstasy in the sight of all. Like the Apostle of the Nations, Rose never revealed "the secret words which it is not granted to man to utter,"[12] but ever after she never hesitated to continue hidden in the world as a simple Tertiary of Saint Dominic. Without any further hesitation, then, she was professed a member of the Third Order.

Many holy women now began to frequent the home of the de Flores family to find guidance and encouragement in the spiritual life from the words and example of the Saint. Among these pious ladies was the wife of the wealthy Gonzalez de Massa, who took an almost motherly interest in the young Tertiary. Although Rose enjoyed the spiritual companionship of these good women, yet she deemed it incompatible with her state in life that so much time should be occupied in these visits to her home. Her heart, like the hermits of the

[12] 2 Cor. xii, 4.

Thebaid, longed for solitude, that she might uninterruptedly commune with the Maker of the Universe. She realized what Saint Bernard expressed in his memorable words: "O beata solitudo! O sola beatitudo!" So Rose's thoughts turned to a favorite retreat or shrine of her childhood's days, situated in the garden, where she used to steal away from her companions to offer up her youthful devotions. Why could she not have a similar, though a more substantial, cell erected for herself? Rose determined to ask her mother for the desired hermitage. Maria, however, gave her a decided refusal. Nothing daunted, she had recourse to the Mother of Good Counsel, and, having been miraculously confirmed in her determination, she begged her confessor, Father Lorenzana, and the de Massas to obtain the consent of her mother. Without protest the coveted permission was granted and the little abode that was to be the scene of so many miracles, both of nature and of grace, was soon built in a comer of the garden. It was small indeed, being only five feet long and four in width. When her confessor commented upon its size, Saint Rose gaily responded: "It is large enough for the Beloved of my soul and me."

Here, in this little retreat, Rose was accustomed to spend the livelong day, returning to the house only at nightfall. Her whole day was one of ceaseless activity, taken up with her devotions and mortifications, her sewing and making nosegays of her flowers. After she had received the white habit of the Order of Truth, she daily recited the Divine Office. We can but faintly imagine the joy and peace that flooded her soul as she chanted the praises of her Love and meditated on the wonders of God in His saints. What devotion, what eager care and attention, she must have given to this labor of love can be fully realized only by those who have drunk deep of the waters of eternal life and have, like her, tasted and seen how sweet the Lord is.

Moreover, as a child of Mary, Rose especially loved the Little Office of the Blessed Virgin and daily recited it in honor of the Mother of her Spouse. Particularly pleasing must this beautiful trait be to the members of the Third Order, whose daily task it is to render these praises to the Immaculate. But the most wonderful characteristic of the Flower of Christ was her extraordinary application to *mental* prayer. Her constant recollection, "her deep, earnest, and all but perfect union with God," [13] may be compared to a sweet odor perpetually exhaled by this Rose of surpassing beauty. Her entire life was a seeking of her Last End, a lifting of her heart and mind to God. He was ever present in her thoughts; He was the constant motive of her every act, and her pure soul never ceased longing for union with Him.

We have seen the tender love and confidence that the Saint reposed in the Mother of God, and are not surprised to find that especially noteworthy was her constancy in reciting the chaplet of Our Lady. She endeavored also to make others acquainted with this efficacious form of prayer. Another favorite devotion peculiar to this Spouse of the Crucified was the recital of one hundred and fifty Divine Perfections, which were written down for her by her confessor. These she loved to repeat, meditating the while on the power and goodness of the bountiful Creator. Saint Rose also weaved spiritual garments for the Christ Child and His ever-blessed Mother. These resembled what we today style spiritual bouquets. They consisted of prayers, good works, acts of mortification, strokes of the discipline—all arranged in a definite and suitable order to represent a garment.

Perhaps it may have occurred to the reader that our Saint was more of a Carthusian, living as she did, alone in her little hermitage, than a Dominican, whose duty it is to combine the active with the contemplative life. This objection, however, might be answered by recalling to mind that Rose was a model of unflagging industry; and we must also remember that God alone knows the innumerable hosts of souls that are saved by those who, hidden in the cloister, constantly pray for the world's salvation. But Rose was a Tertiary,

[13] Capes, F. M.: l. c., p. 15.

not a cenobite, and her love for the conversion of sinners, for whom her Spouse had died, soon found a means for external activity. Her heart instinctively turned to the poor Indian women, outcast and in direst poverty, diseased and often still unconverted. Rose therefore asked her mother to allow her the use of some empty rooms in the house, that she might bring these unfortunates thither, nurse them, and instruct them in their religious duties. At first her mother was enraged at the proposition, but Rose pleaded so earnestly for these poor creatures that the permission was given her. Moreover, this winsome child often succeeded in coaxing her mother to supply her with clothing, bandages, and other necessities. Rose also sought out those families of noble extraction which had suffered a reverse of fortune and were in the greatest need, and who, like the unjust steward, were ashamed to beg. She tactfully attended to their wants without wounding their sensibilities.

Many and astounding were the miraculous powers that our Lord bestowed upon this apostolic maiden. She had the gift of penetrating the hearts of sinners, and frequently made use of the gift of prophecy to assist her friends when they were in difficulty. Thus, when the de Massas were perplexed over an appointment to a distant city that would necessitate a long separation from the family, Rose assured them that the commission would never really be undertaken. Especially noteworthy was the prophecy which Saint Rose made in regard to a convent for Dominican Sisters. She foretold that such a convent would be erected in Lima and dedicated to God under the patronage of her own Saint Catherine. When her mother chided her for making a fool of herself and her family by her idle talk, Rose told her in her own charming, simple way that she would say no more about it, but added that Maria would live to see the accomplishment of the prophecy, and would, moreover, become a religious within its walls. As we may well imagine, these words did not please her very much, but time proved that Rose was no senseless prattler.

When our Saint was in her twenty-fifth year, a great number of the native Peruvians rebelled against their Spanish conquerors and, withdrawing to the wilds, returned to their former savagery and idolatry. Saint Turibius, the Archbishop of the city, did his utmost to show them the folly of their ways; but in vain. It would seem that the demons of hell were allowed to concentrate their energies to destroy Lima, for a wave of irreligion and crime swept over the city, so that even the civil authorities feared lest it should be chastised by the Hand of God. Holy men, inspired by an all-wise Providence, came to preach penance to the wanderers. But their words, replete with the terrors of the awful Judgment, served only to fill the hearts of the transgressors with consternation, and thus augmented the confusion and disorder already existing in the erring city. It was then that Rose, seeing the just demands of an all-merciful God, offered herself as a victim for the unhappy people. Scourging her innocent body till her blood reddened the earth, she prayed unceasingly that the city of her birth might be spared. Her heavenly Spouse was pleased to accept this self-immolation of His beloved, and vouchsafed peace to the afflicted metropolis. The Holy Spirit breathed like a gentle zephyr upon the hearts of the rebellious people, moving them to repentance and to return again to their former allegiance. Thus, like our latest saint, the Maid of Domremy, Rose did her part to save her beloved land from the armies of Satan:

"And when the solemn and deep church-bell
    Entreats the soul to pray,
The midnight phantoms feel the spell,
    The shadows sweep away.

"Down the broad Vale of Tears afar
    The spectral camp is fled;
Faith shineth as a morning star,
    Our ghastly fears are dead." [14]

---

[14] "Longfellow: "The Beleaguered City."

As the earthly life of Saint Rose began to draw to a close, she redoubled her penances. Instead of the knotted cords, two chains were fashioned into a discipline and in the solitude of her cell she was able to inflict this form of voluntary punishment upon herself unmolested. For days at a time she would partake of no food at all, especially before receiving Holy Communion, for often she was deprived of this Heavenly Bread because she had no one to accompany her to the church, and it was an ironbound rule of those times that no young girl should appear in the streets unescorted. Often, as she approached to the Holy Table, she was so weak and emaciated that her brother had to assist her to the altar rail; but no sooner had she partaken of the Sacred Host than her physical strength was restored. Her countenance was suffused with a supernatural light and glowed with such an exquisitely attractive love that it seemed to those beholding her that she was made a partaker, even while still in this vale of sorrow, of the vision of the Blessed.

When her confessor, at her mother's request, forbade her to use the iron chain as a scourge, our Saint employed it as a girdle around her waist, drawing it tightly and fastening it with a little lock. She then threw the key away, lest she should be tempted to remove it. Moreover, the metal crown that she devised in her girlhood days she deemed insufficient, as the sun of her earthly existence began to set; so she had a triple circlet of silver fashioned for her, with thirty-three sharp spikes—in honor of our Lord's years on earth—in each metal ring. Thus her weary head was constantly pained in ninety-nine distinct places. It is distressing for us even to read the vivid descriptions of Rose's bodily macerations as left us by her more detailed biographers, and if we are at times tempted to think that she was imprudent in the use of these instruments of penance, let us remember that God was well pleased with these conquests over flesh and blood, undertaken for love of Him and for the souls that He had died to save. The iron girdle was preserved as a relic after the Saint's death and emitted a heavenly fragrance, and, moreover, God granted that three strokes upon this fearful headgear in honor of the Most Holy Trinity would relieve Rose from the assaults of the Evil One.

This true spouse of the Heavenly Bridegroom, in her desire to watch with our Lord, kept up an incessant battle against sleep, and before her death she had reduced the hours given to rest to two only. But let us not imagine for a moment that this did not entail an heroic struggle. We saw the bed of pain rather than of repose that she made for her tired body, even as a young girl. That, however, was not sufficient to assist her to victory; for, besides the natural inclination to sleep increased by the heavy and oppressive climate of the country, Rose had also to battle with the wiles of Satan. With hell-defying courage, this intrepid heroine would extend her arms on a large cross, so as to sustain her weight, deal her sleepy head pitiless blows, or, as a last resort, she would fasten the little hair she had left of her once flowing tresses to a large nail that was driven in the wall, so that the moment she began to drowse the pain awakened her.

To these exterior sufferings Rose received from on high a still more soul-searching trial. She experienced all the mental agonies of what is known as the "night of the soul." It would require the pen of a learned mystic to describe the terrible anguish that the soul of the Saint endured during these trials, which extended, at intervals, over the long period of fifteen years. During these hours of abandonment Saint Rose felt all the awful separation from the Eternal Goodness that is experienced by the damned in hell. She felt as though her Redeemer had deserted her forever and as though He actually hated her. Moreover, the enemy of man's salvation afflicted the Saint in every way possible, suggesting temptations to despair and even inflicting physical blows upon her. But, relying upon her Saviour and confiding in His glorious Mother, the humble maiden succeeded in vanquishing the hosts of perdition.

Our Divine Lord, however, never permits Himself to be outdone in generosity. After these afflictions with which He tried Rose's heart, as gold in the fire, He showered upon her manifold graces and blessings. Frequently the Blessed Virgin visited this handmaid of the Lord and helped her in many ways. Saint Catherine, her own special patroness, would spend long hours with her to instruct and guide her in the rugged ascent up Mount Calvary. Nor are we surprised to hear that her angel-guardian was almost always visible to her and granted her many spiritual favors. But most of all do we love to think of the many times that the Divine Child came to cheer this childlike Saint. The Christ Child often spent long hours in conversation with this lily-hearted Rose, encouraging her and assuring her that she would one day be forever united to Him in heaven.

Indeed, like her model-saint, she, too, was destined to be espoused to the King of Eternal Glory even while in this vale of sorrow. The great day of her mystical betrothal to the God of Heaven and earth was a Palm Sunday a few years before her death. It happened in this wise: Rose, with the other Tertiaries, was in the Church of Santo Domingo assisting at the solemn services. The sacristan distributed the waving palm branches, but somehow missed Rose. When the procession had formed, the saintly maiden took her usual place and modestly accompanied the others, humbling herself before God and accusing herself of having too eagerly desired the palm branch. So when she came before the miraculous statue of the Queen of the Rosary she begged for pardon. Then the figure became animated and smiled upon the humble child. Rose, touched to the very depths of her soul by this kindness, cried out: "Nevermore, O dearest Lady, will I take a palm branch from the hands of man, for thou, O Palm of Cades, wilt give me a never-fading one!" The Blessed Virgin then turned to the Child Jesus and asked a favor; then Rose experienced a thrill of holy joy, and ecstatic emotion filled her inmost soul, as the Divine Infant spoke these words to His beloved: "Rose of My heart, be thou My spouse!" With a heart overflowing with love and tender gratitude, and overwhelmed by a realization of the greatness of the favor, and of her own unworthiness, she modestly bowed her head, giving vent in tears of thankfulness to the great joy that came over her, while she promised eternal fidelity to her heavenly Suitor.

Rose had been supernaturally enlightened as to the time of her death; she knew that she would never live to see her thirty-second year; and so, when in her twenty-eighth year, she was taken down with what seemed so mortal a sickness that her confessor began to say the prayers for the dying and to urge her to final perseverance, she gently told him not to be alarmed, for her death hour had not yet come. Though the servant of God recovered from the illness, her strength was well-nigh spent, and soon after she left her chosen cell and the home of her parents to dwell in the house of her friends, the de Massas. Her confessor bade her mitigate the severity of her penances and gave her mother leave to destroy the bed of pain that Rose had used all through these years. In the home of her friends the Saint chose the smallest attic-room, and there continued her prayers and mortifications, though the latter were somewhat softened in their rigor. Rose now obeyed Maria de Massa as her mother, and by her charming holiness taught the children of the family the happiness of virtue.

Toward the end of July, 1617, Rose, feeling that her earthly career was drawing to a close, paid a last visit to her parents and her little retreat in the garden. Finally her last sufferings set in on the night of July 31st. She had retired as well as ever, but was found seized with an inexplicable illness that caused her body to become rigid; and she appeared like one in the agony of death. Her mother was immediately sent for, and in the morning her confessor and doctor were summoned. Though there were no signs of physical sickness save those effects mentioned, our Saint described her sufferings when requested to do so by her confessor. She seems to have had a share in the awful tortures that the sensitive body of our Saviour experienced while on the Cross; she felt as though the very marrow in her bones was being burned with fire. After a week of this anguish, bodily ailments were added to Rose's agony. A complication of diseases set in: pneumonia, asthma, gout, rheumatism, and fevers tested the patience of this Job-like maiden. These were the means used by a loving God further to purify the soul of His faithful child. Through it all she ever showed herself the same patient, edifying sufferer, always thinking of others and confident that God would grant her final victory. Three weeks this terrible malady consumed the emaciated body of our heroine, whose pure soul the while was sustained by a joyous serenity that enabled her to bear the excruciating pains.

On the eve of Saint Bartholomew she told her folks that she was to die that night, begged for her parents' last blessing, took an affectionate leave of her friends, exhorted all to a greater love for God, and humbly begged pardon for her faults and the annoyance that she had caused them by her sickness. At 8 o'clock she said that she would die at midnight, and obtained a final absolution from Father Lorenzana, who had to leave for the choral office. As the appointed hour approached, the dying Saint asked her brother to remove the mattress and pillow, that she might die like her Redeemer on the hard wood. Then, having received a blessed candle and fortified with the Sign of the Cross, the First Flower of the New World breathed her last. Those at her side caught the last word of this mystic flower: "Jesus, Jesus, be with me!" In death as in life, her one inextinguishable desire was to be united to the Sacred Heart; and so

"No longer grieving for her Love,
Joy now o'erflows her faithful heart!
Eternal anthems hymned above,
And pure delight her blessed part."[15]

[15] From Vesper Hymn of Saint Rose's Feast.

The news of the Saint's death spread with lightning rapidity, and when day dawned a great throng sought admittance to the house to behold the dead Saint, whose youthful features were restored to the emaciated countenance. Innumerable miracles were granted to those who implored her intercession, and her funeral was rather a triumphal pageant, for no one could feel grief that another saint had been crowned in Heaven. For days the Friars could not bury the sainted remains because of the ever-increasing crowds that came to see the valiant soul's earthly habitat. Finally they succeeded in entombing the sacred corpse in the cloister of the convent.

Besides the cures and favors granted through the Saint's intercession, the great change for the better that swept all over Latin America clearly manifested Rose's continued interest in her countrymen. Nor did these spiritual showers of roses cease as the years lengthened into decades; and so, in 1671, Pope Clement IX announced to the whole of Christendom that Rose de Flores was to be honored as a saint in Heaven, and proclaimed her the special Advocate of the Western Hemisphere. And so each year Holy Mother Church commemorates the victories of this lily-maid on the 30th of August, hailing her with this beautiful antiphon: "O sweet-smelling Rose, scattering everywhere the perfume of virtues, help us to be sharers of the light and fragrance which you enjoy!" [16]

BIBLIOGRAPHY

Florence M. Capes: St. Rose of Lima—The First Flower of the New World. Benziger Brothers, 1913.

The Oratorian Life of St. Rose, edited by Father Faber. This is a translation of the French life by Feuillet, O. P.

Thos. M. Schwertner, O. P.: America's First Saint and Protectress—Rose of Lima. This short sketch of the Saint's life contains the only novena ever written to her in the English tongue. The Rosary Magazine, 1917.

[16] Benedictus Antiphon for Saint Rose's Feast.

Bollandists: Acta Sanctorum. Cf. Tom. V, August 26th, not 30th. The Latin Life, by Father Leonard Hansen, O. P., called "Vita Mirabilis," is incorporated in the Bollandists.

J. B. Feuillet, O. P.: The French Life, of which the Oratorian Life is a translation.

Vte. De Bussierre: Le Pérou et Ste. Rose de Lima. This work is said to very useful to obtain the historical background of the times of Saint Rose.

A French translation of Hansen's Latin Life. Said to be a very free rendering.

A Spanish transalation of Hansen's Latin Life, by Parra.

Alban Butler, Vol. III

Catholic Encyclopedia, Vol. XIII, 192.

Other Saintly Dominicans

In this seventh centenary year since the death of the illustrious Founder of the Order of Friar Preachers, it is meet not only to sing the praises of that mighty athlete of Christ, but also to eulogize those generations of men and women, renowned for their sanctity, who rejoice in calling Saint Dominic Holy Father. God has manifested His glory through the magnificent gifts of holiness and learning with which He has endowed so many wearers of Dominic's chaste white garb. Some of his sons, men of great power, have worn the tiara and ruled the Church with wisdom; others have set a new standard for thought in philosophy and theology; a great number by contributions from their pens have shed an undying luster on various branches of learning, especially Scripture, canon law, history, and literature; many talented in music have arranged inspiring melodies adapted to the words of the Old and New Testaments; not a few sculptors and artists have left immortal monuments to their skill and genius, while those who were rich in virtue, whose lives were studies in the mirrored excellence of the soul, are computed by the thousands. These distinguished sons and daughters of the saintly Guzman gained glory and were lauded mightily in their day; nor did their greatness perish with them. They that came after them down through the centuries have perpetuated their names, and their merits continue to be related. Even those whose names have passed from the memory of many have not lived in vain, for they were all men of mercy, whose godly deeds have not failed; the good things they did live on, and we, their posterity, reap an abundant harvest from the seeds which they have sown.

Over and above the great number of Dominicans upon whose sanctity the Church has set the infallible seal of her approval, there are thousands of others who for generations have been enshrined in the hearts of men. Pius the Ninth affirmed that "from the midst of the family of the Friar Preachers, as from a mine replete with riches, there cease not to come forth men renowned for sanctity. Truly the Almighty has wrought great things in favor of that Order and has enriched it with saints." "Do not ask me," Clement the Tenth once said, "how many saints the Order of Saint Dominic has given to Heaven; count, if you can, the stars which gleam in the firmament, and then you will know the number of saints among the descendants of Saint Dominic." Notable among these worthy sons of our Holy Father are innumerable martyrs. The capitular fathers gathered at London ordered a catalogue to be made of the brethren who had won the crown of martyrdom during the century dating from 1234 to 1335. When the entries were counted, this roll of honor was found to include 13,370 names. The sixteenth century, an age of a mighty religious cataclysm, demanded the life blood of 26,000 of Saint Dominic's children in defense of the true faith. Each decade of years since the inception of the Order has given an increase to the multitude already inscribed among the martyr-sons of the great scion of Calaruèga.

Who will number those of the noble Guzman's posterity who have made a sacrifice of their lives on the altar of duty; those myriads of toilers in the Lord's vineyard—missionaries, confessors, and professors; men and women caring for the sick, teaching, or doing the more humble chores of the house; and last, but not least, those heroic nuns, hidden behind convent walls, engaged perpetually in reciting the Rosary or adoring our Eucharistic King, thus drawing down from Heaven the power by which their brothers in pulpit and confessional captivate souls and turn them toward God? True, these slaves to duty in the various activities of the Order suffer not a martyrdom of blood, yet they spend their lives and are spent just as efficaciously for the cause of faith.

To Saint Thomas Aquinas it was revealed that few, if any, of his brethren would fail to enter the Kingdom of Heaven. Who was better able to determine whether or not such revelations be worthy of communication to others? May we not, then, compute the number of those who have attained sanctity through the observance of the rule and constitutions of the Dominican Order by a record of its members? It would be a giant task, if not an impossible one, to fix precisely how many persons have worn the chaste habit of Saint Dominic. In the year 1245 the Order is said to have embraced more than 30,000 religious. An actual census taken of the First Order alone, early in the eighteenth century, contained the names of approximately 40,000. Based upon these figures, we may safely say that no less than several hundred thousand Dominicans have lived, labored, and passed to their reward before the advent of this generation. As to the number of members of the Second and Third Order who have found the rule of Saint Dominic a guide to holiness, we will not venture to say, since they may be counted only by the millions.

After these generalizations upon the holiness of Saint Dominic's numerous disciples, we turn to a more particular consideration of those of his followers who have been approved by the Church as being worthy of the special veneration of the faithful. Besides the fourteen canonized saints whose lives have been briefly sketched in the pages of this book, the names of 287 illustrious Dominicans are inscribed among the Blessed. From an ecclesiastical viewpoint, there is a well-defined distinction between these two classes of God's chosen children. Canonization and beatification, generally speaking, may be defined as a decree regarding the public ecclesiastical veneration of an individual. This veneration may be permissive or perceptive, may be universal or local. If the decree contains a precept and is universal, in the sense that it binds the whole Church, it is a decree of canonization; if it only permits such worship, or if it binds under precept, but not with regard to the whole Church, it is a decree of beatification. The difference between the two forms of decrees lies in this, that beatification implies a locally restricted, not a universal, permission to venerate, while canonization implies a universal precept. This should always be kept in mind, that the Church forbids, and hence makes it unlawful, to pay to the person known as a Blessed public reverence outside of the place for which the permission is granted. It is otherwise with canonization, which is a precept of the Roman Pontiff commanding public veneration to be paid an individual by the Universal Church.

It is further worthy of note that the restriction as to the veneration of the Blessed is only applicable to a public manifestation of such reverence; the individual is left to follow his own conscience as to the private invocation of, or honor given to, the beatified.

Among the Blessed are to be found many the story of whose lives will appeal just as readily to the faithful as that of the saints. It is our purpose here to make the reader acquainted with the names of only a few beatified Dominicans, chosen at random, so that if he cares to learn more about them he may follow up this introduction and procure longer treatises on the subject.

True it is that the saints are regarded as the heroes in the history of all religious orders. They are, as it were, the leaders; behind them troop the rank and file, in whose vanguard are the Blessed. In their struggle for pre-eminence in sanctity, the canonized Dominicans were ably assisted by the beatified members of that vast army of white-robed knights. Who can even conjecture the extent of the mighty influence that a Blessed Albert the Great brought to bear upon the formative state of the giant intellect with which Saint Thomas Aquinas was endowed, or well weigh the power for good which the spiritual direction of a Blessed Raymond of Capua brought into the life of Saint Catherine of Siena. Nor can we consider it a mere coincidence that a single novitiate under the mastership of Blessed Lawrence of Ripafratta gave to the Church a Saint Antoninus, a Fra. Angelico, and a Blessed Peter Capucci. We could well fill pages with citations of these coadjutor saints. But among Dominicans there are many types of sanctity which demand at least passing recognition. Each exhibits in its own peculiar way the unsearchable designs of the Almighty and bears witness to the truth that "there is no respect of persons with God" (Col. iii, 25).

Blessed Margaret of Hungary is noted for her regal lineage. She was the patroness of many princesses. The daughter of a king, she refused to leave her cloister to marry the ruler of Bohemia, although a papal dispensation had been obtained for her to do so. Her antithesis in worldly estate is presented to us in the person of Blessed Sibyllina, a woman of lowly birth, uneducated and blind. She rose to a height of sanctity as exalted as her rank in the social world was humble. Known to have left the place of her abode but once in sixty-four years, many domestic servants became devoted to her, establishing a confraternity in her honor. The fact that her body remains still incorrupt is taken as a special proof of a virtuous life.

Blessed Ægidius was a nobleman, highly educated, and, besides being a cleric, was especially conspicuous for his knowledge of philosophy and medicine. He led a worldly life in his youth, going so far as to sell his soul to the devil, writing the contract in his own blood. Warned in a vision of the fearful fate awaiting him if he persevered in sin, he began a life of prayer and penance, eventually becoming as famous for his sanctity as he had been notorious for his iniquity.

Blessed John Massias was born of practically indigent parents. He was untutored in the arts and sciences, but from the earliest years was endowed with extraordinary grace and was preserved in such probity of life and purity of heart as to permit Holy Mother Church to say upon his death that he had passed to his eternal reward with his baptismal innocence unsullied.

Blessed Albert of Bergamo entered the Order after the death of his wife. He was famed for the patient and silent way in which he had borne the vexatious domestic persecutions of his spouse.

Among the beatified Martin of Porres holds a unique place because of his being a mulatto. The color of his skin, however, was not indicative of the quality of his heart. His love of neighbor, especially the sick and abandoned, was most ardent. Kindness to dumb animals led him to such an extreme that he could not bear to see even rats or mice killed.

Blessed Imelda offers a charming study in child sanctity. At the early age of nine she entered the Dominican convent near Bologna. The one great desire of her life in those young days was to receive within her breast her sacramental God. Custom had established the age of twelve as the proper time for little ones to receive First Holy Communion, and the convent chaplain would not listen to a suggested deviation from this rule. Frequently did the child beseech her confessor for permission to approach the divine banquet table, only to be repulsed. On May the 12th, 1245, the community partook of the Eucharist in a body, leaving Imelda alone in her choir stall. Her frail body shook with emotion, tears flowed down her babelike face, and with a voice that trembled with grief she asked to be fed upon the Body of her Lord. No attention was paid to her. The Mass came to a close. The religious left the choir. But Imelda remained behind uncomforted. Suddenly a sweet fragrance, as of roses, filled the air and was seemingly wafted throughout the monastery. The nuns, tracing its source, returned to the chapel, and there, to their astonishment, beheld a Sacred Host suspended in the air above the head of the weeping maiden. The priest who had just celebrated Mass came, paten in hand, and, with holy impatience, awaited developments. The Host slowly descended, rested on the paten, and from the hands of the chaplain Imelda received her Eucharistic God. The transport of love which took possession of her little heart at this longed-for moment was too great for a finite being. She died from sheer joy and made her thanksgiving for First Holy Communion among the angels in Heaven. The cultus of this young Blessed has grown so popular that a confraternity for First Communicants has been established in her honor, and the last Eucharistic Congress held in Bergamo passed a resolution petitioning for her solemn canonization.

Having given you now, good reader, a taste of the spiritual sweetnesses to be found in the consideration of the lives of the Saints and Blessed of the Order of Friars Preachers, we bid you Godspeed, and sincerely hope that the perusal of these pages has aroused within your soul the desire to emulate the virtues of those heroic followers of Christ whose noble deeds are portrayed thereon.

Encyclical Letter

To the Patriarchs, Primates, Archbishops, Bishops, and other Ordinaries in peace and communion with the Apostolic See on the occasion of the seventh centenary of the death of Saint Dominic.

BENEDICT XV, SUPREME PONTIFF

Venerable Brethren, Health and the Apostolic Benediction:

At the approach of the happy day, when seven hundred years ago, that light of holiness, Dominic, passed from this world's sorrows to the home of the blessed, it is a joy to Us who have so long been amongst his most devout clients, more especially since the day when We began to govern the Church of Bologna which religiously guards the Saint's remains, it is a great joy to Us, We say, to be able to call upon the faithful from this Apostolic See to keep the memory of so great a saint. And in doing so we are not only yielding to feelings of personal piety, but also performing a duty of gratitude to the Founder and lawgiver and to his renowned family.

Dominic was wholly and thoroughly a man of God: so too was he perfectly a man of the Church, and the Church has ever found him an unconquered champion of the Faith and his Order a stout bulwark of defence. Wherefore not only did Dominic *in his days fortify the temple,*[1] but he took thought for its lasting defence, according to the prophetic words of Honorius III, uttered when he confirmed the Order, "the Brethren of thy Order are to be the champions of the Faith and the true lights of the world."

[1] Ecclus i, 1.

As all are aware, Jesus Christ made use of no other means for the spreading of the Kingdom of God than the preaching of the Gospel, that is, He used the living voice of his heralds for scattering broadcast the Divine teaching. *Teach all nations,*[2] He said. *Preach the Gospel to every creature.*[3] Thus by the preaching of the Apostles, especially of Saint Paul—to which preaching the doctrines of the Fathers and Doctors have always adhered—men's minds have been enlightened by the light of truth and their hearts enkindled with the love of virtue. This was the very means Dominic himself used and proposed to his brethren in order to work for the salvation of souls, *to give to others the fruits of contemplation*. With this end in view, besides the obligations of poverty, purity of life and religious discipline, he gave a solemn and sacred command to his children ever earnestly to devote themselves to the study of doctrine and the preaching of truth.

And, indeed, in Dominican preaching three features have ever shone out conspicuously: great solidity of doctrine, whole-hearted loyalty to the Apostolic See, and eminent devotion to the Virgin Mother.

Thus, although Dominic early discovered his vocation as a preacher, yet he would not undertake that office until he had laboured much at philosophy and theology in the University of Palencia, and had for a long time studied the Fathers from whom as his masters and guides he drank in the riches of the Holy Scriptures, especially of Paul.

In what good stead his knowledge of divine things stood him was soon apparent in his disputes with heretics; for though these latter were armed with every artifice and device for overthrowing the Christian Faith, yet Dominic stoutly refuted them and put them to confusion in a most wonderful way. He showed his power most conspicuously at Toulouse, which was the headquarters of the heretics and a common meeting-place for his most learned opponents. It is

[2] Matt. xxviii, 19.

[3] Mark xvi, 15.

related that here, he and his first companions, men mighty in word and deed, withstood the insolence of the heretics, broke their assault and, by his eloquence and charity, touched their hearts so effectively that a great number were won back to their Mother, the Church. In Dominic's fight for the faith God most manifestly stood by him. For instance, when the heretics proposed that each party should cast his book into the fire, the saint accepted the challenge and the heretics' book was burnt up and Dominic's alone remained untouched and unscorched by the flames. By Dominic's powerful efforts then was Europe delivered from the Albigensian peril.

This same reputation for solid teaching Dominic wished to see extended to his sons. No sooner had his Order been approved by the Apostolic See and given the noble title of "Preachers," than Dominic determined to establish his religious houses as near as possible to famous Universities. He did this in order that his children might avail themselves the more easily of the instructions there given; he also hoped that thereby many students at the Universities might be moved to join his new Order. The consequence was that from its very foundation the Dominican Order won for itself a reputation for solidity of doctrine. Hence it has always been held to be the especial function of the Order to provide remedies for the various evils which arise from erroneous teaching and to spread abroad the light of the Christian Faith. All are aware that there is no greater hindrance to eternal salvation than ignorance of the truth and obstinate clinging to false opinions. Small wonder, then, that the unusual power of this apostolate, based as it was on the Gospel, on the teachings of the Fathers, and on a wealth of widely extended knowledge, should attract the attention of all.

The Wisdom of God seemed in very truth to speak by the members of the Order. Amongst them ranked such famous heralds and defenders of Christian wisdom as Hyacinth of Poland, Peter Martyr and Vincent Ferrer; in their ranks, too, stood such eminent men of genius, such men of prodigious learning as Albert the Great,

Raymond of Peñafort and Thomas Aquinas. It was by Thomas, that greatest son of Saint Dominic, that God *deigned to illumine His Church.* The Order has, indeed, always been held in the highest esteem for its doctrinal teaching of the truth, and its especial glory lies in the fact that the Church has declared that Thomas's doctrine is Her own, and she has made this same Doctor, honoured as he has been by the most remarkable eulogiums from the Supreme Pontiffs, the master and the patron of Catholic Schools.

Side by side, too, with this exceeding zeal for upholding and defending the Faith, Dominic was always conspicuous for his devoted loyalty to the Apostolic See. Thus we hear of his prostrating himself at the feet of Innocent III and dedicating himself to the defence of the Roman Pontiff; and that very night the same Pontiff, Our Predecessor, saw him bearing upon his shoulders the tottering Basilica of the Lateran. History also tells us that when Dominic had trained his first disciples in Christian perfection it occurred to him to gather together from amidst pious and religiously-minded lay-folk a sacred militia whose aim should be to defend the Church's rights and stoutly combat heresy. Hence the well-known Third Order of Saint Dominic which, by popularizing the ideals of a life of perfection among those living in the world, was to provide for Holy Mother Church both rare jewels for her adornment and sturdy bulwarks of defence.

True heirs of their Father, the sons of Dominic have always shown themselves zealously devoted to the Apostolic See. Whenever through the mental darkness that springs from error the Church has had to suffer owing to popular uprisings or the violence of princes, the Apostolic See has always found in the children of Saint Dominic men who under the standard of truth and justice were ever ready to support her supreme authority. Everyone, for example, knows the noble part played in this connexion by the Dominican maiden, Catherine of Siena. For she—urged as she was by the love of Christ Jesus—overcame incredible difficulties and induced the Supreme Pontiff to do what none heretofore had been able to do, namely return to his See of Rome after an absence of seventy years; and when Catherine had secured this result she succeeded in keeping within the Faith, and in obedience to the legitimate Pope, great numbers of the faithful at a time when the Western Church was torn by terrible schism.

Many things We must omit, yet We must not pass over the fact that of Saint Dominic's children there have come four Roman Pontiffs of great renown. By far the most famous of these, Saint Pius V, deserves the undying remembrance of the civil as well as of the Christian world; for by dint of urgent and repeated exhortations he induced the Catholic princes to combine their forces, and thus was able at Lepanto finally to break the Turkish hordes, and this he did by the help and prayers of the Virgin Mother of God whom he bade us henceforth hail as *Help of Christians*.

In this last fact we have a good example of what We termed the third feature of Dominican preaching: an intense devotion to the Mother of God. For we are told that Saint Pius was divinely informed of the victory won at Lepanto at the very moment when devout Associations of the faithful throughout the Catholic world were imploring the help of Mary by reciting the Rosary which the Founder of the Friar Preachers had taught and which he and his sons after him had been at pains to propagate far and wide. For Dominic loved the Blessed Virgin as his mother; consequently it was with special reliance on her protection that he undertook his task of defending the Faith. When confronting the Albigensian heretics who, in addition to their attacks upon other points of the Faith, more especially heaped contempt on the Divine Motherhood and Virginity of Mary, Dominic upheld these particular doctrines with all his might. This led him to invoke the help of the Virgin Mother by the frequent use of the invocation: "Deign to let me praise thee, O most holy Virgin; give me strength against thine enemies." How gratifying to the Queen of Heaven was this devotion of her servant is seen from the fact that She made use of him to teach to the Church, the Spouse of her Son, the most holy Rosary. This is a form of prayer which combines the use of mind as well as lips; for in it we contemplate the principal mysteries of religion while at the same time repeating the "Our Father" fifteen times and fifteen decades of "Hail Mary's." Hence it is well calculated to stir up devotion and nourish all virtues among God's people. With justice, then, did Dominic bid his sons lay great stress on the use of this form of prayer when preaching the word of God to the people. He well knew that such was Mary's influence with her Son that whatsoever graces He gives to men it is really Mary who administers them. He knew, too, that so kindly and loving a mother is she that, while always more than ready to help those in trouble, she can never turn a deaf ear to those that appeal to her. Hence the Church has ever been wont to hail her as *Mother of grace and Mother of mercy*, and has ever found her to be such in reality, more especially when appealed to through the Rosary. It is for this reason that the Roman Pontiffs have never let pass any occasion for highly praising Mary's Rosary and have enriched it with many indulgences.

Now, as you, Venerable Brethren, well know, Dominic's Order is no less suited to the needs of the present day than to the times when it was founded. How many there are today who, deprived as they are of the bread of life, or heavenly teaching, are practically perishing of hunger! How many too who, deceived by error under the guise of truth, are kept from the Faith by the many errors that are prevalent! For priests to cope satisfactorily with the needs of all these by preaching the word of God, they must needs be not only eager for the salvation of souls but also well grounded in the knowledge of divine things. How many thankless and forgetful children of the Church have turned their backs on Christ's Vicar either through ignorance or perversity! Yet all these have to be brought back to the bosom of their common Parent. How sorely we need Mary's motherly protection if we would heal these and the many other wounds of the present day!

Saint Dominic's children have then a practically limitless field in which they can most fruitfully toil for the salvation of mankind. Wherefore We most urgently exhort all such as belong to this Order to take occasion from these present solemnities and so renew their spirit after the example of their most saintly Founder. They must strive day by day to make themselves still more worthy children of their great Father. It is but fitting that the children of his First Order should lead the way and should consequently devote themselves with ever-growing keenness to preaching the divine word; from this there will spring up in men, in addition to devotion to the Successor of Saint Peter and love of the Blessed Virgin, knowledge of and watchful care for the truth. From Saint Dominic's Tertiaries, too, the Church expects abundant usefulness, provided, that is, they strive with ever-growing diligence to confomr themselves to the spirit of their Founder by instructing in Christian doctrine the ignorant and illiterate of Christ's flock. In this task We earnestly desire to see a large band of them working assiduously; for this is a task of immense importance for the salvation of souls. Finally, We wish all Saint Dominic's children to make it their particular task to familiarize Christ's flock with the use of the Holy Rosary. We Ourselves, following in the footsteps of Our Predecessors, more especially of Leo XIII of happy memory, have given the same advice to the people and most earnestly urge it now in these days of bitter affliction. If this practice be inculcated, then We shall feel that these present celebrations have been most fruitful.

Meanwhile, as a pledge of God's gifts and a proof of our kindly feelings, We bestow upon you, Venerable Brethren, and on all your clergy and people the Apostolic Blessing.

Given at Saint Peter's, Rome, June 29, the Feast of the Princes of the Apostles, 1921, in the seventh year of Our Pontificate,

Benedict XV,
Supreme Pontiff.

Chronological List of Dominican Saints and Blessed

		Order.	Date.	Feast.	
1.	Blessed Jane of Aza, Mother of Saint Dominic		About 1190	Aug.	2
2.	Blessed Reginald of Orleans, C........	1st	1200[1]	Feb.	12
3.	Our Holy Father, Saint Dominic, C....	1st	1170–1221	Aug.	4
4.	Blessed Mannes de Guzman, C........	1st	1155–1230	July	30
5.	Blessed Bertrand de Garrigua, C.......	1st	1230	Sept.	6
6.	Blessed Diana de Andalo, V.	2nd	1236	June	9
7.	Blessed Cecilia, V....................	2nd	1202–1290	June	9
8.	Blessed Amata, V	2nd	13th Cent.	June	9
9.	Blessed Jordan of Saxony, C...........	1st	1190–1237	Feb.	15
10.	Blessed John of Salerno, C	1st	1190–1242	Aug.	9
11.	Blessed Ceslaus Odrowatz, C	1st	1180–1242	July	18
12.	Blessed William Arnauld, M..........	1st	1242	May	29
13.	Blessed Bernard Rochefort, M	1st	1242	May	29
14.	Blessed Garcia of Aura, Lay-brother ...	1st	1242	May	29
15.	Blessed Guala de Roniis, C............	1st	1244	Sept.	3
16.	Blessed Isnard, C.....................	1st	1189–1244	June	17
17.	Blessed Peter Gonzalez, C	1st	1246	April	14
18.	Saint Peter of Verona, M..............	1st	1205–1252	April	29
19.	Blessed Zedislava of Berka, Matron....	2nd	1210–1252	Nov.	28
20.	Blessed Nicholas Palea of Giovinazzo, C	1st	1255	Feb.	14
21.	Saint Hyacinth Odrowatz, C..........	1st	1185–1257	Aug.	16
22.	Blessed Gonsalvo of Amarantha, C....	1st	1259	Jan.	10
23.	Blessed Sadoc and 48 companions, Martyrs..........................	1st	1260	June	2

[1] Where only one date is given, it is the date of death.

The companions of Blessed Sadoc are:

24. Blessed Paul, Vicar.
25. Blessed Malachy.
26. Blessed Andrew.
27. Blessed Peter.
28. Blessed James, Novice Master.
29. Blessed Abel, Procurator.
30. Blessed Simeon, Confessor.
31. Blessed Clement, Deacon.
32. Blessed Barnabas, Deacon.
33. Blessed Elias, Deacon.
34. Blessed Bartholomew, Deacon.
35. Blessed Luke, Deacon.
36. Blessed Matthew, Deacon.
37. Blessed John, Deacon.
38. Blessed Philip, Deacon.
39. Blessed Joachim, Deacon.
40. Blessed Joseph, Deacon.
41. Blessed Stephan, Deacon.
42. Blessed Thaddeus, Sub-deacon.
43. Blessed Moses, Sub-deacon.
44. Blessed Abraham, Sub-deacon.
45. Blessed Basil, Sub-deacon.
46. Blessed David, Cleric.
47. Blessed Aaron, Cleric.
48. Blessed Benedict, Cleric.
49. Blessed Onophis, Cleric.
50. Blessed Dominic, Cleric.
51. Blessed Michael, Cleric.
52. Blessed Matthias, Cleric.
53. Blessed Timothy, Cleric.
54. Blessed Maurus, Novice.
55. Blessed Gordian, Novice.
56. Blessed Felician, Novice.
57. Blessed Marc, Novice.
58. Blessed John, Novice.
59. Blessed Gervase, Novice.

60. Blessed Christopher, Novice.
61. Blessed Donatus, Novice.
62. Blessed Medard, Novice.
63. Blessed Valentine, Novice.
64. Blessed Daniel, Novice.
65. Blessed Tobias, Novice.
66. Blessed Macarius, Novice.
67. Blessed Raphael, Novice.
68. Blessed Isaias, Novice.
69. Blessed Cyril, Lay-brother.
70. Blessed Jeremias, Lay-brother.
71. Blessed Thomas, Lay-brother.

		Order.	Date.	Feast.
72.	Blessed Egidius of Portugal, C.	1st	1190–1265	May 14
73.	Blessed Bartholomew Breganza, B. C	1st	1270	Oct. 23
74.	Blessed Margaret of Hungary, V.	2nd	1242–1271	Jan. 26
75.	Saint Thomas Aquinas, C. D..	1st	1225–1274	Mar. 7
76.	Saint Raymond of Pennafort, C.	1st	1175–1275	Jan. 23
77.	Blessed Innocent V, P. C	1st	1225–1276	June 22
78.	Blessed Albert of Bergamo	3rd	1214–1279	May 13
79.	Blessed Albert the Great, B. C.	1st	1193–1280	Nov. 15
80.	Blessed John of Vercelli, C.	1st	1283	Dec. 2
81.	Blessed Ambrose Sansedonio, C.	1st	1222–1286	Mar. 22
82.	Blessed Benvenuta, V..	3rd	1250–1292	Oct. 29
83.	Blessed James of Voragine, B. C	1st	1230–1298	July 13
84.	Blessed Dominic, C..	1st	13th Cent.	April 26
85.	Blessed Gregory, C.	1st	13th Cent.	April 26
86.	Blessed James of Mevania, C.	1st	1220–1301	Aug. 23
87.	Blessed Benedict XI, P. C	1st	1240–1304	July 7
88.	Blessed Jane of Orvieto	3rd	1264–1306	July 23
89.	Blessed Jordan of Pisa, C.	1st	1311	Mar. 6
90.	Blessed James Salomonio, C.	1st	1231–1314	May 31
91.	Blessed Emily Bicchieri, V.	3rd	1238–1314	Aug. 17
92.	Saint Agnes of Montepulciano, V.	2nd	1268–1317	April 20
93.	Blessed Simon Ballachi, C., Lay-brother	1st	1319	Nov. 3
94.	Blessed Margaret of Castello, V.	3rd	1287–1320	April 13
95.	Blessed Augustine of Lucera, B. C	1st	1260–1323	Aug. 8

		Order.	Date.	Feast.
96.	Blessed Imelda Lambertini, V.	2nd	1322–1333	Sept. 16
97.	Blessed James Benefatti, B. C.	1st	1338	Nov. 29
98.	Blessed Dalmatius Moner, C.	1st	1291–1341	Sept. 26
99.	Blessed Villana de Botti, W.	3rd	1332–1360	Feb. 28
100.	Blessed Peter of Ruffia, M.	1st	1320–1365	Nov. 7
101.	Blessed Henry Suso, C.	1st	1365	Mar. 2
102.	Blessed Sibyllina Biscossi, V.	3rd	1287–1367	Mar. 18
103.	Blessed Anthony Pavone, M.	1st	1326–1374	April 9
104.	Saint Catherine of Siena, V.	3rd	1347–1380	April 30
105.	Blessed Marcolino of Forli, C.	1st	1317–1397	Jan. 24
106.	Blessed Raymond of Capua, C.	1st	1330–1399	Oct. 5
107.	Saint Vincent Ferrer, C.	1st	1350–1419	April 5
108.	Blessed Clara Gambarcorti, W.	2nd	1362–1419	April 17
109.	Blessed John Dominici, B. C	1st	1355–1419	June 10
110.	Blessed Alvarez of Cordova, C.	1st	1420	Feb. 19
111.	Blessed Maria Mancini, W.	2nd	1355–1431	Dec. 22
112.	Blessed Peter Capucci of Tiferno, C.	1st	1390–1445	Oct. 22
113.	Blessed Stephan Bandelli, C.	1st	1369–1450	June 12
114.	Blessed Andrew Abellon, C.	1st	1375–1450	Mar. 17
115.	Blessed Peter de Jeremia, C.	1st	1381–1452	Mar. 10
116.	Blessed Lawrence of Ripafratta, C.	1st	1359–1457	Feb. 18
117.	Saint Antoninus, B. C	1st	1389–1459	May 10
118.	Blessed Anthony of the Church, C.	1st	1395–1459	July 28
119.	Blessed Anthony Neyrot, M.	1st	1460	April 10
120.	Blessed Margaret of Savoy, W.	2nd	1382–1464	Nov. 27
121.	Blessed Bartholomew of Cerverio, M.	1st	1420–1466	April 21
122.	Blessed Matthew Carrerii, C.	1st	1470	Oct. 7
123.	Blessed Andrew of Peschiera, C.	1st	1480	Jan. 19
124.	Blessed Constantius of Fabriano, C.	1st	1481	Feb. 25
125.	Blessed Christopher of Milan, C.	1st	1484	Mar. 1
126.	Blessed Damian Furcher, C.	1st	1484	Oct. 26
127.	Blessed Bernard of Scammacca, C.	1st	1486	Feb. 9
128.	Blessed Jane of Portugal, V.	2nd	1452–1490	May 12
129.	Blessed James of Ulm, C., Lay-brother	1st	1407–1491	Oct. 12
130.	Blessed Augustine of Bugella, C.	1st	1493	July 27
131.	Blessed Aimo Taparelli, C.	1st	1495	Feb. 21

		Order.	Date.	Feast.	
132.	Blessed Sebastian Maggi, C	1st	1412–1496	Dec.	16
133.	Blessed Mark of Modena, C.	1st	1498	July	3
134.	Blessed Columba of Rieti, V.	3rd	1467–1501	May	20
135.	Blessed Magdalen Pannatieri, V	3rd	1443–1503	Oct.	14
136.	Blessed Osanna of Mantua, V	3rd	1449–1505	June	18
137.	Blessed John Liccio, C	1st	1400–1511	Nov.	14
138.	Blessed Dominic Spatafora, C.	1st	1521	Dec.	19
139.	Blessed Stephana of Soncino, V.	3rd	1457–1530	Jan.	16
140.	Blessed Lucy of Narni, V.	3rd	1476–1544	Nov.	16
141.	Blessed Catherine of Racconigi, V	3rd	1486–1547	Sept.	5
142.	Saint Pius V., P. C	1st	1504–1572	May	5
143.	Saint John of Cologne, Martyr of Gorcum	1st	1572	July	9
144.	Blessed Maria Bartolomea Bagnesi, V	3rd	1514–1577	May	28
145.	Saint Louis Bertrand, C	1st	1526–1581	Oct.	10
146.	Saint Catherine de Ricci, V.	3rd	1522–1589	Feb.	13
147.	Saint Rose of Lima, V.	3rd	1586–1617	Aug.	30
148.	Blessed Alphonsus Naverette and companions, MM.	1st	1511–1617	June	1

The 109 Martyr Companions of Blessed Alphonsus are:

149. Blessed John of Saint Dominic, Priest, 1619, 1st Order.
150. Blessed Lewis Flores, Priest, 1622, 1st Order.
151. Blessed Francis Morales, Priest, 1622, 1st Order.
152. Blessed Angelo Orsucci, Priest, 1622, 1st Order.
153. Blessed Alphonsus de Mena, Priest, 1622, 1st Order.
154. Blessed Joseph of Saint Hyacinth, Priest, 1622, 1st Order.
155. Blessed Hyacinth Orphanel, Priest, 1622, 1st Order.
156. Blessed Thomas of the Holy Ghost, Priest, 1622, 1st Order.
157. Blessed Peter Vasquez, Priest, 1624, 1st Order.
158. Blessed Lewis Bertrand, Priest, 1627, 1st Order.
159. Blessed Dominic Castellet, Priest, 1628, 1st Order.
160. Blessed Alexis, Novice, 1622, 1st Order.
161. Blessed Thomas of the Rosary, Novice, 1622, 1st Order.
162. Blessed Dominic of the Rosary, Novice, 17th Century, 1st Order.
163. Blessed Mancio of Saint Thomas, Novice, 17th Century, 1st Order.
164. Blessed Dominic, Novice, 17th Century.

165. Blessed Mancio of the Cross, Lay-brother, 1627, 1st Order.
166. Blessed Peter of Saint Mary, Lay-brother, 1627, 1st Order.
167. Blessed Thomas of Saint Hyacinth, Lay-brother, 1627, 1st Order.
168. Blessed Anthony of Saint Dominic, Lay-brother, 1627, 1st Order.
169. Blessed Gaspar Cotenda, Lay-brother, 1627, 1st Order.
170. Blessed Francis Curobiori, 17th Century, 3rd Order.
171. Blessed Caius Jemon, 17th Century, 3rd Order.
172. Blessed Magdalen Chiota, 17th Century, 3rd Order.
173. Blessed Frances, 17th Century, 3rd Order.
174. Blessed John Tomachi, 17th Century, 3rd Order.
175. Blessed Dominic, age 16, son of John Tomachi, 17th Century, 3rd Order.
176. Blessed Michael, age 13, son of John Tomachi, 17th Century, 3rd Order.
177. Blessed Thomas, age 10, son of John Tomachi, 17th Century, 3rd Order.
178. Blessed Paul, age 7, son of John Tomachi, 17th Century, 3rd Order.
179. Blessed John Imamura, 17th Century, 3rd Order.
180. Blessed Paul Aybara, 17th century, 3rd Order.
181. Blessed Romanus of Japan, 17th Century, 3rd Order.
182. Blessed Leo of Japan, 17th Century, 3rd Order.
183. Blessed James Fayaxida, 17th Century, 3rd Order.
184. Blessed Matthew-Alvarez, 17th Century, 3rd Order.
185. Blessed Micahael Jamada, 17th Century, 3rd Order.
186. Blessed Lawerence, his son, 17th Century, 3rd Order.
187. Blessed Louis Nefaci and two sons, 17th Century, 3rd Order.
188. Blessed Francis, age 5, 17th Century, 3rd Order.
189. Blessed Dominic, age 2, 17th Century, 3rd Order.
190. Blessed Louisa of Japan, 17th Century, 3rd Order.
191. Blessed Michael Fimonoia, 17th Century, 3rd Order.
192. Blessed Paul Fimonoia, 17th Century, 3rd Order.
193. Blessed Dominic Xobiori, 17th Century, 3rd Order.
194. Blessed Gaspar Fisogiro, Member of Rosary Confraternity, 17th Century.
195. Blesssed Andrew Gioscinda, Member of Rosary Confraternity, 17th Century.
196. Blessed Andrew Tocuan, Member of Rosary Confraternity, 17th Century.
197. Blessed Cosmus Taquea, Member of Rosary Confraternity, 17th Century.
198. Blessed John Xoum, Member of Rosary Confraternity, 17th Century.

199. Blessed Dominic Georgi, Member of Rosary Confraternity, 17th Century.
200. Blessed Bartholomew Xequi, Member of Rosary Confraternity, 17th Century.
201. Blessed Anthony Chimura, Member of Rosary Confraternity, 17th Century.
202. Blessed John Juananga, Member of Rosary Confraternity, 17th Century.
203. Blessed Alexis Nacamura, Member of Rosary Confraternity, 17th Century.
204. Blessed Leo Nacanisci, Member of Rosary Confraternity, 17th Century.
205. Blessed Michael Tascita, Member of Rosary Confraternity, 17th Century.
206. Blessed Matthias Coxaca, Member of Rosary Confraternity, 17th Century.
207. Blessed Romanus Matevoia, Member of Rosary Confraternity, 17th Century.
208. Blessed Matthias Nacono, Member of Rosary Confraternity, 17th Century.
209. Blessed John Motaiana, Member of Rosary Confraternity, 17th Century.
210. Blessed Thomas Cotenda, Member of Rosary Confraternity, 17th Century.
211. Blessed Simon Quiota, Member of Rosary Confraternity, 17th Century.
212. Blessed Magdalen (wife of B. Simon Quiota), Member of Rosary Confraternity, 17th Century.
213. Blessed Thomas Guengoro, Member of Rosary Confraternity, 17th Century.
214. Blessed Mary (his wife), Member of Rosary Confraternity, 17th Century.
215. Blessed James (their son), Member of Rosary Confraternity, 17th Century.
216. Blessed Joachim Firayama, Member of Rosary Confraternity, 17th Century.
217. Blessed Leo Suqueiemon, Member of Rosary Confraternity, 17th Century.
218. Blessed John Foiamon, Member of Rosary Confraternity, 17th Century.
219. Blessed Michael Diaz, Member of Rosary Confraternity, 17th Century.

220. Blessed Mark Xineyemon, Member of Rosary Confraternity, 17th Century.
221. Blessed Thomas Coyanagui, Member of Rosary Confraternity, 17th Century.
222. Blessed Anthony Giamando, Member of Rosary Confraternity, 17th Century.
223. Blessed James Densci, Member of Rosary Confraternity, 17th Century.
224. Blessed Lawerence Rocuiemon, Member of Rosary Confraternity, 17th Century.
225. Blessed Paul Sanciqui, Member of Rosary Confraternity, 17th Century.
226. Blessed John Jago, Member of Rosary Confraternity, 17th Century.
227. Blessed Bartholomew Mofioie, Member of Rosary Confraternity, 17th Century.
228. Blessed John Kangata, Member of Rosary Confraternity, 17th Century.
229. Blessed Paul Nangaxi, Member of Rosary Confraternity, 17th Century.
230. Blessed Thecla (his wife), Member of Rosary Confraternity, 17th Century.
231. Blessed Peter (their son), Member of Rosary Confraternity, 17th Century.
232. Blessed Magdalen Sanga, Member of Rosary Confraternity, 17th Century.
233. Blessed Paul Tanaca, Member of Rosary Confraternity, 17th Century.
234. Blessed Mary (his wife), Member of Rosary Confraternity, 17th Century.
235. Blessed Elizabeth Fernandez, Member of Rosary Confraternity, 17th Century.
236. Blessed Ignatius (her son), Member of Rosary Confraternity, 17th Century.
237. Blessed Apollonia, Member of Rosary Confraternity, 17th Century.
238. Blessed Anthony of Corea, Member of Rosary Confraternity, 17th Century.
239. Blessed Mary (his wife), Member of Rosary Confraternity, 17th Century.
240. Blessed John, age 12, Member of Rosary Confraternity, 17th Century.
241. Blessed Peter, age 3, (their son), Member of Rosary Confraternity, 17th Century.

242. Blessed Dominic Xamada, Member of Rosary Confraternity, 17th Century.
243. Blessed Clara (his wife), Member of Rosary Confraternity, 17th Century.
244. Blessed Mary, wife of B. Andrew Tocuan, Member of Rosary Confraternity, 17th Century.
245. Blessed Agnes, wife of Cosmus Taquea, Member of Rosary Confraternity, 17th Century.
246. Blessed Dominic Nacano, Member of Rosary Confraternity, 17th Century.
247. Blessed Bartholomew Xichiemon, Member of Rosary Confraternity, 17th Century.
248. Blessed Damian Jamichi, Member of Rosary Confraternity, 17th Century.
249. Blessed Michael (his son), Member of Rosary Confraternity, 17th Century.
250. Blessed Thomas Xiquiro, Member of Rosary Confraternity, 17th Century.
251. Blessed Rufus Iscimola, Member of Rosary Confraternity, 17th Century.
252. Blessed Mary, wife of B. John Xoum, Member of Rosary Confraternity, 17th Century.
253. Blessed Clement Vom, Member of Rosary Confraternity, 17th Century.
254. Blessed Anthony (his son), Member of Rosary Confraternity, 17th Century.
255. Blessed Dominica Ongata, Member of Rosary Confraternity, 17th Century.
256. Blessed Catherine, Member of Rosary Confraternity, 17th Century.
257. Blessed Mary Tanaura, Member of Rosary Confraternity, 17th Century.

		Order.	Date.	Feast.
258.	Blessed Martin Porres, C.	3rd	1569–1639	Nov. 5
259.	Blessed Francis de Capillas, M.	1st	1649	Jan. 15
260.	Blessed John Massias, Lay-brother	1st	1585–1656	Oct. 3
261.	Blessed Francis Possadas, C.	1st	1644–1713	Sept. 20
262.	Blessed Lewis Mary Grignon de Montfort, C.	3rd	1673–1716	May 23

	Order.	Date.	Feast.
263. Blessed Peter Sanz and four companions, MM.	1st	1680–1747	May 27
The four companions of B. Peter Sanz are:			
264. Blessed Francis Serrano, M.	1st	1695–1749	May 27
265. Blessed John Alcober, M.	1st	1694–1749	May 27
266. Blessed Joachim Royo, M.	1st	1691–1749	May 27
267. Blessed Francis Diaz, M.	1st	1713–1749	May 27
268. Blessed Ignatius Delgado and 25 companions, MM.	1st	1761–1838	July 11

Blessed Ignatius Delgado's companions are:

269. Blessed Joseph Fernandez, Vicar Provincial.
270. Blessed Vincent Yen, Priest.
271. Blessed Dominic of God, Priest.
272. Blessed Peter Tu, Priest.
273. Blessed Thomas Du, Priest.
274. Blessed Dominic Doan, Priest.
275. Blessed Joseph Hien, Priest.
276. Blessed Dominic Trach, Priest.
277. Blessed Dominic Tuoc, Priest.
278. Blessed Joseph Nieu, Priest.
279. Blessed Bernard Due, Priest.
280. Blessed Peter Tuan, Priest.
281. Blessed Dominic Henares, Bishop.
282. Blessed Joseph Cauh, Secular Tertiary.
283. Blessed Francis Chien, Secular Tertiary.
284. Blessed Joseph or Peter Uyen, Secular Tertiary.
285. Blessed Thomas Thoan, Secular Tertiary.
286. Blessed Francis Xavier Mau, Secular Tertiary.
287. Blessed Dominic Uy, Secular Tertiary.
288. Blessed Augustine Moi, Secular Tertiary.
289. Blessed Stephan Vinh, Secular Tertiary.
290. Blessed Dominic or Nicholas Dat, Secular Tertiary.
291. Blessed Augustine Huss, Secular Tertiary.
292. Blessed Nicholas The, Secular Tertiary.
293. Blessed Thomas De, Secular Tertiary.

	Order.	Date.	Feast.
294. Blessed Jerome Hermosilla, B. M., and Companions	1st	1800–1861	Nov. 6
The seven companions of B. Jerome are:			
295. Blessed Francis Gil de Federich, M....	...	1702–1745	
296. Blessed Matthew Alonzo Leziniana, M............................	...	1702–1745	
297. Blessed Hyacinth Casteneda, M.......	...	1743–1773	
298. Blessed Vincent Liem, M	...	1731–1773	
299. Blessed Valentine Berrio-Ochoa, B. M.	...	1827–1861	
300. Blessed Peter Almata, M..............	...	1830–1861	
301. Blessed Joseph Klang, M..............	...	1832–1861	

Summary.

13th Century, 85; 14th Century, 21; 15th Century, 27; 16th Century, 13; 17th Century, 114; 18th Century, 7; 19th Century, 34.

Italy, 68; France, 8; Spain, 40; Germany, 6; Hungary, 50; Poland, 2; Lusitania, 3; Belgium, 1; Peru, 2; Japan and Tonquin, 121.

Martyrs, 208; Confessors, 65; Virgins, 22; Matrons, 3; Widows, 3.

Saints, 14; Blessed, 287. Total, 301.

OTHER TITLES AVAILABLE FROM ST. AIDAN PRESS

View a sample chapter from each title at www.staidanpress.com.

THE STORY OF THE WAR IN LA VENDÉE

by George J. Hill, M. A.

The brave French Catholics of the Vendée and neighboring provinces rose up in arms when the revolutionary government replaced their priests with clergy who had renounced the Pope. Though they lacked money, allies, and were divided by disputes, they did not cease to fight until they had secured the open practice of their Faith. Here is the story of their devotion and courage against the advocates of liberty, equality, fraternity, and death.

$18.00 — 342 pages. Available at amazon.com.

CATHOLICISM AND SCOTLAND

by Compton Mackenzie

Much has been written about the desperate fight that English Catholics waged to keep the Faith, but Scotland's Catholic history is little known. Have you ever heard of David Beaton, Cardinal Archbishop of St. Andrews, and his struggles? Or of Fr. Ninian Winzet, who boldly challenged Calvinist champion John Knox to a public debate? Read this book and find out about the Scots who sought to defend their country and their Faith from the onslaught of Protestantism.

$12.00 — 138 pages. Available at amazon.com.

FICTION

THE QUEEN'S TRAGEDY

by Msgr. Robert Hugh Benson

"Upon the publication of former books of mine several kindly critics remarked that the reign of Mary Tudor told a very different story with regard to the Catholic character. It is that story which I am now attempting to set forth as honestly as I can."

$19.00 — 364 pages. Available at amazon.com.

THE NET

by Agnes Blundell

Roger felt a freezing dew break out upon his forehead. The net was over him it seemed; in vain he told himself that he could establish his identity. His head was worth forty pounds to the vile creatures at the stair foot, and once in their clutches who knew if he could ever communicate with his friends? . . . Gaolers and pursuivants alike fattened on the traffic in human life and divided the spoils. Judges were as careless as callous."

$16.00 — 264 pages. Available at amazon.com.

THE ANCHORHOLD

by Enid Dinnis

Editha de Beauville had all that the world could offer: wealth, wit, and beauty. Yet a chaplain's sermon drove her to give up all this, and enter the religious life. But could a proud, strong-willed noblewoman accept and embrace the poverty and self-abnegation of the religious life, particularly that of full seclusion in an anchorhold? A difficult path lay before Editha. Read on to learn how she fared, and how her life affected those around her, including Sir Aleric, her erstwhile suitor, now a crusader knight; Fr. Nicholas, a young priest who was quite bright, and thought so too; and Fiddlemee, the witty yet wise court jester whose past held a surprising secret.

$14.00 — 194 pages. Available at amazon.com.

THE SHEPHERD OF WEEPINGWOLD

by Enid Dinnis

Sir Robert Luffkyn, rich grandson of a peasant, has purchased the manor of Weepingwold from the noble but impoverished de Lessels, intending to make the renamed Luffkynwold a busy center of his tanning trade. He sends Petronilla, last de Lessels, to Gracerood, intending her for its future Abbess, and plucks little Brother Kit from the cloister to become the new parson of the long-abandoned church. How will Father Kit fare with the parish and his own soul? Will Petronilla find her true vocation? And is there really a witch in the parish?

$14.00 — 202 pages. Available at amazon.com.

SCOUTING FOR SECRET SERVICE

by Fr. Bernard F. J. Dooley

Frank and George are going to spend their summer vacation in the Adirondacks, thanks to Frank's uncle Ed. But once they get there, they realize something fishy is going on. Can they trust Pete, their Indian guide, or is he mixed up in it too? And is Frank's mysterious uncle really behind it all?

$14.00 — 188 pages. Available at amazon.com.

THE MASTERFUL MONK

by Fr. Owen Francis Dudley

Brother Anselm comes back to England to counter the Atheist's efforts to destroy the influence of Catholic morals. Between his lectures he is drawn into a struggle for the soul of Beauty Dethier, who is Catholic but fascinated by the "freedom" of the world and the Atheist. It will take more than argument to save her from disaster.

$18.00 — 342 pages. Available at amazon.com.

WILL MEN BE LIKE GODS? & THE SHADOW ON THE EARTH

by Fr. Owen Francis Dudley

Father Dudley's first two books on human happiness are published together here—his rare collection of essays together with a novel which illustrates the essays and introduces his most famous character, the Masterful Monk.

$15.00 — 216 pages. Available at amazon.com.

CANDLELIGHT ATTIC AND ODD JOB'S

by Cecily Hallack

Here are seven true stories in honour of the Seven Joys of Our Blessed Lady, and ten more invented ones about the delightful Barnabas Job, to make a comfortable book for those who are afraid of the dark.

$14.00 — 192 pages. Available at amazon.com.

THE HAPPINESS OF FATHER HAPPÉ

by Cecily Hallack

Shingle Bay did not know what to make of Fr. Savinius Happé. He was a cheerful, rotund Franciscan, a famous author of books on everything from Etruscan civilization to Alpine meadows to beetles, and someone who had never quite mastered the English language. His jovial demeanor concealed a wisdom that alternately bewildered, astonished, but ultimately won over the people of Shingle Bay.

$10.00 — 112 pages. Available at amazon.com.

CON OF MISTY MOUNTAIN

by Mary T. Waggaman

"It had been a long night for Con. Just what had happened to him he was at first too dazed to know. Dennis had flung him into the smoking-room with no very gentle hand, turned the key and left him to himself. And, sinking down dully upon a rug that felt very soft and warm after the hard flight over the mountain, Con was glad to rest his bruised, aching limbs, his dizzy head, without any thought of what was to come upon him next."

$14.00 — 190 pages. Available at amazon.com.

www.ingramcontent.com/pod-product-compliance
Lightning Source LLC
Chambersburg PA
CBHW020148090426
42734CB00008B/732

* 9 7 8 1 9 6 2 5 0 3 0 3 7 *